1994

RETHINKING
PEACE

RETHINKING PEACE

edited by
Robert Elias & Jennifer Turpin

Lynne Rienner Publishers ▪ Boulder & London

Published in the United States of America in 1994 by
Lynne Rienner Publishers, Inc.
1800 30th Street, Boulder, Colorado 80301

and in the United Kingdom by
Lynne Rienner Publishers, Inc.
3 Henrietta Street, Covent Garden, London WC2E 8LU

Library of Congress Cataloging-in-Publication Data
Rethinking peace / by Robert Elias & Jennifer Turpin, editors.
    p. cm.
   Includes index.
   ISBN 1-55587-482-7 (alk. pap.)
   ISBN 1-55587-488-6 (pbk.:alk. pap.)
   1. Peace. I. Elias, Robert, 1950– . II. Turpin, Jennifer E.
JX1963.R47 1994
327.1'72—dc20   93-38657
                                                          CIP

British Cataloguing in Publication Data
A Cataloguing in Publication record for this book
is available from the British Library.

Printed and bound in the United States of America

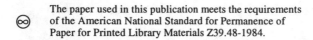
The paper used in this publication meets the requirements
of the American National Standard for Permanence of
Paper for Printed Library Materials Z39.48-1984.

To

Lester Kurtz and Richard Falk,
for changing the way we think

John Harris,
for launching *Peace Review*

Rachel Smith and Patricia Barcel,
for being our wonderful sisters
and for their zest for life

CONTENTS

Regional Challenges

Part 3 New Ideas: Creating New Models 175

New Consciousness

PREFACE

The writer Kurt Vonnegut once claimed that "thinking doesn't seem to help very much. The human brain is too high-powered to have many practical uses in this particular universe." To the contrary, real thinking can help quite a lot. But, as psychologist Erich Fromm once suggested, we have to begin applying it more to creating "human utopias," rather than only "technical utopias." Our minds, not merely our hearts, can make a more peaceful world.

As we write, our hearts are saddened by the course of global affairs. Not only do deep-seated problems remain but the prospects for change—promised by the revolutionary events of recent years—are at risk. Seeing the New World Order shaping up as little different from the old, and seeing—from the U.S. vantage point—the Clinton administration promoting many of the same policies as did the Bush and Reagan administrations before it, we are concerned about lost opportunities for a better future.

As the essays in this book suggest, we believe that new ideas can make a difference. But we do not offer naive promises of a bright new century ahead. Instead, we offer some new thinking to challenge outmoded ways of running our societies.

The writer James Baldwin once said, "We take our shape, it is true, within and against that cage of reality bequeathed to us at our birth; and yet it is precisely through our dependence on this reality that we are most endlessly betrayed." We want to offer a reality different from the one that has ruled this century—arguably the most violent century in history. In this book, our writers provide a wealth of new ideas and information, but as Albert Einstein once suggested, "Imagination is more important than knowledge." *Rethinking Peace* is designed to provoke our imaginations too.

The idea for *Rethinking Peace* came from the frequent comments we received from professors and others who told us it would be valuable to collect the best *Peace Review* essays in one volume. In the short years since its birth in 1989, *Peace Review* has tried to challenge conventional thinking, even within peace studies, and certainly within mainstream policymaking circles. We have tried to make our journal international in scope: We examine issues from around the world, our subscribers live in forty different countries, and our writers represent even more. Rather than dry, footnoted articles, we print essays designed to present new ideas and perspectives, not merely new data. Our essays are written to be read: They are short, provocative, jargon-free, and accessible to the expert and lay public alike. Our hope is to attract a large readership from many walks of life.

We think this book will be useful to researchers, activists, and policymakers, but our greatest concern is for students. We hope *Rethinking Peace* will reach them not only in peace studies courses but also in courses in sociology, politics, international relations, and even expository writing—where the book would provide a wealth of stimulating writing topics. Also, because the essays are short, we have covered far more issues than the typical edited collection, a real advantage for any conscientious educator.

Not surprisingly, we have many people to thank for helping us, directly or indirectly, put this book together. We appreciate the support provided by our families, including Solveig Turpin, Bill Turpin, Rachel Smith, Jeff Turpin, Tony Turpin, Bill Turpin, Jr., Herb Eling, André Elias, Patricia Barcel, Madeline Foran, and August Elias. And we want to also thank our supportive friends: Bill Hoynes, Deirdre Burns, Valerie Forman, Joanne Ford, Pam Kettle, Thais Austin, Behesha and Ed Grist, Sonia Doyle, Burke Forrest, and Kelley Hargrave.

We thank our writers for their new thinking about peace. We are grateful for the various supporters of *Peace Review* over the last several years, including our advisers, directors, subscribers, and other readers. We note especially our editors and friends: Mary Friedland, Lois Lorentzen, Richard Arum, Stephanie Vandrick, Karen Musalo, Martha Henderson, and Scott McElwain.

We thank John Harris for founding *Peace Review,* for his tireless work in making it a success, and for making us his colleagues. We are grateful to Ralph Lane for standing by his conviction that our work is important and worth supporting. And we appreciate Lynne Rienner, our publisher, and Gia Hamilton, our editor, and their staff, for making *Peace Review* even more successful and for making this book project possible.

Many thanks to our friends and colleagues who have influenced our thinking on these issues, including Lester Kurtz, James Skelly, Sandy Gottlieb, Thomas Cushman, Joseph Fahey, Elise Boulding, Paul Joseph, Richard Falk, Kevin Clements, and Ralph Summy.

We are grateful as well to other colleagues and friends (besides those already mentioned) at the University of San Francisco, including William Edwards, Tony Fels, Else Tamayo, Miriam Feldblum, Tami Spector, Andrew Goodwin, Larry Wenner, Jack Elliott, Barbara Bundy, Uldis Kruze, and Mike Webber. We appreciate the support of Dean Stanley Nel and Associate Dean Gerardo Marín. And for keeping us optimistic about the future, we thank our students.

Jennifer Turpin
Robert Elias
Mill Valley, California

1

INTRODUCTION: THINKING ABOUT PEACE

ROBERT ELIAS
JENNIFER TURPIN

The details of a new order of life cannot be known to us. We must shape them ourselves. Life consists solely in the search for the unknown, and in our work of harmonizing our actions with the new truth.—Leo Tolstoy

I have to cast my lot with those who, age after age, with no extra-ordinary power, reconstitute the world.—Adrienne Rich

If the hope of the world lies in human consciousness, then it is obvious that intellectuals cannot go on forever avoiding their large share of responsibility for the world. . . . Intellectuals should constantly disturb, should bear witness to the misery of the world, should be provocative by being independent, should rebel against all hidden manipulations, and should be the chief doubters of power and its incantations.—Vaclav Havel

With the development of the atomic bomb, Albert Einstein argued that everything had changed except our thinking about the world. Einstein and Bertrand Russell warned us that "we have to learn to think in a new way . . . shall we put an end to the human race; or shall mankind renounce war?"

Unfortunately, humans have not renounced war. Even though, with a couple of catastrophic exceptions, we have avoided wars fought with atomic or hydrogen bombs, more people have died, directly and indirectly, from wars since Einstein and Russell's warning than in all wars fought up until that time. The Cold War, which so routinely produced surrogate hot wars of enormous destruction, pitted the United States against the Soviet Union for over forty years. It changed practically none of our thinking about international relations; rather it intensified our old thinking in a dangerous, nuclear age.

In the last couple of years, we have witnessed another turning point in

world history. The Cold War has largely ended. Extensive changes have
occurred in the Soviet bloc. We in the West no longer consider the former
USSR as the enemy. Ostensibly, the basis for our continued madness, and
headlong drive for war, has disappeared. Yet again we risk being in a period of monumental change, which we may shortchange by our refusal to
think differently. Rather than ending wars, the Cold War's decline might
well be taken as an opportunity to escalate our hot wars. Witness the
slaughter of 200,000 people in the recent Gulf War, where the destructive-
ness of our conventional weapons seemed almost as devastating as what we
always feared from nuclear wars. We find new pretexts for continued wars:
fighting drugs, regional policing, curbing nuclear proliferation, ethnic conflicts, counterinsurgency, and so forth. Thus, we approach the end of this
century with a world of change now in our grasp yet refuse to think in new
ways.

The dramatic events unfolding in the last few years, not only in Eastern
Europe but also in Latin America and elsewhere, should encourage us.
Change is possible, and new possibilities for peace and justice have
emerged.

   Nevertheless, formidable forces still impede a more just and peaceful
world. Militarism and violence continue despite the end of the Cold War,
with militaries inventing new tasks—such as drug wars—to maintain their
budgets. The United States has adopted an even more aggressive role as the
world's policeman in places like the Persian Gulf and Latin America—
coopting the United Nations along the way. Civil war, "ethnic cleansing,"
and systematic sexual assault ravage Bosnia and other war-torn corners of
the globe. Repression lingers, both East and West, and there are more
refugees than ever before. Racism and sexism plague the world community.
The gap between rich and poor nations widens, leaving malnutrition, homelessness, disease, premature death, and other destitution, such as the starvation in Somalia. Third World communities in the developed world suffer as
well. Stronger nations keep intervening, economically and militarily, into
weaker nations. Nuclear weapons are still aimed at old Cold War enemies,
and nuclear capabilities proliferate to new nations. Crime and other domestic violence escalates. The new nationalism promotes racial and ethnic conflict and erodes the possibilities for democracy in Europe, Africa, and Latin
America. And environmental decay has reached crisis proportions, from oil
spills to the greenhouse effect.

   While some are new, these problems have long plagued the world and
have long been unresolved by the theory and practice of conventional international relations. Can peace studies provide an effective alternative
model? We think so.

   But how can peace studies meet these challenges? About four years
ago, the journal *Peace Review* was established to answer this question. It

encouraged writers and readers to think in new ways. Our objective was to offer greater access to peace research to academics, policymakers, and the lay public. Built on a sixty-year legacy of peace research, and based on rigorous, scholarly work, our essays have promoted an open, public discourse on new strategies for promoting a more peaceful world. We have printed the best of these essays in this book. We can only hope that the time has come for these ideas to be finally heeded.

In our essays, we have wondered why conventional politics and generations of peace movements have not quelled our fascination with militarism and the false security it affords. To reflect our changing times, we have run essays that have looked at the barriers to peace and justice in new ways. We want to know how we got to where we are now. What kind of thinking has kept leading us to war? And we want to know how we can fundamentally change our thinking so that a peaceful future is more than simply a pipe dream.

I n sum, we want to "rethink" peace in light of the emerging New World Order. But how much real rethinking can be accomplished? According to *Newsweek* columnist Meg Greenfield, the answer is "not much." She argues:

> Rethinking is what we always announce we are doing when the big picture changes traumatically in a kind of "death rains down on the dinosaurs" way . . . [But] no good ever came of rethinking. This is mainly because so little rethinking ever came of rethinking—it is mostly another kind of activity altogether, something more like rearranging things so that you or your think tank or your agency will not lose position or power or— God forbid—your entire reason for being, under the changed conditions.

With these words, Greenfield provides a useful warning. But rather than give up the ship, we have resolved to meet her challenge. While through the years, we have seen enough peace studies papers or conferences that insist that we are "at the crossroads," and that purportedly tell us "where we go from here," some eras really *are* a crossroads. In his book *The Imagination of the New Left,* George Katsiaficas tells us why only a few select years qualify as "revolutionary" in modern history. Along with his 1789, 1848, 1905, 1917, and 1968, we must include 1945—the birth of the Nuclear Age, and 1989—the end of the Cold War. Not coincidentally, as Fritjof Capra argues in his book *The Turning Point,* a radical change of thinking, both in concepts and values, is needed to solve the unprecedented problems of our world today. This change, he claims, must be from a mechanistic worldview to an ecological one. It is necessary because all the current problems around the globe are interconnected—they are systemic. They comprise what Paul Joseph, in his *Peace Politics,* calls our "shared fate."

There is little doubt that things have changed profoundly, ameliorating certain problems while provoking others. Although Greenfield is no doubt right about there being few "grand thinkings," the essays that follow are more than "rearranging" old ideas. At least a few will likely serve as landmarks in genuinely rethinking the world's future. Yes, as Greenfield argues, rethinking will always have to be rethought. Indeed, as Vaclav Havel has suggested, that is precisely the task of intellectuals in the modern era. We have gathered here a diverse group of intellectuals who, without apologies, are quite eager to accept this responsibility.

Elsewhere, David Meyer has recently suggested the "paradox of open windows." It is ironic, he argues, that the peace movement—of which peace scholars are a part—seems to be mobilized the most when the possibilities for peace and change are the worst, and vice versa. As the window of opportunity for transformation opens wider, it seems that the window of new thoughts and action closes down. Our task, therefore, is to throw open the window of ideas before the window of change begins to close. We approach this endeavor soberly: Although we are positive about what we can accomplish, we realize there are as many barriers as opportunities.

*R**ethinking Peace* fits into a rich and lengthy tradition of peace scholarship. To understand that tradition, we will first examine what we mean by *peace,* and then what we mean by *peace studies.*

There is no universal concept of peace but we can identify several different perspectives. The longest-standing notion of peace is "negative" peace, or the absence of war and other direct violence. Some define peace even more narrowly to include only the absence or prevention of nuclear war. But arguably, this is a definition more appropriate to security studies or traditional international relations. Those fields, relying on the so-called realist school of thought, generally focus more on war than on peace, and more readily accept the inevitability of warfare. Peace studies, of course, does not. Going in the other direction, some have expanded the notion of negative peace to include (the absence of) other forms of direct violence, both organized and random.

Still others describe peace even more broadly, as "positive" peace: the presence or promotion of social justice. Under this conception, a peaceful society or world requires the absence of war and other direct violence but also requires the protection of human rights. Here again, we can see both narrower and broader conceptions. Western societies (and particularly the United States) have confined themselves to political and civil rights, or those rights of political and personal freedom with which states should not interfere. Here, the absence of state repression, for example, would be a sign of peace. In contrast, Eastern societies (and particularly the former Soviet Union) and developing societies have emphasized economic, social, and cultural rights, or those rights of human welfare that states have an obligation to provide. Here, the absence of structural violence, such as underdevelopment and institutionalized poverty, would be a sign of peace.

Some societies, like most of the European nations and also Canada and New Zealand, have accepted both definitions of human rights as crucial to a peaceful world. And yet a third conception of human rights has also recently emerged. It includes a more explicit right to peace, as well as rights to development and environmental preservation.

Concepts of positive peace generally accept all these definitions of human rights. Rather than taking the position—as do U.S. officials—that economic rights contradict political rights, advocates of positive peace believe that they are complementary and that more just ways of organizing societies and the world can be devised.

Likewise, we can see how negative and positive peace complement each other. The presence of war and other direct violence (the absence of negative peace) not only disrupt the immediate "peace" but also promote social injustice (the absence of positive peace), since they promote widespread violations of human rights in all its definitions. The Gulf War, for example, not only brought the relentless violence of U.S. weapons immediately upon the Iraqi people, but it also generated other violence (such as an escalation in sexual assaults against women), further eroded their political and civil freedoms, and, even more seriously, undermined their economic well-being—leaving widespread disease, starvation, and homelessness in its wake. It also devastated Iraq's progress toward development, as well as the natural environment of the entire region.

But the reverse is also true: The presence of social injustice (the absence of positive peace) provides not only the immediate violence of repression and oppression but also the breeding grounds for the development of war or other direct violence such as crime. For example, the widespread social injustice in Central America and the Caribbean has led to the development of revolutionary movements for change. Reacting to years of structural violence, populations rise up, often producing civil wars where the state attempts to beat back challenges to its rule. Similarly, years of economic deprivation, social neglect, and racial or class injustices can provide the breeding grounds for greater direct violence—in the form of crime—in any society. In other words, if you want peace, you have to have justice, and vice versa.

Simply put, peace studies is the systematic study of the causes of war and violence and the conditions of peace. Peace studies encompasses at least peace research and peace education and arguably also peace action. The study of peace, however, has progressed through various stages. Carolyn Stephenson has identified three "waves" of peace studies.

The First Wave: The first wave began in the 1930s with the quantitative analyses of war conducted by Quincy Wright and Lewis Richardson. But peace research institutes did not emerge until the mid-1940s in France, the Netherlands, and the United States. In 1945, the *Bulletin of the Atomic Scientists* was founded. In the early 1950s, the Research Exchange on the Prevention of War began publishing its *Bulletin,* which led to the creation at the University of Michigan of the *Journal of Conflict Resolution,* under the influence of Kenneth Boulding, Herbert Kelman, and Anatol Rapaport. This was also the base for the Center for Research on Conflict Resolution, and the Correlates of War Project—under the direction of J. David Singer. In 1959, the Richardson Peace Research Centre was formed in Lancaster, England, and Alan and Hanna Newcombe formed the Peace Research Institute in Dundas, Canada, which emphasized a "negative" definition of peace. That same year, Johan Galtung established the Peace Research Institute of Oslo, in Norway, which adopted a radical new "positive" definition of peace. In 1964, it began publishing the *Journal of Peace Research* and, a bit later, the *Bulletin of Peace Proposals* (now *Security Dialogue*). The Stockholm International Peace Research Institute, which emphasized armament and disarmament, was also founded in the early 1960s.

International societies also emerged, such as the Peace Research (now Science) Society (International), which was begun by Walter Izard in Sweden in 1963. The International Peace Research Association (IPRA) emerged from the Quaker International Conference in Clarens, Switzerland, in 1963 and held its first conference at the Polemological Institute of the University of Groningen, Netherlands, under the direction of Bert Roling. National peace associations also emerged, such as the Council on Peace Research in History, which formed in 1963 in response to the John Kennedy assassination and the escalation of U.S. involvement in Vietnam. In 1972, it began *Peace and Change,* which was later jointly published by the Consortium on Peace Research, Education and Development (COPRED). The Japan Peace Research Group was founded in 1964, and the Canadian Peace Research and Education Association was formed in 1966.

The Second Wave: The second wave of peace studies began in the late 1960s. The reaction to Vietnam led to radical peace research in northern Europe, and to the emergence of peace education in the United States. Peace research was for the first time introduced extensively into the undergraduate classroom. Manchester College in Indiana had established the first peace studies program in 1948, but the big surge in programs began in the early 1970s.

Many were spurred by two organizations: the Institute for World Order (now the World Policy Institute, which has moved from education to research, publishing *Alternatives*—jointly with the Centre for the Study of Developing Societies in India—and the *World Policy Journal,* presently based at the New School for Social Research), which was established in New York by Richard Falk and Saul Mendlovitz; and COPRED, founded by Elise and Kenneth Boulding in 1970. Both organizations helped develop new university programs at places such as Syracuse, Manhattan, Akron, Kent State, and Gustavus Adolphus. The first chair in peace studies was established at Colgate in 1971. Unlike earlier education efforts, which emphasized graduate studies (at places such as Northwestern, Stanford, and Yale in the United States, and Lund, Gothenburg, and Uppsala in Sweden), the new programs focused on undergraduates and numbered about 100 by the end of the 1970s. The University of Bradford in England offered both graduate and undergraduate studies and established Britain's first peace studies chair in 1973.

This period broadened peace studies from the examination of war to the examination of other kinds of violence and injustice. The rise of various movements, such as those for civil rights and feminism, and against the Vietnam War, produced an internal, radical critique of peace studies. Some felt that peace studies was underestimating the violence done by structures of power. Decolonization, and then the oil crisis, led to an increasing emphasis on Third World development in peace studies, including questions of poverty, inequality, and malnutrition. A questioning of "objective" science promoted a greater emphasis on values.

The Peace Education Commission of IPRA was founded in 1973 to help make peace research more accessible and to promote experiential learning and democratic pedagogy. The Japanese Peace Studies Association began in 1973. In the United States, the International Studies Association and the American Sociological Association formed subsections on peace studies, and peace issues helped motivate the development of the Caucus for a New Political Science—an alternative to the conservative American Political Science Association. In 1974, The Latin American Council on Peace Research was formed in Mexico, and the Asian Peace Research Association was formed in Japan.

The Third Wave: The third wave of peace studies began in the early 1980s, less from the research and education community, and more from peace movements and the escalating threats to world peace such as that posed by the nuclear arms race. Antinuclear concerns generated organizations such as Physicians for Social Responsibility, the International Physicians for the Prevention of Nuclear War, and Artists for Social Responsibility. These led to educational organizations such as Educators for Social Responsibility and United Campuses Against Nuclear War, and to groups who allied with older institutions such as the Center for the Teaching of International Relations at the University of Denver, the Peace Education Program of the Teacher's College at Columbia University, the Center for Global Responsibility, and the Peace Education Network of COPRED.

The surge in programs began with the threat of nuclear war, but it again broadened to examine military intervention and other forms of direct violence, repression, and injustice. Researchers examined structural alternatives designed to influence or transform political systems, such as nonviolent sanctions, nonoffensive defense, and conflict resolution. The conditions of peace joined the causes of war as a major emphasis of the field.

In 1980, UNESCO held the first Disarmament Education Conference. Gene Sharp's work on nonviolent action and civilian-based defense gained publicity, partly through the Program in Nonviolent Sanctions established at Harvard. Work on alternative defense, or nonoffensive defense, began in Europe and then spread to the United States by the mid-1980s. The Institute for Defense and Disarmament Studies, founded by Randall Forsberg, promoted research to both compete with mainstream "bomb counters" and to help develop the nuclear freeze movement—jointly devised by Helen Caldicott and her Women's Action for Nuclear Disarmament (WAND).

Conflict resolution and mediation surged in importance during this period. Programs were devised for conflicts ranging from the interpersonal to the local to the national to the international levels. Groups such as the National Institute on Dispute Resolution, the Society of Professionals in Dispute Resolution, and the National Conference on Peacemaking and Conflict Resolution were started. Conflict resolution programs were begun at places such as Hawaii, Michigan, Minnesota, George Mason, Wisconsin, Syracuse, Colorado, and the Harvard-based Boston university negotiation consortium.

Regional organizations of peace faculty began in the mid-1980s in Indiana, Hawaii, New England, New York, Ohio, Oregon, and Wisconsin. New peace studies programs began at places such as Tufts, Oregon, Brandeis, the University of California at Berkeley, Notre Dame, and the Five College Consortium in Amherst. By the late 1980s, the number of programs had increased to 250. In 1987, the Peace Studies Association was formed at a meeting at the University of California, Irvine, and based first at Bethel College in Kansas and then at the University of Colorado, Boulder. In 1984, the magazine *Nuclear Times* was established. In 1989, *Peace Review* was established at Stanford University and then moved to the University of San Francisco.

Governments began institutionalizing peace research and education in states such as California, Hawaii, New Jersey, Ohio, and Wisconsin, and in countries such as New Zealand. National institutes emerged, such as the United Nations University for Peace in Costa Rica, the Austrian Peace Research Institute, the Canadian Institute for Peace and International Security, the Australian Peace Research Centre, the U.S. Institute for Peace, the European Center for Peace Studies in Austria, the Soviet Research Council on Peace and Development, and the Peace Research Unit of the Czechoslovak Academy of Sciences.

This brief overview of the evolution of peace studies shows us roughly where we have been. It represents more than half a century of focused research and education designed to explore the conditions and correlates of peace. But that exploration has not been without its opponents. Peace studies has been periodically assaulted by mainstream policymakers and journalists, conservative university faculty and administrators, and the political right. When not outright prevented, peace studies has always been starved for resources. It has been condemned as unpatriotic and un-American and as a field falling outside the supposed "value-free" objectivity of mainstream academia. Despite the challenges, peace studies has always reemerged arguably stronger in each succeeding era. Although it has not always been a smooth and continuous development, much progress has been made. The world is still fraught with violence, but many believe that peace studies has made some important contributions toward a more peaceful future.

To address that future, peace studies must adapt, once again, to changing circumstances. What does peace studies represent in the post–Cold War New World Order? Arguably, we must move into yet another stage: a *fourth wave* of peace studies. *Rethinking Peace* contributes precisely to this task.

To launch a new wave of peace studies, we must begin with the foundations that have gotten us this far. And then we must break new ground. For example, peace studies must continue to emphasize subfields such as violence and warfare, militarism, nuclear weapons, global conflict and cooperation, racism and sexism, class and underdevelopment, human rights and repression, and global movements and social change. But it must also address itself more directly to questions of common security, economic justice, racial and ethnic conflict, nuclear proliferation, military conversion, violence against women, cultural violence, North-South and South-South conflicts, and especially interrelationships among problems such as "the bomb, the debt, and the rainforest," or among gender, militarism, and development. Peace studies should develop more sophisticated theories of social change. It should reexamine the role of supranational organizations such as the United Nations and of transnational organizations such as Amnesty International and Oxfam. And peace studies should explore new innovations in peacemaking.

Likewise, the fourth wave of peace studies should begin with the methods that have distinguished it from traditional international relations and security studies and then expand them in new directions. For example, peace studies should keep promoting critical thinking, a consideration of competing perspectives, and the questioning of the conventional wisdom. It should remain multidisciplinary, involving as many fields as possible in the study of peace. It should be global—avoiding ethnocentrism, celebrating cross-cultural linkages as well as differences, and emphasizing the interconnectedness of the world's peoples and problems. Peace studies should also keep promoting social responsibility: a sense of global citizenship, the

motivation toward service and public participation, and the quest for positive social change.

But methodologically, peace studies can do even more. It must put a
greater emphasis on diversity, in both who does peace studies and in who
peace studies focuses upon. The threat of nuclear war seems secondary, for
example, to those who live under such dire and violent structural conditions
that they believe the bomb has already been dropped on where they live.
The development of new associations, such as the African Peace Research
Association and the expanded Asia-Pacific Peace Research Association, is
an encouraging sign in this regard.

Peace studies must also move from being merely multidisciplinary to
being more interdisciplinary. The field must become more integrated and
better able to make connections among its diverse strands and subfields.
Peace studies should put conflict and its resolution into perspective. Not all
conflict is bad; peacefully managed, some conflict is healthy. In particular,
as Joseph Fahey argues, peace studies should not let its preference for nonviolence turn into passivity, especially in confronting the state structures
that routinely prevent a peaceful world. And not all conflict resolution
should be so readily accepted, especially when it masks power disparities
and helps coopt rightful claims for greater justice and well-being.

Peace studies must also recognize that only fundamental change will
eliminate the war system. Some reforms might be welcomed, and change
might require intermediate steps, but we cannot achieve a genuinely peaceful world with our current structures and ideologies. And peace studies
must better integrate its key components: Peace research and peace education must be more closely linked, and both must lead more readily to productive peace action.

We believe that *Rethinking Peace* can help peace studies move in these
new directions. We would like to see peace studies undergo a kind of glasnost (opening up) and perestroika (restructuring). We have adopted a social
problems perspective on peace in the essays that follow. In other words, we
contend that the barriers to peace are not biological or natural. Rather, they
result from failed social structures and arrangements, within societies and
within the international system itself.

To help set peace studies off in new directions, we look both back-
wards and forwards. We want to know what kind of thinking has gotten us
to this point, but we are even more interested in where new thinking can
take us. Based on the latest developments, *Rethinking Peace* tries to take
some classic debates into the twenty-first century. We are interested in disputes about the nature of progress and human nature, about the relationship
between masculinity and war, and about which economic structures promote the greatest justice. What happens to the debate between "realism"
and "idealism" in international relations in the post–Cold War period? Has
there really been an end to ideology, or has it simply been masked to justify

the New World Order? And what is the role of "civil society" as an alternative to societies and a world now dominated by states?

More specifically, *Rethinking Peace* begins by examining some of the "old thinking" about international relations that underlie our violent and militarized world. It reviews the assumptions and strategies behind the war system and how they have influenced not only policymakers but people around the world. We will examine the presumptions behind phenomena such as national security, nuclear war planning, and military adventurism.

Next, we want to take stock and rethink contemporary models of war and peace. We present critical approaches, which challenge this old thinking, and confront the conventional national and international policies that threaten or violate the peace. We will examine current dilemmas such as the new nationalism, the cooptation of the United Nations, and the plight of women in the developing world. And we will examine the new challenges to various regions of the world, from Europe to the Middle East to Africa to Asia-Pacific.

Then, *Rethinking Peace* explores various new ideas for peace and new models for understanding both the causes and cures for violence. Rather than merely criticizing current thinking, how can we think differently and more positively about a better future for both domestic and international relations? And how can we more peacefully promote a greater public participation in shaping a better world? This endeavor begins with developing a "new consciousness," such as by carving out new roles for the arts, education, the media, and other components of our cultures. It also asks us to listen more carefully to voices that are usually ignored, such as those of women and people of color. And that new thinking can lead to new models for peace, such as a more participatory economics, a revitalized civil society, and alternative approaches to development and security.

Finally, *Rethinking Peace* promotes new strategies for converting new thinking into effective peace action. We emphasize practical approaches for social change, from the local to the global. This begins with strategies for peace action such as grassroots organizing, citizen assemblies, and municipal diplomacy. And then we examine the state of several contemporary peace movements, in places like the United States, Japan, and Africa.

We have developed *Rethinking Peace* by relying on unprecedented diversity. Our authors represent a wide spectrum of race, gender, and ethnic backgrounds; they are drawn from many different nationalities, spanning virtually every region of the world. Also, rather than being confined to a few, predictable disciplines, *Rethinking Peace* is highly interdisciplinary. It brings together writers in fields as diverse as sociology, politics, law, philosophy, writing, English literature, history, theology, psychology, education, economics, linguistics, criminology, fine art, media studies, modern languages, women's studies, international relations, and environmental studies.

In sum, *Rethinking Peace* provides a unique and stimulating perspective on the barriers and prospects for global peace. We hope the essays that follow will open whole new worlds for those who read them.

We would like to thank Carolyn Stephenson for her analysis (from which we have borrowed liberally) of the various "waves" of peace studies, in "The Evolution of Peace Studies," in Daniel C. Thomas and Michael T. Klare, eds., *Peace and World Order Studies* (Boulder: Westview Press, 1989).

PART 1
OLD THINKING: HOW DID WE GET HERE?

OLD THINKING:
HOW DID WE GET HERE?

Great minds against themselves conspire
And shun the cure they most desire.

—Anonymous

The quest for security is a natural one. Yet, arguably, the realities we have created for ourselves about what will produce that security have led us repeatedly down roads that have been counterproductive to that end. How could even "great minds" have devised means to peace that have been so consistently violent?

This section provides an overview of the old patterns of thinking that have produced our violent, militarized world. We will examine the assumptions and strategies behind the war system and how they have entered our collective consciousness.

How, for example, has our national security become associated with the attributes of "real men," and how has masculinity become equated with the willingness to be violent? How did emerging "fantasies of power" help fuel our destructive militarism, especially the promotion of nuclear weapons? How did "security studies" emerge, and how has it come to dominate and limit our sense of what is possible and impossible in international relations? How have we been ingrained in the routine belligerency and purported superiority of Western civilization? And how has the missionary zeal of the Christian Crusades in Europe been transplanted, beginning with Columbus, in the Americas, and particularly in U.S. foreign policy?

2

REAL MEN, WIMPS, AND NATIONAL SECURITY

MYRIAM MIEDZIAN

If we stop imbuing our boys with the values of the masculine mystique, we'll end up raising nice, decent, sensitive men who will do just about anything to avoid war and violence. But what about the Hitlers, the Khomeinis, the Husseins, and the rest of the belligerent unliberated world? They'll go on raising strong, tough men ready to fight at the slightest provocation—or without any provocation at all. Our nice wimpy leaders will be sitting ducks. We can't afford this kind of experimentation, the "realists" will say; our national security is at stake.

I wanted to put this type of objection to rest. But the more research I did the clearer it became that our national security was already endangered. The "real men" who run our country are handicapped by the values of the masculine mystique in their ability to make rational foreign policy decisions.

These values also serve as a facile cover for self-serving economic interests. They help mask the fact that many national defense decisions have more to do with economic interests of the military-industrial complex than with defense needs. This further endangers our national security.

The masculine mystique hampers the real men in our government in their ability to deal rationally with national security issues. It influences many citizens to support wars unquestioningly, and encourages young boys to sacrifice their lives in them, often unnecessarily.

Through much of our history, the failure to place pragmatic over moral concerns, the failure of a person in government to fully embrace a policy of unquestioning belligerence and/or full-scale war toward whoever the enemy might be has led to that person being called soft, weak, unmanly, unpatriotic, an abettor of the enemy, and most recently wimpish.

This essay is excerpted from Myriam Miedzian, *Boys Will Be Boys* (New York: Doubleday, 1991).

In 1848, then Congressman Abraham Lincoln was vilified in the Illinois press for his stance against the Mexican-American War, a war waged by the United States in order to take from Mexico some of its provinces.

When Woodrow Wilson showed reluctance to enter World War I, Theodore Roosevelt charged that Wilson has "done more to emasculate American manhood and weaken its fiber than anyone else I can think of."

New York Times columnist Tom Wicker recalls that during the Vietnam War he was regarded by many as being unpatriotic because he opposed the war, but columnist Joseph Alsop, who supported the war, was not considered unpatriotic: "You can't be considered unpatriotic if you're for a war." To be deeply committed to negotiations, to be opposed to a particular war or military action, is not only considered unpatriotic, it also casts serious doubt on one's manhood.

I n his book *The Best and the Brightest,* David Halberstam informs us that "the thing [Lyndon] Johnson feared most was . . . that his manhood might be inadequate." When Johnson was told that a member of his administration was going soft on the war, he dismissed him with the comment "Hell, he has to squat to piss." According to Halberstam, "Manhood was very much in the minds of the architects of [the Vietnam War]. They wanted to show who had bigger balls."

Paul Warnke, chief American negotiator of the 1979 Salt II Arms Control Treaty remembers being called a "weak wimp" by the Committee on the Present Danger, which succeeded in preventing the ratification of the treaty by the Senate.

In the Contragate secret jargon, the name for the State Department was "Wimp." This was due to then Secretary of State Shultz's disapproval of the sale of weapons to Iran and diversion of profits to the Contras.

When TV interviewer Larry King asked Speaker of the House Tip O'Neill why the President [Reagan] wanted to intervene in Nicaragua, O'Neill responded, "It's his being a man. [The President believes] America has to show a firmness of manhood."

After the 1989 United States military intervention in Panama, the *New York Times* ran a front-page story entitled, "War: Bush's Presidential Rite of Passage." The article pointed out that "for better or for worse, most American leaders since World War II have felt a need to demonstrate their willingness to shed blood. . . . All of them acted in the belief that the American political culture required them to show the world promptly that they carried big sticks." A year later, the press was discussing President Bush's need to prove his manhood as a motivating factor in his threats to go to war with Iraq [emphasizing], for example, Bush's tough talk about Saddam Hussein getting "his ass kicked."

R ichard Barnet describes the inner sanctums of power: "One of the first lessons a national security manager learns after a day in the bureaucratic climate of the Pentagon, State Department, White House, or CIA is that toughness is the most highly prized virtue. . . . The man who is ready to recommend using violence against foreigners, even where he is overruled, does not damage his reputation for prudence, soundness, or imagination." On the other hand, "the man who recommends putting an issue to the UN, seeking negotiations, or horrors of horrors, 'doing nothing' quickly becomes known as 'soft.'"

Barnet points out that since the onset of the Cold War "the outstanding bureaucratic casualties . . . have all been men who took modest risks to promote conciliation rather than confrontation. In the 1950's George Kennan, father of our Soviet "containment" policy, lost political influence when he expressed the view that the Soviets did not represent a serious military threat in Europe and that negotiations with them were preferable to continued confrontation. In 1962 Chester Bowles developed a reputation for "woolliness" because of a plan he proposed for the neutralization of Southeast Asia. For this Bowles soon lost his position as Undersecretary of State. Barnet points out that "ten years later [Bowles's plan] would look like a blueprint for a US victory."

It is difficult to think clearly and rationally, to entertain all the possibilities objectively when taking "wimpish" positions endangers one's high position in government and one's livelihood, and puts one at risk of being considered unpatriotic. Only men of exceptional courage will do so.

As long as those who favor negotiations and are reluctant to enter armed conflicts are put on the defensive are considered "wimps," it will be exceedingly difficult to pull away the cloak of patriotism in which our military-industrial-congressional-academic complex is wrapped, and clearly analyze our military needs for the future.

Barnet is convinced that our national security managers suffer from a severe handicap in conducting foreign relations because they have no "training or incentive to develop understanding, compassion, or empathy for people in different circumstances from their own."

An important part of what enabled Chester Bowles and other wimps like him to foresee that getting involved in a war in Vietnam would be a calamitous mistake was their ability to empathize with the Vietnamese people, see things from their perspective. They understood that Ho Chi Minh was a national hero for the Vietnamese, and that the Viet Cong, which was the offshoot of the revolutionary army, had the enthusiastic support of the Vietnamese people. Because they understood this, they realized that it would be close to impossible for the United States to win in Vietnam.

To the architects of the Vietnam War, empathy was a "soft, irrational, effeminate" quality antithetical to their "rational, hard-nosed" thinking.

And so they were unable to develop a realistic understanding of the situation.

During much of our history, the tendency has been to identify political rationality with hard positional bargaining and the willingness to go to war when such bargaining fails. Being weak, irrational, and wimpish has been identified with soft positional bargaining and a disinclination toward war.

But if we look carefully at the distinction between weak positional bargaining and principled bargaining, we realize that many of the men maligned as being wimps have in fact been much closer to the latter in their way of thinking about foreign policy than the former. They have been aware of the need to understand and empathize with the other side in order to arrive at a realistic long-range solution. They shun the kind of macho posturing and concern with ego that characterize hard positional bargaining.

Ron Kovic, the Vietnam War veteran whose autobiography *Born on the Fourth of July* was made into a film, returned from the war a paraplegic, and became increasingly enraged as he realized that his sacrifice had been unnecessary. He writes:

> We had never been anything but a thing to them, a thing to put a uniform on and train to kill. . . . They were smooth talkers, men who wore suits and smiled and were polite, men who wore watches and sat behind big desks sticking pins in maps. . . . They had never seen blood and guts and heads and arms. They had never picked up the shattered legs of children and watched the blood drip into the sand below their feet.

S aving lives is not a top priority in the halls of power. Being compassionate and concerned about human life can cause a man to lose his job. It can cause a woman not to get a job to begin with. Women's reputed empathy and compassion are viewed by many as rendering them unqualified for high offices that involve "tough" international decision-making.

David Evans, a former Marine lieutenant colonel who is now the military correspondent for the *Chicago Tribune,* vigorously rejects this callous, unempathetic attitude. He is convinced that it leads to a thoroughly unrealistic foreign policy based on fantasy and denial, and that direct involvement in combat leads most men away from a macho, belligerent response to political conflict. War becomes a nightmarish reality, not a patriotic, flag-waving, exciting demonstration of manhood. A relatively small percentage (Oliver North comes to mind) are excited by battle and cannot get enough of it.

Evans points out that many of the men in our government who take the toughest, most macho positions on foreign policy and nuclear strategy have never seen any form of combat. McGeorge Bundy, Robert McNamara, and Walt Rostow served in World War II, but their service was limited to planning and analysis. They all supported the Bay of Pigs invasion of Cuba and the Vietnam War.

In the Reagan administration, Pat Buchanan, Elliot Abrams, and Richard Perle favored support for the Contras and more American involvement in Nicaragua. They took "tough" positions on the nuclear arms race. None of them has been in the service.

The social conditioning that romanticizes war and teaches young boys to repress empathy, to be tough, to be fearless, not to cry, to value winning more than anything, leads to the development of "mental machismo" among politicians who make decisions unencumbered by moral scruples. Their machismo requires the courage to make decisions without concern for the human suffering they will bring to others. This "detached" decision-making, which is in fact deeply attached to the values of the masculine mystique, is then viewed as the epitome of male rationality.

A fter having spent three years at the Pentagon, Evans is convinced that our most dangerous failure to deal with reality is in nuclear policy. He describes the men who develop our nuclear strategy and defense policy as suffering from severe "denial psychosis." The fact that most of them have never experienced any war first hand makes it easier for them to shield themselves from any concrete sense of what fifty million casualties or the destruction of ten of our major cities might really mean.

Their tendency to look at war "as a huge football game" further facilitates avoidance: An advertisement by the manufacturer of the F-15 fighter compares its uses to football plays, stating that "we've gone to a long deep pass from a nuclear line of scrimmage." Star Wars is perceived as "blocking the kick."

The briefcase that contains the secret codes needed to authorize the launching of our nuclear weapons follows the President everywhere, enabling him to react immediately in case of nuclear attack. This all-important briefcase, whose contents hold the key to destroying all life on earth, is called the "football." In the Vietnam War, the May to October 1972 bombing of North Vietnam was named "Linebacker I"; the December bombing was "Linebacker II."

In describing the White House reaction to Mikhail Gorbachev's July 1985 announcement of a unilateral nuclear test ban, then National Security Adviser Robert McFarlane stated that it led to "a sense that they were more agile now, so we had to become agile ourselves. It's like being a member of the Notre Dame football team and you're used to playing Davidson. And all of a sudden Davidson recruits some players from the New York Giants. You have to adapt and move quicker yourself."

The obsession with winning, and the notion that you can never go wrong being too tough, owe much to the training in extremely competitive sports that so many American boys receive from the youngest age, both as participants and as spectators. In sports, there is no further goal beyond winning. For many men in government the goal of "winning," of having more than "they" do, becomes a substitute for a carefully considered foreign policy [which analyzes] the effects that various policy decisions are likely to have on human beings.

A uthor Carol Cohn likewise argues that the thinking of nuclear theorists is based on the avoidance of nuclear reality. Both the limited subject matter they deal with—in their "war games," nuclear strategists are concerned primarily with survival of weaponry, not human beings—and the techno-strategic language they have created make it possible for these normal, decent men to plan nuclear holocaust as though it were just another job.

The use of abstraction and euphemism allows them to talk about nuclear holocaust without having to deal with the reality behind their words. In their language the incinerating of cities is referred to as "countervalue attacks." "Collateral damage" refers to human deaths. A "surgically clean strike" refers to "attacks that can purportedly 'take out'—i.e., accurately destroy—an opponent's weapons or command centers without causing significant injury to anything else."

The nuclear strategists' theorizing is about weapons, not about people. If asked about human survival, they will explain that they don't deal with those issues. They consider the separation of technical knowledge and theorizing from social, psychological, or moral issues to be legitimate and necessary. This separation enables them to talk about weapons that are supposed to protect people "without actually asking if they can do it, or if they are the best way to do it, or whether they may even damage the entities you are supposedly protecting."

T he masculine mystique teaches men to be tough, to repress empathy, and to not let moral concerns weigh too heavily when the goal is winning. These qualities have become identified with political realism.

But what is rational or realistic about not allowing the human cost of war to be a major factor in political decision-making? Why is not weighing the suffering of the Ron Kovics who fight wars or of the civilians who are innocent victims, a condition of rationality? Why does political realism require a lack of concern with moral issues?

Could it be that if politicians allowed themselves to feel empathetic they would feel so sorry for the soldiers who might be maimed or killed in war that they would be paralyzed, unable to do what [is] necessary to defend our nation against dangerous enemies? Would moral concerns about killing civilians lead them down an irrational road to enslavement?

The answer is clearly no, for the tendency to defend oneself against attack is so strong, both in terms of individuals and groups, that it is almost unthinkable that leaders imbued with moral concern would allow our nation to be attacked and not respond. The bloody history of our species suggests that much greater effort is required to restrain violent response than to encourage it.

The claim that theirs is an "instrumental" rationality that does not get involved in questions of values detracts from the fact that the values [of men in power] are almost entirely limited to what they take to be national power, prestige, and economic interests [which] often grow out of their own ego needs, their need to prove [their] manhood, or their desire to secure positions of power. Instrumental rationality permits them to avoid fundamental questions. For example, if our national interest is related to the welfare of our citizens (isn't that what the Constitution tells us?) then what could be more contrary than a cavalier disregard for the lives of young Americans who fight in wars whose need has never been rationally assessed?

T he belligerent policies of the "real men" in power are made possible through public support given by citizens raised to believe that being patriotic means supporting their nation's wars and military actions without question. The values of the masculine mystique prepare boys, from the youngest age, to someday willingly risk their lives in battle. Boys find out at a very early age that war is respectable. There are endless role models of great conquerors, heroic warriors, and brave soldiers.

It is not only patriotism that leads so many parents to acquiesce in the sacrifice of their sons in unnecessary wars, but also pride in their sons manhood. (Many young women raised with the image of men as tough and dominant find men in uniform sexy, thus further reinforcing these values.)

In a letter published in the *Ladies Home Journal* during World War I, a father writes to his son: "Don't forget that the biggest thing that a war can do is to bring out that man [in you]. That's really what you and the other chaps have gone over for, to demonstrate the right kind of manhood."

The opportunities for demonstrating manhood in a major war are greatly diminished in a nuclear age, but excitement over violent conflict continues. In 1984, when my younger daughter's sixth-grade class voted on a nuclear freeze (after having studied the issue), out of twelve girls, eleven supported a nuclear freeze, one was undecided. Out of seventeen boys, six were pro-freeze, three were undecided, and eight opposed a freeze. "Nukes all the way!!!!!" one boy wrote. "I say yes to total Global Thermonuclear Missiles build up (in other words NUKES)," wrote another.

In the film of *Born on the Fourth of July,* when Kovic visits the family of one of the men in his battalion who died in Vietnam, the soldier's father confesses that he doesn't understand what his son gave his life for; he doesn't grasp the purpose of the Vietnam War. But he does not question any further. He proudly tells Kovic that his own father fought in the First

World War and that he fought in the Second. On screen we see his young grandson, who will never know his father, practicing with his toy rifle for his turn to prove patriotism and manhood.

Like this young boy—like most young boys—Kovic started his practice for war at a very young age. The film opens with him and his friends playing war in the woods with their toy machine guns, helmets, grenades. Later we see Kovic's high school physical education teacher calling the boys "ladies" and screaming at them to sacrifice their bodies. (In the book it is the drill sergeant in boot camp who constantly threatens the young marines' manhood by calling them "ladies.") We also see a young Kovic despondent when he loses a wrestling match and jubilant when he plays an important role in winning a baseball game. This constant competition prepares boys to think in us/them and win/lose terms. They become so imbued with the glory of winning that it hardly matters to them, later, what military contests are about. They are mainly a chance to fight and win.

The romanticization of war through war toys, in books, in films, on TV, and the extreme emphasis on competitiveness, winning, and sacrifice in sports, all prepare young men to sacrifice their bodies and often their lives years later in warfare.

For his book *A Choice of Heroes,* Mark Gerzon interviewed a large number of Vietnam War veterans. He found that living out a John Wayne fantasy was foremost in the minds of many of those who had embraced the war. Typical was author Phil Caputo, who enlisted because he had wanted "the chance to live heroically. . . . I saw myself charging up some distant beachhead, like John Wayne in *Sands of Iwo Jima,* and then coming home a suntanned warrior with medals on my chest." Gerzon tells us that "the John Wayne syndrome is an explicit, if unwritten, code of conduct, a set of masculine traits we have been taught to revere since childhood." These traits include being "hard, tough, unemotional, ruthless, and competitive."

Author William Manchester, who fought in Asia in World War II, tells us that when his rifle company was polled on why they had joined the Marines, a majority cited a war fantasy with John Wayne called *To the Shores of Tripoli.*

Manchester recalls, "After my evacuation from Okinawa, I had the enormous pleasure of seeing Wayne humiliated in person at Aiea Heights Naval Hospital in Hawaii. . . . Each evening, Navy corpsmen would carry stretchers down to the hospital theater so the men could watch a movie. One night they had a surprise for us. Before the film the curtains parted and out stepped John Wayne, wearing a cowboy outfit—10 gallon hat, bandanna, checkered shirt, two pistols, chaps, boots and spurs. He grinned his aw-shucks grin, passed a hand over his face and said, 'Hi ya, guys!' He was greeted by a stony silence. Then somebody booed. Suddenly everyone was booing."

"This man was a symbol of the fake machismo we had come to hate, and we weren't going to listen to him. He tried and tried to make himself heard, but we drowned him out, and eventually he quit and left."

"Real men" seem unable to distinguish between (on the one hand) boldness in the ability to make decisions that are difficult precisely because of human concerns, and (on the other) making decisions without empathy for those who will suffer the consequences. They have mistakenly confused the latter with manliness.

(There is a certain irony that men, who in the political arena dismiss a concern with human morality as soft, are outraged—or at least claim to be—by crime, rape, and domestic violence: for it is the same values that guide them that also lead to male brutality in the home and crime in the street.)

If the so-called wimps are often ineffectual in changing our foreign policy, it is not for lack of determination, but because they are struggling against the values of the masculine mystique which are deeply embedded in our political establishment.

W e have come full circle. If the major objection, from a national security perspective, to our moving away from the masculine mystique and rearing sons who will not place intrinsic value on toughness, dominance, emotional detachment, and fierce competition is that such men will not be able to defend our nation in the real world, then our response is that the actions of the men who determine our national security policy now are based on confused thinking and self-deception that grows out of their attachment to the values of the masculine mystique.

Just like a John Wayne war movie, it's all fake machismo. Real strength, real courage, are based on dealing with reality, not denying it. The thinking of the real men who are supposed to be defending our national security is based on avoidance. All their talk about toughness is a form of verbal swaggering as unconnected to reality as John Wayne's physical swaggering on the screen.

3

FANTASIES OF POWER

—————————— H. BRUCE FRANKLIN ——————————

The year is 1910. A young Missouri farmer carefully copies down ten lines of science fiction poetry from Tennyson's *Locksley Hall* and places them in his wallet. The lines depict ultimate aerial superweapons of the future, waging a terrible climactic war in the skies:

> . . . there rain'd a ghastly dew
> From the nations' airy navies
> grappling in the central blue. . .

The horrors of this scientific warfare bring about universal peace and world government:

> . . . the war-drum throbb'd no longer,
> and the battle-flags were furl'd
> In the Parliament of man,
> the Federation of the world.

Now it is July 1945. The same Missourian, on his way to a historic conference in Europe, believes that he is about to gain control over the ultimate aerial superweapon. He pulls that now-faded slip of paper from his wallet, where he had been carrying it for thirty-five years, and recites those lines to news reporter A. Merriman Smith.

If Harry Truman believed that the atomic bomb might bring an end to war, it was not just because of a poem. As a very typical American, he had grown up in a cultural matrix bubbling with fantasies of ultimate weapons. Appearing first over a century ago as American science fiction, these fantasies were to shape the nation's conceptions of nuclear weapons and responses to them, decades before they materialized.

———————

This essay originally appeared as "Fatal Fiction: A Weapon to End All Wars," in the *Bulletin of Atomic Scientists* (November 1989). Copyright © 1989 by the Educational Foundation for Nuclear Science, 6042 South Kimbark, Chicago IL 60637, U.S.A. A one-year subscription to the *Bulletin* is $30.

S uch fantasies were kindled by the advent of modern technological warfare, which burst upon the world between 1861 and 1871 in the US Civil War and the Franco-Prussian War. In the 1870s, a new literary genre was born: fiction envisioning future wars. The typical European fantasy was militaristic propaganda designed to terrify its newly-emerging mass reading audience with a specter of their ill-prepared homeland invaded by some likely enemy, often armed with a deadly new weapon. But American authors churned out hundreds of novels and stories imagining future wars from a peculiarly American perspective. In this fantasy, the emergent faith in American technological genius wedded to an older faith in America's messianic destiny, engendering ecstatic visions of made-in-America super-weapons that would allow America to defeat all evil empires, wage war to end all wars, and make the world eternally safe for democracy. In the decades leading to World War I, this fiction was a main dish in the cultural diet of what is now called middle America.

Even before the discovery of radioactivity, American fiction was imag-ining weapons equal to nuclear weapons not only in explosive force but also in political and cultural power. A most revealing example is Frank Stockton's 1889 novel *The Great War Syndicate.* When war breaks out between England and the United States, twenty-three great capitalists form a syndicate, "with the object of taking entire charge of the war." The Great War Syndicate develops the *Motor Bomb,* with the explosive force of an atomic bomb. Merely demonstrating this dreadful weapon brings victory. England is then allowed to join the Syndicate of War as a junior partner, and the world submits to the Syndicate's benevolent rule. In the novel's final words:

> . . . all the nations of the world began to teach English in their schools, and the Spirit of Civilization raised her head with a confident smile.

T he mercy shown toward the British did not apply when superweapons were used against non-whites, especially Asians. The fate of Hiroshima and Nagasaki was foreshadowed decades earlier in dozens of future-war novels and stories that raved about the Yellow Peril. For exam-ple, Jack London's 1910 short story *The Unparalleled Invasion* predicts that in 1975, when the world seems doomed to be overrun by hordes of Chinese, it is saved by a secret weapon developed by an American scientist. Fleets of airships shower China with missiles loaded with "every virulent form of infectious death," exterminating the entire Chinese population with "bacteria, and germs, and microbes, and bacilli, cultured in the laboratories of the West." This is, as London so aptly says, "ultra-modern war, twenti-eth-century war, the war of the scientist and the laboratory." Once the Yellow Peril is entirely expunged, ". . . all survivors were put to death

wherever found," the world becomes a virtual utopia for the victorious
forces of progress, led by America. London's story is a twentieth-century,
American version of Tennyson's "ghastly dew" that rains from airships,
thus ending war and bringing about a prosperous, unified world. It
appeared in 1910, the very year that Harry Truman placed Tennyson's lines
in his wallet. It was published in *McClure's,* a magazine that young
Truman avidly devoured. As he wrote to his sweetheart Bess in 1913, "I
suppose I'll have to renew my subscription to *McClure's* now so I won't
miss a number."

T he situation in which the President saw himself in August 1945 is
forecast by the first novel to imagine radioactivity used as a weapon
of war: Roy Norton's 1907 *The Vanishing Fleets,* which was serialized in
the *Associated Sunday Magazines,* a Sunday insert carried by most leading
American newspapers (the *Parade* of its day). Japan launches a sneak
attack. But American scientists invent "the greatest engine of war that science has ever known"; giant radioplanes powered by radioactivity and
capable of sweeping away whole fleets of warships. The President, "his
Americanism exceeded only by his humanitarianism," decides that his
solemn duty to humanity is to use this weapon in war—in order to end war.
He explains why secrecy is imperative:

> If our secret becomes known . . . the Japanese might not continue the war,
> thereby depriving us of the opportunity to actually use this . . . most dead-
> ly machine ever conceived . . . thereby ending wars for all time. . . . Let us
> bear with fortitude whatever reproaches may be heaped upon us, for we
> are the instruments of God.

After American fliers win "the last great battle in history," the
President announces: "The United States, having faith in the Anglo-Saxon
race as the most peaceful and conservative, has formed an alliance with
Great Britain." Thus comes the end of war; American-Anglo hegemony and
perpetual peace are guaranteed by the eternal American monopoly on the
superweapon produced in secret by American ingenuity and merging air
power with radioactivity.

The first truly nuclear weapon of war appeared in Godfrey Hollis'
1908 novel *The Man Who Ended War.* An American scientific mastermind
invents a focused beam of radioactive waves which instantly disintegrates
the atoms of all metals into subatomic particles. When the big powers fail
to comply with his ultimatum demanding immediate universal disarmament, he begins annihilating their fleets with his radioactive beam weapon.
The nations disarm. The "man who ended war" then destroys his machine,
his plans, and himself, so that no one will obtain the secret of the weapon
and the world will therefore be permanently at peace. This characteristical-

ly American fantasy presents a striking contrast to H. G. Wells' 1913–1914 novel *The World Set Free,* which imagines atomic bombs not as peacemakers but as the instruments of global Armageddon. Unlike Wells, who was to recognize that the scientific knowledge required to produce atomic energy or weapons could never be kept private or monopolized, *The Man Who Ended War* promulgates the myth of the atomic secret, which would have a critical influence on American politics and culture beginning, as we shall see, in 1940 and extending through the Rosenberg case and beyond.

T he American mode of atomic fantasy evolved further in *The Man Who Rocked the Earth,* by Arthur Train and Robert Wood, which was serialized in 1914–1915 by the *Saturday Evening Post,* another magazine whose fiction was read eagerly by young Truman. It opens with the World War hideously stalemated, as millions are slaughtered by a multitude of novel weapons. Then appears an American scientific wizard who calls himself PAX. PAX's ultimate weapon is a radioactive beam which can annihilate mountain ranges or armies. He fires this atomic weapon from an airship powered by atomic energy generated by uranium forced into rapid disintegration. His atomic attacks produce scenes interchangeable with descriptions recorded by survivors of Hiroshima, including detailed accounts of death from radiation sickness. Armed with atomic weapons, PAX declares that "either war or the human race must pass away forever." Of course in the fantasy it is war that becomes extinct. Faced with the peacemaker's atomic arsenal, the nations destroy their weapons, abolish armies, and form a world government to guarantee perpetual peace.

Atomic energy and weapons remained a popular subject of fiction through 1940. Science, politics, and the mass media were not too far behind. By the end of 1939, World War II had begun in Europe and physicists in Germany, Great Britain, the United States, the Soviet Union, Japan, and other nations were working on atomic energy. That year, scientists published almost a hundred articles on nuclear fission. By 1940, American newspapers and magazines—from *Popular Mechanics* to *Time* and *Newsweek*—were exciting their readers with fantasies about the wonders to come from splitting the atom. The public was told that the nuclear chain reaction essential for atomic energy, and possibly even atomic bombs, now depended mainly on developing practical means for producing significant quantities of the unstable isotope Uranium-235.

S imultaneously, a serialized science-fiction novel read by millions of Americans developed both the doctrine of US global supremacy through nuclear weapons and a proposal for institutionalizing this hegemony—later to be presented as the Baruch Plan. This was *Lightning in the Night,* which ran in weekly installments during the pivotal months of

August to November 1940 in *Liberty,* one of America's top three magazines.

The action begins five years in the future, after Germany and its allies
have conquered Britain and France. Japan and the Soviet Union carry out a
sneak attack on Hawaii. Formations of Soviet, Japanese, and Nazi bombers
devastate American cities. Hordes of Reds, Japanese, Mexicans, and
Germans invade on three fronts, inflicting on an unprepared United States
the "macabre nightmare of modern warfare" (October 19 installment).

As the US fights back, the Nazis arrange a meeting with the American
president. Hitler begins by explaining the theory of atomic energy and sum-
marizing the history of atomic research. The Nazi leader recalls that "by the
year 1939 the physicists of the Reich, of Denmark, and of America were
frantically at work attempting to free and harness atomic energy"
(November 9).

"The secret of world mastery," Hitler continues, of course would go to
the nation that "first could produce great quantities of pure U-235," the uranium isotope sufficiently unstable to sustain an explosive chain reaction.
The Reich, he announces, has discovered this key to atomic energy, and has
begun production of pure U-235, with its "destructive power beyond present-day comprehension . . . the power to blow entire cities off the face of
the earth. . . . Within one month, that devastating power can be unleashed
against your cities, your people," Hitler boasts, so "further resistance
becomes utterly foolhardy." After this month of grace he will unleash "literal and total annihilation."

The President concedes that a nation without atomic weapons would be
helpless against a nation with them, and so this installment concludes with
the United States apparently ready to surrender to the Nazis. Thus the millions of readers of *Liberty* in 1940 confront a picture of their future if
America were to lose a nuclear arms race with the Nazis.

But the final installment reveals that the United States had secretly
been working on its own atomic weapons. Great cyclotrons and other mar-
velous equipment had been provided to the nation's "most ingenious and
resourceful scientists." The President expounds America's vision of atomic
energy, a vision like that of 1940 articles in *Harpers, Collier's,* and the
Saturday Evening Post, a fantasy that would reappear after Hiroshima and
Nagasaki under the slogan "Atoms for Peace":

> We saw its potentialities as a weapon of war, but even more clearly as an
> unlimited source of heat, of light, of power for peaceful production and
> transportation—all this at an almost incredibly low cost . . . poverty would
> vanish from the earth. So would war itself; for the economic causes of war
> would no longer exist . . . that Utopia, if you like, was what we envi-
> sioned: a free world of free peoples living in peace and prosperity, facing
> a future of unlimited richness.

Although the Nazis now have the secret of the ultimate weapon, they are too late. At this very moment, "50,000 feet over the Atlantic, great United States stratospheric bombers," specially modified for intercontinental flight and carrying atomic bombs, are "heading for every great city in Germany."

The President next presents the American proposal for peace and atomic disarmament. (This turns out to be the same as the only proposal for nuclear disarmament ever actually offered by the United States, the Baruch Plan of 1946: a body dominated by American scientists would control both the world's supply of uranium and the licensing of nuclear energy facilities to other nations; the United States would maintain its monopoly on nuclear weaponry until some unspecified date in the future when it would be turned over to an international agency):

> We have no wish to assume for long the task of policing the world. When the world is restored and made free, a Council of Nations shall take over the task we inaugurate now.

Germany surrenders. Japan and the Soviet Union capitulate a day later, after an American bomber drops one nuclear bomb on the deserted Russian steppes. The American atomic bomb has brought the utopian *Pax Americana* to the planet.

The nation's motives for developing atomic weapons in the novel are precisely those of the Manhattan Project: to forestall Nazi use and to achieve a lasting peace. Like those who later were to make the decision to use atomic bombs, *Lightning in the Night* assumes that the first nation to deploy atomic weapons wins and ends the arms race. The fictional President, like his actual counterpart in 1945–46, fails to realize that this might just accelerate the race for nuclear superweapons and open an epoch ever more dominated by them.

I n the fall of 1940 the US government began to wrap atomic research in a shroud of secrecy. Even the secrecy itself was a secret. Newspapers, magazines, news services, and radio broadcasters were soon ordered not to mention atomic power, cyclotrons, betatrons, fission, uranium, deuterium, and thorium. Army Intelligence later even attempted to block access to back issues containing popular articles on atomic energy in order "to wipe the whole subject from memory."

Thus ended the free exchange of knowledge that had symbolized the community of science, to be replaced by one of the grotesque features of our times: the attempt to transform vital parts of human knowledge into secrets whose existence is to be classified by the state and kept inviolate by the secret police. When the seventeenth-century Church authorities forced

Galileo to stop promulgating Copernicanism, at least they claimed they were prohibiting the dissemination of false belief. The US government, however, was consciously outlawing scientific truth about the fundamental nature of the universe. As early as 1941, John J. O'Neill, president of the National Association of Science Writers, charged that this censorship on atomic research amounted to "a totalitarian revolution against the American people." Pointing to the devastating potential of an atomic bomb utilizing Uranium-235, O'Neill asked a fateful question: "Can we trust our politicians and war makers with a weapon like that?"

So for the crucial years 1941–1945, public discussion of atomic weapons was banished from the nation that claimed to be leading the fight for democracy and freedom, while a handful of men secretly spent two billion dollars of public funds to develop these weapons. During these years, the only Americans exposed to public thoughts about atomic weapons were readers of science fiction. At first the government disregarded atomic weapons in science fiction, which was considered a subliterary ghetto inhabited by kids and kooks. But then it became alarmed by every science-fiction atomic bomb. So even though there already had been widespread public discussion of the two main technical problems of atomic bombs—isolating sufficient quantities of the fissionable isotope Uranium-235 from Uranium-238 and achieving critical mass suddenly enough to set off an explosive chain reaction—government censorship clamped down on the imagination of fiction writers. When Philip Wylie submitted his novella *The Paradise Crater* in early 1945, he was placed under house arrest; an Army Intelligence major informed him that he was personally prepared to kill the author if necessary to keep the weapon secret. Even science-fiction comic strips were censored. On April 14, the McClure Newspaper Syndicate ran strip one of *Atom Smasher,* a new Superman series pitting America's favorite superhero against a cyclotron. The Office of Censorship promptly forced the running of a substitute series (in which Superman played a baseball game singlehanded).

The only citizens left to contemplate the consequences of atomic weapons were the readers of *Astounding Science-Fiction,* which stirred up a major security investigation when it published Cleve Cartmill's *Deadline* in the March, 1944 issue. The story suggested that the anti-fascist Allies would never use an atomic bomb because they realize that nuclear weapons could eventually threaten the existence of the entire race, leaving nothing but dust and rocks. This was not the view of the men who did decide to drop the bombs.

Today few serious historians accept the original public position, still widely shared, that the atomic bombs significantly shortened the war, eliminated the need to invade Japan, and thus saved hundreds of thousands of American lives. The historical debate has tended instead to focus on the motives of the decision makers, principally President Truman himself. Truman was aware of Japanese peace feelers. And he had been guaranteed that the Soviet army would launch an all-out assault on the main surviving Japanese forces between August 8 and 15. Since he believed that the Soviet attack would end the war ("Fini Japs when that comes . . . about," he secretly recorded), did he have other motives?

The debate has tended to polarize between two positions. One suggests that Truman and his advisers intended the atomic bombs on Japan as what many believe they turned out to be—the opening shots in the Cold War against the Soviet Union. The other argues that the decision was made by default, through bureaucratic inertia and myopia, that there was just never any doubt that the bomb would be used. But the President may have had another incentive as well. For Harry Truman and his key advisers evidently believed that destroying cities with atomic bombs might bring an end to war itself.

Thus President Truman reenacted the role of the President in *The Vanishing Fleets,* the novel that first imagined the United States wielding a weapon based on radioactivity, who decides that only by using this most deadly machine ever conceived can he end wars for all time. Defending his role in the decision to use atomic weapons, Secretary of War Stimson explained that he was persuaded "that the bomb must be used" because "that was the only . . . way to awaken the world to the necessity of abolishing war altogether. No technological demonstration . . . could take the place of the actual use with its horrible results." Edward Teller argued that the bomb was so horrible that it might actually help get rid of wars, so "[f]or this purpose actual combat-use might even be the best thing."

It was on his way to Potsdam that President Truman recited those lines from Tennyson prophesying that ghastly combat waged by airships would "still the war-drum" and bring about "the Federation of the world." Given details of the Alamogordo test, Truman recorded in his diary his thoughts about the atomic bomb: "It seems to be the most terrible thing ever discovered, but it can be made the most useful." When he learned of the devastation of Hiroshima, he proclaimed: "This is the greatest thing in history." Echoing the President in *The Vanishing Fleets,* who declared that America must "bear with fortitude whatever reproaches may be heaped upon us, for we are the instruments of God," President Truman called the atomic bomb "an awful responsibility which has come to us," and told the nation: "We thank God that it has come to us, instead of to our enemies; and we pray that He may guide us to use it in His ways and for His purposes." Did the President believe that he now possessed what Americans had long fantasized, the absolute weapon that could achieve perpetual peace under the global hegemony of the United States?

W ithin months of Hiroshima came the Baruch Plan, which some see
      as merely an ultimatum to the Soviets to forswear nuclear weapons
or be destroyed. But the Baruch Plan—virtually identical to the atomic ultimatum issued by the President in the 1940 novel *Lightning in the Night*—
may be comprehended more deeply as an expression of the treacherous
mirage of the ultimate weapon endemic in American culture.

On June 14, 1946, the United States, represented by Bernard Baruch,
dramatically announced that the only way the nations of the world could
choose "World Peace" rather than "World Destruction" would be by sub-
mitting to a new international agency, not subject to veto, to be staffed by
personnel with proven competence in atomic science, and empowered to
evoke the immediate, swift, and sure punishment of any nation violating its
orders. They must do so, Baruch declared, because America is now in possession of the absolute weapon. No nation would be allowed to have
nuclear weapons except for the United States, which would keep producing
them until it had "a guarantee of safety, . . . not only against the offenders
in the atomic area but against the illegal users of other weapons bacterio-
logical, biological, gas—perhaps . . . against war itself." Here is the culmi-
nation of that great fantasy, from the motor bomb of *The Great War
Syndicate* in 1889 through the atomic bomb of *Lightning in the Night* in
1940. By wielding the ultimate weapon, the United States forces the world
to end war for all time.

4

THE DICTATOR'S FURNACE

DONNA U. GREGORY

The role of war's machines in causing wars is no simple issue. It is often treated simply, though, both by those who condemn weaponry as war's provocateur and by those who hail it as war's preventive. Instead, attitudes toward weapons are part of an intricate set of beliefs both about science and technology and about our powers of initiative as human beings. One's view of war technology is part of a larger view. It matches one's picture of how political cultures work, one's sense of human agency, and one's model of the cosmos and humanity's place in it.

During World War II, the new "realists" in the United States shared a view that distanced the human agent both from the new war technologies and from responsibility for human history. In urging a stronger defense, both during the war and after, these Nuclear Age realists punctuated their discourse with phrases like "this is not of our choice" and "this is the truth, however tragic." They spoke of the need for more military preparedness in peacetime as a tragic imposition of fate. But fate, it seemed, prevented much analysis of how much preparedness we needed, particularly after the atomic bomb. The force that so compelled us to acquire a boundless nuclear arsenal was not reality or fate or even the threat of Total War. It was a metaphor. A metaphor, however, that encompassed a dazzlingly intricate set of assumptions, packing together anxieties so intense that it had the power to both represent and create a whole world.

We must unpack this metaphor. Once we are aware of how it works, we can reread Nuclear Age history. Reexamining key documents from this perspective reveals some strange dimensions of our nuclear estate.

In the late 1950s, during the nuclear strategists' purge of expository prose in favor of mathematical models, Rand Corporation strategist Albert Wohlstetter condemned most early nuclear strategy as being in the essay tradition. Yet that tradition allows lay readers to understand thinking about nuclear weapons in a way that they cannot understand today's tech-

---

This essay was first published in *Peace Review* 1:1 (1989).

nologized analyses. Obscured beneath today's arcane vocabulary, the basic
principles of nuclear strategy haven't changed since they were first articulated during the 1940s and the early 1950s. Indeed, the first strategic
nuclear analysis came from a man schooled in the classic liberal arts,
Bernard Brodie, whose book *The Absolute Weapon: Atomic Power and
World Order* was published in 1946. Still considered both the best of all
strategic thinkers and the father of strategy's moderate wing, Brodie spans
the evolution of military strategy from prenuclear to nuclear thinking, with
writings from 1941 until his death in 1978.

Using some simple tools, we can decode meaning in these writings to
see how Brodie's representation of military force reflects a coherent vision
of the world. This vision explains why the political realists saw fate dictating our pursuit of the ultimate nuclear arsenal, rather than believing that we
had a wide range of choices and the ability to discriminate between them.

One of Brodie's earliest essays, in which he argues that we need a radically new strategy to replace "defense," which will be called "deterrence,"
opens as follows:

> Under conditions existing before the atomic bomb, it was possible to con-
> template methods of air defense keeping pace with, and perhaps even out-
> distancing the means of offense. Long-range rockets baffled the defense,
> but they were extremely expensive per unit for inaccurate, single-blow
> weapons. Against bombing aircraft, on the other hand, fighter planes and
> anti-aircraft guns could be extremely effective.

This passage describes how things were in a time *before* the atomic
bomb. In this time, it says, we could realistically expect that we could
depend on air defense to counter offensive strategies. The next paragraph
will tell us how things have changed *after* the atomic bomb—we cannot
depend on air defense any more.

At first glance, the passage is straightforward and its meaning clear.
The language is concrete, descriptive, and action packed. Weapons systems
are identified by concrete nouns: the atomic bomb, rockets, bombing aircraft, fighter planes, antiaircraft guns. Weapons systems stand as the
subject of all the clauses after sentence one. A race metaphor structures
the action throughout. This metaphor describes how, in those days, means
of defense could race against offensive systems and beat them. Air
defense could "keep pace" with and even "outdistance" most bomber
aircraft. Long-range rockets alone had "baffled" defensive countermea-
sures; but these rockets were insignificant because they were not cost-
effective.

The meanings in the passage, however, are not fully encompassed in
this account. When we think about it, the terms "offense" and "defense" do
not refer to weapons engaged in a contest, as the passage purports to have
it. Rather, they refer to "functions" weapons may serve in a war strategy.

Here, then, the terms are metaphors for such strategic functions. They represent what human beings must conceptualize when they want to develop one weapons system to counter another weapons system. The passage literally refers not to a war of weapons but to the military strategists' cognitive experience—they are anticipating the next combat to which their skills will be called. But it also points to something in addition to the strategists' cognitive experience. By using offense and defense in this way, and by adding the "race" metaphor to provide a pattern for the weapons' interactions, Brodie turns weapons research and development into a cosmic drama. The entire passage reifies the weapons design process, speaking about that complex human process as if it were accurately representable as a natural, concrete thing.

This linguistic reification distracts us readers and thereby leads us to think through the issue incompletely. Images of weapons racing each other draw our inner eye to pictures of aerial combat and mechanical armies in the sky. So engaged, we are unlikely to think about people making and implementing decisions in scientific research labs or government offices down on earth. The real-world referent fades, dominated by a more vivid, more graspable picture. Thus, while such metaphorical representations of the design process fascinate us, they contribute nothing to our understanding of that process. In fact, they actually hinder our understanding by obscuring the process. Our vision of an arms race becomes transposed onto our understanding of strategic necessities, which finally displaces any detailed awareness we might otherwise have had of a normal research and development process. Only now are all the meanings of this simple passage decoded and its effect on us elucidated. The way has been paved to institutionalize an arms race.

Besides obscuring the complexities of the R&D process, the reifications have another effect. While making human beings and their activities invisible, they raise into the foreground a fictional world of smart, fast machines. These machines are not merely the ones we know in the real world. Through the magic of metaphor, these war machines acquire consciousness and will. They engage in battles, run races, and act intelligently without human agency. They do things humans do while the humans watch, like parents at their children's dance recital. Machines excite, fire our concern, and perform to the thunder of our admiring applause. Mechanical power substitutes for the living world's own vitality. And while we watch them perform, we forget that we take these embattled machines seriously precisely because they are represented as if they were people. In our mind's eye, they have been anthropomorphically transformed.

In combination with this transposition of human qualities onto weapons, the reifications have a third effect. They render human beings passive against this backdrop of superior vitality and power. Brodie's representations give the weapons great power and diminish human power. Consider how small is the hint of human presence in Brodie's first line. Before the atomic bomb, Brodie says, "it was possible to contemplate" defense as a viable strategy. What we contemplate "under" is the "existing conditions" weapons systems impose, their cumulative force and the technological means of producing them. These conditions are "over" us, controlling us, dictating to us the terms of our being. The capabilities of weapons systems determine the range of possible strategies for using them, a fact that we are not expected to dispute. Though we ought to react with surprise if strategic "conditions" are taken as given rather than as implicated in man-made processes.

Moreover, such conditions are no small matter, given or not; for though the strategic conditions existing at a given time matter greatly to defense policies, the significance of these conditions is not restricted to policies. The weapons systems are seen as determining also the broader conditions for life, since weapons ultimately guarantee the natural state or fail to do so. To Brodie, we now will owe our very existence to possessing the atomic bomb; therefore the conditions the atomic bomb imposes seem rightfully to command our contemplation. Then, to represent human beings as fate's humble servants makes even more sense after the bomb's advent. The bomb will impose conditions commanding our servitude.

M ilitary force, then, in Brodie's early writings, is represented in some striking ways. It is ever increasing in power, exciting, clever, intelligent, autonomous, mysteriously generated (perhaps even transcendent)— and it determines human destiny. Admirable human qualities are displaced onto weapons, while humans have become relatively impotent. In all, technological progress, depicted as having its own momentum, seems never to have been under human control. Rather, in their military research, development, and procurement, and in their security policies, it is human beings that are underlings to a technological imperative holding sway over human society.

The view that human beings serve some technological diktat greater than themselves was already quite apparent in Brodie's dissertation *Sea Power in the Modern Age,* written in 1941. The book examines nineteenth and early twentieth century naval interventions and assesses their influence on war, state policy, and military strategy. It views technological progress in weaponry as unrelenting, a fact to which humanity must be alert and responsive. New weapons arise to counter enemy weapons, themselves originally counters to another enemy's countertechnology, and so on. It is an endless dialectic in which "each Power finds it necessary to further these inventions to avoid falling hopelessly behind in the inexorable race for technical advantage." War's own logic makes weapons evolution inevitable, and through this evolution, war technology achieves an autonomous life.

Brodie represents this "necessity," this bondage to the "inexorable race for technical advantage," by an arresting figure of speech: "the insatiable appetite of the ship's furnace." The furnace's appetite explains and stands for inexorable weapons production. Thus, the metaphor of the ship's furnace substitutes for a causal theory. The furnace is what drives weapons evolution always toward weapons more violent. From sail to steam to armor-hulled battleships and ultimately to submarines, naval weapons progressed in only a century; by 1941 the furnace had produced a weapon—the submarine—that could for the first time "menace a whole world order." War could now be "total war." This metaphor, then, concertizes the process of technological change, rendering that process itself machinelike. The furnace is a weapons producer whose products ever increase in destructive power and whose numbers and kinds increase at an ever hastening rate. Here is how Brodie deploys the furnace, in the concluding paragraph of *Sea Power:*

> Sail gives way to steam and timber walls to iron, vessels of war take cover in the depths of the sea and spread their wings far above the crests of the waves, but naval war remains much the same in its purposes and in its accomplishments. Yet how different may be the conditions under which sea power fulfills its mission! The insatiable appetite of the ship's furnace alters the strategy of nations. The submarine attaches to itself the far-ranging eyes of the airplane and threatens a whole world order, including much that was never menaced before. And no-one in the day of crisis can be certain that it will be parried.

At the propositional level of meaning, the passage simply sums up the book's argument: War's own logic makes weapons evolution inevitable.

There is more in it, however, than this. There is a reality less recognizable than the one we see at first glance. Consider the verbs describing the actions of these machines. The military technologies function both as the grammatical subjects and as the agents of all this activity. By implication these machines have amazing powers that are autonomously directed.

In this passage, the war machines are not merely anthropomorphized, however. They have exotic attributes. The submarine acquires the "airplane's eyes" and this hybrid monster then "threatens a whole world order." The metaphors and syntactic constructions create a picture of powerful creatures imbued with humanlike will and intelligence.

As in the 1946 essay, human beings themselves are all but absent. Not until the final sentence does Brodie shift away from animal activities to human states of mind. The sentence raises a question about "certainty." Human subjects emerge as very small and insignificant against the backdrop of mechanized power and activity that dominates the preceding sentences. And no wonder: Ultimately the contest of giants will decide the war's outcome. We—the "no-one"—cannot even know how they will interact. All we can do is facilitate their being by serving the furnace's hungry demands.

B rodie's view that the genesis of war technology eludes human control was, then, an attitude he had held for some years. In fact, it was a commonplace attitude and remains so today in the military and strategic communities. The furnace metaphor expresses this attitude, but it also blinds Brodie to the question of causalities and control. The furnace metaphor helps neither to identify causes nor to analyze them, and at the same time it obscures the problem questions. "War's own logic" is not enough to explain the process, because this too is a metaphor.

Besides obscuring the pressures generating the weapons and allegedly necessitating vast numbers of them, the furnace metaphor is so captivating an image that it even obscures its own implications: It does not invite us to ask whether the furnace has a thermostat, and if so, how it's set, and if not why we don't add one. If we search hard, we find in *Sea Power* an important clue about the thermostat. There is one, but it has been cranked up as high as it can go, the act has been thoroughly justified, and it has been long forgotten. The thermostat represents the perceived need for national power to provide national security, measured in military terms. Brodie argues that in prenuclear times, at any rate, military victories produced national prestige, which was (and remains) the main currency of state power. Power, after all—a state's power to impose its will, as Clausewitz put it—is the purpose of that inexorable pursuit of technological advantage. "Power" is another name for what the ship's furnace produces.

The ship's furnace is a power generator driving the Ship of State, stocking its arsenals with the means to ensure its survival and well-being. The furnace is a transformer; it is an alchemist's alembic, where gold and lead are transmuted. It is both belly—consuming national resources—and womb—generating war machines. The alembic transmutes natural, financial, and human resources into war power. How much power, scaled on a nonexistent thermostat, is decided not by a democratic legislature, but by the Dictates of National Security. This is the most pervasive metaphor of all in the realist literature. National Security, the dictator of national policy, has needs as gargantuan as technology's furnace. It imposes terms and conditions under which we are bound by the bomb. The Dictator's rule is as absolute as his judgment is inscrutable. Inaccessible to ordinary citizens, the Dictator needs an army of handmaidens, the national security establishment, to encode, translate, scramble or pronounce his dictates.

In this "reality," the war machines become an inexorable force that humankind serves. War machines are the given, the changing but positive fact that determines human history. The ultimate verbal alchemy has occurred. A world has been made, and no one is responsible. In literal terms, "reality" gets reflected in our language, which in turn strongly tends to confirm our particular perception. Similarly, policies created out of a particular perspective will tend to create conditions in reality that confirm that view. If countertechnology drives war machine production in fact, this situation partly results from our having assented to and confirmed this fact. In this situation, our language is what compels our beliefs about reality, not an objectively existing reality that commands perception and belief. Understanding how our language works can, therefore, give us more options in the world we make and to which we assent.

One task for the peace movement is to focus on a richer analysis than realism provides of the living dynamic between our belief systems and perceptions and our actions in the world. Most particularly, this means publicizing the ways our language can reinforce our beliefs and compel our actions.

Four practical approaches suggest themselves. All focus on the kind of cosmos implied in Brodie's realist discourse. As we have seen in this brief analysis, it is a cosmos of classical mythology, where things happen in a domain somehow separate from our control. Though this dimension is seen to affect us intimately, it is not seen as of our making. It is imposed on us, and our primary task is to survive it. The first approach, then, involves examining the "realist" assumption about hostility and aggressivity as inevitable and as determining.

The second approach involves examining the implied cosmos itself. It resembles the science fiction world of an embattled adolescent. Could it be that many of our policy intellectuals are immature?

Third, how is it that our policy intellectuals and the faculty of the elite institutions who train them are predominantly "realists"? Are "we" helpless in this, or merely unaware?

Fourth, "realists" note that countries typically get power through military prestige—either through actual victories or through conspicuous displays of force. Is this fact not determined at the level of popular culture? It is not so much militarism or even weapons fetishism that we need to look at. We need to ask what kind of people do it, how they are raised and schooled, what toys they are given as children, and what they do for fun.

Questions as mundane as these appear to be the key to changing the ideology whose metaphors currently drive our national security policy.

5

WAR, PROPAGANDA, AND CIVILIZED VALUES

CYRUS VEESER

In many universities in the United States, students are required to take certain core courses, which are intended to provide a common grounding of culture. Typically these courses are given the title Western Civilization and are based on a study of the works of major authors, from Plato to Marx, who are judged to have made major contributions to the culture of Western Europe. Recently, at some U.S. universities, where students with European ethnic roots may no longer be predominant, faculty and students have argued that these courses are too narrowly based and that the authors chosen are too often exclusively white, and male.

In this debate, the defenders of tradition, including former U.S. Secretary of Education William J. Bennett, have sought the high ground of objectivity, arguing that Western Civilization's critics are politicizing a subject that by its nature transcends politics. The *New York Times,* reporting Bennett's verdict that by revising its course Stanford University had caved in to a "campaign of pressure politics and intimidation," offered a capsule history of curriculum changes. "In the early 1970's," said the *Times,* "often under pressure from students, many colleges reduced or abandoned requirements for basic courses in the humanities that for centuries had been considered a part of a college education." The *Times* presumed that basic courses like Western Civilization have been required "for centuries," validating the myth that such courses are an organic, and thus unalterable, part of college and university curricula. In fact, there is nothing natural or traditional about the present-day Western Civilization offerings. These classes are, in fact, the offspring of a government-sponsored propaganda course launched after the United States entered World War I.

The First World War was a war involving the mobilization of entire populations in order to meet the need for an immense expansion in the output of munitions and to provide personnel for the vast armies engaged.

This essay was first published in *Peace Review* 1:1 (1989).

As a consequence, it was to a large degree a war of ideas—not primarily an ideological war between the Central and Allied powers, but a battle by each belligerent to activate its civilian population through the force of propaganda. Well before the United States entered the war in April 1917, the main European combatants had launched massive "information" campaigns. The United States followed suit and quickly outdid the efforts of the Old World. The Committee on Public Information (CPI), headed by George Creel, distributed some 10 million of its various patriotic pamphlets, in addition to producing films, sponsoring lectures, and monitoring the foreign language press. Besides this official government agency, numerous private groups boosted the war. One, the National Board for Historical Service (NHBS), put the nation's leading historians "at the service of the government," as the board itself said. The NBHS historians worked closely with Creel's committee, writing many of the CPI's highly partisan pamphlets.

In the summer of 1914, U.S. professors had been shocked at the publication of *To the Civilized World,* a manifesto asserting that Germany was defending the West against the barbarian, signed by ninety-three of that nation's leading scholars, including Karl Lamprecht, Max Planck, and Gerhart Hauptmann. Yet when their own nation was called to arms, U.S. professors, historians in particular, willingly lent their professional services to the state. Officially, both the CPI and the NBHS urged the maintenance of scholarly standards. The NBHS warned against "the perversion of history in the interest of any particular creed, whether that creed be pacifism or militarism, nationalism or internationalism." In practice, however, the historian's attempts to shed light on the "present war" through an exposition of the past veered away from impartiality. Historians in fields far removed from current events, including classical, medieval, and colonial American history, strained common sense as well as professional ethics as they tried to bring their special expertise to bear on the war effort.

The wartime articles produced by historians reveal how accommodating the ideal of objectivity proved to be. Tracing the roots of pan-Germanism, historian James Westfall Thompson of the University of Chicago found that, through the ages, Germans had been uniquely warlike and expansionist. In medieval times, Thompson pointed out, French bestiaries gave "French names to the finer kinds of animals, and German names to the wolf, the ass, etc." Another Chicago historian, in an essay called "The Repulsiveness of the German State," suggested that "President Wilson's distinction between the German government and the German people" had lately been superseded. The new and more correct view, according to George H. Mead, found that the "German government is an entirely natural expression of the German community, its people and its history. . . . Just as the German government and the German people," continued Mead, "have never been able to understand that America is not preparing to use its force for the purpose of exploiting Mexico and the Central and South

American countries, simply because our fundamental political habits do not allow us to undertake to control other peoples against their own wills, just so it has been next to impossible for the Americans to comprehend how naturally and how logically the German community conceive of the use of force."

While the CPI and the NBHS diffused this sort of analysis, the War Department was drawing up plans that would, by the last months of the war, militarize postsecondary education across the country. The Students Army Training Corps (SATC), piloted in the summer of 1918 and instituted in 516 colleges and universities that fall, put nearly every U.S. male undergraduate in uniform. The SATC killed two birds with one stone. Colleges and universities had suffered dramatic revenue shortfalls in the academic year 1917–1918 as a result of army enlistments. By allowing young men to attend college and draw $30 a month salary as recruits, the War Department was effectively subsidizing U.S. colleges while guaranteeing for itself a large pool of officers if the war continued.

Nearly every institution that was eligible participated in the SATC, with only Haverford College declining on ethical grounds. The curriculum, taught by the regular faculty, included such familiar courses as English, German, French, mathematics, physics, chemistry, meteorology, and so on, with the addition of a mandatory course called War Issues. War Issues was a key component of the SATC. The War Department's committee in charge of education "felt that the soldiers should know something about the historical and economic causes of the war, the problems of the government which have played so important a part in it, and the national ideals of the various countries engaged in the struggle." As described by the War Department, War Issues would cross disciplinary boundaries, combining geography, economics, political science, history, and philosophy to illuminate the causes of the war.

The War Department left each college to organize the War Issues course its own way, although instructors were provided with a suggested syllabus and district directors visited many of the schools to see how the course was progressing. Like scholars involved with the National Board for Historical Service and the Committee on Public Information, those who helped organize War Issues expressed themselves as advocates of fair-mindedness and high academic standards. "A dogmatic presentation of material," cautioned a letter from the War Department to schools taking part in the SATC, "would be fatal to the success of the work; on the contrary the attitude of the instructor should be fair and patient; his aim should be to present facts rather than propaganda, resting our cause upon its solid basis of truth and justice."

A glance at the materials recommended to the War Issues instructors shows again the fragile nature of impartiality. A booklet called "Questions on the Issues of the War" provided teachers with 112 queries distilled from thousands that arose during the summer pilot of the SATC. The booklet listed articles and books about the war and provided annotations to help instructors prepare answers. Many citations referred to pamphlets of the government's Committee on Public Information; most of the other works cited had been published since the war's outbreak and had such titles as "Germany's Madness," "Germany's Civilized Barbarism," and "The Octopus of German Culture." A sampling of the annotations gives a sense of the book's tone. In response to the question "Why does Germany want to rule the World?" an article titled "The Philosophy of Terrorism" was recommended as "showing the essential paganism of the German intellect." To help explain what was meant by *Kultur,* the booklet noted that "perhaps the best definition of *Kultur* in brief compass shows that Germany has singularly little 'culture' properly so-called."

T he ten district directors of the War Issues course, all professors, including two each from Harvard and the University of Chicago, were nearly unanimous in finding that the course was well received by students and faculty alike. The course appealed in part because it was not simply a rehearsal of facts. "Mere knowledge itself was not all the aim," F. S. Bogardus of Indiana State Normal School and director of District 6 wrote in his final report. "There was a desire to arouse a feeling of personal responsibility for a victorious ending of the war as a struggle between right and wrong." For Bogardus, the effectiveness of the course was measured in part by whether the students became "possessed of an overmastering desire to take some action."

The district directors of War Issues agreed on another point: Although the armistice was signed before even one semester of War Issues had been completed, many colleges seemed interested in continuing the course—perhaps even making it permanent. "The attitude toward making it a permanent feature of the curriculum is favorable," reported M. L. Bonham, Jr., of Louisiana State University. Another director suggested that the War Department take definite steps to see that the course was institutionalized. The course had proved itself, W. E. Hocking felt, to be "a concrete center for various abstract disciplines." Hocking was certain that colleges would react favorably to suggestions about how to conduct the course because he sensed "the endless appetite everywhere for direction."

The inspiration for a way to incorporate War Issues into the curriculum was not to come from the War Department, however, but from Columbia University. Columbia's own War Issues course had conformed to the national paradigm. The first paragraph of Columbia's outline of its course Issues of the War stated frankly: "At the outset of the course it is important to show . . . the undeniable responsibility of Germany and Austria-Hungary for initiating hostilities." Subject headings in the topical outline included:

"Barbarous and Illegal Conduct of the German Invaders," and the narrative referred to "the bestial and sacrilegious practices of . . . German soldiers."

Columbia's faculty and deans took War Issues as a model for an innovative course called Introduction to Contemporary Civilization. The course, wrote Columbia dean Herbert E. Hawkes, "is a lineal descendant of a course called the *Issues of the War*." Like administrators at other colleges, those at Columbia appreciated the way War Issues gave students a common background of ideas that spanned disciplines. As important as offering a certain body of knowledge, however, was the goal of anchoring students' beliefs to a particular worldview. "The main purpose of the course," announced Columbia's president, Nicholas Murray Butler, "is to lay a foundation for intelligent citizenship." Butler and Hawkes were unequivocal about their political ends. "For those college students who are enamored of the cruder and more stupid forms of radicalism, every instruction in the facts of modern civilization, and the part that time plays in building and perfecting human institutions, is of the greatest value," Butler wrote. Conservative students, on the other hand, would learn that "movement and development are necessary for progress."

C onceived in wartime, Contemporary Civilization was brought forth during the Red Scare of 1919. Dean Hawkes clearly considered Bolshevism a greater threat than Kaiserism. This deadlier and more subtle disease called for a more effective inoculation. "Even though we are no longer in danger either from the military force or from the propagandism of Germany, the coming years show a menace no less real and perhaps more difficult to meet," wrote the dean. "It is no longer possible," he continued, "to prepare a man to meet the arguments of the soap box orator, shallow and short-sighted though they may be, with the economic theory of Adam Smith. Nor is it possible to substitute in the minds of some of our students who are already in the second generation of radical thinkers, a sounder philosophy than by a study of the economic and governmental problems which now confront us, in the light of their development."

C ontemporary Civilization would accomplish its daunting task by applying, as had War Issues, a study of the geography, economics, politics, philosophy, and history of Western nations to "the insistent problems these nations must face." The comprehensive and carefully guided approach promised to yield students having "a common starting point and a single point of vantage," from which to understand world problems. Such a course, Dean Hawkes explained in *Educational Review,* "is transcendentally important at just this moment in our history." Contemporary Civilization, asserted the dean, would create students "who shall be safe for democracy." Columbia's course became the prototype for similar offerings at colleges and universities around the country. Over time, these courses left behind the momentary relevance of Contemporary Civilization, and became the class in great books so familiar today. As colleges moved away from applying the best thought of the past to current issues, any recollection was lost of the course's provenance in a wartime crusade.

It might be argued that, regardless of its origin, the Western Civilization course in its modern form is far removed from, and indeed above, politics. But, if the jingoism and flag waving of the War Issues course today seem so clumsy and obvious, it is necessary to remember that few contemporaries found the course objectionable. Today, the politics of the Western Civilization course is perhaps better camouflaged. At Columbia, and other universities, it has become the most dignified, the most objective, and the most immutable of courses. Far from applying philosophical truths to contemporary issues, Western Civilization now removes a carefully chosen corpus of great works (or ideas or thinkers) from time, place, and history. By requiring instructors and students to approach the canonical works without secondary sources, and without even the pretense of understanding the historical moment in which, say, Aristotle, Augustine, or Hegel wrote, the Western Civilization course guarantees in advance a separation of ideas from the world. Students are taught only that certain works of the Western European tradition have a transcendental value to which writings from other cultures cannot hope to aspire. They also learn that the greatest accomplishment of scholarship is to detach ideas from the pressures and contradictions of time, place, class, race, and gender; even though these forces acted powerfully on the canonical authors.

Western Civilization, even in its present overtly apolitical form, does send out an indirect message to those trying to sort out the confusions of the present. If the goals of U.S. foreign policy in Central America, for example, are consonant with the transcendental ideas—the fostering of democracy and self-determination—then evidence to the contrary, such as the killing of civilians by U.S. mercenaries, must be quite simply erroneous.

Ideals, like the "Great Books" themselves, safely exist in a distant and hermetic realm. George H. Mead, writing for the NBHS in 1918, was evidently convinced of the virtue of his own culture: "Our fundamental political habits do not allow us to undertake other peoples against their own wills." Mead and the NBHS authors stated directly what today's Western Civilization classes accomplish through the reification of ideals and the corresponding negation of reality.

Writing on the function of the humanities generally in the present time, Edward Said has noted: "It is my conviction that culture works very effectively to make invisible and even 'impossible' the actual affiliations that exist between the world of ideas and scholarship, on the one hand, and the world of brute politics, corporate and state power and military force on the other." What is true of humanistic study in general has special application to Western Civilization courses. Today, these courses self-consciously erase affiliations between ideas and the world, both in the past and in the present. It is doubly ironic that Western Civilization, which presents itself as the study of transcendental ideas, precious of themselves, in fact traces its roots to an unabashed effort at enemy formation in the service of war mobilization.

6

COLUMBUS AND THE CRUSADES

JOSEPH J. FAHEY

It is astonishing to observe how many wars have been waged and how much violence has been committed in the name of Jesus Christ. It is astonishing because Jesus himself never sanctioned violence: he stood in the Hebrew prophetic tradition, which believed that the peaceful messianic age would "bring good news to the poor," "set at liberty the oppressed," and cause nations to "beat their swords into plowshares, and their spears into pruning hooks." Concerning any kind of violence, Jesus urged an end to the "eye-for-an-eye" ethic through his instruction in the Sermon on the Mount to "love your enemies, do good to those who hate you, bless those who curse you, and pray for those who attack you."

Before his crucifixion at the hands of the Romans, Jesus bestowed "peace" upon his followers, but the supreme irony is that the peace of Jesus has consistently been invoked by the followers of Jesus to justify the slaughter of innocents for the past seventeen hundred years. What brutal wars, pogroms, crusades, and inquisitions have been carried on in his name. Millions of soldiers, as they died of war wounds, devoted their last words to a prayer to this simple Hebrew pacifist, asking God's blessing on the butchery of spiritual brothers and sisters. Slavery, torture, rape, and pillage have been committed in his name. When Christians fought each other—as they frequently have—both sides claimed that Jesus had blessed their cause. Old worlds (which Christians called new worlds) were invaded (discovered) in the name of Jesus, and indigenous people, cultures, religions, and histories were sacrificed for gold, silver, and slaves on the altar of oblivion.

It is in the context of the history of Christian attitudes toward conquest and war that "High Admiral of the Sea and perpetual Viceroy and Governor of all (discovered) Islands and Continents" Christopher Columbus must be understood. With Admiral Columbus, eleven hundred years of messianic and military history arrived in what would be called the

This essay was first published in *Peace Review* 4:3 (1992).

Americas on that fateful day in the fifteenth century, C.E. On October 12, 1492, the Arawak people who warmly greeted the Spanish ships met not merely Christopher Columbus—their real encounter was with Christopher Columbus and the Crusades. Essential to understanding the Columbian invasion of the Western Hemisphere is that combination of apocalyptic vision, messianic imperative, financial reward, and territorial expansion that characterized the medieval Crusades and Inquisitions and that molded the worldview of the Europeans of Columbus's age.

To understand Christopher Columbus as crusader, a discussion concerning the origins of the "just war" and the Crusades in Christian history will be helpful. While Christianity had been a pacifist religion for its first three centuries (based on the Christian Scriptures), a dramatic change occurred in the fourth and fifth centuries when Ambrose of Milan and Augustine of Hippo justified war as a Christian enterprise. The fourth century began with the prohibition of Christian service in the Roman armies, and it ended with only Christians being permitted to serve as Roman soldiers. Christian participation in war became possible when: Emperor Constantine accepted Christianity as a legitimate religion within the Roman Empire in 313; Augustine and other theologians abandoned the biblical ideal that a peaceful and socially just Reign of God was possible on this earth; and early Christian theologians came to believe that the Pax Romana (Roman Empire) was the divinely established vehicle to hasten the spread of the Pax Christiana (Christian Church) throughout the entire pagan world. Only when the world was totally Christianized could history be ended through the triumphant Second Coming of Christ. Apocalyptic theology and millenarian theology were always near the surface of Christian missionary and colonial activity.

This union of God and Caesar resulted in the Christian embrace of the "just war" principles that had earlier been enunciated by Plato, Aristotle, and Cicero. Some Christians believed they had to "defend" Caesar's realm in order to spread the realm of God to all the earth. But the cold eye of history tells us that offensive wars and invasions are always fought in the name of defense; hence, the just war principles have very often been used to rationalize offensive or total war. Augustine himself, for example, although he cautioned that war should be fought with a mournful attitude, nevertheless believed that the just war principles could be used to justify an assault against heretics (the Donatists) as well as for the defense and expansion of the empire. Hence, the subsequent theological, political, economic, and cultural union of the Pax Romana with the Pax Christiana, along with the justification of violence in God's name, made violence, repression, conquest, and war inevitable in what was to become in 800 C.E. the Holy Roman Empire. In this political, economic, and theological union of God and king were planted the seeds of the Crusades abroad (eleventh through seventeenth centuries) and Inquisitions at home (twelfth through nineteenth centuries).

T he Crusades were initially holy wars fought in God's name by popes who, with the support of nobles and kings, attempted to capture the Holy Land from the followers of Islam. But the Crusades soon broadened to include the domination of Eastern Christianity (which had split from the papacy in 1054), the acquisition of territory and wealth from the East, and the persecution of Jews and heretics in Europe.

The first Crusade was initiated in medieval Europe in 1095 by Pope Urban II at Clermont, France, when he urged the reestablishment of the Truce of God (which limited fighting to the period between Easter and Advent) and the Peace of God (which severely limited those who could fight) at home in order to "succor your brethren in the East." Urban reportedly stated: "Recall the greatness of Charlemagne, O most valiant soldiers. . . . Let all hatred depart from among you, all quarrels end, all wars cease. Start upon the road to the Holy Sepulchre to wrest that land from the wicked race and subject it to yourselves." *"Deus vult!"* ("God wills it!") was the crowd's response. Not only the pope, but God, had declared war on the Muslims.

Those who participated in the Crusades fought in the name of the pope, were granted a papal indulgence for the remission of sins upon taking a *votum crucis* (vow) to go on a Crusade (the indulgence was later granted whether or not one actually went on the Crusade since it was possible to pay another to take one's place), and wore a cloth cross on the shoulder of their garment as a symbol that they had taken up the cross. Crusaders received the *privilegium crucis* (papal protection of their property) and a moratorium on the payment of debts and on the debts' interest; and Crusaders could be judged only by ecclesiastical rather than civil tribunals.

Since the Crusades were holy wars, the restrictions of the just war and the limitations of the Truce of God and the Peace of God were generally ignored, killing was indiscriminate, and victory was often celebrated as "the justification of all Christianity and the humiliation of all paganism." Indeed, even some clerics participated in the killing, and new militant monastic orders were founded to participate in the Crusades. Those "infidels" who were not crucified or mutilated or disemboweled or hanged were often enslaved, tortured, and raped, and their possessions were, of course, stolen from them. Concerning the capture of Jerusalem in 1099, for example, Raymond of Agiles reported that "piles of heads, hands, and feet were to be seen in the streets of the city. . . . It was a just and splendid judgment of God, that this place should be filled with the blood of the unbelievers, when it had suffered so long from their blasphemies."

The first Crusade restored Nicea to the Byzantine Empire (1097), occupied Edessa, Syria (1097), conquered Antioch (1098), and captured Jerusalem (1099). As a result, the Latin Crusader states in the Middle East were formed. But the followers of Islam (most notably under the leadership of Saladin in the twelfth century) eventually recaptured these states, and from a religious and political viewpoint, the eight Crusades to the Middle East from the twelfth to the fourteenth centuries were considered to be failures. (An especially tragic affair was the Children's Crusade in 1212, in which German and French children were sold into slavery or shipwrecked on their way to the Holy Land.)

Clearly, however, the Crusades were not economic failures; they stimulated trade, shipping, banking, and satisfied the desire for new lands and wealth on the part of the European Christians. Especially desired was a different passage to the riches of the East. In addition, the popes frequently gave indulgences to those who would wear the cross of the Crusader to do combat with the pope's theological or political enemies. Consequently, the Crusades continued in Europe for several hundred years after they ceased in the Middle East.

While many historians treat the Inquisitions in Christian Europe as separate historical entities from the Crusades, in reality the Crusades and the Inquisitions are merely two sides of the same theological, economic, and political coin. Like the Crusades, the Inquisitions were wars fought and persecutions conducted in God's name, for God's gain, and for God's glory. The Inquisitions often accomplished at home what the Crusades ultimately failed to accomplish abroad: the destruction of pagans and heretics, the acquisition of wealth and property for pope and king, and the neutralization and elimination of political enemies. The Inquisitions (one of which was actually declared as a Crusade by Pope Innocent III in 1207–1208) were church-sanctioned holy wars against the Cathari, Albigensians, Waldesians, Moors, Jews, liberal theologians, homosexuals, witches, and other heretics who threatened the political and economic power of pope and king.

Major Inquisitions took place in France, Spain, and Germany; only England and Scandinavia were spared this reign of terror. Most often, one only had to be accused (accusers were granted anonymity) of some kind of heresy in order to be declared guilty and be burned at the stake. While the Inquisitors (who normally were directly responsible only to the pope) were despised by the people, they were nevertheless successful for quite a long period of time in stifling dissent, creativity, individuality, and independence of thought. Three inquisitorial tribunals were appointed to Spanish America and displaced the bishops in the control of heresy after 1569. Indeed, the methods of the Inquisitions were even to be used by both sides during the period of the great Christian Reformation in Europe, which began in the sixteenth century.

T he invasion of Christopher Columbus and those who followed him to the Western Hemisphere must be understood in the context of the Christian acceptance and glorification of war (the Crusades) and persecution (the Inquisitions). The Spanish throne from whom Columbus received the funds for his four voyages to the West had just conquered the Moors in southern Spain, and in 1492 ordered the expulsion of all Jews from Spain as part of the Spanish Inquisition. Columbus himself witnessed the end of the 700-year war with Islam when he observed "the royal banners of your majesties planted by force of arms upon the battlements of the Alhambra" and saw "the Moorish King come forth from the gates of the city and kiss the royal hands of Your Highnesses." Spain had long conducted its own crusade against Islam.

Columbus capitalized on the success against the Muslims in Spain to request support from "Your Highnesses, as Catholic Christians and defenders of the Christian Faith against the doctrines of Mohamet and all other idolatries" to fund "a westerly route" to the Orient which would, in part, provide gold for the great Crusade to finally recapture Jerusalem and eliminate the Muslims.

When Columbus reached what he believed to be the islands off Japan and China, his own actions toward the indigenous people and environment and those of the conquistadors who followed him continued to a remarkable extent the legacy of the Crusades and Inquisitions that existed in Spain and other parts of Europe. The following points will illustrate:

• As a youth in Genoa and as a young sailor, Columbus was exposed to merchants who lived off the sea and profited from the territorial expansion and new markets established during the Crusades: Genoese traders sought riches and gold from Europe, Africa, and the Middle East. In Columbus's words: "Genoese . . . and all the people who have pearls, precious stones and other valuable things, take them to the end of the earth . . . to convert them into gold."

• Prior to his voyage, Columbus came to strongly believe in the apocalyptic teachings of Franciscan Antonio de Marchena: the "heathen" must be converted to Christ; Jerusalem's holy places must be recovered from the Muslims; the "end times" when Christ would come again were imminent.

• Columbus was deeply convinced that he was divinely supported in his quest for riches and conversions in the East, and he eventually determined that there remained only 150 years to convert the heathen before the Second Coming of Christ. "God," he later stated "made me the messenger of the new heaven and the new earth. . . . He showed me where to find it."

• The finances provided for the voyage of Columbus's three ships were made available from the keeper of the privy purse, Luis de Santangel (a converted Jew), who was treasurer, with the Genoese Francesco Pinelli, of the Fund for the Crusades.

• Probably the first symbol the Arawak Indians saw on Columbus's ships was the cross of the Crusades emblazoned on the sails. Columbus also wore the Crusader's cross on his tunic.

• Despite the known presence of people on Guanahani (the first island Columbus sighted), according to Columbus: "The Admiral went on shore in the armed boat . . . bore the royal standard" and "took possession of that island for the King and Queen" of Spain.

• Columbus, while impressed with the simplicity and friendliness of the people he encountered, immediately thought of making them slaves and converting them to Christianity: "It appears to me that the people are ingenious and would be good servants, and I am of opinion that they would very readily become Christians, as they appear to have no religion."

• The day after landing on Guanahani, Columbus "took some of the natives by force . . . to learn if they had any gold." He continued: "Seeing some of them with little bits of metal hanging at their noses, I gathered from them by signs . . . there would be found a king who possesses great cups full of gold, and in large quantities."

• Concerning the people, Columbus observed that "the people here are simple in war-like matters as your Highnesses will see by those seven which I caused to be taken and carried to Spain" and concluded, "I could conquer the whole of them with fifty men and govern them as I please." He returned with more than 1,200 men on his second voyage.

• In 1495, on the present island of Haiti, all indigenous people over fourteen years of age were to produce a quota of gold every three months; those who failed (and most did) had their hands cut off.

• When he found that gold was scarce in the islands, Columbus engaged in a slave raid that captured 1,500 Arawak men, women, and children, 500 of whom were sent back to Spain (200 died en route) to be sold at auction.

• When the Arawaks organized an army of resistance, they were burned at the stake, hanged, and tortured in inquisitorial fashion. Mass suicides began among the Arawaks and they killed their own infants rather than let them grow up to face the Spaniards.

• Columbus founded the *encomiendas,* which were huge Spanish-run estates worked by the slave labor of the indigenous people and African slaves who began arriving during Columbus's lifetime. The *encomiendas* survived Columbus and were for centuries a major source of exploitation of people and land in Latin America.

A major source of information on the violence and exploitation of the Columbian-inspired exploitation of the indigenous people—and a powerful source of opposition to it—is the work of Dominican priest Bartolome de Las Casas. Perhaps his most brilliant and persuasive work is *In Defense of the Indians.* Las Casas, a contemporary of Columbus in the

"New World," and other missionaries, spoke vigorously against the numerous crimes that were committed against the "Indians" in the name of God, and the priest makes a powerful case that de facto genocide did indeed occur very early on after the Columbian invasion. Although these and other missionaries were not to prevail in urging humane and equitable treatment of the Indians, their voice is an important one because it documents that humanity, compassion, and authentic Christianity existed in the midst of the terrible events of the fifteenth, sixteenth, and seventeenth centuries in the New World.

PART 2
TAKING STOCK: RETHINKING CONTEMPORARY PARADIGMS

TAKING STOCK: RETHINKING CONTEMPORARY PARADIGMS

If you want to make frozen circumstances dance, you have to sing to them in their own music.—Karl Marx

Our old thinking about peace and security has not only guided our approach to the world, it has numbed us to other possibilities. We have become frozen in outdated models for conducting human and international affairs even long after they have proven unworkable. Our task is to thaw these circumstances as soon as we can.

This section takes stock of where we have been as a result of the old thinking that has guided international relations for the last century and a half. It surveys a series of critical approaches and vehicles for challenging the conventional national and international policies that have routinely threatened or violated the peace.

We begin by examining current assumptions and dilemmas. For example, we often hear that violence and aggression are natural to humans and therefore inevitable; but is that really true? Does the emerging New World Order promise a more peaceful world, or rather only a new model of conquest dominated by a single superpower? Our concerns about nuclear and conventional arms buildups usually focus on the weapons themselves as they accumulate in ever larger numbers; but has our preoccupation with stockpiles blinded us to more fundamental causes and problems? Just as nationalism seemed to be loosening its grip on world affairs in favor of greater international cooperation, a "new nationalism" has emerged with a vengeance; is it the same as the "old" nationalism, and will it last? Along with nationalism, a heightened sense of ethnicity has emerged not only in Europe, but also in Africa and other parts of the world; how does it threaten the peace, and what can be done about it?

We consider other global dilemmas as well. While we typically define other nations as our enemies, the deterioration of the world's environment—to which most of us contribute—may actually be a much greater threat. But the New World Order threatens not only the environment indirectly but people even more directly. Women, who constitute more than half the world's population, are the hardest hit; we should take more seriously their plight (and their struggle against it), especially in developing regions of the world such as Africa.

Our new era has also produced unprecedented numbers of refugees, or people fleeing from threats such as war and repression; yet refugees are now welcomed less by other nations than at any time in recent memory. Also, criminal violence threatens us as much as war and other violence, yet our wars against crime are invariably ineffective and counterproductive. Why then do we keep fighting them, and what role do the media play in locking us into these outmoded responses?

In this section, we also examine the new developments and challenges unique to various regions of the world. What have been the implications of glasnost and perestroika for the former Soviet bloc, and for other regions as well? Has the euphoria over the changes in Eastern Europe been warranted; what are the limits and possibilities? How has violence developed in one corner of this region, in the former Yugoslavia, and can conflict resolution effectively address the ethnic and other tensions that underlie it? Also, what will be the role for Asia-Pacific in the new era? Can confidence-building measures diffuse nationalist conflict? And, what does the future hold for the Middle East; are there realistic alternatives after all these years of bloodshed?

TAKING STOCK:
CURRENT DILEMMAS

7

WAR AS A SOCIAL PROBLEM

SAM MARULLO
JEN HLAVACEK

"Human nature being what it is, there will always be war." Public opinion polls have found that roughly 60 percent of the U.S. population agrees with this statement. Yet contrary to this belief, war is a social problem rather than a natural or biological state of affairs. There are no genes destining humans to fight wars, nor has there been evolutionary selection for aggressive traits in human groups. This is the conclusion of the *Seville Statement on Violence,* endorsed by the United Nations Educational, Scientific and Cultural Organization (UNESCO) in 1989.

The statement was written to summarize the state of scientific knowledge concerning the roots of war, repudiating common misconceptions about its biological or genetic basis. Its basic propositions can be summarized as follows: It is scientifically incorrect to say that we have inherited a tendency to make war from our animal ancestors; it is scientifically incorrect to say that war or any other violent behavior is genetically programmed; it is scientifically incorrect to say that human evolution has selected for aggressive behavior; it is scientifically incorrect to say that humans have a violent brain; and it is scientifically incorrect to say that war is caused by instinct or any single motivation.

In contrast to these faulty biological presumptions about war and violence, it may be more productive to adopt a social science perspective that views wars as social events that vary over time and place. They are social phenomena to be explained within their context by other social factors. By adopting such a perspective, we are encouraged and empowered to find solutions to end wars and to create the social conditions that make them less likely to occur in the future.

In January 1991, the American Sociological Association (ASA) endorsed the Seville Statement. In elaborating the reasons for sociologists to make such an endorsement, the ASA Section on the Sociology of Peace

This essay was first published in *Peace Review* 4:3 (1992).

and War issued its own statement on the sociological dimensions of violence and conflict. Their statement, drafted by then section chair Louis Kriesberg, acknowledges the lack of humans' genetic programming to do violence to each other and insists that we look to social processes and conditions to explain violence, conflict, and war. Even these concepts, it notes, have a cultural interpretation that implies social disapproval, since killing someone may not be considered violence when it is done by persons who are regarded as having the authority to commit the act. For example, executing a prisoner sentenced to death is part of the lawful duties of some correctional officers rather than an improper act of violence.

The ASA Section on Peace and War statement contains five major propositions. First, violence occurs in a wide variety of settings and forms, e.g., interpersonal fights, family feuds, organizational rivalry, class-based revolutions, communal riots, and state-based international wars: No single set of genetic predispositions, social conditions, or social processes accounts for this great variety of ways in which people injure or kill each other. Second, violence, war, and conflict can be best understood in the context of the full range of human relations, including cooperation, love, and mutual dependency. Third, violence and war in part arise from and are exacerbated by forces internal to the perpetrators, whether individuals, groups, organizations, or countries. Fourth, the social system within which potential antagonists exist greatly influences the likelihood of violence and war. And, finally, social, cultural, and economic integration among potential antagonists reduces the risk of violence and war.

Thus, although war and militarism may at first appear to be innate characteristics of humans, we see from these propositions that they are in fact social creations, shaped by their social context and intended as methods to achieve social, economic, or political goals. Cast in this light, the social problem of war and violence reminds us of another social institution that one time was widely thought to be based on innate human characteristics, and about which it was widely believed to be inevitable—the institution of slavery. Slavery too had a long history, during which many believed that some humans—particularly those with dark skin from Africa—were biologically inferior and thus destined to be slaves. Economies were built to depend on slave labor, which then became defined culturally as being fundamental to the well-being of others in the society.

Today we are appalled by the concept of slavery and wonder how this peculiar institution could have been accepted as *natural* for its centuries-long history. We can hope that someday in the not-too-distant future, we will look back on previous human history in horror at the ready resort to mass violence as a means of resolving differences. In the short run, we must use our scientific knowledge to better understand the social forces that lead us to accept violence and war as natural states of human affairs and hinder the development of alternative means of settling disputes. As the sociologists' statement concludes, "There is, then, much we can do to make the world safer and less violent."

8

THE SEVILLE STATEMENT ON VIOLENCE

DAVID ADAMS ET AL.

Believing that it is our responsibility to address from our particular disciplines the most dangerous and destructive activities of our species, violence and war; recognizing that science is human cultural product which cannot be definitive or all-encompassing; and gratefully acknowledging the support of the authorities of Seville and representatives of the Spanish UNESCO; we, the undersigned scholars from around the world and from relevant sciences, have met and arrived at the following Statement on Violence. In it, we challenge a number of alleged biological findings that have been used by some in our disciplines to justify violence and war. Because the alleged findings have contributed to an atmosphere of pessimism in our time, we submit that the open, considered rejection of these misstatements can contribute significantly to the International Year of Peace.

M isuse of scientific theories and data to justify violence and war is not new but has been made since the advent of modern science. For example, the theory of evolution has been used to justify not only war, but also genocide, colonialism, and suppression of the weak.

It is scientifically incorrect to say that we have inherited a tendency to make war from our animal ancestors. Although fighting occurs widely throughout animal species, only a few cases of destructive intra-species fighting between organized groups have ever been reported among naturally living species, and none of these involve the use of tools designed to be weapons. Normal predatory feeding upon other species cannot be equated with intra-species violence. Warfare is a peculiarly human phenomenon and does not occur in other animals.

The fact that warfare has changed so rapidly over time indicates that it is a product of culture. Its biological connection is primarily through language which makes possible the coordination of groups, the transmission of technology, and the use of tools. War is biologically possible, but not inevitable, as evidenced by its variation in occurrence and nature over time

This statement was published in *Peace Review* 4:3 (1992).

and space. There are cultures which have not engaged in war for centuries, and there are cultures which have engaged in war frequently at some times and not at others.

It is scientifically incorrect to say that war or any other violent behavior is genetically programmed into our human nature. While genes are involved at all levels of our nervous system function, they provide a developmental potential that can be actualized only in conjunction with the ecological and social environment. While individuals vary in their predispositions to be effected by their experience, it is the interaction between their genetic endowment and conditions of nurturance, that determines their personalities. Except for rare pathologies, the genes do not produce individuals necessarily predisposed to violence. Neither do they determine the opposite. While genes are co-involved in establishing our behavioral capacities, they do not by themselves specify the outcome.

It is scientifically incorrect to say that in the course of human evolution there has been a selection for aggressive behavior more than for other kinds of behavior. In all well-studied species, status within the group is achieved by the ability to cooperate and to fulfill social functions relevant to the structure of that group. "Dominance" involves social bondings and affiliations; it is not simply a matter of the possession and use of superior physical power, although it does involve aggressive behaviors. Where genetic selection for aggressive behavior has been artificially instituted in animals, it has rapidly succeeded in producing hyper-aggressive individuals; this indicates that aggression was not maximally selected under natural conditions. When such experimentally-created hyper-aggressors are present in a social group they either disrupt its social structure or are driven out. Violence is neither in our evolutionary legacy nor in our genes.

It is scientifically incorrect to say that humans have a "violent brain." While we do have a neural apparatus to act violently, it is not automatically activated by internal or external stimuli. Like higher primates and unlike other animals, our higher neural processes filter such stimuli before they can be acted upon. How we act is shaped by how we have been conditioned and socialized. There is nothing in our neurophysiology that compels us to act violently.

It is scientifically incorrect to say that war is caused by "instinct" or any single motivation. The emergence of modern warfare has been a journey from the primacy of emotional and motivational factors, sometimes called "instincts," to the primacy of cognitive factors. Modern war involves institutional use of personal characteristics such as obedience, suggestibility, and idealism, social skills such as language, and rational considerations such as cost calculation, planning, and information processing. The technology has exaggerated traits associated with violence both in training of actual combatants and in the preparation of support for war in the general population. As a result of this exaggeration, such traits are often mistaken for the causes rather than the consequences of the process.

We conclude that biology does not condemn humanity to war, and that humanity can be freed from the bondage of biological pessimism and empowered with confidence to undertake the transformative tasks needed in this International Year of Peace and in the years to come. Although these tasks are mainly institutional and collective, they also rest upon the consciousness of individual participants for whom pessimism and optimism are crucial factors. Just as "wars begin in the minds of men," peace also begins in our minds. The same species who invented war is capable of inventing peace. The responsibility lies with each of us.

Signatories: David Adams, Psychology, Wesleyan University, Middletown (CT) USA; S. A. Barnett, Ethology, The Australian National University, Canberra, Australia; N. P. Bechtereva, Neurophysiology, Institute for Experimental Medicine of Academy of Medical Sciences of USSR, Leningrad, USSR; Bonnie Frank Carter, Psychology, Albert Einstein Medical Center, Philadelphia (PA) USA; José M. Rodríguez Delgado, Neurophysiology, Centro de Estudios Neurobiológicos, Madrid, Spain; José Luis Díaz, Ethology, Instituto Mexicano de Psiquiatría, Mexico D.F., Mexico; Andrzej Eliasz, Individual Differences Psychology, Polish Academy of Science, Warsaw, Poland; Santiago Genoves, Biological Anthropology, Instituto de Estudios Antropológicos, Mexico D.F., Mexico; Benson E. Ginsberg, Behavior Genetics, University of Connecticut, Storrs (CT) USA; Jo Groebel, Social Psychology, Erziehungwissenschaftliche Hochschule, Landau, Federal Republic of Germany; Samir-Kumar Ghosh, Sociology, Indian Institute of Human Sciences, Calcutta, India; Robert Hinde, Psychology, Cambridge University, UK; Richard E. Leakey, Physical Anthropology, National Museum of Kenya, Nairobi, Kenya; Taha M. Malasi, Psychiatry, Kuwait University, Kuwait; J. Martin Ramírez, Psychobiology, Universidad de Sevilla, Spain; Federico Mayor Zaragoza, Biochemistry, Universidad Autónoma, Madrid, Spain; Diana L. Mendoza, Ethology, Universidad de Sevilla, Spain; Ashis Nandy, Political Psychology, Center for the Study of Developing Societies, Delhi, India; John Paul Scott, Animal Behavior, Bowling Green State University, Bowling Green (OH) USA; Riitta Wahlstrom, Psychology, University of Jyvaskyla, Finland.

Organizational endorsements

American Anthropological Association (Annual Meeting, 1986); American Orthopsychiatric Association (1988); American Psychological Association (Board of Scientific Affairs, Board of Social and Ethical Responsibility for Psychology, Board of Directors, and Council, 1987); Americans for the Universality of UNESCO (1986); Canadian Psychologists for Social Responsibility; Czechoslovak UNESCO Commission (1986); Danish Psychological Association (1988); International Council of Psychologists

(Board of Directors, 1987); Mexican Association for Biological Anthropology (1986); Polish Academy of Sciences (1987); Psychologists for Social Responsibility (US, 1986); Society for Psychological Study of Social Issues (US, 1987); Spanish UNESCO Commission (1986/1987); World Federalist Association (US, National Board, 1987).

9

SOCIOLOGICAL STATEMENT ON WAR AND VIOLENCE

How people define and use the terms "violence," "war," and "conflict" significantly affects their social conduct. They use the terms to make sense of social events and to influence these events. Violence is conventionally regarded as illegitimate hurting of people. Thus, even killing someone may not popularly be considered violence, when it is done by persons who are regarded as having the authority to commit the act. The word is often used as a way of claiming or denying legitimacy of various acts. Social scientists usually regard conventional definitions as part of the explanation for variations in the use or threatened use of coercion which physically harms other persons. War popularly refers to all kinds of large-scale intense conflicts, but generally is understood to be struggles conducted by governments employing organized armed forces against each other. Sociologists add that it is a particular social-cultural institution, a social invention.

Conflicts are conventionally viewed as disruptions of order in which antagonists seek to harm each other. Sociologists, however, generally regard conflict as an inherent aspect of social life and a way of changing relations among adversaries. It does not necessarily entail physically damaging others since conflicts can be waged in many different ways.

V iolence occurs in a wide variety of settings and forms, e.g., interpersonal fights, family feuds, organizational rivalries, class-based revolutions, communal riots, and state-based international wars. No single set of genetic dispositions, social conditions, or social processes accounts for this great variety of ways in which people injure or kill each other. Thus, relatively elaborate and extensive forms of violence require explanations about the boundaries of group identifications, coalition promotion, norms about what violence is legitimate, and obedience to authority. Of course, these same matters are as relevant to peacemaking and cooperation as to violence and conflict. Whatever relevance humans' genetic makeup may

This statement was first published in *Peace Review* 4:3 (1992).

have for interpersonal or even interfamilial violence, it contributes little to explaining the great variations in large-scale socially constructed forms of conflict such as wars. They are sustained by cultures and social organizations which greatly vary.

V iolence, war, and conflict are best understood in the context of the full range of human relations, including cooperation, love, and mutual dependency. Certainly people relate to each other in struggles, but most social life is cooperative, and social interaction always blends both conflict and cooperation. Moreover, it is possible to wage fights without violence or war, by using nonviolent coercion, persuasive appeals, and by offering benefits for cooperation. Violent forms of conflict survive largely because they receive some form of social legitimation. Wars, for example, are an institutionalized way of conducting conflict among peoples whom governments direct. Even interpersonal and intergroup violence is most often carried out by people doing what the groups to which they belong regard as appropriate conduct. Those kinds of violence which are not socially approved are considered deviant and have different sources.

V iolence and war in part arise from and are exacerbated by forces internal to the perpetrators, whether individuals, groups, organizations, or countries. The forces which support violence are social, cultural, and economic, as demonstrated in research on areas such as the military-industrial complex, gender socialization, group solidarity, socialization into group identities—including nationalism, and collective behavior and social movements.

T he social system within which potential antagonists exist greatly influences the likelihood of violence and war. Norms and values about violence and the availability of institutionalized means for resolving conflicts shape the strategies adversaries choose to pursue their goals. In every society, systems of dispute settlement, including elaborate legal systems, provide nonviolent means of managing conflicts. The limited nature of such systems globally, and the lack of confidence in their efficacy, contribute to making war and large-scale violence more likely. Over the past two centuries, there has been a trend of increasing attempts to institutionalize international systems for the prevention or control of war and other forms of violence.

S ocial, cultural, and economic integration among potential antagonists reduces the risk of violence and war. Mutual dependency, crosscutting identities and bonds, and cultural and political similarities also lessen the likelihood of violence and war. In contrast, socialization of group members which emphasizes ingroup virtues and outgroup vices increases the likelihood of violence and war, as does the perception of injustice or illegitimate inequality. There is, then, much we can do to make the world safer and less violent.

10

THE GULF WAR AND
THE NEW WORLD ORDER

JOSEPH GERSON

*No country has ever managed to be a great power and a great
debtor at the same time, and two great powers—Britain in this
century and Spain in the 16th century—lost their stature as world
leaders when they moved from creditor to debtor status.*
— Joint Economic Committee of the U.S. Congress, 1988

The United States has a new credibility. What we say goes.
— George Bush, speaking at a U.S. military base, February 2, 1991

More than a year after the collapse of the Berlin Wall and the Soviet
Union's Eastern European empire, the pace of history remains stuck on fast
forward. The Bush administration's Gulf War has not only exacted an enormous toll in human life and spirit, it has moved to impose itself as the only
force to be reckoned with in the global balance of power, thus creating
what Bush has called a New World Order.

On the night of January 17, 1991, George Bush's New World Order
manifested itself as Baghdad was devastated by a barrage of 400 sea-
launched cruise missiles. This was followed by more than 100,000 aircraft
attacks that, according to UN observers, bombed Iraq back into the "prein-
dustrial age." Though the hastily mobilized U.S. movement to protest
Washington's military intervention and offensive forced a debate in
Congress and almost carried the Senate, the Bush administration's commitment to fight an offensive war against Iraq prevailed. On the home front,
the administration's public relations offensive and its manipulation of the
news won the hearts and minds of people in the United States, many of
whom anxiously sought reassurance that the United States was, in some
way, still Number One. The human and environmental consequences of the

This essay was first published in *Peace Review* 3:2 (1991).

"apocalyptic" assaults that destroyed primary life-support systems of the industrial age—water, sewage, and electricity—were ignored. Contrary to popular thinking in the United States, the dawn of the new order came with the devastation of Iraq and Kuwait and between 100,000 and 350,000 war dead—depending on whether one was more inclined to believe the U.S. military in Riyadh or the *Bulletin of the Atomic Scientists.*

It was a war for oil and for making the world safe for feudalism, but it was more. From the beginning, the Bush administration used Saddam Hussein's brutal and cruel invasion and occupation of Kuwait, and the subsequent U.S. intervention, to shape the post–Cold War order. It was a war to reconsolidate U.S. control over the oil of the Middle East in order to reaffirm its control of this lever of power over its competitors and allies— Japan and Western Europe. In a world of three economic superpowers and only one military superpower, the Bush administration demonstrated that U.S. military power would reshape the world in what Michael Klare has described as Pax Americana II. The war was used to ensure that the United States' trilateral allies would be more deeply integrated into the U.S.-led structure. On the morrow of the military victory, the new wisdom in Tokyo was that "Japan is Number Two." Across the Atlantic, Jacques Delors concluded that unless Europe developed an integrated and independent military by 1995, it would not be able to compete with the United States. Those who feared that the collapse of the Cold War would cost them their power or position in the "national security" establishment and military industries have been temporarily reassured that while everything changes, everything stays (sort of) the same.

I t is by using a global geostrategic lens that we can understand the Bush administration's rush to war (Thomas Friedman and Patrick Tyler report in the *New York Times* that the offensive strategy and commitment were in place no later than August 2), its cynical use of UN economic sanctions and Arab League resolutions to provide political cover for its military intervention, and its double standards on aggression, occupation, and sanctions. Were this a war against aggression as the administration claimed, the United States could not have fought the war with Turkish, Syrian, Israeli, and Moroccan allies—all of which are still occupying and integrating lands and people conquered since 1967. This geostrategic framework also helps to explain the distinct lack of enthusiasm of the United States' trilateral allies (particularly Japan and Germany) for funding, not to mention fighting, this war. They need the oil, but the question of which foreign power— the United States or Iraq—has its hand on the tap has not been seen as a matter of life and death to them. They have economic, social, and political agendas, not military ambitions, to pursue.

On September 11, in a speech to Congress, President Bush attempted to sell his nearly unilateral military intervention into the Gulf in the guise of building a "New World Order." He also said the United States was "shoulder to shoulder" with twenty-six nations in the Saudi desert, yet when the fighting began in January only the armies of the United States and the former colonial powers Britain and France were seen to play major roles. With nary an acknowledgment of the Reagan administration's refusal to recognize the standing and legitimacy of the World Court, a decade of conscious U.S. neglect of, and opposition to, the United Nations, the terrorizing war the United States imposed on Nicaragua, or last year's invasion of Panama, President Bush told the world that he was opposed to aggression and that his goal was the establishment of a New World Order based on collective security within the framework of the United Nations.

The president's limited commitment to collective security revealed his advertising slogan for the slick copy that it is. His concept of collective security was not extended to the nations conquered and occupied by the United States' allies in this war, nor did it emerge from atonement after a painful reexamination of the history and current U.S. policies of aggression, occupation, and annexation. Bush's New World Order is old-fashioned gunboat diplomacy fought with Vietnam era and New Age technology.

King Hussein was not the first to describe the aims of the U.S. intervention as the recolonization of the region. He was, however, clearer than most when he said the division of the Arab world created by this war would be worse than that resulting from the secret Sykes-Picot agreement of 1916. During World War I, people were told that it was "a war to end all wars." In the Middle East it created the "peace to end all peace." As A. J. P. Taylor, David Frankin, and other historians have described in considerable detail, World War I was fought primarily to determine whether Britain and France or Germany would carve colonies out of the dying Ottoman Empire. The French and British won, and the Sykes-Picot agreement, reached two years before the war's end, divided the region into British and French colonial spheres.

The Bush administration's Gulf War was fought to reconsolidate U.S. control over the oil of the region, "one of the greatest material prizes in the history of warfare." For the last forty-five years, since it came to dominate the Middle East as a result of the collapse of the British and French empires, the United States has used the Cold War; its nuclear arsenal and nuclear threats; the buying, selling, and subversion of governments by the CIA and other U.S. agencies; the bombardment of Lebanon, Libya, Iran, and now Iraq; the Nixon, Carter, and Reagan doctrines; and Israel to retain its regional dominance.

S ince the end of the U.S. war in Indochina, it has been clear to policymakers in Washington that U.S. global power has been declining relative to that of Japan and Western Europe, and more recently in relation to some Third World nations like Iraq. By 1970, Japan and Western Europe had rebuilt their nations and their economies after the devastation of World War II. Herman Kahn had written *The Emerging Japanese Superstate,* and when Nixon promulgated his doctrine at the 1969 summit meeting with Prime Minister Sato, power sharing with Japan was also proclaimed. Across the world the European Economic Community was beginning to merge the industrial power and markets of Europe to resist what J. J. Servan-Schreiber described as the American Challenge.

Nelson Rockefeller, Zbigniew Brzezinski, and other "national security" planners feared that the growing economic competition of the North could lead, as it did in 1914 and again in the 1930s, to world war. Thus, the concept of trilateralism was born. The trilateral allies—the United States, Japan, and Western Europe—were to be integrated under U.S. leadership in order to minimize conflict among these economic powers and to reinforce U.S. power. The Trilateral Commission, first headed by Brzezinski, included Jimmy Carter and George Bush among its early members. During the Carter administration, and to a lesser extent during the Reagan years, serious progress was made in institutionalizing trilateralism. U.S. and Japanese military strategies were more deeply integrated. When the West grappled with the meaning of glasnost and perestroika, Henry Kissinger, Valéry Giscard d'Estaing, and Yasu Nakasone were dispatched as a group to meet with Mikhail Gorbachev. Early in the Bush administration, the U.S. House of Representatives endorsed "burden sharing," an important element of trilateralism. U.S. allies were to subsidize U.S. militarism by paying for U.S. military forces based in their countries.

About the same time that Paul Kennedy was writing *The Rise and Fall of Great Powers* and the Joint Economic Committee of Congress was issuing the report quoted above, the Pentagon addressed the same concerns. Recognizing that the Reagan era military spending spree could not continue indefinitely, that the United States could not control all of the world, and that as many as forty nuclear powers might emerge over the next twenty years, the Pentagon understood that difficult strategic choices lay ahead. It therefore assembled the Commission on Integrated Long Term Strategy, which included Henry Kissinger, Zbigniew Brzezinski, Samuel P. Huntington (of Vietnam War fame), Generals Andrew Goodpastor and John Vessey, and others to provide a strategy for "the long haul."

Among the panel's conclusions, published in a report titled *Discriminate Deterrence,* were that the United States must retain power over the Persian Gulf, the Mediterranean Sea, and the Pacific Ocean. Even before the collapse of the Berlin Wall, the commission concluded that the primary threat to U.S. global power came not from the Soviet Union but from the South. While it recommended continued modernization of U.S. nuclear weapons, the panel recommended that spending for high-tech weaponry, for low-intensity warfare, and for rapid deployment to the Third

World through greater airlift and sealift capabilities be the government's priorities when hard financial choices had to be made in Congress. Thus were the seeds for the Bush administration's Gulf War planted.

President Bush has moved to master the "vision thing" and has developed a militarized geopolitical strategy consistent with *Discriminate Deterrence*. To understand what the world looks like from the White House, it is worth turning to the writing of the economist Walter Russell Meade and to the itinerary of our president's recent travels. For reasons that were not clearly explained in the press, in December 1990, the president followed his diplomatic journey to the Middle East with a sojourn in Latin America. The purpose of travels in Latin America—to accelerate progress on creating a free trade zone in the Americas—was strategically related to his preparations for war in the Middle East.

W riting in the *Atlantic Monthly* a year ago, Meade brilliantly described the forces at work in creating the Bush administration's vision of a New World Order. While the United States is seeking to create a trilateral world order dominated by the Northern industrialized nations, it may not succeed. Three currency zones, Meade explained, may be emerging. The European Community is about to create the ECU, the European Currency Unit, which will contribute to the further integration of a market of 500 million consumers. An ECU trade zone would draw on Europe's extraordinary technological resources. In Asia and the Pacific, a yen zone also appears to be a possibility, based on an even larger market and more advanced technological resources. Even if the United States could unify the Americas into a dollar zone (and the history of Latin American resistance to U.S. intervention will not help), it could not compete in market size or technological resources.

The dollar zone, Meade argued, could compete with the ECU and yen zones, only if it continued to dominate the oil-rich Middle East. If oil continued to be traded in dollars rather than ECU or yen, and—just as John D. Rockefeller had understood—if the United States could keep its hand on the petroleum tap, it had a chance of competing in the event of the collapse of trilateralism. It is worth remembering that the dollar has lost 50 percent of its value against the yen and deutsche mark over the last five years. Were oil traded in DMs it would cost U.S. consumers and industry twice as much as it does now without the cost of oil rising even one pfennig on the international market. And, if the United States maintained its ability to control the flow of Middle Eastern oil, it would retain control over a lever that has given it significant influence over European and Japanese economic and political life.

It seems unlikely that the Bush administration has thus far been forced to choose between world orders based on trilateralism or competing trade zones, though the recent collapse of the Uruguay Round of the GATT

(General Agreement on Trade and Tariffs) was not a good sign for trilateralism. The Bush administration is holding its options open and seeking to reconsolidate U.S. power on as many fronts as possible in these opening moments of the post–Cold War era. It used and demonstrated its awesome military power to intimidate Japan and Western Europe to accept and finance U.S. global leadership in the coming period.

Although we do not know if the Bush administration consciously invited Iraq's brutal invasion of Kuwait through a plot that has been described in some considerable detail by Jordan's King Hussein, we do know that it has seized upon the invasion to erect the structures of the post–Cold War era, much as it seized upon the Greek civil war in 1947 and North Korea's invasion of South Korea in 1950 to build the necessary structures to win the Cold War.

Other dimensions of the New World Order can be seen in the deals that were made to win the United Nations Security Council's endorsement of the Bush administration's Gulf offensive. Several billion dollars flowed from Gulf coffers to breathe life into the dying Soviet economy. The Soviets also won diplomatic space for its military interventions into the Baltic states and Soviet streets. China's abstention on the Security Council vote was won when its foreign minister was invited to visit Washington, effectively breaking the international isolation that followed the 1989 Beijing massacre. As U.S. tanks rolled toward Iraq, democratic and nonviolent activists of Tiananmen Square are being tried and sentenced to more than a decade in jail. France did seek to differentiate its policies from those of Washington but found little room to maneuver. After three catastrophic wars with Germany in little more than a century, it is struggling to integrate a reunited and powerful Germany into the European Community by balancing German power in Europe with that of the United States. The French government fears that if it alienates itself too much from Washington, it will find itself again facing Europe's greatest power alone.

The United States' trilateral allies have reaffirmed their willingness to participate in financial burden sharing. After much arm twisting—including implied threats to Japan's access to U.S. markets and to Japanese security—Japan agreed to contribute $13 billion to the war effort, nearly the same amount that President Bush has said the war will cost the United States. (Among the many hidden costs to U.S. taxpayers was the write-off of Egypt's $7 billion debt to the United States and Israel's request for an additional $13 billion in economic subsidies.) After German jets were dispatched to the Turkish front of this war as a result of U.S. pressure, the German financial contribution to the war was set at just under $9 billion. The precedent for the use of U.S. bases in Japan, Britain, Spain, Italy, Germany, Greece, Portugal, and Turkey for NATO out-of-area operations in the post–Cold War era has been made. While France has yet to reopen itself to U.S. bases, it did join the New World Order with troops in the Gulf and with U.S. access to French air space for B-52 bombing raids originating in Britain.

In the Middle East, the Bush administration has laid the groundwork for a new alliance structure built on the integration of Egyptian and Syrian military power and the financial and strategic resources of the oil-rich nations' Gulf Cooperation Council. This structure will work in tacit alliance with Israel and Iran. While most U.S. ground troops will be withdrawn from the region, U.S. planes and ships will continue to be deployed and based in the region to serve as a reminder of the coercive underpinnings of the New World Order. As General Schwartzkopf has announced, it is likely that these forces will be augmented by the forward deployment of the Central Command's headquarters and more visible bases on the ground through which U.S. forces can be rotated in the context of "military exercises," as they were in Honduras during the war against the Sandinistas.

The administration has also been clear that it is in no hurry to address the increasing misery of Palestinians suffering from the Israeli military occupation. Rather than reopen the dialogue with the PLO, the preferred U.S. solution to the Israeli-Palestinian conflict continues to exclude an independent Palestinian state. There will be considerable motion around a "peace process" to pacify the Arab street, but with political debts to pay for Israel holding its fire during the war, the break in relations between many conservative Gulf states and the PLO, and the 1992 presidential elections approaching, the Bush administration is likely to focus on negotiations that stabilize relations between Israel and neighboring Arab states and not the more central Palestinian question.

T he majority of Europeans and Japanese have profited from their rejection and containment of militarism, their attention to long-term economic planning, and (to a lesser extent) their greater attention to social justice. Their people and societies are more secure than our own. By opting to shape the world through U.S. military power, rather than on the basis of common or collective security, democratic values, diplomacy, and U.S. economic viability, President Bush has opted for a new domestic order for the United States, that of a garrison state. The combination of military spending, reinforced by triumphalism, and the refusal to create industrial and energy policies other than military spending will accelerate the decay and decline of the U.S. economic and social infrastructures. Europe and Japan will not finance U.S. militarism and U.S. debts indefinitely.

Then we will find ourselves dancing to the piper's tune, one not to our liking. There is increasing talk in Japan of the need for "power sharing," the logical consequence of trilateralism. And in Europe, increasing numbers of politicians are following Jacques Delors's lead by calling for the construction of an independent European military, built within the framework of the Western Economic Union. German Foreign Minister Hans Dietrich Genscher has called for "Europe to act as one in the fields of foreign security, economic and monetary policy." History need not repeat itself—even in new forms.

The Joint Economic Committee of Congress was right. We cannot long survive as a great power and as a great debtor. Valuable time, political imagination, and essential financial and economic resources, as well as hundreds of thousands of human lives, were wasted with the Gulf War and are being sacrificed to the Bush administration's vision of a New World Order. Industrial planning and investment is deferred in the name of laissez-faire capitalism and the reality of state subsidies for the wasteful Military-Industrial Complex. Our society grows sicker—unable to provide for the real security of its people. The president's energy policy follows in the footsteps of his predecessor: "Consume today for tomorrow we will no longer be held accountable." And all the while, the ecological clock— above all, the threat of global warming—continues to tick away.

11

HARDWARE IS NOT THE PROBLEM

WILLIAM A. SCHWARTZ
CHARLES DERBER

Basic changes in analysis and action are required, we believe, if those of us working to avoid a nuclear holocaust are to make much of a difference. To see the problem, consider two recent events: the signing of the INF (Intermediate Nuclear Forces) treaty and the explosion of the war in Afghanistan into Pakistan.

The INF treaty received vast news coverage and academic commentary and provoked intense political reactions. Boston University president John Silber says the treaty "endangers the free world." Most others think the treaty makes the whole world safer. The U.S. and Western European peace movements unsuccessfully opposed deployment of the U.S. Euromissiles and applauded their imminent demise. Reagan and Gorbachev received nominations for the Nobel Peace Prize. The *Bulletin of the Atomic Scientists* rolled back the hands of its "doomsday clock."

Of course, arms control is better than no arms control. But the treaty's concrete importance is in fact minimal. Even if the INF treaty actually lived up to the superpowers' advertised 5 percent cut in nuclear arsenals, it would have no discernible effect on the consequences or the risk of nuclear war. With or without the Euromissiles, obviously, a major nuclear war would probably mean the destruction of human civilization. With or without the Euromissiles, neither side could launch a first strike without almost guaranteeing its own destruction in return. With or without the Euromissiles, conventional war in Europe would gravely risk escalation, whether intended or not, to a nuclear cataclysm.

In fact, every target previously covered by the missiles banned under INF can be covered by other superpower missiles and aircraft. The superpowers have about 50,000 nuclear weapons, enough to annihilate us all many times over. The INF missiles were redundant from the moment they were installed. Their purposes were always political, not military, as

---

This essay was first published in *Peace Review* 1:1 (1989).

Richard Burt, then assistant secretary of state, unwittingly confirmed; responding to a possible delay in Pershing II deployment because of technical problems, Burt reportedly said, "We don't care if the goddam things work or not . . . what we care about is getting them in."

And INF, as a result of a U.S. stipulation, does not actually require the destruction of even a single nuclear warhead; the Pershing II, the cruise missile, and other warheads will be retained and could legally be mounted on other weapons not covered by the treaty. Moreover, even as the press dramatically photographs technicians dismantling INF missiles, the superpowers are busy building new weapons systems with far greater capabilities—Trident II ballistic missiles and sea-launched cruise missiles in the United States, for example. The United States is, in fact, now rapidly expanding its nuclear arsenal (reversing a historical trend dating from 1967), even as President Reagan takes credit for reducing nuclear weapons.

As the INF treaty was urgently debated around the world, a real threat to the planet passed almost without comment. Despite urgent warnings from the CIA, the Reagan administration completed its plan to convert Pakistan into a giant base camp for the Afghan guerrillas and a source of devastating U.S.-supplied weapons, including the shoulder-fired Stinger antiaircraft missile. As the guerrillas accomplished spectacular feats—both on the battlefield and in terrorist attacks against airliners and other civilian targets—the Soviet Union tried perhaps its only remaining alternative to withdrawal: It expanded the war into Pakistan, just as the CIA warned it would. Soviet pilots flying jets with Afghan air force markings have violated Pakistan air space hundreds of times, in many instances bombing and strafing rebel bases, refugee camps, and civilian villages—sometimes as far as thirty or forty miles past the border. Dogfights have left planes downed and Soviet airmen in Pakistani custody.

The Soviet-Pakistani violence received little news coverage and commentary compared to the INF treaty, and almost no one has warned of a nuclear danger. But the danger was real, and at this writing still is so. Senior Pakistani and U.S. officials even discussed a plan for U.S. pilots to fly reconnaissance missions on the Afghan-Pakistani border, which could have led to the first direct Soviet-U.S. combat of the Nuclear Age. As it was, considering the convincing evidence that Pakistan can now rapidly make several nuclear weapons, the border violence was apparently one of the few instances in history in which two nuclear armed states have fought. Had the Soviets expanded their attacks, a major crisis could easily have erupted, perhaps in conjunction with an internal explosion in unstable Pakistan and perhaps involving nuclear armed India as well.

The United States has long regarded a Soviet attack on Pakistan as one of the acts that could prompt World War III. In 1980, for example, the *Los Angeles Times* reported that "White House and other officials dealing with national security," said in a press backgrounder that "if the Soviet Union carried its expansionism into Iran or Pakistan, the United States would have little choice but to oppose it militarily." Such an event, the officials said, "would almost certainly become a nuclear war."

Technical matters of minimal importance like the INF treaty have long distracted the nuclear debate from the real conflicts and violence that could actually ignite a global cataclysm. The 1950s and 1960s saw many serious nuclear danger points—for example, in Korea (in the two intense Taiwan Straits crises), in Lebanon, in the Suez, in Vietnam, in Cuba, and in the 1967 Middle East war. None of them concerned the largely technical matters that dominated the public nuclear debate—such as backyard fallout shelters (which were useless) and the Limited Nuclear Test Ban Treaty (which served public health by banning atmospheric nuclear tests but did not diminish the danger of nuclear war).

In the 1970s, those concerned with nuclear war were largely transfixed by the SALT and ABM treaties—which were specifically designed not to restrict any weapons system either superpower really wanted. As George Rathjens observes, the SALT treaties have not "had any significant effect on the magnitude of damage that would be expected should a nuclear war occur, and it is doubtful if either has significantly enhanced deterrence or strategic stability." The same is true of the ABM treaty. Meanwhile, dangerous crises burned around the world with little comment from those seeking to avoid nuclear war. Examples are the 1970 War of Attrition crisis (which included direct combat between the Soviet Union and Israel, apparently nuclear armed by then), the Black September crisis in the same year in Jordan (of which Nixon said: "It was like a ghastly game of dominoes, with a nuclear war at the end"), and the 1973 Middle East war (when Henry Kissinger and other aides ordered a massive U.S. nuclear alert while the president, overwhelmed by Watergate, slept).

In the early 1980s, debate raged about the MX missile, which supporters term the "Peacekeeper" and opponents call a major threat to world peace. It is neither. The Soviet first-strike threat that some said the MX would counter does not exist, and never did, and neither does the U.S. first-strike threat that others say the MX would enhance. The Scowcroft Commission finally acknowledged that regardless of the MX, the Soviets had no way to launch a nuclear war without inviting its own annihilation. And now that the MXs are sitting in their silos, only a madman could doubt that the United States remains totally vulnerable to Soviet retaliation in case of nuclear war, just as it was before MX.

A real danger knocked at the door during the MX debate, but it had nothing to do with the missile. In 1982, Israel invaded Lebanon, apparently with tacit U.S. permission, provoking serious hostilities with Syrian forces and moving within shelling distance of Damascus. The foreign ministers of the European Community warned of "a generalized war" in the Middle East, widely regarded as perhaps the most likely spark for a nuclear catastrophe. As Ambassador Ghassan Tueni of Lebanon told the United Nations General Assembly session on disarmament in June 1982, "the war in Lebanon was becoming a threat not to Lebanon alone, but to others as well, and probably to the entire world." In 1983, the United States intervened directly in the war with Marines and a naval armada—probably nuclear armed—thus inviting a repetition of the sea power confrontations that have plagued every major Israeli-Arab war since 1956. William Ury, director of Harvard's Nuclear Negotiation Project, writes: "The Soviet description of Berlin in 1958 as a smoldering fuse connected to a powder keg could have applied just as well to Lebanon in 1983."

The pattern just described reflects a basic misunderstanding of the sources of nuclear danger. The U.S. political right, center, and left alike have long claimed that the nuclear problem is essentially a problem of the arms race. They have disagreed mainly over how the arms race should be run—whether the United States should try to win it through rearmament, rationalize it through arms control, end it through a freeze or a comprehensive test ban, or reverse it through huge cuts in nuclear arsenals. Indeed, the arms race has become virtually synonymous with the problem of nuclear war. One bumper sticker sums up a common peace movement position: "Stop the Arms Race. Save the Human Race."

It is natural to assume that enlarging and refining nuclear arsenals somehow makes the danger worse. But nuclear weapons are so powerful that, beyond a point, increases in either numbers or technological wizardry mean little. McGeorge Bundy writes: "A decision that would bring even one hydrogen bomb on one city of one's own country would be recognized in advance as a catastrophic blunder; ten bombs on ten cities would be a disaster beyond history and a hundred bombs on a hundred cities are unthinkable." Even if Bundy exaggerates, the arms race ceased to matter greatly to the nuclear danger many years ago. Even in the 1950s the U.S. Strategic Air Command planned to reduce the Soviet Union to a "smoking radiating ruin at the end of two hours." By 1960, President Eisenhower was "shocked and angered by the level of overkill envisioned" in the official U.S. plan for nuclear war. That same year, the U.S. Air Force concluded that depending on who struck first, a Soviet nuclear attack would already kill between 110 and 150 million in the United States, most of the population.

Little has changed since 1960, except perhaps the number of times we can bounce the radioactive rubble of the world. The total explosive yield of the stockpile has in fact declined, as warheads have become smaller and more accurate. According to the 1984 annual report of the U.S. Department of Defense, "the total number of [U.S.] Megatons was four times as high in

1960 than [it was] in 1980." Until the Reagan buildup, the number of U.S. warheads also decreased slightly after 1967. The numbers are simply irrelevant.

Most people know that nuclear weapons are tremendously powerful and that the superpowers achieved massive overkill years ago. But few recognize the full implications. Many assume, for example, that the amazing advances in missile accuracy and other technical characteristics of the last few decades have somehow undermined the nuclear balance of terror. The right periodically warns that new Soviet weapons pose a grave first-strike threat against the United States, while the left warns of an emerging U.S. first-strike threat to the Soviet Union. But when a single warhead can level a city and render it uninhabitable for thousands of years, neither side can pull off a successful first strike, no matter what weapons are at hand.

A successful first strike is virtually a logical impossibility in the Nuclear Age. General David Jones, former chairman of the U.S. Joint Chiefs of Staff, says: "I don't know any American officer, or any Soviet officer, who believes either superpower can achieve a true first-strike capability, that one side could ever so disarm the other as to leave it without the ability to retaliate . . . [both] strongly agree that neither side can win a nuclear war in any meaningful sense."

With only a few exceptions, the new generations of weapons on each side waste billions of dollars but do not change the balance of power or the risk of war. As Admiral Noel Gaylor, former commander in chief of U.S. forces in the Pacific, writes: "A tired old Bear bomber, and a maneuvering hypersonic re-entry vehicle . . . [either one] can destroy New York just as well." And a tired old B-52 can incinerate Moscow as well as a B-1 or Stealth bomber, or an MX, Trident II, or Midgetman missile. Star Wars—praised by some as a defense against nuclear war and condemned by others as a grave threat to peace—would also change nothing important to deterrence. Defense against nuclear war is simply impossible, as almost every competent scientist agrees. A defense that can't work doesn't make things better, and it doesn't make things worse. It is just a waste, and a distraction from real dangers.

Short of nearly complete nuclear disarmament, which is not in sight, arms control likewise can do little to affect the dangers of nuclear war. Even the proposed START treaty to substantially cut strategic nuclear arsenals, however satisfying in principle, would only eliminate weapons that are redundant to begin with. Unlike START, INF, and prior arms control treaties, the nuclear freeze or the comprehensive test ban treaty might at least put a cap on technological improvements in nuclear weapons and delivery systems, and hence could save a lot of money. But the balance of terror would remain. We see little reason to expect that the risk of nuclear war would change for the better, as arms control advocates hope, or for the worse as the opponents warn.

Logic, then, suggests that the arms race and arms control are largely irrelevant to the nuclear danger. So does history. Apart perhaps from the early years, when the United States considered using its vast nuclear superiority to level the Soviet Union, none of the many nuclear danger points of past four decades resulted from the size or the technical characteristics of the superpowers' nuclear arsenals. Even the 1962 Cuban missile crisis—the only crisis that even remotely concerned the arms race—had little to do with the real military balance of power or the integrity of deterrence. Kennedy confronted Khrushchev for political reasons, to prevent the Soviet leader from scoring a symbolic Cold War victory. And, as six of Kennedy's senior advisers wrote in 1982, "The balance of terror so eloquently described by Winston Churchill seven years earlier was in full operation . . . no one of us ever reviewed the balance for comfort in those hard weeks. The Cuban missile crisis illustrates not the significance but the insignificance of nuclear superiority in the face of survivable thermonuclear retaliatory forces."

Other crises have followed the same pattern. Particularly since 1960, leaders on both sides have always assumed that nuclear war would be a complete catastrophe for all concerned. They have often risked nuclear war because they have been insanely reckless, willing to run the risk of planetary destruction to achieve their goals, not because they thought new weapons might give one side a usable advantage or a way to escape apocalyptic damage in case of nuclear war

Weaponitis, as we call the obsession with technical matters of the arms race, is not only an error in thought. The error is politically convenient because the alternative to picturing the nuclear problem as a problem of the arms race is confronting the real danger: the aggressive and reckless foreign policies of the United States and the other nuclear powers. In the United States, the foreign policy mainstream, whether consciously or not, finds in weaponitis a way to talk about and purportedly deal with the peril of nuclear war without calling into question risky U.S. actions in Lebanon, the Persian Gulf, Afghanistan, Cambodia, and other Third World flashpoints. Liberal politicians, in particular, can earn excellent antinuclear war credentials by promoting arms control without breaking out of the long-standing U.S. foreign policy consensus.

Around 1980, the U.S. peace movement likewise made a pivotal political decision—partly conscious, partly not—to avoid a controversial critique of U.S. foreign policy and to focus instead on questions of hardware like the MX, the Euromissiles, and the Freeze. Partly as a result of that decision, the peace movement achieved respectability and gentle treatment—in the press, in establishment foundations, in Congress, and else-where—rare in the history of oppositional U.S. mass movements. But the cost was great: remaining silent about most of the real violence that endangered the planet in the 1980s.

A few, like Noam Chomsky, had long warned that superpower-sponsored conflict and intervention in the Third World posed grave nuclear dangers. After the Israeli invasion of Lebanon, and the peace movement's failure to respond to it, more movement activists, scholars, and leaders began to recognize the need for a change of course. Initially under the leadership of the (Quaker) American Friends Service Committee, the deadly connection between worldwide U.S. militarism and the nuclear danger became a widely discussed rubric for thinking about political challenges to superpower foreign policy to reduce the nuclear threat. The deadly connection idea is the most hopeful development in nuclear politics in many years.

B ut at the moment it is only a beginning. Major antiwar organizations such as the newly merged SANE-Freeze have officially adopted the deadly connection in their platforms but deeds have not followed words, as the nonresponse to the Afghan war shows. It is difficult to recall even one recent Third World conflict that drew serious protest on grounds of nuclear danger. Even U.S. actions with obvious risks of provoking a superpower confrontation—like the massive nuclear-armed naval intervention in the Persian Gulf on the Soviet doorstep, the largest and most dangerous U.S. military operations since Vietnam—did not lead to widespread protest.

Of course, both superpowers and many other nations and political movements contribute to the tensions and conflicts that could lead to a nuclear confrontation. U.S. citizens, however, have primary responsibility for the actions of their own state. We have much to learn, and do, about our government's part in the real political conflicts that could one day lead to the launching of thousands of nuclear weapons that—with or without INF, MX, Star Wars, or a Freeze—could reduce our planet to "a smoking radiating ruin at the end of two hours."

12

THE NEW NATIONALISM IN EUROPE

MARY KALDOR

Far from ending, history seems to have accelerated since the revolutions of 1989. Germany has unified; the Soviet Union, Yugoslavia, and Czechoslovakia have fallen apart. A major war is taking place in the middle of the continent, with tens of thousands of deaths, millions of refugees, and the destruction of whole villages, towns, and historic buildings. Anti-Semitism, antigypsyism, and other forms of xenophobia are on the rise again almost everywhere in Europe.

Did those of us who devoted so much of our lives to the goal of ending the Cold War make a mistake? Was it worth being a dissident or a peace activist if this was to be the final outcome? Why did we assume that everything could be solved if the division of Europe were removed? Cold War apologists, such as John Lewis Gaddis or John Mearsheimer, told us that future generations would look back nostalgically on the period of the Cold War as a golden era of stability—the "Long Peace," they called it. Eastern European officials used to warn us that democracy was impossible because nationalist and racist feelings would be revived. Were they right after all? Was nationalism kept in check, "deep frozen" as many commentators would have it, only to reemerge when the Cold War ended?

I do not think we were wrong. People's behavior is conditioned by their immediate experience, not by memories of what happened to previous generations. Of course, those memories are rekindled and used in every nationalist conflict, but it is the current context that determines the power of memory to shape politics. I would like to argue two propositions: First, far from having been suppressed by the Cold War, the new nationalism is a direct consequence of the Cold War experience. Without the Cold War, the current wave of nationalism would not have happened, at least not in the same way and with the same virulence. Second, the new nationalism that is sweeping through Central and Eastern Europe is different from the nationalism of previous epochs, although it may share some common features. It is a contemporary phenomenon, not a throwback to the past.

This essay was first published in *Peace Review* 5:2 (1993).

N ationalism is a relatively recent phenomenon that arose in the late eighteenth century. It is extremely difficult to disentangle the concept of a nation from the concept of a nation-state. Definitions of a nation vary: a common linguistic group, inhabitants of a particular territory, an ethnic group, a group with shared cultural traditions, religion, or values. In practice, a group of human beings that define themselves as a nation usually do so because they are citizens of a particular state, because they are discriminated against by a state, or because they are interested in establishing their own state.

All nationalisms share two common features. First is the notion of citizenship—the idea that sovereignty, i.e., control of the state, is vested in the nation rather than in, say, the monarch—as in eighteenth-century Western Europe or nineteenth-century Central Europe—or foreign oppressors, as in the Third World or in the Soviet empire.

Of course, concepts of citizenship varied. Historians often distinguish between Western and Eastern nationalism—in particular, the French and the German variants of citizenship. In France, the citizens were the inhabitants of French territory. There was a notion that being French was associated with French language and culture. But this could be acquired; immigrants and minorities could assimilate. By contrast, the German notion of citizenship was ethnic. Even today, anyone of German ethnic origin can claim German citizenship.

Second, nationalism involves a sense of distinct group identity, which is defined in contrast to other groups. The rise of nationalism was linked to the rise of written vernacular languages, which in turn was linked to the expansion of the intellectual class. The discovery of print technology made the written word far more widely accessible. New publications such as novels and newspapers gave rise to new identities and communicative networks. Benedict Anderson uses the term "imagined community" to describe the way in which the people who had never met or who were not related could develop a sense of community because they read the same newspapers and novels. But it is in war that the idea of a nation is the most substantiated. The existence of an enemy, real or imagined, is an important element in forging a sense of national identity.

During the Cold War years, national sentiment seemed superseded by bloc sentiment, at least in Europe. In the East, the language of Marxism-Leninism displaced the language of nationalism as a legitimizing principle. And in the West, vague commitments to democracy and the Western way of life seemed more important than national interest. The idea of an ideological enemy seemed more convincing than a national enemy. Many commentators talked about the post-1945 European era as "postnationalist." This turned out to be wishful thinking.

M ax Weber defined the state as an organization "that [successfully] claims the monopoly of the legitimate use of physical force." Pierre Bourdieu, the French sociologist, has extended that definition to cover what he calls symbolic violence, by which he means the use of language as a form of domination. It is in both the symbolic and physical senses that the state has collapsed or is collapsing in much of the postcommunist world.

The current wave of nationalism has to be understood in terms of the collapse of the communist state. First, the language of domination—the Marxist-Leninist discourse—has been totally discredited. More important, no alternative language exists that is capable of reconstructing legitimacy, i.e., mobilizing a consensus about the political rules of the game. During the communist period, there were no public political debates and no autonomous political movements or parties. There was no mechanism through which political ideas, principles, values, political groups, or even individuals could gain respect or trust in society.

To some extent, Europe, understood as a haven of peace, prosperity, and democracy and identified with the European Community, constituted a political alternative. But it soon became clear that only rich countries could join the European Community. The experience of market reform, which was associated with Western countries—especially in the former Yugoslavia, Poland, and Slovakia—quickly dispelled the mobilizing potential of the European idea. Because all politicians made use of the language of democracy, markets, and Europe and nobody really understood what it signified, it lacked the substantive content upon which to base new forms of authority.

In the aftermath of the 1989 revolutions, there were no tried and tested politicians, no established routes to power. There was a generalized distrust of politicians and parties. Given the huge expectations generated by the 1989 revolutions, every politician was bound to be disappointing.

In these circumstances, the appeal to an untainted, uncompromised ethnic, religious, or linguistic identity is one of the most effective ways to win power. In large parts of the postcommunist world, it is nationalist parties that have won elections. You vote for a politician because he (and it almost always is not she) is a Serb or a Slovak or whatever like you. The mobilization of fear, the notion that you and your people are threatened, the creation of a war psychosis in the time-honored communist tradition are all mechanisms to stay in power, to reestablish authority, to reclaim control over the means of symbolic violence. Both communist and nationalist discourse require an other—imperialism or an enemy nation. But the communist rhetoric could claim a monopoly over discourse because it was based on universalist values. The problem with the nationalist rhetoric is that it is inherently exclusionary. By nature, it is fragmentary—stimulating counter-claims to the control of symbolic violence.

Of course, there were differences among nationalist parties. Some were anticommunist and called themselves democratic. Others were simply revamped communist parties, as in Serbia or Azerbaijan. Some nationalist parties made efforts to include minorities in their nationalist project, as in the Ukraine. Others were openly exclusivist. Many commentators suggested that these differences were important. Nationalism is said to be Janus-faced. A sense of national identity is a necessary precondition for establishing democracy, for opposing totalitarianism, and for rebuilding a sense of civic responsibility. The movements in Poland, the Baltic states, and Slovenia were compared to liberation movements in the Third World. Yet sadly, the ugly face of nationalism has shown itself much more frequently than the pleasing face. In Slovenia and Croatia, and in the Baltic states, ethnically based citizenship laws have been introduced. Everywhere xenophobia and chauvinism are on the increase. In many places, paranoia about the other is whipped up and human rights are violated in the name of national security.

I n addition, the Cold War machines are disintegrating. The arms buildup over the last forty years profoundly influenced economies and societies. It was naive to suppose that this process could be reversed merely by cutting defense budgets. Large parts of the postcommunist world are flooded with surplus weapons, unemployed soldiers, and arms producers. It is easy enough to form a paramilitary group by putting on a homemade uniform, buying weapons on the black market, and perhaps even employing an ex-soldier or two as mercenaries. The wars in the former Yugoslavia or the Transcaucasian region are being fought this way.

In the Croatian-occupied part of Bosnia-Herzegovina, known as the Croatian Community of Herzog-Bosne, there are, for example, several military groups. There is the official Croatian-Bosnian army, the HVO; the Muslim territorial defense force known as Armija; the extreme right-wing Hos, who wear black in memory of the Ustashe (Croatian Nazis) who ruled Croatia in 1941–1945; and a number of smaller free-lance armies such as the Croatian Falcons or the Yellow Ants. Each group has its own chain of command, sources of supply, registered license plates, and roadblocks. Similar groups can be found in the Serbian parts of Bosnia-Herzegovina and, with the breakdown of lines of command, the Yugoslav army (the JNA) has come to look more and more like a collection of paramilitary groups.

Much the same situation can be found in Transcaucasia. In Georgia, all the political parties, except the Greens, have their own militias. Shevardnadze has tried to reestablish a monopoly over the means of violence by trying to weld together these militias into a regular army. It is this ragbag of armed bands that is currently facing defeat at the hands of the Abkhazian National Guard. In Ngorno Karabakh, you see everywhere young men in various uniforms lolling around waiting to be sent to the front. They are all unpaid volunteers. The minister of defense of Ngorno Karabakh, a former Intourist guide, told me he thought it would become easier to create a regular army now that there was a "real war." In Azerbaijan, the government is employing Russian ex–Soviet army officers on yearly contracts to create a regular army. All the same, the Ministry of Defense official spokesman described the war with Armenia as a "citizens struggle. . . . We have no army and they have no army—this is a citizens struggle. All the fighting is done by irregular troops."

Private armies exist as in feudal times, but no single grouping has the legitimacy to reestablish a monopoly. None, be it an elected government or a disaffected minority, can command widespread trust in society. In these circumstances, government troops become just another paramilitary group.

In societies where the state controlled every aspect of social and economic life, the collapse of the state means anarchy. The introduction of markets actually means the absence of any kind of regulation. The kind of self-organized market institutions that are the precondition for a market economy simply do not exist. The market does not, by and large, mean new autonomous productive enterprises. It means corruption, speculation, and crime. Many of these paramilitary groups are engaged in a struggle for survival. They use the language of nationalism to legitimize a kind of primitive accumulation—a grab for land or capital. The nationalist conflicts in the former Yugoslavia and Soviet Union cannot be understood as traditional power politics; that is, not as conflicting political objectives defined by parties to the conflict, which are, in principle, amenable to some kind of compromise solution. Rather, they have to be understood as a social condition—a condition of laissez-faire violence.

Many of the characteristics of this social condition exist throughout the postcommunist world. But the situation is more extreme in the former Yugoslavia and Soviet Union, for historical and geographical reasons. Both regions are a patchwork of ethnicities; the countries of Central Europe are much more homogeneous. Both regions have histories of ethnic conflicts that politicians can easily use. This is especially true in Yugoslavia, where memories of atrocities inflicted on all communities, and especially the Serbs, during the Second World War are still vivid. And in both regions, the communist regimes—Stalin in the Soviet Union and Tito in Yugoslavia—exploited national questions in order to sustain their rule.

The new nationalism is different from the old nationalism. First, the new nationalism is antimodern, whereas earlier nationalisms were of modernization. Nationalism has, of course, always harked back to some idea of a romantic past, but the old nationalism was an essential component of modernity: It was linked to the rise of the modern state and industrialization. The early nationalists were functionalist: Nationalism, for them, was part of the march toward progress. The nation-state was a viable political unit for democracy and industry, not merely a natural institution for a historically established national community. It was a stage in human evolution, from local to national and eventually to global society. Mazzini, for example, did not support Irish independence because he thought Ireland was not viable as a nation-state. Similarly, nationalists in the Third World viewed national liberation as a precondition for modernization and development.

In contrast, the new nationalism is antimodern, not only because it is a reaction against modernity, but also because it is not a viable political project—it is out of tune with the times. This is why it is antimodern rather than postmodern. The rediscovery of cultural identity is often considered an element of postmodernism. This implies some possibility of moving beyond modernity, whatever that may involve. The new nationalism offers no such prospect. In a world of growing economic, ecological, and even social interdependence, the new nationalism wants to create ever smaller political units.

Earlier nationalisms incorporated different cultural traditions. The new nationalism is culturally separatist. It is often said that Yugoslavia was an artificial creation because it contained so many different linguistic, religious, and cultural traditions. But all modern nations were artificial. The national language was usually based on a dominant dialect, which was spread through the written word and education. At the time of Italian unification, only between 2 percent and 3 percent of Italians spoke Italian. At the first sitting of the newly created National Assembly, Massimo d'Azeglio said: "We have made Italy, now we have to make Italians." The Yugoslav project was less successful than earlier national projects, perhaps because it was attempted too late or too quickly. The new nationalism is a reaction to the cultural hegemony of earlier nationalisms. It is an attempt to preserve and reconstruct preexisting cultural traditions, said to be national, at the expense of other traditions.

T he new nationalism emphasizes ethnos. Cultural traditions are a birthright; they cannot be acquired. This is reflected in the citizenship laws in the Baltic countries or in Slovenia and Croatia, which exclude certain minorities and which distinguish between autochthonous, i.e., indigenous, and other minorities. There were, of course, elements of ethnicity in earlier nationalisms, especially in Germany. But now the emphasis on ethnos combined with cultural separatism contains an inherent tendency toward fragmentation. Every excluded minority discovers it is a nation. The former Yugoslavia is not only divided into Slovenia, Croatia, and Bosnia-Herzegovina, and so forth. Croatia is also divided into a Croatian and Serbian part; in Bosnia and Herzegovina, there is now a Bosnian Croatian state and a Bosnian Serbian state; and there are now distinctions between Bosnian Muslims who were once Croat and Bosnian Muslims who were once Serbs.

The antimodernism of the new nationalist movements is also reflected in their social composition. The earlier nationalist movements were more often urban and middle class, although they did become mass movements in the twentieth century. Although it is difficult to generalize, the new movements often include an important rural element. Susan Woodward has characterized the war in Bosnia-Herzegovina as a socioeconomic war, in which rural nationalists control multiethnic townspeople. In Serbia, the main support for Milosovic comes from industrial workers who live in the countryside and maintain their own smallholdings. In the nineteenth century and in Third World national liberation movements, intellectuals were extremely important. There are still, of course, nationalist intellectuals, but in today's world, where the opportunities to travel and collaborate with intellectuals in other countries have greatly increased, it is much more common to find intellectuals in Green, peace, and human rights movements that have a global consciousness. The expansion of education, and scientific and office jobs, has greatly increased the number of people who can be called intellectuals and who have international horizons. In Serbia, it is the students and the Academy of Sciences that constitute the main opposition to Milosovic. In the Transcaucasian region, it is Armenian and Azerbaijani intellectuals, supported by Russian intellectuals, who are working the hardest to overcome national conflicts.

A postmodern project would be integrating rather than unifying or fragmentative. It would emphasize cultural diversity rather than cultural homogeneity or cultural divisiveness. It would encompass the growing educated strata in society. Some people argue that the new nationalism has the potential to be integrating. Scottish nationalists talk about Scotland in Europe. Likewise, the new nation-states in Eastern Europe all say that they want to "join Europe." Indeed, the main motivation for nationalism in Slovenia and Croatia and also the Baltic states seems to have been that these people believed their chances of joining the European Community would be greater if they were unencumbered by their large backward neighbors, i.e., Russia and Serbia. Fashionable European concepts like "subsidiarity" or "Europe of the Regions" offer the possibility of combining local and regional autonomy with Europewide cooperation. But this is completely at odds with the ethnic principle of citizenship and even with the territorial sovereignty that is an essential element of all nationalisms. In practice, the new nationalism has shown itself to be closed to the outside world. New nationalist governments are reimposing control over the media, especially television; they are renationalizing rather than privatizing industry; they are introducing new barriers to travel, trade, and communication

by increasing frontiers. As such, the new nationalist project is unviable; it
is incapable of solving economic and environmental problems, and it is a
recipe for violent unrest and frequent wars.

T he second way the new nationalism differs from earlier nationalisms is
  the use of new technology. If the new nationalism is antimodern in
philosophy, it is modern or even postmodern in technique. In place of the
novels and newspapers that constructed the earlier nationalism, the new
nationalism is based on new communicative networks involving television,
videos, telephones, faxes, and computers. These techniques extend the possibilities for mobilizing, manipulating, and controlling public opinion. New
neo-Nazis in Germany circulate anti-Semitic videos, and they use CB
radios to orchestrate their demonstrations.

   The use of new technology had led to the rise of transnational "imagined communities." Groups of exiles in Paris, London, and Zurich have
often played an important role in national movements. But ease of communication and the expansion of expatriate communities in new countries such
as the United States, Canada, or Australia have transformed the new national movements into transnational networks. In almost every significant
national movement, money, arms, and ideas are provided by expatriates
abroad. Irish-American support for the IRA has been well documented.
Other examples include Canadian mercenaries in Croatia, American
Macedonians calling for the unification of Macedonia and Bulgaria, and the
Armenian diaspora supporting the claim to Ngorno Karabakh. The new
nationalism has resulted, in part, from the loss of cultural identity in the
anonymous melting pot nations of the New World. The dreams of the expatriates, the longing for a "homeland" that does not exist, are dangerously
superimposed on the antimodern chaotic reality they have left behind.
Radha Kumar has described the support that Indians living in the United
States give to the Hindu nationalist movement: "Separated from their countries of origin, often living as aliens in a foreign land, simultaneously feeling stripped of their culture and guilty for having escaped the troubles
'back home,' ex-patriates turn to diaspora nationalism without understanding the violence that their actions might inadvertently trigger."

   Another aspect of the new technology is, of course, modern weapons.
Modern military technology is immensely destructive. Even without the
most up-to-date systems, villages and towns in Croatia, Bosnia, and
Herzegovina have been razed. It is the combination of an antimodern philosophy with modern technology, in both military and communicative
terms, that makes the new nationalism so dangerous.

T he new nationalism is a dead-end phenomenon. It is a reaction to the
  oppressive nature of modernity, especially its statist Eastern European
variant, and a rationale for a new gangsterism. It will lead at best to small,

autarchic, authoritarian, poor states, and at worst to endemic, continuous violence. The conflict in Northern Ireland can be viewed as a foretaste of the new nationalism; it is a mistake to view the events in Ulster as a reversion to the past, although the various parties to the conflict—especially the various paramilitary groups—do make use of tradition. Rather, it is a contemporary antimodern phenomenon with many similarities to the new nationalisms in Eastern Europe.

The new nationalism is unviable because the nation-state as a form of organization, with extensive administrative control over clearly defined territory, is no longer an effective instrument for managing modern societies. In fact, this was already the case before World War I. The bloc system, which emerged after the Second World War as a result of the Cold War, established for a while some sort of stability, albeit oppressive, because it overcame some of the nation-state's shortcomings.

The nation-state is both too large and too small. It is too small to cope with economic interdependence, global environmental problems, and destructive military technologies. It is too large to allow for democratic accountability, cultural diversity, and the complex decisionmaking needed in the economic and environmental realms. The blocs offered a method of dealing with the problem that the nations were too small. But they greatly exacerbated the problems arising from the fact that nation-states were also too large. The new nationalism has reacted to these problems by trying to make ever smaller nation-states.

We now need a break with the idea of territorial sovereignty—the notion of more or less absolute control by a centralized administrative unit over a specific geographic area. We need greater autonomy at local and regional levels to enhance democracy, to increase people's ability to influence their own lives, to foster cultural traditions and diversity, to overcome the sense of anonymity caused by modernity, and to make sensible decisions about local economic and environmental problems. But we also need international institutions with the real power to intervene at local levels to protect human rights and democracy, to uphold environmental and social standards, and to prevent war. In other words, we need layers of political organization crisscrossing both territory and fields of activity.

I s this a utopian idea? Actually, elements of this approach already exist. The most important example is the European Community (EC). The EC is not the forerunner of a European nation-state; it is a new kind of political institution with elements of supranationality, that is, sovereignty in certain fields of activity, which allows it to interfere in member-state affairs and overrule them on some issues. The EC could become an institution capable of dealing with Europewide problems while also enhancing local and regional autonomies. The same evolution could occur in other international institutions, such as the United Nations or the CSCE (Conference on

Security and Cooperation in Europe). These organizations now get their power from the nation-states, which severely limits what they can achieve. If their roles are to be extended, it will have to come from new forms of transnational political pressure.

New forms of communication have helped develop transnational networks. In certain fields, especially intellectual and managerial activity, people communicate more—through telephone, fax, and frequent travel—with others in their same field around the world than with their neighbors or their fellow nationals. If these networks have created transnational "imagined communities" based on ethnicity, they have also created more globally conscious "imagined communities." Two types of networks have a common interest, together with international institutions, in curbing the administrative sway of nation-states.

One type of network involves local layers of government: municipalities and regional governments. Since the early 1980s, local governments have become much more involved with foreign policy issues through twinning arrangements, nuclear-free or violence-free zones, and other initiatives. Organizations such as the Association of Nuclear-free Authorities, the Standing Council of Local Authorities of the Council of Europe, and the Association of European Regions potentially represent new types of transnational pressure groups.

A second type of network has emerged from the single-issue social movements of the 1970s and 1980s. These groups were much more successful at local and transnational levels than at national levels. Not able to break the grip of traditional political parties on national politics, they were much more effective than parties at creating transnational constituencies. Organizations like Greenpeace, Helsinki-Watch, Amnesty International, Oxfam, and the Helsinki Citizens Assembly can cross national boundaries and operate internationally. To these groups should be added trade unions, churches, and academic institutions, which have greatly increased their international networks in recent years. Together, they are forming what could be called transnational civil society.

Throughout Eastern Europe and especially in areas of conflict, brave groups of people, often intellectuals, are struggling to provide an alternative to violence and ethnic nationalism. They use the language of citizenship, civil society, nonviolence, and internationalism. They are supported by transnational networks such as those mentioned above. The main hope for an alternative to nationalism lies in constructing a new political culture, a new legitimate language, that might be based on an alliance between the emerging transnational civil society and international institutions.

The Balkan war provides an example of what could be done. The activities of international institutions are now greatly hampered because they are intergovernmental, which means they are seeking solutions "from above."

This is because they can only make decisions based on compromise between member states, and often the compromises satisfy no one. They also assume that their negotiating partners should be the representatives of states or embryo states, yet these are the aggressive nationalists who are breaking all the norms of international behavior. Thus, international institutions are becoming parties to ethnic partition, which could mean, among other things, a loss of legitimacy for the institutions themselves.

T he new nationalism is a social condition arising from the collapse of communist state structures. The new politicians may have been elected, but they do not have the legitimacy to be considered "representative" of the people because they practice exclusionary policies. There are also, in the Balkan region, municipalities, civic groups, and individuals who are trying to keep multiethnic communities together, to prevent the spread of war, to support refugees and deserters, and to provide humanitarian aid. These groups are helped by municipal and civic transnational networks, but their resources are extremely meager. If international institutions could make those groups and institutions that uphold international standards their primary partners, and could condemn all those who violate international norms, it could begin the reconstruction of legitimate political culture "from below."

The forerunners of the new groups in Eastern Europe are the dissidents of the 1970s and 1980s. Their political discourse can be traced back to the dialogue between peace groups and democracy groups across the East-West divide. In the long run, that dialogue should be remembered not for its role in ending the Cold War and ushering in a new period of turbulent nationalism, but rather for its role in establishing a new way of thinking about politics and political institutions.

13

ETHNICITY'S THREAT TO PEACE

ABDUL AZIZ SAID
ABDUL KARIM BANGURA

Ethnicity is a major political and human fault line in Africa. For centuries before European colonialism, ethnic allegiance set the boundaries of communal loyalties and the framework in which political dynamics transpired. While the nation-state is relatively new in Africa, being largely a European phenomenon, multinational groupings have historically been common. Great empires such as Ghana, Mali, and Songhay ruled subjugated peoples of different nationalities long before the arrival of the Europeans.

At the Berlin West African Conference in the winter of 1884–1885, European powers carved up various parts of Africa, creating national borders that cut across cultural and linguistic communities. Today these borders, products of an intricate diplomatic charade, challenge African stability, economic development, and integration. The Europeans later helped Africans create new frameworks for interaction beyond ethnic groups, but they failed in many instances to fully integrate diverse people with distinctive traditions and histories of separateness into the new nation-states. As a result, throughout Africa ethnicity has become a force of political instability that threatens the survival of nations.

The nation-state is the typical arena of ethnic conflict. State governments often try to ignore and suppress the aspirations of individual ethnic groups or impose the values of the dominant elite. In response, ethnic groups mobilize and place demands upon the state, ranging from representation and participation to protection of human rights and autonomy. Ethnic mobilization takes a variety of forms, ranging from political parties to violent action.

International relations are changing from the historic predominance of nation-states toward a more complex order where ethnic groups compete for influence. The new global system is simultaneously more parochial and more cosmopolitan than the international system of nation-states we are leaving behind. For example, while in Western Europe culturally diverse

This essay was first published in *Peace Review* 3:4 (1991).

peoples are uniting, in Eastern Europe bonds of culture and language are clashing with territorial state lines.

There is no place on earth where this clash is more visible than in Africa: Yalunka and Koranko peoples straddle the borders of Guinea and Sierra Leone. Golas, Gallinas, Kroos, and Vais straddle borders of Liberia and Sierra Leone. Kissis and Konos cross borders of Liberia, Guinea, and Sierra Leone. Mandingo and Susu territory crosses the borders of Côte d'Ivoire, Senegal, Mali, Gambia, and Sierra Leone. Wolofs inhabit both Gambia and Senegal. Hausas cross borders of Ghana and Nigeria. Ashantis cross borders of Ghana and Côte d'Ivoire. Fulani communities span most West African countries. Kikuyus inhabit Tanzania and Kenya. Bushmen cross borders of Malawi, Mozambique, and Zambia. Sindebeles span Botswana and Zimbabwe. According to David Laitin, three of the five points of the star on Somalia's flag are said to point ominously to Ethiopia's Ogaden region, Kenya's Northeastern province, and Djibouti. These regions are largely inhabited by Somali peoples, and the Somali government longs to get them back.

The influx of refugees escaping from Liberia's ongoing civil war into Sierra Leone complicates traditionally good relations between these two nations and within the Mano River Union economic agreements of these countries and Guinea. It challenges the security of Sierra Leone's eastern borders. News accounts in the *Sierra Leone Newsletter* reveal that one Foday Sankannah Sankoh, a reported convicted felon from Sierra Leone's foiled 1971 military coup who served a five-year prison term and now leads the Revolutionary United Front (RUF), an offshoot of Charles Taylor's National Patriotic Front of Liberia (NPFL), has been named "Governor of Sierra Leone" by Charles Taylor. It is alleged that Sankoh was trained alongside Taylor's troops in Libya. However, in a recent BBC interview, Taylor denied the claim. He argued that had he been involved, he would now be in Freetown, Sierra Leone's capital. He admonished President Momoh of Sierra Leone for treating Sankoh's incursion with levity, as the late President Doe of Liberia did when his (Taylor's) and Prince Johnson's (now a rival to Taylor for the Liberian presidency) troops attacked. He concluded that Momoh is seeking international sympathy from the foreign news media.

S ocial science scholars have developed many and varied theories around ethnicity. John Stack says that ethnicity is a "group identity that is essentially fluid, depending upon how the boundaries of an ethnic group are drawn in a specific context, and hence, the precise context of ethnic identity is defined in relation to distinct external stimuli." Thus, nation-states use ethnicity to legitimize their existence. Somalia emphasizes its Arab character to distinguish itself from non-Arab Ethiopia and Kenya and thus mobilizes Arab support on behalf of its struggle to redeem Somali-speaking provinces in the Horn of Africa. The government of Sudan also emphasizes its Arab character to distinguish itself from non-Arab Sudanic, Nilotic, Nilo-Hamitic, and Bantu groups in the south and thus mobilize Arab support of its struggle to smash the rebellion in the south.

Clifford Geertz develops a primordialist theory that integrates religion, language and territory, and social practice. Ethnicity and sectarianism are interwoven, he says. Other social scientists, such as Anthony Smith, argue that ethnicity is symbolic; it is mythic in character and therefore can be used as a force to make people question older assumptions about their nationality and heritage. Smith too feels that ethnicity lies within the primordialist roots of religion, language, territory, and social practice. Yet he asserts that religion is the most cohesive element of ethnicity, being associated with community; thus it diminishes political and ethnic boundaries.

Milton Gordon uses the term "ethnic group" to embrace unities of race, religion, and national origin that together create a consciousness of "peoplehood." This use of the term broadens its meaning beyond the traditional reference to national origin. Gordon says that raising peoplehood consciousness directly affects people's social, economic, and political behavior.

Clifford Geertz elaborates on a component of ethnicity he refers to as "communalism," a shared identity and a feeling of common aspirations. Applying Geertz's framework to Africa, we discover that communalism is based on tribe, language, and national origin (e.g., in the small African state of Gambia, Sierra Leonean businessmen identify with one another; in Sierra Leone, Nigerian businessmen do likewise). Divisions based on economic class or political disaffection may be harbingers of civil strife. But alienation based on culture, language, or nationality can become a focus of authority and patriotism within a state that the state seeks to replace, or from which the state seeks to disassociate. The Somali government, as noted above, emphasizes its Arabism in Horn of Africa conflicts, but the Ethiopian and Kenyan governments have argued that legitimizing one ethnic secession would effectively legitimize such movements in general, to the detriment of the entire African continent.

Geertz identifies several ascriptive characteristics around which many ethnic conflicts have revolved: Assumed blood ties, language, and culture are major ones. These characterized the ethnic genocide that took place in Burundi in 1972. Approximately 3.5 percent of the country's total population of 3.5 million was slaughtered in a period of a few weeks in a tortuous competitive struggle between the country's two major ethnic groups, the Hutu and the Tutsi. Race, a volatile element in transactions between former colonial powers and former colonized peoples, remains a serious political factor in South Africa, despite the Pretoria government's claims to the contrary. As the late prime minister of Sweden and peace activist Olaf Palme stated at the United Nations Security Council meeting of March 25, 1977,

South African apartheid is "a weird dictatorship of the minority [whites] for social and economic exploitation. . . . It also has a unique feature. Apartheid is the only tyranny branding a person from birth according to the color of the skin. From the very moment of conception the child's destiny is determined. A Swedish author has called this system spiritual genocide."

A wareness of one's ethnicity may be, to a great degree, a function of coercive assimilation fostered by modernization. When social groups are mobilized, congeniality and cooperation do not necessarily occur. Increased contact, exposure, and communication among ethnic groups may exaggerate one's self-image, magnify cultural differences, produce conflict, and induce political disassociation. Ghanaians expelled from Nigeria a few years ago felt, on returning to Ghana, alienated from the tribal cultural setting they had come to know in Nigeria. At the height of the oil boom, these Ghanaians were welcomed with opened arms to the degrading jobs many Nigerians did not want. As the Nigerian economy worsened, due to declining oil prices caused by the oil glut of the 1980s, the Ghanaians were violently chased out of Nigeria.

Economic development—an increase in material goods and services—does not immunize a number of African societies from ethnic conflict. Kenya, one of the flourishing economies on the African continent, is not free from ethnic conflicts, as minority ethnic groups there decry Kikuyu dominance in economic life, especially in the main cities and in government. A typical Kikuyu businessman sees a better future in continued Kikuyu predominance than he sees with a shared destiny with, say, a Luo businessman.

Structural anthropology, social anthropology, and psychological anthropology provide valuable insights for analyzing ethnic conflicts. The structural anthropologist Claude Levi-Strauss defines culture as "the complex whole which includes knowledge, belief, art, morals, custom, and other capabilities and habits by man as a member of society." He identifies structures common to societies—diacritical features, language, conscious and unconscious levels of operation, kinship patterns, and myths. Implicit in his analysis is the notion that culture is not only a static structural phenomenon, but a salient one as well. An ethnic group is a culture and yet may "belong to" a larger culture. The Mandingo inhabitants of Sierra Leone, Guinea, Côte d'Ivoire, Gambia, Senegal, and Mali identify with the larger Mandinka culture. Now, more than ever, larger numbers of African Americans, African Caribbeans, African Cubans, African Brazilians, and African Europeans are identifying with various African cultures. A complex hierarchy of potential identification exists, but Frederick Barth suggests that "ethnic identity is superordinate to most other statuses, and defines a way an individual operationalizes and externalizes his reference group norms."

According to Francis Hsu, psychological anthropology plays an important role in the configuration and matrices of ethnic interaction. It focuses on the roots of ethnic conflict and the fundamental differences between ethnic groups. Psychological anthropology explores the relationships of human beings, their levels of interaction, and the effects of crosscurrents such as social change and economic development. Predictability of ethnic conflict appears linked to the varying intensities of those levels of articulation between cultures that are effective and those that are decreasingly utilitarian. One might not expect conflict between ethnic groups A and B, even if group A has a predominant advantage in political representation, if ethnic group B is not politicized. Tanzania, for example, has since its independence in 1961 adopted an African brand of socialist ideology referred to as *Ujamaa* to bypass ethnic issues. Nigeria, which subdivided its states and introduced constitutional arrangements to minimize the impact of ethnicity on its politics, has seen ethnic feelings survive to a considerable extent; the persistence of ethnic differences marked the civil war of 1966 to 1970 over the attempt to establish a Biafran republic.

Whether we are dealing with Morocco's suppression of Polisario forces struggling to gain independence, the Zairian government's suppression of small ethnic groups aspiring for greater political and economic participation, or the present conflict in Liberia (which has spread into Sierra Leone), we are naturally attracted to an anomaly of the twentieth century—the impulse for Western modernization and the accelerating consciousness for self-determination among various linguistic and geographical ethnic groups. These conflicts underscore tensions between state, modernization, and human rights. While a state must assimilate ethnic groups within its borders in order to provide them with the modern economic, health, and social resources they deserve as citizens of the twenty-first century, the ethnic groups tend to resist the devaluation of their ethnic identity. African governments have responded by forcing secessionist ethnic groups to adapt to the political economy of the state. African states racked by ethnic conflict, such as Angola, Nigeria, Ethiopia, and Sudan, are less inclined to view claims of self-determination and secession as expressions of some transcendent human struggle than are states like Algeria and Zimbabwe, whose level of ethnic conflict does not approach disassociation. In all cases, however, the human rights of ethnic groups have been compromised.

The likelihood of Africa's ethnic conflicts widening is closely related to the distribution of resources, modernization and development, and the prospects for political pluralism. Increasingly, issues of economic equity, political participation, and retention of traditional cultural values arise. Where governments are found wanting, whether through misunderstanding, arrogance, or misapplication of resources, alienation between the central authority and ethnic forces crystallizes.

The result, almost ineluctably, is conflict, violent expression of opposition, and/or the emergence of separatist movements that threaten national cohesion. In such circumstances, ethnicity issues are transformed into security issues, and the military is called upon to suppress dissidence. The Moroccan government suppresses the Polisario movement in the name of national security; the Zairian government suppresses opposing ethnic groups in the name of national cohesion.

G iven the inadequacies of African nation-states in the face of ethnic challenges, there is a need for discussion and action that does not assume the continued utility and viability of the nation-state system. We should explore moving away from conceptual regimes of "statehood" to "peoplehood" and from "state rights" toward "rights of people." We should explore recognizing the legitimacy of cultural differences and instituting structures with local geographical authority with regard to social and religious affairs.

This essay is an exercise in forecasting; as such, its hypotheses need to be rigorously tested: Economic development and mass media exposure exacerbate, and to some degree intensify, ethnic consciousness and subsequent fragmentation more than they contribute to political consolidation and social integration. The concept of "development," long seen as an increase in GNP and per capita income, or a rise in production and consumption, may be redefined as liberation from externally imposed values, socioeconomic-political inequities, and the suppression of cultural expressions.

The nation-state may lessen as an entity of reference, as the perceived nexus of development, and as the sine qua non of political identification. Consequently, the concept of national interest may become more nebulous and less useful in predicting political behavior.

14

WHO ARE THE ENEMIES?

MICHAEL RENNER

Wendell Berry, noted American writer and farmer, has asked: "To what point . . . do we defend from foreign enemies a country that we are destroying ourselves? In spite of all our propagandists can do, the foreign threat inevitably seems diminished when our air is unsafe to breathe, when our drinking water is unsafe to drink, when our rivers carry tonnages of topsoil that make light of the freight they carry in boats, when our forests are dying from air pollution and acid rain, and when we ourselves are sick from poisons in the air. Who are the enemies of this country?"

It may be that ecological threats generate less attention because often they are homespun. Countries are prepared to make considerable sacrifices to defend their national sovereignty and territory. Environmental degradation is a more fundamental, if sometimes subtler, threat to the security of virtually all nations. It undermines the very support systems on which human activity depends and eventually manifests itself as a threat to economic well being. But most countries are doing precious little to preserve their environmental security. The United States, for example, spent some $273 billion in 1986 to defend against poorly defined foreign military threats, but only $78 billion (of which $60 billion were private funds) to deal with very concrete environmental pollution threats.

But pollution respects no human-drawn borders; it jeopardizes not only the security of the country from which it emanates, but also that of its neighbors. There is thus a fundamental contradiction between the illusion of national sovereignty and the reality of transboundary environmental degradation. *Our Common Future,* the report of the World Commission on Environment and Development (the Brundtland Commission), put the dilemma succinctly: "The Earth is one but the world is not. We all depend on the biosphere for sustaining our lives. Yet each community, each coun-

This essay is excerpted from Worldwatch Institute, *State of the World 1989* 1:2 (New York: W. W. Norton, 1989).

try, strives for survival and prosperity with little regard for its impact on others."

Throughout human history, struggles over access to and control over natural resources—land, water, energy, and minerals—have been a root cause of tension and armed conflict. But disputes over the allocation of resources are increasingly aggravated by the rapid deterioration of resource quality. In some cases, environmental degradation is rapidly becoming a prominent source of international tension.

Border transcending environmental degradation most immediately affects neighboring countries, as illustrated by disputes over water resources. An estimated 40 percent of the world's population depends on the 214 major river systems shared by two or more countries for drinking water, irrigation, or hydro-power; 12 of these basins are shared by five or more countries. Disputes revolve around water diversion or reduced water flow, industrial pollution, the salination or siltation of streams, and floods aggravated by soil erosion.

For example, control over the Nile waters is a matter that casts a long shadow over relations between Egypt, the Sudan, and Ethiopia. Boutros-Ghali, Egypt's Foreign Minister, warned in early 1985: "The next war in our region will be over the waters of the Nile, not politics." Similar disputes simmer in virtually all regions of the world, from the valley of the Rhine in Europe to that of the Ganges in India and Bangladesh.

Soil erosion might seem less directly implicated as a source of tension between nations, yet silt accumulation can lead to more frequent and devastating floods. This has happened in Bangladesh, for instance, where years of deforestation in the Himalayas have led to increased soil erosion and, as a consequence, to siltation of the rivers entering that country. The latest flood, in September 1988, is now considered to be the worst ever. Such catastrophes can only be effectively counteracted if Bangladesh, India, Nepal and China all agree to cooperate in reforestation and reduction of soil erosion—a task that seems daunting indeed.

The rapid evaporation of the Aral Sea in the central Asian region of the Soviet Union (due to excessive draining for irrigation purposes of the rivers feeding the sea) is having detrimental effects on regional agriculture, fisheries, vegetation, and climate patterns. The climatic impact might well be felt as far away as Afghanistan and Iran, for the Aral Sea absorbs solar energy, thus moderating the winters and making possible a longer growing season.

Transboundary air pollution provides another example, with perhaps even more worrisome consequences. Acid rain is destroying aquatic life and forests throughout central Europe and North America. Massive damage from acid deposition in Canada (more than 50 percent of which comes from US sources) has caused considerable diplomatic frictions between Canada and the United States, because the latter has doggedly refused to consider additional measures to reduce emissions of sulfur and nitrogen oxides.

Toxic clouds carrying hazardous substances can traverse the entire globe before dispersing or falling down to earth. A case in point is the pesticide DDT. Though its use has been prohibited in the United States since 1972, it is nevertheless still produced and exported to many developing countries, where no laws govern its use. DDT sprayed in Central America is known to have contaminated the upper Great Lakes in the United States, and the pesticide even returns in imported agricultural produce. Similarly, insecticides from Asia and southern Europe are found in Arctic and Antarctic waters.

Increasingly, environmental degradation is having a truly all encompassing global effect, in the sense that no single nation can hope to escape the danger. The growing hole in the ozone layer poses grave threats to human health, agricultural productivity, and marine fisheries. Similarly, the build up of carbon dioxide and other trace gases is leading to rising global temperatures and potentially catastrophic temperature shifts. The security of entire nations is compromised by the impending dangers of shifting precipitation patterns, rising sea levels, and disrupted crop-growing regions. While all of humanity will suffer from the repercussions, ozone depletion and global warming are caused primarily by industrial countries, which account for 84 percent of chlorofluorocarbon production and 69 percent of carbon dioxide emissions.

The contradiction between national sovereignty and the international impact of environmental degradation is exacerbated by the wide discrepancies in the stage of industrial development and the capacity for effective action between different countries. For example, strict regulations, increased public opposition to landfills and incinerators, and consequently rising costs for hazardous waste disposal in industrial countries have led to a proliferation of legal and illegal shipments to developing nations, particularly those on the African continent, with little or no environmental legislation. The dumping of Italian toxic wastes in Nigeria in 1988 cast a spotlight on such shadowy deals.

Conflicts over the allocation of natural resources have historically lent themselves to military solutions. But in the face of transnational pollution, a zero sum game is transformed into a no-win situation. National defense establishments are powerless against environmental threats. As technologically sophisticated as they may be, military means cannot reverse resource depletion or restore lost ecological balance. In fact, an emphasis on military strength compounds the problem. The ability to deal effectively with the challenges arising from environmental degradation is compromised by the continued arms race.

After a decade of runaway military spending, the nineties may provide an opportunity for redirecting security policies. More stringent US federal spending limits, the Gorbachev disarmament overtures, the onerous debt burden in the Third World, and perhaps most important, the popular yearning for a less heavily armed world could set the stage for far-reaching arms reductions. Reversing the global arms race not only promises greater security, but also allows governments to free the resources needed to address pressing social, economic, and environmental problems across the globe.

The record of traditional arms control is not reassuring. Instead of putting a brake on military competition, superpower agreements have served as a smokescreen for relentless war preparation; tailored to establish weak limits for aging weapons systems, they stimulated the development and deployment of more sophisticated technology. Since 1972, the Strategic Arms Limitation Talks treaties allowed the superpowers to add almost 13,000 warheads to the strategic nuclear stockpiles.

Cloaked in secrecy, arms negotiations tend to get bogged down because there is little pressure to compromise. Independent initiatives may prove more fruitful. Taken outside the realm of formal bargaining sessions, they seek to bring the weight of public opinion to bear on the process. Either the US or the Soviet Government, for example, might publicly announce that it will refrain from testing and employing any new nuclear weapons for a specified period. If reciprocated by the other government, that constraint could be extended for an indefinite period, and at a later point be codified in a formal accord.

The greatest hope for reining in the arms race lies with the vocal and insistent pressure that has emerged from the grassroots, paralleling the movement in the environment and development field. People everywhere are less and less inclined to leave the responsibility for defining security to governments. The agenda ranges from traditional peace movement actions to innovative acts of citizen diplomacy. The Natural Resources Defense Council, by persuading Soviet authorities to let it establish seismic monitoring stations near the nuclear testing grounds at Semipalatinsk, helped compel the Reagan administration to reopen talks with Moscow about nuclear test ban verification. The Campaign for Peace and Democracy/East and West and the European Nuclear Disarmament campaign seek to counter the arms race by building a grassroots alliance of peace and human rights groups straddling the military blocs in Europe.

As far back as in the Bible, people have been urged to cast down their arms, to be done with war and to labor instead with plows and pruning hooks. The advice is even more appropriate today, when threats to natural life-support systems are the whole world's enemy.

It is important for nations to devote greater resources to environmental protection. But in the face of transnational environmental problems, national efforts are likely to prove fruitless without the cooperation of neighbors. Indeed, as awareness of the transnational character of environmental degradation has grown and as remedies became more urgent, an increasing number of international conventions have been concluded, with varying degrees of national commitment and success.

The United Nations Environment Programme (UNEP) has served a useful function in laying the groundwork for additional treaties. Its most celebrated achievement to date is the Montreal Protocol that calls for a 50 percent cut in CFC production by 1999. But UNEP's mandate remains limited, and there are no firmly established international mechanisms to address ecological problems. For example, several of UNEP's attempts to draft rules on international responsibility for transboundary responsibility have failed.

Ironically, transnational coordination of environmental policies can occasionally be a two edged sword. The consensus building process within the European Economic Community, for example, has at times inhibited individual countries from taking stricter national action. This was the case with automobile emissions.

As in the field of disarmament, the inertia of formal international conferences may be overcome by the independent actions of one or more like-minded countries. They could commit themselves to reduce their fossil fuel consumption, cut their CFC production, or stop ocean dumping, and then invite other nations to adopt similar policies. Such environmental alliances—formed to act against a common threat—could tie together nations that share ecosystems, countries that are geographically distant but bear primary responsibility for global environmental threats, or military rivals that may have little else in common than an interest in avoiding environmental catastrophes.

T hese alliances are already becoming a reality. In 1984, nine European countries and Canada formed a "30 percent club." Aware that vast amounts of airborne pollutants drift across national borders, these nations committed themselves to reduce their 1980 levels of sulfur dioxide emissions, a chief culprit of acid rain, by at least 30 percent by 1993. A total of 19 countries (including the Soviet Union, but not including the United States) have joined the club so far. A similar pledge to cut nitrogen oxides by 30 percent by 1998 was made by 12 European nations in 1988.

Environmental alliances that run across adversarial military blocs can fulfill a valuable role by strengthening the common interests of opposing camps. Europe has been divided into East and West for four decades now, but joint policies to cope with environmental threats may help in breaking down ideological barriers. Tanks and planes might fend off a military attack, but no technology exists to repel the air- and water-borne pollutants that cross borders with impunity. East-West environmental cooperation first became manifest in the 1979 Convention on Long Range Transboundary Air Pollution, which gave rise to the 30 percent club. Both sides are now showing considerably greater interest in enhanced cooperation.

One specific alliance might evolve among the countries that share the Elbe. This river—severely polluted with cadmium, mercury, lead, phosphates, and nitrates—flows through heavily industrialized parts of Czechoslovakia and East Germany before streaming through Hamburg, West Germany, and emptying into the North Sea. Because West Germany has an obvious interest in seeing the river cleaned up, it is considering funding a water treatment plant in East Germany. By similar logic, the country earlier agreed to pay for some sulfur dioxide scrubbers on Czechoslovakian power plants in an effort to reduce the air pollution wafting across the border.

The newfound urgency to counteract global problems like the greenhouse effect and ozone depletion may also bring change in US-Soviet relations. As early as 1972, the superpowers signed an Agreement on Cooperation in the Field of Environmental Protection. But activities carried out under the accord have been starved for funds. Now, without government sponsorship, scientists from the Soviet Union and the United States are beginning to collaborate more closely on measures to cope with the greenhouse effect, in an effort dubbed greenhouse *glasnost.*

A unique environmental alliance is shaping up in war-torn Central America. Governments agreed in 1988 to establish a series of peace parks, designed to preserve the region's fast disappearing rain forests and to help promote sustainable development, straddling the borders of Costa Rica, El Salvador, Honduras, Guatemala, Nicaragua, and Panama. Nicaraguan official Lorenzo Cardenal hopes that these biosphere reserves will become "a worldwide model of sustainable tropical forest development."

As with war and peace issues, citizen diplomacy is playing an increasingly important role in pushing governments to stem environmental degradation. In widely different ways, environmental groups have sought to link up with overseas counterparts or influence national policies affecting the global environment. The Rainforest Action Network, for instance, is pressuring development banks not to fund projects that destroy the remaining tropical forests. The Environmental Project on Central America is organizing US support for the Central American peace parks.

Today's threats to environmental security may supplant concerns about intractable issues of military security, even as the world takes halting steps toward disarmament. Growing environmental awareness is spawning a new willingness to collaborate on a global basis. If nations can work together to solve common ecological problems, if multilateralism works, then we stand a chance of overcoming the many other issues that divide us.

15

ON THE STATUS
OF SOUTHERN WOMEN

LAYI EGUNJOBI

Generally speaking, women the world over have lagged behind their male counterparts in terms of status, prestige, power, and esteem. Consequently, women, as a group, have been given appellations such as unequal partners in development, a neglected or forgotten resource in development, or an untapped source of power. Although this situation is changing rapidly in economically developed countries, where women have already achieved a high level of parity with men in many spheres of life, there is still a very wide gap between men's and women's status in developing countries. This is particularly so in Africa. Here, tradition and culture, as well as historical antecedents, have combined to set the status of African women at a very low ebb.

Paradoxically, African women are well known for their enormous contributions to the economic survival of their societies. Women not only contribute significantly to national development, they also perform leading roles in the organization and sustenance of families. All these contributions augment the reproductive role bestowed on them by nature. Hence, African women are both producers and reproducers. At the same time, they constitute the majority of both rural and urban poor, they are the least educated, and they participate less than men in political activities.

African women have not been unaware of this predicament; of course, they are conscious of men's long-sustained dominating role, and they have continuously challenged men's dominance. Frictions, struggles, agitations, conflicts, and even rebellions have been inspired and spearheaded by African women. It is against this background that the implications of the paradox of the creative role that African women play in the process of development and their low status in society can be appreciated.

A few background statements about the political, geographical, and cultural life of Africa can help illuminate a discussion of African

This essay was first published in *Peace Review* 3:4 (1991).

women. In the last quarter of the nineteenth century, the African continent
was partitioned and subsequently colonized by European powers, in accordance with the Berlin Conference of 1884. Hitherto, Africans had lived in
kingdoms linked by trade. Their economy was based essentially on agricultural cultivation, livestock, and fishing. Community life was based on
extended families more than on the nuclear family. Most activities, including agriculture, construction of dwellings, and caring for the sick, were
communal. Religion played a significant role in traditional African people's lives, influencing birth, marriage, travel, war, and burial.

The advent of the colonialists monetized the African economy and
introduced new crops, religions, and systems for education, health care
delivery, and government. Today the impact of colonialism is noticeable
everywhere one goes in Africa, in modernization and its accompanying
sociocultural and environmental side effects.

Most colonized African countries attained political independence in
the early 1960s. Agriculture still remains the bedrock of their economies,
although growing commercial and industrial activities are diversifying economic life. Population continues to grow while urbanization proceeds at a
high rate.

The bane of most African countries today is their debt burden, an offshoot of their declining economies. Although some progress can be recorded, poverty is still the lot in life for a significant proportion of the populations. A look at the situation from the focal lens of gender shows that
women, compared to men, bear the brunt of poverty. With the exception of
a few matrilineal societies, women's traditional position is to be seen and
not heard. Western education is changing this tradition, but the rate of
change has not been as fast as the need demands.

African women contribute substantially to agriculture. In about half of
African societies, women predominate in agricultural production.
Men and women contribute equally in some other societies; in only a few
societies do men predominate in agricultural production. In Tanzania, over
90 percent of economically active women engage in some form of agricultural production. Among the Haya people of this country, women generally
work longer hours on the farms than men. The Haya husband may own two
farms, with a wife on each. Even though the wives are responsible for farm
management, the husband controls the farms and collects the income.

A big impact on women's agriculture roles in many African countries
comes from the high degree of semipermanent migration of men from rural
to urban areas. The proportion of female-managed rural households in
Africa ranges from 5 percent in Niger to as high as 45 percent in Kenya,
according to information presented at the African Population Conference in
Dakar in 1988; and these rates are increasing. As heads of rural households,
women make all important agricultural decisions and carry out all agricul-

tural tasks, including plowing and planting, which are traditionally regarded as belonging to men.

It is against this background that the following recommendation was made at a seminar on the Rights of African Rural Women held in Lagos, Nigeria: "Rural women should be accorded more recognition for their roles because when the men migrate to the urban centers, it is these women who are left to continue tilling the soil and keeping the property usable." Despite African women's agricultural contributions, they generally lack access to credit and land titles. In some provinces in Kenya, for example, the criterion for qualifying farmers for agricultural credit is the title of land ownership, which traditionally remains in the hands of the husband.

African women also make notable contributions in the informal sectors of their economies. In West African countries such as Nigeria, Côte d'Ivoire, Ghana, and Senegal, women dominate informal commercial activities. Throughout urban and rural Africa, women constitute a far larger proportion of the daily and periodic markets than men. They create traditional savings and credit societies, which help them expand their trading activities, undertake building projects, or pay their children's school fees. These "market women," as they are usually referred to, have also formed pressure groups for social and political change.

Women hold essential household responsibilities. It is the woman's responsibility to fetch water, which may be several kilometers away from home, and firewood, which as a result of drought and rapid desertification is fast becoming a scarce source of fuel. Perhaps the most astonishing aspect of the African woman's capacity to carry a huge work load is the way she combines economic production with child care and household chores. It is not uncommon to find a woman tilling the ground with a child mounted on her back. Unfortunately, women receive little or no recognition or reward for carrying these gigantic burdens of responsibility with remarkable degrees of courage and determination.

A tradition of relegating women to the background, present in most African societies, contributes the most to women's continued low status. In no area of human endeavor is an African woman supposed to put herself on equal footing with men (although in exceptional cases women have been made chiefs, founded new settlements, or led wars). While some traditional African gods exhibit either female symbolism and prowess, they are certainly not on parity with male gods.

A poll taken among the Chagga people in Tanzania aptly summarizes the traditional relationship between menfolk and womenfolk. Both men and women expressed the view that "a woman should not aspire to tasks which would elevate her above the male authority in the home." In traditional Africa, the wife is subordinate to the husband and in some cases refers to her husband as "master." A wife does not normally address her husband by name. The man's apartment in most African homes is separate from that of his wife or wives. Children mostly stay with their mothers; the man's apartment is the most revered compound of the house.

A bias exists in contemporary Africa toward formal education of females. Faced with a choice of which child to send to school, the boy or the girl, a typical African family usually sends the boy, while the girl remains at home helping with the chores. The wide gap between male and female school enrollment explains why women lag behind men in organized labor participation, representation in legislative bodies, and leadership roles. In many African countries, the male child is seen as the only legitimate family successor. The female child is considered no more than a productive mother and keeper of the home.

In Nigeria, parental prejudice to female education is compounded to a considerable extent by a traditional social stigma. It is generally believed that highly educated women are prone to assert their rights and claim equality with their menfolk, attitudes believed to be inimical to stable marriage. In a society where unmarried women are generally looked down upon, girls may not be keen on pursuing higher education for fear of not securing future male partners.

The age-old bias against womenfolk was recently illustrated in Nigeria by the Advisory Judicial Committee's decision to bar Ms. Idongesit Ntem, the solicitor general of Akwa Ibo State, from being appointed a state judge because she is a single mother. The National Commission for Women argued against this decision. Nonetheless, Ms. Ntem's experience represents only one out of the countless instances of the social discrimination that African women suffer as a result of being born female.

The incongruousness between the status accorded African women and their contributions to social and economic life raises the question of whether or not women are aware of their position—and whether or not they have been doing something about it. African women have always been aware of the dominating role of men and have often challenged this unsatisfactory relationship. It is important to note that a feminist struggle for women's rights has been going on since the beginning of human society. African women are no exception. In colonial days, African women took part in many wars and revolts against colonial enslavement and exploitation. In Angola in the seventeenth century, Anna Zingha, Queen of Matamba and Central Africa's first political figure, led the fight against the Portuguese colonialists. During this century, African women have played fundamental roles in the struggle for national independence—not only for political independence, but also for clearly defined objectives on issues relating to their rights and needs. Betty Kaunda, secretary of the Chilenjie section of the Women's League of the African National Congress, recalled struggles of the Zambian Women's League on two issues directly affecting them as housewives, the first being about their shopping conditions. At a time when African women were not permitted to enter most shops owned by whites and to select purchases, they maintained that a woman has a right to choose what to buy for her family. Second, they maintained that an African woman is entitled to brew beer for her husband or to sell for household money, in conformity with African custom. Women were not allowed to do this in Lusaka and several other urban areas of Zambia (then Northern Rhodesia); a woman beer-brewer would be arrested and fined ten pounds if caught in the act, and her beer would be confiscated.

Perhaps the most spectacular demonstration of African women's strength and solidarity is the Aba riots of 1929 in Eastern Nigeria against the colonial administration and the native authorities. This event was provoked by a rumor that taxation, hitherto levied only on men, would soon apply to women. An outstanding discontentment spread among women with regard to their economic position, which had been badly affected by a recent fall in the price of palm oil products, coupled with an increase in customs taxes on essential commodities. In a matter of days after the rumor started, thousands of women assembled, then marched on the main roads, attacked the native courts and the colonial administration's district offices, cut telegraph wires, and freed prison inmates. The women were said to have been "led by an old and nude woman of great bulk." Although the colonial army moved in and fired at the women, killing or wounding scores of them, "the Aba riots greatly impressed public opinion in Britain because of the strength and solidarity displayed by the women concerned."

The inconsistency between women's high contributions and low status have very critical implications for peace and conflict within and between nations. What efforts have the public sectors put forth to address this important issue? And to what extent (if any) have these efforts succeeded in changing the low status of African women? One may assert, and correctly too, that awareness is being created regarding this paradox, and efforts are put forth in most countries toward enforcing equal rights for females. In Tanzania, for example, public policies since independence have offered women new opportunities, often by means of legislation. One such law is the Amendment to the Affiliation Act, which allows women to "claim the support of the father for children born outside wedlock if the father's identity can be established." Another example in Tanzania is the Law of Marriage Act of 1971. This gave more women increased security through legal registration of marriages and divorces. It allowed the married couple to determine at the onset whether the marriage would be monogamous or polygamous. If polygamy were chosen, the husband would have to obtain the consent of the first wife or wives before taking an additional wife. One other example of improvements in Tanzanian women's lives is the Maternity Law (Amendment) Act of 1975. This provides maternity benefits for all women regardless of their marital status.

Nigeria provides yet another national example of public policies and programs concerning gender issues. The core of the institutional framework is the National Commission for Women, which promotes political and socioeconomic improvements for women through activities such as the Better Life for Rural Dwellers program. Some measure of progress has been recorded in women's political participation in Nigeria. In the last local government elections, for example, some councils gained at least one female member. A few of the newly elected local government chairs were women. Professional societies of Nigerian women journalists, lawyers, and bankers aim to protect women's rights within the professions and also to assist less privileged women attain improved status commensurate with their contributions.

Although the United Nations Charter of 1945 and the 1948 Universal Declaration of Human Rights have enshrined the principle of equality, little progress has been achieved in the area of equality between men and women in Africa. The contradictory situation in Africa today places women as important producers and reproducers on the one hand, and as political, social, and economic subordinates on the other. Resolving this paradox is the most challenging need facing African women today. African women, even of the most traditional sectors, have the capacity to rid themselves of all forms of deprivation. The way forward is to empower women to find solutions to their own problems. This, however, requires strong political will on the part of African governments to create the necessary administrative and legislative infrastructure. A solution demands popularizing the education of women; this is the most potent weapon in the struggle for their improved status.

16

THE DILEMMAS OF FLIGHT

ARTHUR C. HELTON

More people are now in flight from persecution, war, repression, and other events disturbing the public order than at any time since World War II. The Office of the United Nations High Commissioner for Refugees (UNHCR) reports over 17 million refugees worldwide—people who have crossed a border and who have a fear of persecution upon return. This population includes those fleeing atrocities in Bosnia-Herzegovina, near anarchy in Somali, and similar depredations around the world.

According to the UNHCR, the largest concentration of refugees, about 6 million people, is found in Southwest Asia, North Africa, and the Middle East. This includes over 5 million Afghans in Pakistan and Iran, the largest single displacement of a national group. Some of these refugees have returned, but many still await stability and an end to renewed conflicts in Afghanistan. Others have fled anew. Africa has the largest numbers of dispossessed, including 6 million refugees and over 13 million people displaced internally. Many of those displacements are in the Horn of Africa and in the countries bordering Liberia.

The term "refugee" has a specific legal connotation. The 1951 United Nations Convention on Refugees, and its 1967 update, Protocol Relating to the Status of Refugees, define refugee as a person who is outside the country of nationality (or, for stateless people, the place of last habitual residence), and who has a well-founded fear of persecution on account of race, religion, nationality, political opinion, or membership in a particular social group. If an individual cannot meet this definition, then he or she is not entitled to protection under the treaties.

Traditionally, therefore, refugee protection is reserved for those who have left their countries of origin. The decision to leave and cross a national border can transform an individual into an object of concern under international refugee law. Refugees thus are those who have lost protection under law in their country of origin and who need another source of protection.

This essay was first published in *Peace Review* 5: 3 (1993).

Under the international regime, those individuals who flee across a border from the generalized threats posed by war or civil disturbance are outside the ambit of refugee law. These people are not considered to have a sufficiently individualized fear of persecution. Member states of the Organization of African Unity have adopted a broader refugee definition, which includes war and civil disorder. Governmental and expert discussions in Asia and Latin America have also recognized the advantages of a broader definition.

There are also ambiguities in the refugee definition. The UNHCR offers an interpretation in its guidelines. "Persecution," for example, usually includes a threat to an individual's life or freedom. A deprivation of liberty must be significant, that is, lengthy or onerous. Under certain circumstances, discrimination or the denial of other basic rights can constitute persecution. For example, the inability to earn a living, to receive an education, or to have a normal family life can constitute persecution, even if the deprivation does not threaten life or freedom. Also, various measures not themselves amounting to persecution can, taken together, constitute persecution on "cumulative grounds." But more than harassment is required to constitute persecution.

Also, persecution generally must come from a government source. Under certain circumstances, forces that a government either cannot or will not control can become "agents" of persecution for purposes of refugee protection; they may include death squads or even insurgent forces not susceptible to government control.

As suggested, a person may be entitled to refugee protection if the persecution in question is based on race, religion, nationality, political opinion, or membership in a particular social group. Two basic concepts are involved: group membership and belief. Mere membership is generally not sufficient to warrant refugee protection. The individual must show a nexus between himself or herself and the possibility of persecution. In certain circumstances, however, where a group has been singled out by a persecutor for abuse, mere membership may be sufficient for protection. A social group may be statistical, social, or associational. Such groups might include women, or certain families or voluntary associations.

With respect to belief—that is, religion or political opinion—it is not absolutely necessary that the individual previously manifest the belief in question. But the belief must be one the authorities in the home country will not tolerate, and it must be held strongly enough that it will likely be expressed in the future, even if it has not been expressed in the past. Under certain circumstances, protection is warranted where authorities attribute a political opinion to an individual, even if the person does not actually hold it.

The term "asylum" is not defined in international instruments, but it can be taken to mean the act of providing "protection" to refugees seeking entry. Under international refugee law, there is no categorical right for a refugee to receive asylum. The concept of "protection"—again not defined—can be taken to mean the act of respecting fundamental human rights, such as the core rights declared in the Covenant on Civil and Political Rights, and the Covenant on Economic, Social, and Cultural Rights.

There is a crisis in refugee protection quite apart from the magnitude of displacement. The demise of the Cold War has changed the context for addressing refugee protection. Governments, particularly those in Western developed nations, are increasingly treating as unauthorized migrants people who used to be considered part of refugee movements. Foreign policy is less of a motivating force for assisting refugees. Instead, budgetary constraints have created a new ideology of migration management. Today, most asylum seekers are considered economic migrants from less developed countries.

Contemporary discussions by policymakers about how to respond to refugee emergencies invariably include one or more of the following three approaches: (1) refugee containment, such as by organizing internal safety zones like those devised in 1991 for Kurds in northern Iraq, and by initiatives like the humanitarian assistance programs in Somalia and the former Yugoslavia, or by summary return programs like that imposed on the Haitian boat people; (2) burden sharing or shifting, such as by imposing regional screening arrangements like those devised in 1989 for Vietnamese and Laotian asylum seekers in Asia; and (3) collective deterrence, such as by promoting various techniques to limit asylum, like those recently pursued by many developed countries in Western Europe and elsewhere.

Let's examine each of these approaches more specifically. First, refugee containment: After the Gulf War ended in 1991, about 2 million Iraqi Kurds and Shiites fled their homes and sought haven in Saudi Arabia, Turkey, Iran, and northern Iraq. Some of the neighboring countries were reluctant to provide asylum, and the efforts by coalition forces and the United Nations to assist these people, in Iraq, were in many aspects unprecedented. Many of those dislocated have returned to so-called safe areas in Iraq where UN "humanitarian centers" have been established. But as conflict flares in Iraq, it is doubtful whether these arrangements for internal protection will endure.

An agreement between the UN and the Iraqi government about humanitarian responsibilities has expired. Assistance activities continue, but we do not know whether these initiatives can be translated into workable arrangements elsewhere in the world. Following the example of these extraordinary measures in northern Iraq, the UN has attempted to make analogous arrangements in Somalia and the former Yugoslavia. Humanitarian assistance is being provided to ameliorate the causes of flight; and the international presence attempts to offer a form of effective protection. And in Haiti, a containment strategy is being pursued by U.S. authorities through a high seas interception and direct return program.

Second, *burden sharing:* In Asia, a UN-sponsored Comprehensive Plan of Action (CPA) has been established to manage the outflow of Vietnamese boat people and Laotian asylum seekers. It features a screening process for refugee status determination and the return of those who do not meet the refugee definition. About 100,000 Vietnamese boat people currently languish, frequently in harsh conditions, in detention camps in the region. Most of them will be rejected for status and resettlement and will remain confined until Vietnam permits their return.

The CPA assumes that individualized applications for refugee status pursued from largely a Western perspective can be implemented in legal systems with no analogous provisions. The experience has been mixed, and the UNHCR has assumed many adjudicative functions, particularly in Thailand, Malaysia, and Indonesia. The deterrent rationale of the CPA, moreover, has resulted in a strict application of conventional international refugee law. No provision is made for permanent asylum in the region or temporary refuge for those who need humanitarian protection. This regional arrangement signals the end to the fairly generous resettlement program that existed for refugees from Southeast Asia after the Vietnam War. But such an approach has yet to be fully emulated elsewhere.

Third, *collective deterrence:* In Western Europe, nations trying to harmonize economic and political systems have introduced measures designed to deter asylum seekers, particularly those from outside Europe. These mechanisms include the narrow application of refugee protection criteria, the identification of safe places for return, the adoption of accelerated procedures and visa requirements, the imposition of fines against airlines for carrying passengers without proper travel documents, and the creation of detention schemes and work restrictions.

The debate on accelerated procedures, for example, typically implicates both minimum international standards, such as those used under the CPA, and national notions of fairness. The legal cultures of certain nations may demand more procedural safeguards than would be strictly required by minimum universal standards. Also, detention schemes may infringe international refugee law and general human rights law when confinement is arbitrary or unnecessary to ensure removal or to protect the community.

According to the UNHCR, Europe has relatively few refugees, about 1 million, mostly resettled under official asylum and admissions programs, although conflicts in the former Yugoslavia are causing significant new displacements. The relaxation of East-West tensions and the political changes in Central and Eastern Europe and in the former Soviet Union may precipitate new movements. Western European governments now fear being inundated with migrants and asylum seekers from the East. The harsh reactions—including summary returns—in 1991 by the Italian authorities to the arrival of Albanian asylum seekers reflect this fear.

At the same time, Central and Eastern European governments, and the emerging new government structures in the former Soviet Union, are trying to cope with new displacements. Laws conferring legal status on displaced persons and refugees, for example, have been enacted by the Russian Federation parliament, which now has also ratified the refugee treaties.

O ver the next decade, much must be done to enhance refugee protection. The following recommendations should be considered. First, 117 governments have now adopted either the 1951 Convention on the Status of Refugees or its 1967 Protocol—the two major, multilateral treaties establishing rights for refugees. But many governments are not yet parties to these treaties; an international campaign should be pursued to generate full support by all nations.

Second, among the signatories to the treaties, many governments fail to completely fulfill their responsibilities. Noncompliance has included forcing refugees to return to places where they may experience persecution or harsh treatment, and unduly restricting access to asylum. Such measures are frequently devised by developed nations to deter the entry of refugees from less developed countries. One such measure is the interdiction (high seas interception) of Haitian boat people by the U.S. Coast Guard. From 1981 to 1992, these Haitians have been summarily examined and returned to Haiti, except for the few who exhibit obvious refugee characteristics. Since May 1992, Haitians have been returned directly without any inquiry into their persecution claims. Such measures violate the basic tenets of refugee protection. An international campaign, headed by the UNHCR and refugee NGOs, should be launched to secure compliance with refugee treaty obligations.

Third, deterrent measures, such as alien detention schemes, are also used against asylum seekers by governments hoping to avoid their arrival. Examples are found among signatories of the refugee treaties, such as the United States and several Western European countries, that automatically detain many arriving asylum seekers. Hong Kong, while not a signatory to the treaties, also has a detention scheme that has arbitrarily detained thousands of Vietnamese boat people. Unnecessary restrictions on movement abound in refugee arrangements in many parts of the world. Given the magnitude of the violations, a special international initiative should be undertaken to eliminate abusive detention practices.

Fourth, the manner in which asylum claims are processed raises additional concerns. There have been promising developments in status determination in some jurisdictions, such as the United States. In addition, the status determination procedures of the CPA for Vietnamese and Laotian refugees provides a valuable laboratory for developing procedural safeguards in refugee adjudication. Additional experiments for improving standards should be conducted, such as providing legal counseling, self-help materials, and an information database for adjudicators.

Fifth, the current judicial remedy for disputes under the Refugee Convention and Protocol is limited to state-initiated actions at the International Court of Justice. This impractical remedy has never been invoked. Instead, new mechanisms should be designed to help promote the human rights of refugees. They might include the creation of a United Nations court on the protection of refugees; similar proposals have been made at the European level. An international court should provide the right of petition by aggrieved individual refugees, or by representative groups, to redress violations of international refugee law and human rights law.

Sixth, fundamental changes are needed in international refugee protection. New instruments to broaden the scope of refugee protection should be formulated, initially at the regional level and inspired by progressive national practices. For example, this process could begin with the member states of the Conference for Security and Cooperation in Europe (CSCE) to address the protection needs of asylum seekers and displaced persons throughout Europe. Or it could begin in Latin America, which has already recognized broad protective principles in the 1984 Cartagena Declaration and in the documents emerging from the 1989 Central American Refugee Conference.

Seventh, international cooperation is needed in managing refugee emergencies. Comprehensive regional arrangements could help, but they will likely remain elusive until all regional members adopt more uniform standards for evaluating refugee status. This must include their reliability and fairness in resolving claims, as well as their meaningful integration of NGOs into the design and implementation of such arrangements.

Eighth, the UNHCR has declared this the "decade of repatriation," the preferred solution for refugees. Guidelines should be developed by the international community to make sure that the return of refugees is voluntary and that repatriation really respects the fundamental human rights of people in the countries to which refugees will be returned.

Ninth, international law now provides inadequate protection for people who are internally displaced. Those who have not yet fled across an international border may need the greatest protection. The work being done by the United Nations Secretary-General's Representative on Internally Displaced Persons should be actively supported by governments to help devise effective intergovernmental mechanisms to protect these people.

Tenth, all existing protections of refugees must be still further enhanced. They should be central to the follow-up work of the World Conference on Human Rights, which was recently held in Vienna, Austria.

17

CRIME WARS FORGOTTEN

ROBERT ELIAS

The press corps is like a pool of stenographers with amnesia.
—I. F. Stone

Historically, U.S. crime policy has remained remarkably consistent, using "get tough" strategies to fight periodic crime wars. Apparently only wars will solve the problem. Yet, just as consistently, this policy has failed: Crime and violence continue unabated. Policymakers shun the systemic changes needed for taking crime seriously: undoing the adverse social conditions that generate most victimization. Obviously, policymakers would rather hide the historic failure of U.S. crime policy. How can they do so?

As with most public policy, the U.S. public learns about government crime policies largely through the media. If the public read the criminological literature, our crime policy's failure would be clear enough. But because most of us do not, we rely on the mass media to tell us whether our policies work, and if not, why not.

Yet the media have, with few exceptions, conveyed official, conservative, law-and-order perspectives with little fundamental analysis of their success or failure. They have repeatedly promoted crime and drug wars, which inevitably fail but which they periodically help resuscitate anew as if these wars had never been fought, and lost, before. The media help promote criminal victimization by failing to hold policymakers responsible for strategies that predictably do not work; indeed, they make the problem worse. The media's amnesia, unwitting or not, encourages people to support policies that promote their own victimization.

When they aren't getting their news from network television, millions in the United States rely on newsweeklies to make sense of their world. The commercials tell us to "read *Time,* and understand." But if we read *Time,* or the two other major newsweeklies—*Newsweek* and *U.S. News and World Report*—will we really "understand"? To find out what they've been telling

This essay was first published in *Peace Review* 5: 1 (1993).

us about crime, we examined every general crime story appearing in the newsweeklies between 1956 and 1991.

The newsweeklies faithfully reproduce the government's biased definitions of crime, focusing on lower- and working-class behavior and mostly excluding harms such as corporate wrongdoing, which are far more costly (in lives, injuries, and lost or damaged property) than common crimes. The newsweeklies help define, and also legitimize, the official version of the crime problem, its seriousness, and its cure.

Without a crime, there can be, officially, no victimization. Having not been defined as crime, the vastly more costly and threatening impact of corporate wrongdoing is not treated as victimization. Even harms like domestic violence and sexual assault, formally defined as crime but only passively pursued by law enforcement, undermine the real victimization involved. The newsweeklies are obsessed with drunk drivers, even though far more deaths and injuries are caused by safety defects and shoddily engineered automobiles. And they are preoccupied with child abductions (even though quite rare), while ignoring the immensely larger problem of child abuse. Without the media questioning crime categories, many genuine victims are ignored—they're cast out of the public's consciousness and out of the realm of public assistance.

Even when the newsweeklies cover white-collar crime, the biases remain. We never see the far greater victimization these kinds of offenses produce. This crime is never portrayed as a structural or systemic problem (stemming, for example, from the injustices of capitalism) but rather only as a matter of deviant individuals such as Michael Milken or Ivan Boesky. *Newsweek* argues that drug dealers and other common criminals must be "mercifully destroyed," but that for white-collar criminals the "harshest penalty is the one they inflict on themselves." Unlike street-crime coverage, suite-crime coverage shows no tearful victims, outraged editorials, or fanciful theories of how Milken's or Boesky's laziness or bad upbringing caused their crimes.

The newsweeklies, like the government, portray crime as one-on-one offenses committed by strangers, even though most violent crime—and much property crime—occurs between people who know each other. The exceptional is stressed over the commonplace: Sensational but unusual crimes get the most attention. Crimes such as mass murders get extensive play while largely missing the real story: Most serial murderers are men and most of their victims are women.

The media typically treat victims as innocent good people and accused offenders as guilty bad people, even though many victims have their own criminal records and even though many offenders have been victimized— by specific crimes and often by the unremittingly harsh environments of their past. The newsweeklies, like so-called "reality television" cop programs, provide a misleading picture of the crime problem.

The newsweeklies portray as criminals only a portion of those committing official crimes. They do not report about all of those committing crimes but rather about those whom police departments emphasize as criminals, whether they are responsible for most crime or not. Minorities are the ones arrested in most drug busts even though whites consume more illegal narcotics. Drug crackdowns have historically followed the changing drug-use patterns of minorities, not the seriousness of the drugs themselves; criminality is largely manufactured for certain groups. The newsweeklies condescendingly lament "black-on-black crime," but ignore its causes and the higher level of white-on-white crime. The media refuse to second-guess our conventional conceptions of criminality. Thus, those portrayed as criminals in the newsweeklies have "changed" over the past thirty-five years: First it was the Negroes. Then it was the Blacks. And now it's the African Americans—even though they and other minorities do not commit most crimes.

In contrast, the newsweeklies picture victims as mostly white people, even though minorities are arguably the biggest victims. Consider the flood of coverage for the Carol Stuart murder case, during which the media cheered the Boston police's "search and destroy" mission to root out the accused black man. Never mind that she was actually murdered by her white husband, Charles Stuart, a far more likely suspect, who fabricated the black assailant story. As if the racism weren't enough, never mind that the real story here was yet another woman victim of domestic violence.

Likewise, when a black man is accused of victimizing a black woman, it is sexism rather than racism that predicts the outcome. Consider the vicious victim-blaming the media dealt to Anita Hill when she reported Supreme Court nominee Clarence Thomas's sexual harassment.

The newsweeklies conceptualize criminals as black people and crime as the violence blacks do to whites. Yet this did not prevent *Newsweek* from running a post–Los Angeles riot story claiming that the public, politicians, and the media have engaged in a "conspiracy of silence" by *not* admitting that they associate crime with black faces!

Who confronts this scourge of African American crime? Accurately enough, the newsweeklies show us white police officers at the front lines. Yet instead of lamenting this suspicious racial confrontation—questioning what pits black offenders against white victims and white cops—the newsweeklies instead let readers draw the inevitably racist conclusions.

Police officers are portrayed as victims of violent crimes and vicious people, even though almost all crimes occur when officers are not around.

The police are also victimized by institutional constraints: The newsweek-lies tell us the police don't get enough resources, even though law enforce-ment appropriations actually keep rising. Police are also falsely described as being handcuffed by soft courts, which restrict police practices and allow rights technicalities to set criminals free.

In contrast, despite persistent cases of police brutality and misconduct, almost no media reports claim the police cause victimization. Even the recent, videotaped beating of Rodney King by Los Angeles police pro-duced only mild rebukes from the newsweeklies. Rather than being exam-ined as a systemic problem, the media focus on deviant officers and the frustrations of police work. There is no consideration of whether the vic-timization the police suffer might come only secondarily from actual crimes and primarily from counterproductive crime policies that ignore crime's fundamental causes and unnecessarily perpetuate violence, routine-ly placing law enforcers in the resulting crossfire.

P olice officers don't cause crime, so what does? According to the newsweeklies, crime is caused by bad people who are naturally evil or are led to wrongdoing by permissiveness and bad upbringings. We will always have criminals; all we can do is be vigilant against them.

Crime, so say the media, is also caused by bleeding-heart liberals who undermine the toughness needed to do the job. We need harshness, includ-ing capital punishment—the only language the "savages" and "monsters" (as criminals are called by *Time*) among us understand—not compassion and rights. This we are told even though the United States has long had one of the world's highest incarceration rates and severity of punishments.

The newsweeklies do not really consider the "causes" of victimization at all but rather only its symptoms. Rather than examining our society or our fundamental institutions, the newsweeklies treat crime as an entirely individualized problem: Everyone has the opportunity to avoid becoming a criminal: it's your choice—except of course for those irretrievably evil people who must simply be put away.

How can we prevent crime? According to the newsweeklies, we must provide endless police resources, abandon rights technicalities, toughen our penalties, build more prisons, harden criminal targets, enlist widespread community subservience, change our careless lifestyles, curb our permis-sive society, and adopt exotic reforms such as bicycle cops, preventive detention, law enforcement ROTC, and boot camp or minefield prisons.

W hen the government launches its periodic crime campaigns, the media dutifully serve as its publicists. Increasingly, these crusades have been launched in the name of victims: We must get tough to help vic-tims. Yet little of this helps victims in any way.

The policies pursued do not work, and arguably they help perpetuate victimization rather than reduce it. Victims are also often mistreated, first by officials and then by the media, even while they are being lauded in these campaigns. Officials, then the media, routinely release the names of victims—even in sensitive cases such as sexual assault and domestic violence—despite the dire consequences. In the recent William Kennedy Smith case, *Newsweek* did not immediately join media outlets such as NBC and the *New York Times* in directly naming the woman, yet it covered the case by advocating the naming of rape victims.

Officials regularly blame victims for the offenses committed against them. Despite sporadic sensitivity training, law enforcers still accuse victims of being in the wrong place, dressing the wrong way, saying the wrong thing. The newsweeklies follow suit.

Victims get the same message when the newsweeklies print the kinds of things "you can do to prevent crime." This resembles the "public service" advertisements that say litter is the main environmental threat: "People start pollution, only people can stop it." It isn't greedy corporations, unregulated industrial capitalism, or a flagging political system that cause pollution or crime but rather careless and irresponsible people.

F or our escalating drug crime, the newsweeklies blame drug use even though drug laws and enforcement are the real cause. Because drugs are, by definition, bad in themselves—even though we have a society only half sober consuming dozens of legalized drugs (thanks substantially to newsweekly advertisements encouraging such behavior)—and because drugs are assumed to produce more crimes, the newsweeklies are led inevitably to the sources of those drugs: Foreigners are the cause of drug crimes.

The newsweeklies have featured a series of foreign culprits. Some, such as the "Red" Chinese and the Cubans, are inherently evil: monsters undermining our way of life for ideological purposes—the evidence against these nations being drug sources notwithstanding. When officials and the media could no longer deny the growing addiction of U.S. soldiers both in Vietnam and after they returned, it was only the fault of the evil Vietcong. Ignored was the CIA's own long-standing involvement in the Southeast Asia drug trade.

Other foreigners are treated more as simply incompetent. We read reports about Burma and Turkey, and about Bolivia and Peru, but especially about Colombia, Mexico, and Panama. None seem able to do the job, so the United States has no choice but to intervene to lend a "helping hand," perhaps even a U.S. military invasion such as our attack on Panama to kidnap Manuel Noriega. Never mind that Noriega ran drugs for the CIA and the White House, and that his U.S.-engineered successors also head drug-laundering Panamanian banks. Whether friends or foes, U.S. policy does not promote the drug flow but rather only the foreign irresponsibility or evilness. Sometimes only force, even war, can make foreigners see how much they are victimizing us here in the democratic United States.

To help explain crime, the newsweeklies have run dozens of anticrime speeches and "exclusive" interviews with the "experts." But the experts are often unqualified, the expertise is dubious, and the perspectives are invariably conservative. In more than eighty-five interviews, only one expert fell left of the middle of the political spectrum. The rest featured practically no one we might even call a moderate; all held strongly conservative, if not reactionary, law-and-order views on crime control. All but eleven of the experts held government positions. Could it be that these officials might not be entirely objective about conventional crime policy— policies for which they are often personally responsible? The newsweeklies never think to ask.

We heard from FBI directors—led by numerous interviews with J. Edgar Hoover—and from conservative senators who are building careers based on get-tough crime policies. We heard from every U.S. attorney general (including John Mitchell before his own imprisonment), except for the only genuine liberals: Ramsey Clark and Bobby Kennedy. The only presidents having enough expertise for interviews were Richard Nixon, who was forced to resign for violating the Constitution, and Ronald Reagan, who led the most criminally indicted administration in U.S. history. Also interviewed were police superintendents and battle-weary police sergeants, get-tough district attorneys, conservative judges, drug enforcers, Justice Department officials, and other enforcement officials.

Those interviewed outside government included a handful of psychiatrists, lawyers, law professors, sociologists, college presidents, and clergy. Virtually all echoed rather than challenged official explanations for crime. Somehow expertise seems confirmed simply by one's appointment or general status. For those few who did have appropriate crime expertise, the newsweeklies could not have chosen more status quo sources. Their "exclusive" interviews—sold as new ideas never seen before to battle crime—offer instead the usual failed clichés.

Even more glaring examples of old ideas paraded as brilliant new solutions are found in the newsweeklies' coverage of wars on crime and drugs. We are all familiar with the Reagan and Bush "wars." Since we apparently cannot "just say 'no,'" the government has been forced to launch a no-holds-barred police and military assault on the problem.

With few exceptions, the newsweeklies have accepted these wars and adopted them for their own, running one story after another, breathlessly reporting the escapades of our caped crusaders. These wars have been presented as new ideas, as policies we have never tried before, even though we *have* launched them before, repeatedly, at least a few in each of the last three decades.

When we examine the crime coverage since the 1950s, we find the newsweeklies knowing all about the government's previous wars on crime and drugs. Indeed, when each new war was launched, the newsweeklies served as faithful cheerleaders. Yet each time, they reported the new war as if they hadn't covered the previous one—a few years earlier. Crime stories are repeatedly recycled: Contents and headlines are almost interchangeable, both within and among the newsweeklies. *U.S. News and World Report* even ran the identical picture of a Los Angeles narcotics arrest twice—ten years apart! This extraordinary amnesia has helped conceal how miserably each of these wars has failed. They are usually counterproductive, producing more—not less—victimization.

Suppose people knew about the persistent failure of crime wars, each using virtually the same strategies as the one before? Would it change how willingly they support these policies? Do the newsweeklies have a responsibility to provide this kind of information? Can we expect the public to have any memory if the media it relies on have a persistent amnesia of their own?

S ince the newsweeklies view people as ultimately responsible for crime, it's not surprising that they feature what ordinary citizens have been doing to "fight back." The citizenry's heightened fear of crime gets the most attention, ignoring, of course, the contribution made by the newsweeklies' own coverage. Citizens are at the "end of their tether," usually disgusted by the criminal justice system's unwillingness to get tough on criminals; inevitably, this forces people to take matters into their own hands.

In principle, the newsweeklies warn against this. Instead, citizens should adopt various self-protection strategies, such as guard dogs, armed attendants, lighting systems, foolproof locks, walkie-talkies, and other crime-control gadgets. Never mind that they are either too expensive or do not work—despite reaping huge profits for the security industry. People should also take self-defense classes and learn how to reshape their lifestyles to avoid crime. Never mind that these strategies avoid crime's fundamental sources and instead ask us to adapt to an inevitably criminal society. Citizens must join a crime-control organization. Never mind that most are run by officials as public relations gimmicks and that crime stoppers and neighborhood watches have little impact on crime. People should monitor the toughness of judges, police, and other officials. Never mind that we already have the world's toughest criminal justice system.

The newsweeklies deplore vigilantism, yet their stories—such as their coverage of Bernhard Goetz, the so-called subway vigilante—help create the environment for precisely that response. It is wrong, they tell us, to start shooting people you imagine might want to victimize you, but after all, what else can we expect from a frustrated citizenry? It is wrong to make Goetz into a hero, but we can't help it if the U.S. public thinks this guy is great—we are just reporters. It is wrong to promote racism, but this was, after all, a matter of black youths with a criminal record who might have attacked a white man—never mind reporting his own criminal record. It is wrong for people to violate gun-control laws, but how can you blame them for trying to protect themselves? The level of crime this case reveals is horrible, but let us focus only on the individuals involved and ignore the problem's systemic roots.

With media encouragement, the people do fight back, but with everything except what would seriously address the problem. With the media's social construction of the crime problem, how else could people be expected to respond?

I n our repeated crime wars, "war" is not merely a strategy, it is a cultural psychology. Taking a problem seriously—even if the resulting policies demonstrably fail—somehow requires us to go to war. We're a culture of violent solutions, even if our violence—from the Persian Gulf to our city streets—accomplishes nothing at all. We "solve" the violence of crime by committing more violence, however counterproductive. When random, official violence does not suffice, only the organized violence of war will do.

The newsweeklies construct for us a world and society where human nature inevitably leads us to evil. Bad people cause crime, and only those who have learned to harness their urges—such as police and other officials who specialize in self-control—can fight the evil individuals among us. At best we can only hold the line against this inevitable evil, and we must respond with the only language it understands: force, and sometimes war.

Reading just the headlines, much less the stories, of newsweekly crime coverage shows how violent we are and how deep-seated is our war psychology. Consider the words repeatedly used in that coverage: WAR, battle, MONSTERS, new frontier, FRONTAL ASSAULT, fryers club, ARMS RACE, strikes back, MELTDOWN, drastic measures, HARDEN HEARTS, force, DEAD ZONES, firing line, SCOURGE, boot camp, FRONT LINES, savages, PLAGUE, attacking, FIGHTING, wimp, GETTING TOUGH, feel the noose, BUSTING, slaughter, MISSION, big guns, TRENCHES, enemy, STRIKING, crackdown, CUTS OFF, battle, FLOOD, dead on arrival, ROTC, crushing, STINGS, up in arms, CURSE, enveloping evil, TARGET, invasion, POTSHOTS, clamp down, SHOOT, hardline, TAKING AIM, menace, ALL-OUT ATTACK, alert, SMASHING, search and destroy, ARMED FORTS, counterforce, BOMBS, bloody, SCORES, kills, WAR AT HOME.

The media reproduce the violent language of officials, but they also embellish the language, finding new ways to represent the violence upon which we so routinely rely. With this bombardment, how could we expect the public to do anything but join in? Having created an environment overwhelmed by violent responses, sure enough public opinion polls show people calling for blood—a charade of democracy paraded as only what the people want.

War, which is inherently immoral and routinely counterproductive, is how we address crime. The lessons this teaches contradict those of a society truly free of crime. Such a society seeks peace, not war, and uses peaceful, not warlike, means. It would not routinely promote war and then enlist the wounded (the victims) in a new round of violence. A peace movement against crime would reflect a significantly different culture than ours—one dedicated to social justice and human rights, the absence of which stimulates most crime and violence.

Officials, knowing the psychological power of language, have begun coopting the language of peace. Police officers are now "peace officers," even as they become progressively more warlike. War making becomes "peace through strength," and offensive weapons are called "peacekeepers." Why do journalists, whose business is language, allow these perversions? When will they find their own voices, their own language, and reveal our crime policies' violent failure?

The mainstream media act like lapdogs, not watchdogs, in their crime reporting. Occasionally, they ask the right questions about crime, implicitly challenging the status quo. But they routinely answer them with the conventional wisdom.

U.S. crime policy does not work. When officials try to convince us it does, it is mere propaganda. Wars on crime and drugs do not succeed; when they are launched, officials know they will fail. Invariably they have purposes other than curbing crime and drugs. But officials succeed in launching successive crime wars only by not being held accountable for past failures. The media—our window on politics and government—let us down. By reproducing official perspectives, the media help spread this propaganda. Their intentional or careless amnesia about past crime wars robs us of our history and our ability to learn from past mistakes. Like in Orwell's *1984,* our consciousness gets tossed down the memory hole, conveniently replaced by official stories. Whether for Gulf wars or for crime wars, it dooms us to repeating wars and policies that do not work and that mask fundamental injustices and ulterior motives.

TAKING STOCK:
REGIONAL CHALLENGES

18

GLASNOST AND THE
END OF THE COLD WAR

JENNIFER TURPIN

The Cold War was a battle of words. While U.S.-Soviet conflict was played out through regional interventions, the primary turf for this war was institutional. Mass media organizations did the most to develop the enemy images that drove the nuclear arms race. International conflict and the mass media are inextricably linked. The media not only inform people about global disputes, they help shape public opinion and political relationships. The media helped launch the Cold War's battle of words, but now they have also helped diffuse it.

In particular, Mikhail Gorbachev has used the media to end the Cold War. He has captivated a global audience in a manner unique in Soviet history. Gorbachev has used the media to promote his social agenda; his ability to continue doing so may determine his eventual success or downfall.

If we now increasingly consider ourselves part of a "global village," it has resulted largely from the proliferation of media technology and the role of the international press. The Information Age has created a world community unique in history; people are promptly informed of worldwide events, vicariously experiencing natural disasters, social unrest, and political change. International relations are played out in the media, both informing and manipulating public opinion. Leaders use the media to promote or discourage social policies and social change. These changes, coupled with Gorbachev's policies, are promoting a revolution in Soviet media.

The state's relationship to the people and the press has been important throughout Soviet and Russian history. We can define freedom of the press only in relation to each society's political and economic system and its cultural context. Unlike the U.S. definition, which measures freedom by the absence of government regulation, the Soviet definition measures freedom by the absence of private, economic control. The history of the Soviet press must be understood accordingly.

This essay was first published in *Peace Review* 2:3 (1990).

A passive conception of human behavior, spawned by loyalty to the Orthodox church under tsarist rule, was undermined by the Bolshevik Revolution. Thereafter, the masses were believed to have the power to alter society through collective behavior. A "people's press" would be sustained along with a philosophy of communal action. Even as early as Lenin, however, the Soviet mass media emerged, instead, as a coercive instrument of mass persuasion. Lenin established the rules of what and who were to be published, conceptualizing the newspaper as a collective propagandist, agitator, and organizer. He argued that

> freedom of the press in the RSFSR [Russia], surrounded by bourgeois enemies of the whole world, is freedom of political organization of the bourgeoisie and its loyal servants, the Mensheviks and SRs [Socialist Revolutionaries]. . . . The bourgeoisie is still many times stronger than we are. To give it still the weapon of freedom of political organization [freedom of the press] means to ease the enemy's cause, to help the class enemy. We do not desire to end in suicide and so we will not do this.

Free press issues remained a subject of debate after Lenin. Trotsky used the press to criticize his opponent; Stalin denounced the press for giving Trotsky coverage. With his power secured, Stalin extended Lenin's theories of propaganda and ruled over the Soviet press with an iron fist. Under his reign, the press superstructure was devised, including agencies that monitored press activities, and organizations, such as Glavlit, that enforced censorship.

Under Khrushchev, the press achieved some greater creativity and initiative. Khrushchev viewed the media as the champion of the workers' cause. Although he used less inflammatory terms, such as "communist education," to describe the press's role, Khrushchev nevertheless argued that since "an army cannot fight without weapons, so the party cannot successfully carry on its ideological work without this sharp and militant weapon, the press." The Soviet press grew markedly from the Khrushchev era to the Brezhnev era; by 1966, the Union of Journalists had become the largest professional union in the country.

The Soviet journalist's role has been historically defined by loyalty to Marxist-Leninist theory. It has been bound by its unconditional party loyalty *(partinost)*, high ideological content *(ideinost)*, patriotism *(otechestvennost)*, truthfulness to Leninist theory *(pravdinost)*, popular character *(narodnost)*, mass accessibility *(massovost)*, and criticism and self-criticism *(kritika i samo-kritika)*. Journalists have been socialized into these principles and into accepting designated press priorities.

An elaborate censorship system was also imposed. Various agencies monitored the Soviet mass media, supplementing the self-censorship already practiced by journalists. To achieve even greater control, the Communist Party's propaganda department, typically supervised by a politburo member, appointed the key members of each editorial and management staff. This produced a revolving door between the party, government officials, and the Soviet press system.

The Soviet press system includes two major organizations: TASS, the official press, and APN *(Agentsvo Pechati Novosti),* the unofficial press agency launched in 1961 to improve Soviet credibility abroad. According to Mark Hopkins, a Soviet expert, "If one were to contrast TASS and Novosti in style and tone of propaganda and information, one might say that TASS is of the Soviet iron age, and Novosti of the nuclear era." Novosti's editorial staff began with intelligence officers trained in disinformation: people such as former British agent and Soviet spy Kim Philby.

Novosti is an enormous and powerful organization, with representatives worldwide. Its commentators boast of influencing political events and discussion in other nations, such as alerting Australians to the consequences of accepting U.S. military bases and advising Scandinavians that joining the Common Market would endanger peace. Novosti journalists have been expelled from Kenya, the United States, and Norway for using their covers for political espionage.

B ut Novosti and the Soviet press more generally have acquired a much different face under Gorbachev. In 1986, for example, he said:

> Broader publicity is a matter of principal to us. It is a political issue. . . .
> When the subject of publicity comes up, calls are sometimes made for exercising greater caution when speaking about the shortcomings, omissions, and difficulties that are inevitable in any ongoing effort. There can be only one answer to this, a Leninist answer: Communists want the truth, always and under all circumstances.

Early in his regime, Gorbachev alarmed the press with some of the controversial issues he raised. His carefully edited speeches were published days after they were actually given. After a few months, however, he consolidated his power over the press. Gorbachev appointed Alexander Yakovlev, former ambassador to Canada, as chief of the Communist Party's propaganda department. As a close Gorbachev ally and former head of the Soviet Institute for World Economy and International Relations, Yakovlev has recently served as Gorbachev's fall guy, taking the blame for leftism, Eastern Europe, and the Baltic crises. As the brains behind the radical democratic faction in the Communist Party, his impact on the Soviet press is noteworthy.

Historically, the Soviet Union has strenuously resisted the Western press and its media style. Yet today, Western sources have been allowed in and Western styles have been borrowed. For example, the Soviets have adopted the Western practice of using the media to advance public opinion, shifting their emphasis from the group to the individual. The proliferation of advertising and public opinion polls reflects this trend.

The Soviet press revolution has baffled U.S. Sovietologists. Public discussion has broadened so dramatically that experts who claim that certain topics are still off-limits are continually disproven. Novosti Press Agency has been radically changed under Gorbachev. Its highly circulated newspaper, *Moscow News,* has shed the rigid propaganda of the 1970s and 1980s to become a vanguard press, providing a valuable testing ground for Gorbachev's early glasnost reforms. Other publications have also increased their range of discussion and confrontation; *Ogonyok,* as another example, is now swamped with letters to the editor, reflecting the changing relationship between the press and the public.

B esides transforming the domestic media, Gorbachev has also used the foreign press like none of his predecessors. His personal style has produced changes in media form and content. Instead of delivering the turgid official speeches of earlier Soviet leaders, he shows more openness in his speech patterns. Rather than authoritarian prescriptions for reforming the USSR, Gorbachev calls for fundamental change while admitting his own uncertainties. His new political thinking has been cleverly packaged to captivate an international audience. What's more, his packages have substance: at Reykjavik, he challenged the prevailing nuclear agenda with a plan to eliminate nuclear weapons by the year 2000. Sparsely covered by the U.S. press, this incident nevertheless characterized Gorbachev's frequent media surprises. The international media now wait, wondering what he will do next.

The Chernobyl disaster made the Soviets more vulnerable to international scrutiny and stimulated a period of media catharsis. In the Soviet and international media, Soviet leaders and citizens began denouncing the Stalinist past, bemoaning internal economic and political problems, rehabilitating former dissidents, and addressing various human rights issues. This humbling of Soviet elites before the world community profoundly affected the Soviet image abroad and undermined Gorbachev's opponents at home. A new Soviet diplomatic persona emerged, exemplified by Vladimir Posner, who was able to present Soviet policy in a Western style on U.S. television.

Gorbachev claims his political thinking is not entirely new. His agenda has deep roots in Leninist theory. While resisting the dogmatic use of the press, he often draws on Lenin to justify his social policies. This seems more than merely a way to quell protests by hardline communists who have accused Gorbachev of selling out to the West. On the other hand, in confronting the Baltic crises, Gorbachev has also invoked Abraham Lincoln, comparing his situation to the United States during its Civil War. Gorbachev was trained as a socialist of the old order, but he now faces the threat of Soviet disintegration. To save the system that nurtured him, he must reform it, fighting off challenges from both the left and the right. His media skills, at home and abroad, may account for his unexpected survival to date.

S oviet conservatives have accused the national media of promoting Gorbachev's reform policies. Indeed, they have. Unlike the grassroots democratization in Eastern Europe, Soviet reforms have emerged from the top down, producing changes filled with contradictions and uncertainties.

The Gorbachev media style contrasts with both old Soviet practice and current Western practice and may be more democratic than either. In the West, the mass media presents news as entertainment, providing what sells and conspicuously undermining a critical appraisal of world events. Information in the United States, for example, passes through filters that allow government and corporate interests to dominate public discourse. As a consequence, the public gets inaccurate and imbalanced information about policy issues and therefore cannot comprehend the underlying causes of events. In the USSR, the threat to freedom of the press has been more directly from government controls. The challenge for the Soviet media is to relieve itself of its Leninist roots while resisting the private elitism of the Western media.

Media glasnost in the USSR can promote democratic expression at home and ameliorate Cold War tensions abroad. Soviet citizens will be freer to examine the underlying causes of peacelessness. Problems such as accidental nuclear war, nuclear proliferation, nationalist violence, repression, and poverty are more readily addressed without a superpower monopoly on media drama. In our shrinking world, critical issues will be played out through the international mass media, and thus it must be emphasized as a powerful force for shaping not only Soviet society but also world events.

19

AFTER THE EUPHORIA

JUDIT KISS

Eastern Europe is a place where layers of unfinished history are crowding upon each other, making the past always present and the present always liable to fall back into the past. Unfinished primitive capital accumulation, industrial revolution, consolidation of a parliamentary democracy, incomplete socialist transformation, and failed national independence all weigh on the social structures and the popular consciousness. Because of this unfinished, amorphous nature of society, elements of all these different historical chapters, ideas, and structures persist, making contemporary social movements extremely complex and unpredictable.

In the euphoric days of 1989, it was possible to dream that a new era was coming. The liberated energy of the people of the countries of the East, coupled with the assistance of the West, would lead to the formation of new societies of economic prosperity and social justice, able to heal the historical frustrations of centuries.

The popular upheavals of the last few years represented an overwhelming negation of the previous regime, which had long ago corroded. The regime was unable to maintain the relative economic security and social equality that had been reached in the golden age of the sixties. Its promises of socialism with a human face had evaporated long ago. The system became an old, rusty, tired machine held together externally by COMECON and the Warsaw Pact and internally by one-party rule and by the centrally planned economy—institutions that seemed to be untouchable. When the sudden upsurge of civil courage sent thousands of Eastern European into the streets, the regime collapsed like a house of cards.

Once the first euphoria was gone, the countries of Eastern Europe had to face a sobering double challenge. They had to redefine themselves as independent national entities and find a place in the emerging new Europe.

The newly elected governments reached back into history in their efforts to create a new identity. Unfortunately, there was very little to build

---

This essay was first published in *Peace Review* 4:4 (1992).

139

on. Many centuries of backwardness and successive waves of occupation by outsiders offered rather limited experience with genuine democracy and economic progress. Decades of state socialism meant that there were no strong civic movements, articulated political parties, or experienced politicians, to say nothing of the absence of a functioning legal system, a democratic constitution, and so forth. Everything had to be built up from scratch, because growing competition among the newly independent states, and the unique possibility for European unification, created an enormous pressure to accelerate the systemic changes. All the newly established democracies soon came to be pulled by two somewhat conflicting forces: a drive to national independence and a need to be dependent on the West.

Instead of creating the Europe of Culture and Civilization in their own countries, the whole of Eastern Europe began a march to Western Europe. In their eagerness to copy the model of the West, Eastern European countries moved to introduce a full-fledged market economy, trying to catapult themselves back into an imaginary nineteenth-century model. Western (that is, Western European and U.S.) systems became so idealized that all doors were immediately open to them; instant trade liberalization was accompanied by a massive inflow of cheap mass culture, from thrillers to pornography. Although the Western influence was acclaimed by the people, it was also used to justify some unpopular measures. In a bizarre shift, the influence of the "comrades from Moscow" was taken over by representatives of the World Bank and the International Monetary Fund, and their blueprints were presented as infallible prescriptions. Nationalism was used to cover up the fact the the new societies still lacked ideological pluralism and alternative strategies for social reformation. In an ominous succession of events, the new people in power, from Serbia to Lithuania, created nation-states with invented glorious pasts and never-ending chapters of historical injustice to be revenged against their neighbors or their ethnic minorities.

Two years after the collapse of the Berlin Wall, anybody can become an enemy in Eastern Europe today. Minorities, foreigners, ex-allies, or just plain others are presented as the cause of the prolonged suffering of the people. In the general xenophobia that spills over the region like a dirty stain, only the president of Hungary, Arpad Goncz, dared to speak out publicly against repeated racist and chauvinist assaults. The newly emerging nation-states, all equally victims of the past, tend in their demands for compensation for real or perceived past injuries to take their revenge for history on one another. Eastern Europe is becoming a bloody battlefield of zero-sum-game players, where everybody tries to win against the others.

From the very beginning, an ill-defined concept of national interest overshadowed the commitment to democracy. The new democratic states tend to define their borders and full-rights citizens on the basis of ethnicity. In Slovenia and Estonia you already have to prove your "blood right" to be allowed to vote. The governing Hungarian MDF is considering ways to increase its voting strength by adding Hungarian emigrants living abroad to the voters' roll. This idea has already been put into action in Croatia, when even Australians with Croatian parents could vote for Mr. Tudjman, the "father of the Croatian nation."

The growing intolerance and nationalist extremism are fueled by another phenomenon. When the Berlin Wall came down, the economies of Eastern Europe had long been in deep crisis. The chaos of transition and the global recession added to the worsening trends and led to a dramatic drop in production and living standards throughout the region. In addition, the hastily adopted Western recipes did not produce the expected miracles. Tragically enough, the victims of shock therapies in Poland, Czechoslovakia, and Bulgaria—the newly poor suffering more grievously because the state welfare systems have collapsed—are the ones who are most easily manipulated by the new power holders. Fooled by nationalist-populist slogans, they stand behind the guns in the former Soviet Union, they want to purge Jews in Poland, and they vote for Meciar's demagogy in Slovakia.

To make things worse, there is real competition among the countries of Eastern Europe for their place in the New World Order. Due to their common history, they share a similar economic structure, so they have fairly similar offers for the picky Western businessman. The West did not prove to be so generous and supporting as it seemed at first. Its own internal problems, its long and deepening recession, and the complexity of the political and economic problems in the East quickly cooled the initial enthusiasm to welcome the newcomers to the free world. It seems as if the least problem atic countries and the most lucrative business ventures will be welcomed into an integrated Europe, while the rest will be left alone to solve their own problems.

As the rhetoric of Cold War conflict evaporated, Eastern Europe had to wake up to the rude realities of life. Instead of sublime ideas of human freedom, it turns out that the Western world is driven by hard economic or strategic interests. The most painful case has been that of the former Yugoslavia. All the military resources built up to defend against the Soviet threat remain unused, while a war launched by a desperate ex-Communist leader takes the lives of thousands. In a recent CSCE meeting, the U.S. representative explained to Mr. Izetbegovic, president of the bleeding Bosnia-Herzegovina, that his country has no oil, nor does it possess nuclear weapons, and therefore it cannot possibly be of primary interest to the United States.

Two years after the historic events of 1989–1990, one can sadly conclude that, instead of a genuine revolution carried out by the will of the people, what is going on during this difficult period of transition is only a change of elites and of governing ideology. Instead of instant market economy and democracy, what is emerging in Eastern Europe is a new hybrid society, with some elements of the free market and of parliamentary democracy, both of which can easily be abused by the new power holders.

I n order to maintain their newly gained power, the emerging new elites recreate authoritarian ways of governing. To secure strong economic bases for their perpetual dominance, they participate actively in a savage fight for capital accumulation that is now going on throughout the region.

The new version of authoritarianism is characterized by national colors and a hasty revision of the history of the recent past. The urge to reject the recent past is extremely strong, due to both the general popular disenchant-ment with the previous system and a bad social conscience. The old regimes were built on coercion, but they also required the cooperation and the silent or vocal complicity of the population. This is the reason why, in almost all of these countries, a noisy witchcraft has been taking place against some of the alleged representatives of the previous regimes. The new power uses the popular sentiments to legitimize itself and at the same time to create its own patronage system. Instead of solid democratic institu-tions, highly personalized new political machines were rebuilt, both to sup-port the new state power and to oppose it.

At the same time, countless former members of the *nomenklatura,* like Milosevic of Yugoslavia, present themselves as new, genuine, nationalist leaders, whose past is ignored. In Romania, only two years after the bloody overthrow of the Ceaușescu dictatorship, the recently elected mayor of Ciui can already proclaim in an interview that: "Ceaușescu was a good Romanian."

In a still immature democracy, the weak coalition governments are tempted to use the recently adopted democratic institutions to cement their emerging domination. Elections are announced hastily, at times convenient for the current power holders. In the absence of efficient social control, new laws that often represent only the narrow interests of the ruling parties are being pushed through the parliaments. This is how new laws on land restitution, privatization, and education are born, without taking into con-sideration the long-term interests of society or the opinion of the citizens. Despite popular disagreement, the male-dominated parliamentary bodies have tried to introduce new, restrictive abortion laws throughout the region. The once most promising Eastern Europe country, Czechoslovakia, has been pushed into a breakup, promoted by a narrow-minded political elite against the popular will as expressed in opinion polls. In the meantime, in Poland, the worsening economic crisis that has followed the rigid imple-mentation of economic shock therapy and the intensifying erosion of the society has led the prime minister to ask for extraparliamentary powers to govern the country.

Once again in Eastern Europe the end justifies the means. Freedom, democracy, and market economics are to be introduced by decree, and voices of criticism are labeled immediately as leftist, antidemocratic, unpatriotic, alien, cosmopolitan, or communist. To maintain the national unity, the new governments increasingly try to restrict their internal opposition, most virulently in the battles that rage over the control of telecommunications and the media, from Belgrade through Budapest to Baku.

The newly introduced elements of the market economy can easily be used by the new elites to reinforce their power. New wealth is created by the quickest and most antidemocratic ways—by looting, by military occupation (and the recentralized military economy in the case of the former Yugoslavia), by the redistribution of geographical and economic assets in the former Soviet Union, and by civilized indirect redistribution in countries like Poland and Hungary.

Privatization was one of the major slogans in the 1989–1990 elections in each country of the region. However, what has been achieved until now is the privatization of only a fraction of the national assets; at the same time, new powerful state bureaucracies have been created. In the most successful case—that of Hungary—about 13 percent of state property was actually privatized in two years, but the newly established property agencies are entitled to interfere in economic issues to a greater degree than at any time since the 1968 economic reforms. In the new hybrid society, both free market and state interventionist arguments are used, depending on the current interests of the dominant elites. The ideology of the market is used when the government is about to reduce social welfare expenditures, whereas state intervention to defend the national interest is advocated when the government is about to rebuild protected military industries.

Eastern Europe's transformation seems to be longer, costlier, and much more painful than it was expected to be two years ago. But at least there is one important lesson that the slowly emerging opposition among civic groups and trade unions seems to understand: Democracy cannot be delivered at one stroke. It will come as a result of a long, slow process of learning, which begins at the grassroots and requires a permanent effort to create a culture of understanding, discussion, and the acceptance of differences. It will be a long time until it becomes the normal behavior, the social reflex, of the societies that will have emerged from the present miseries of Eastern Europe.

20

CONFLICT MITIGATION
IN FORMER YUGOSLAVIA

JAN ØBERG

Since 1945, the United Nations has tried to keep the peace basically by practicing nonviolence. The blue helmets have served as cease-fire monitors, buffer zones, or intermediaries in conflict hotspots. UN soldiers have been armed only with what might be necessary for pure self-defense of the personnel. The rule of thumb has been that the United Nations must be perceived by all parties as impartial and must not take part in any military action. But it has now become involved in fighting in Somalia, and recently the Security Council authorized the use of force to protect so-called safe havens in Bosnia-Hercegovina. Five thousand additional troops will also be backed by air power. The mandate permits not only self-defense if under attack but also the use of force against those who might attack safe havens.

Another mandate the Swedish and other governments have been asked by Secretary-General Boutros-Ghali to prepare is that of protecting one party and fighting against paramilitary units and others who do not abide by decisions of the Security Council. In light of this development, we should remember the years 1960–1964 in Congo/Katanga, when the UN was involved as a peacekeeper and did engage in fighting for a short while. The person who undoubtedly remembers better than most is Brian Urquhart, then UN Undersecretary-General, the person who has taken key responsibility in most UN peacekeeping operations. In his autobiography, *A Life in Peace and War* (1987) , he writes about those who recommended the heavy use of force:

> They simply did not want to understand either the principle involved or the bottomless morass into which they would sink if they descended from the high ground of a non-violent international peacekeeping force and began fighting for life against the numerically superior local troops. . . . The military often wants heavy or offensive weapons, but I have always been firmly against their use in a peacekeeping UN operation. The real

This essay was first published in *Peace Review* 5: 4 (1993).

strength of such an operation is not found in its ability to use weapons but, rather, in not using them and in thereby remaining outside the conflict and preserving the unique position and prestige of the UN. The moment the UN starts killing people it becomes part of the conflict it is supposed to be controlling, and therefore part of the problem. It loses the one quality which distinguishes it from, and sets it above, the people it is dealing with.

In the wake of the Iraqi/Gulf War and in light of the circumstances in Somalia and former Yugoslavia, Urquhart has recently suggested a third way between traditional peacekeeping and large-scale collective enforcement (as in the Gulf)—something that would "essentially be armed police actions." The forces would be small and representatively international and would not have military objectives as such. They would put an end to random violence and bring a degree of peace and order to promote humanitarian relief work.

Urquhart is correct in believing that one can face situations where violence must be used: for instance, where a couple of renegade generals kill thousands and destroy a country in their personal war *and* where there are firm reasons to believe that preventive military measures would save more lives than they would cost. Also, impending genocide by a dictator should move the world community to take action. Even Mohandas K. Gandhi would probably have subscribed to such action.

But this is something entirely different from what is now being discussed in the case of former Yugoslavia, for a number of reasons. The people shot at by UN forces will fight back and feel justified in doing so. It is more difficult to fire—and legitimize firing—at someone who does not threaten or do violence to you. The moment UN peacekeepers point their guns at some party, they take sides; the fine nonpartiality, prestige, and confidence of their mission is compromised. It cannot lead to disarmament or demobilization of any party, only to escalation and potentially to spreading the conflict, for instance by drawing in new parties or weapons from outside; it will also lead to a closing of ranks behind the real troublemakers.

Peace *enforcement* also prevents the continued peace*keeping*. For instance, Canadian peacekeeping blue helmets cannot do their job if they risk being hit by Canadian peace-enforcing troops under NATO command. If engaged in war, the UN cannot keep peace, make peace, or build peace. Peace enforcement is nonsensical, an absurdity. No one can force people to be peaceful if they firmly believe that they are fighting because their very existence is at stake. Peace must always build a strategy that addresses the root causes of conflict and violence in the first place.

Do we have a moral obligation? I do not think so. The moment we use force—whether in the name of international law, human rights, or some other well-intended purpose—we have failed to address the problem adequately. The extremely counterproductive European and U.S. handling of former Yugoslavia has aggravated the original situation almost beyond the point of recognition. They turned a situation from bad to worse and have no moral right to set things right with or against any party.

Should we use the UN for peace enforcement out of humanitarian concern? Hardly, there are so many humanitarian hotspots the world community does not even address. There were twenty-four conflicts going in 1992, with more than 1,000 dying in battle. Why have we not intervened in those disputes?

There is something very strange, indeed absurd, about this faked New World Order. It directs itself selectively against various types of *direct, manifest* violence—for instance, when serious human rights violations have taken place or the parties have slid into open warfare.

Yet the truth is that much of this direct violence is caused by *underlying economic malfunctioning, and social and cultural structures,* such as cultural deprivation, economic maldevelopment, or ever deepening gaps between the rich and poor. This underlying problem is caused predominantly by the very same big powers, their historical rule and role, and their contemporary modes of operation. Probably 20 million people die each year unnecessarily from preventable diseases and the denial of basic needs worldwide due to the extreme and widening disparities in development and life opportunities. Yet nobody talks about "peace enforcement" against this, against the Great Makers of Violence.

The situation in former Yugoslavia lends, it seems, very little moral credibility to any high-powered, "civilized" Western UN-NATO peace enforcement. We should remember what a Danish journalist wrote way back in 1915, namely that "the Balkans are the change big powers have used in their transactions throughout history."

Will we ever be able to create a fairer global community if the UN is placed—or places itself—at the forefront of an uncivilizing mission in the Balkans? It is worth remembering that the first sentence in the United Nations Charter states that "we the peoples of the United Nations determined to save succeeding generations from the scourge of war" and that Article 1 states as the first purpose of the UN "to maintain international peace and security, and to that end: to take effective collective measures for the prevention and removal of threats to the peace . . . and to bring about by peaceful means, and in conformity with the principles of justice and international law, adjustment or settlement of international disputes or situations which might lead to a breach of peace."

It is true that Chapter VII does specify the circumstances under which military force—collective security—can be employed under UN guidance. But this is something very different from peace enforcement and, as yet, Chapter VII is not applicable to the situation in former Yugoslavia.

C onflict mitigation is a concept and a methodology the Transnational Foundation for Peace and Future Research (TFF) has developed during the last two years for its project in former Yugoslavia (Croatia including Krajina, Slovenia, and Bosnia-Hercegovina). It is intended to serve a number of purposes.

First and most important, it wants to help ease—mitigate—the situation and enable the parties themselves to solve their own conflicts to the largest extent possible. Because people "own" their conflicts, the task of third parties is not to present ready-made solutions, but to listen and help them solve their own problems. Mitigators play the role of "conflict doctors" rather than "judges." We at TFF deliberately use the concept of mitigation rather than of solution or mediation. It signifies a modest indirect approach, which provides perspectives, concrete proposals, and some tools that can be used by the parties themselves.

This is down-to-earth empirical *field research* rather than simulation, pure theory development, or workshop seminars conducted at a comfortable physical and academic distance. The world is an ongoing laboratory experiment in conflict management, and although it is not without danger to visit areas with tense conflicts or even open violence, this is what we feel must also be done by conflict resolution scholars.

One of the things many find somewhat strange is that, as experts in conflict analyses and mitigation, we profess committed neutrality between conflicting parties. This implies that the conflict mitigation team does not take sides for or against any actor; instead it takes sides against violence and all other types of inefficient conflict resolution. Some would say it is immoral not to take a stand against an actor that commits serious crimes. This is perfectly understandable—and very compatible with Western, Christian ethics. But it is a firm conviction of those of us engaged in conflict mitigation that we should not act like judges; we should denounce only the wrong (violent) deed, not the doer. Conflict resolution experts get who absorbed into taking sides will be unable to build the confidence needed on all sides for achieving a settlement. It does not prevent the mitigator from asking critical questions or from clearly stating that violence is unacceptable because other alternatives should have been tried.

Most people seem to believe—falsely—that their own indignation must be brought to the fore, and that they contribute something important to addressing the conflict when they identify who is guilty or who took the fatal first step. We believe otherwise. One must approach and, where necessary, work with all sides—help them to recognize that violence is counterproductive and that there are alternatives available to them.

This, admittedly, implies a kind of detachment—namely from promoting one's own emotions the moment one sits face-to-face with war criminals. To the mitigator it is a first priority to understand why violence is so fascinating to those persons rather than telling them how immoral they are. We are reminded of Mohandas K. Gandhi's pragmatic rule that "a burning passion coupled with absolute detachment is the key to all success."

U nfortunately, conflict mitigation goes against the code of our civilization. It is considered weak, unrealistic, idealistic—whereas violence is applauded and understood as a sign of bravery. Throughout the Yugoslav crisis, the cry has been that "we must do something." Yet to use violence is to do exactly nothing for conflict resolution. Rather, it just satisfies one's own passion for revenge and action and one's need to show (moral) superiority. Conflict resolution is not about harming or killing people. It is about killing problems and harnessing the human and circumstantial attraction to violence. Violence is always part of the problem, never the solution.

The mitigation team works without invitation, at least in the initial stage. Why? It is to secure that the team is totally independent and unbiased and maintains the freedom to seek interviews with any party in any region. This is particularly relevant in complex conflicts with more than two parties. Furthermore, the sense of being "at service"—a goodwill mission—is increased, and so is the likelihood that various parties will see the team as a natural third party to rely on.

Our studies and missions serve as early-warning, preventive (citizens) diplomacy, and as multitrack diplomacy. Representatives of governments and international organizations such as the UN certainly perform a very important function in many cases of conflict management and peacekeeping. But they would be the first to admit the limitations. They usually get into a conflict when it has already become "hot" and even violent, and they are often prevented from developing a real understanding of all the essential parties involved. Likewise, with the exception of a few recent conflicts, they cannot get access to internal disputes nor approach the problems without the prior consent of the parties.

NGO experts and independent groups can get access to these parties and provide helpful insights precisely because they are informal. They can analyze conflicts, find facts, and suggest creative violence-preventive measures at an early stage; and they can, in principle, get into any society, start interviewing various actors, and feed the information into governments, other NGOs, the United Nations, and humanitarian organizations.

T hen there are the problems of peace*making* and peace *building,* the whole negotiation and mediation process—internationally, in the region, and locally—the top-down and the bottom-up that are linked to reconciliation and to changing the root causes of the violence. The international community, particularly the European Community (EC), has been taken by surprise since the format of the Yugoslav conflict did not "fit" any of the Cold War institutions the "new Europe" has maintained even though the Soviet Union and the Warsaw Pact have disappeared.

Thus, one of the world's most complex conflicts was instead initially placed in the hands of two capable statesmen, Lord Carrington and Cyrus Vance. With the exception of the United Nations—which has never become what it should but has done less harm and more good than any other actor in the crisis—there existed no procedures, no organization, no budget, no experience relevant for "helping" the peoples in former Yugoslavia solve their problems. The international community basically wanted to *tell* the Yugoslavs what they should do—and what would happen if they did not comply.

The recent field work of the TFF makes it abundantly clear that although the UN peacekeepers, UNPROFOR, are in place in Croatia, there is no agent in charge of getting the former combatants into a process of reconciliation, structural change, and peaceful coexistence. The UN keeps the peace, but how will future violence be prevented when the peacekeepers have to withdraw? At present there are no local, regional, or international efforts that aim at real peacemaking: changing the structures and perceptions that lead to war in the first place. On the contrary, Serbia as well as Croatia increasingly seem to view the UN deployment as part of their future politico-military designs—something that has already spilled over into the Bosnia-Hercegovinian war zone.

Mitigation work can contribute to peacemaking and peace building precisely because it seeks a broader social understanding and better understands the peacemaking potential of "civil society." Again, conflicts like these belong to entire societies, not just decisionmaking elites. Conflict mitigation is an open and open-ended process. Traditional conflict resolution experts and mediators work with small selected groups, usually at the top decisionmaking level. They take them to faraway pleasant surroundings and help them deal with psychological barriers and successively learn to cooperate and see mutual interests. We respect those who achieve important, lasting results by such methods but remain skeptical about actual implementation and about the elitist assumptions underlying this approach.

In contrast, conflict mitigation places social diagnoses and policy proposals at the disposal of everyone in the conflicting society who wants to listen. We make deliberate use of mass media as well as an expanding network of personal contacts. Next, the reports (or executive summaries of them) are placed at the disposal of the United Nations, fed into the particular bodies that deal with the situation in this particular country. The reports are also sent to other international organizations, to embassies, to the relevant media, to humanitarian organizations, and to the scholarly community.

Although it may sound overambitious, it is important to help not only the conflicting parties but also the international community to better understand the complexities of the conflict. That will increase the likelihood of avoiding steps that are clearly counterproductive to peaceful conflict resolution. The Yugoslav conflict makes it abundantly clear that this is needed within the international community.

Where feasible we work with drafts or interim reports, which the conflicting parties are invited to comment on. At the same time, it is crucial that the team, being an unbiased, nonparty to the conflict, present its own creative approaches to future solutions that polarized parties will usually not see themselves precisely because they are locked into the conflict.

This has a considerable potential for building goodwill among all sides in a conflict. If there is one thing people lack in tense situations it is proposals for how to avoid violence or to stop warfare. High-level politicians and many others throughout former Yugoslavia have willingly shared their time and expressed their appreciation for the mission's work. Although it is impossible to measure, we believe that the types of proposals we have delivered to various parties have made a positive contribution and, in former Yugoslavia at least, struck a positive note of hope with otherwise war-weary people.

If the circumstances so permit, the goodwill character of the mission is likely to lead to an informal third party role. Thus, the TFF has been involved in creating contacts between the FRY Panic government and the Kosovo-Albanian leadership and serves informally as consultants to the latter. During 1993 it has planned a series of consultations between the Croatian government and the opposition and between members of the leadership and the opposition in the Serpska Krajina Republic (RSK) in Knin.

C onflict mitigation is a craft as well as an art. Here are the principles we practice and try to teach. If more internal and external actors in the Yugoslav crisis had embraced them, we believe everyone would have been better off.

Conflict mitigation means helping others solve their problems, not imposing solutions, but it insists on nonviolence or peace with peaceful means. Conflicts in and of themselves are positive—a precondition for pluralism, growth, and freedom of the mind. However, some ways we choose to handle conflicts are a problem. It is more important to determine what a conflict is about than who is guilty. Even if the guilty disappeared, the problem would often still be there. Chasing the guilty means revenge or tit-for-tat and propels actors further away from a solution.

It is necessary to get to the roots of the conflict and let off steam. But only constructive views of a common future—not quarrels about the past—inspire viable solutions. To solve a conflict, the parties must perceive it in new ways, think in new ways, and start acting in new ways. Verbal commitment is not enough. Identifying interests is more important than locking oneself up in a position. Keeping alternatives open is a safe way. Blocking communication and stereotyping others is a recipe for deadlocking the conflict.

Procedures, negotiations, and the solutions must be based on objective standards, applying to all sides. There is usually your truth, their truth, and a larger truth—and people know it. Means are goals-in-the-making. Good goals cannot be achieved through bad means. There is our side and their side and the relationship. Taking steps to harm or humiliate the other is counterproductive and not in our interest. Taking steps that help us and do not harm the relationship is wiser.

It is wise to develop one's own strategy, stick to it, and propagate it, inviting the other side to do the same. Just reciprocating or reacting to the other is dangerous. Imitating the wrongdoer makes our deeds wrong. An eye-for-an-eye will one day make the whole world blind. Conflicts not only split people, they also unite them. Opponents may disagree on everything, but they share the judgment that what their conflict is about is important to them. That is the key to peace: recognizing that there is a common problem to be solved. Peace and conflict resolution, therefore, do not imply that we give in or accept being bullied.

Power should not be used to punish or kill but to achieve one's own goals together with others, without harming them and without hindering them from realizing their objectives. The use of violence—whether physical, psychological, direct, or structural—is proof of incompetence and powerlessness in the face of conflicts. Violence never solves a conflict; it breeds aggression and more violence. Problems solved by violence always reappear later.

To solve a conflict implies voluntary agreement on how to achieve a future that is better for each party and for the relationship. A good solution does not appoint a winner and a loser. It transforms the issue and the perceptions, attitudes, and behavior of the parties. A good solution can also consist of agreeing to disagree and of separating from each other in a civilized manner, minimizing pain on all sides. Mitigators do not take sides between parties, much like a good doctor does not scold patients even if they are carrying a disease. Mitigators are "conflict doctors" who help patients recover from the disease and prevent relapses. Mitigation is urgent care and prevention all in one.

We at TFF have often been asked: If you are so critical of what has been done in the Yugoslav case, what would you want instead, and how would you achieve it? Obviously we do not have all the answers. There are no ideal solutions anymore. But we do believe that the "paradigm" underlying what has been done is wrong. Some basic, pragmatic questions have apparently not been asked: What kind of problems are being faced in former Yugoslavia, what are the root causes? What is the best approach, the most productive way of offering help to the conflict-stricken people who live there?

Instead, virtually every leading actor has jumped to conclusions and transformed Yugoslavia into a much larger problem—such as its role in the power configuration among countries in "new Europe," or in the post–Cold War struggle between Europe and the United States, or in the future of the UN. Yugoslavia became somebody else's conflict, snatched from the 24 million whose future is actually at stake.

Do sanctions work? Shall we intervene? Shall we give Muslims (more) weapons? How do we get consensus in the Security Council? How do we signal that this and that is unacceptable in Europe? How do we stop the genocide? All these are questions relating to the core issues: the very nature of Yugoslavia and why it had to break apart, how to help the peoples themselves dissolve and transform their societies peacefully and create a sustainable development beyond tomorrow.

We should stop believing only in peace "packages" and big integrated peace "plans" from above and think also of many actors at many levels who can do many different things in many different spheres of the conflict-ridden society. The great plans are predicated upon the typical linear idea that we must first take step 1, then proceed to step 2, and so forth. But they usually stall because step 1 is not taken by any or all actors.

It is useful to think of peace processes as multidimensional experiments in social development. Human beings are more prone to say why things will not work than to say, let's try. So, redundancy in peace initiatives and an unconventional mixing of steps and processes are essential. If one thing does not work, we try five others—we keep attacking the problem, not the people. Without creativity we shall go wrong.

I n simple terms, if you want to help stop a war, two things are needed. First, find out what the root causes are as seen by the actors as well as by third parties and address them. Second, propose to the parties ideas and concrete steps in the direction of solutions in such a manner that they will recognize that peace is more attractive than continuing warfare. We have to address both the past and the future to help people at war move away from it. Unless we succeed intellectually and propose better futures in a convincing manner, warfare will be their preferred option.

What do we do about the criminals and renegades who will not even listen? The wrong answer is: Meet them on their own ground and fight them with their own means. In the process we will unavoidably become war criminals ourselves and legitimize spiraling violence. Our use of counterviolence will confirm their belief that they have their backs against the wall.

The better answer is: Help the people who have lent their support to the renegades; people most often do so because no other actors provide them with security. The peasants who have lost everything in the country-side may say that they want their local commander to smash the neighboring village inhabited by "the others." If you tell them that UNPROFOR's security covers both sides—provided both sides are disarmed—and that that will open up the possibility of negotiating local normalization; restoring their houses, the village water supply, electricity, communications; repatriating refugees, reuniting families, and providing the opportunity to resume farming, then people are provided an alternative that will make them see that the renegade's "vision" is not in their best interest.

D emilitarization, disarmament, and demobilization are essentially political concepts. The political disarming of renegades—the real political jiujitsu—is much more important than physical disarming. We must play a different game than the renegade's, undermining his perceived power by opening the eyes of his constituency with the realistic promise of a better future. An integrated approach must be taken between cease-fires, disarmament, peacekeeping, peacemaking, and peace building. This is what the principled third party, including the UN, can do—and do best unarmed.

Generally speaking, the world community cannot promote a policy of punishing the bad—and the worst—only. If we want to reward and help those 90 percent of the citizens all over former Yugoslavia who want nothing but normalization, peaceful reconstruction, and postwar socioeconomic development after the living hell they have been experiencing, we must get the renegades and criminals to simply give up. The gross mistake is that they alone are the ones to whom we have appealed. Their language is violence, sometimes uninhibited cruelties. Why did we not appeal to all the others, to dissidents, to decent and tolerant forces of "civil society" who, beyond doubt, still make up the majority?

S o what could be done differently in the former Yugoslavia? Here are some examples of what might be done, by both formal and informal third parties. First, they should address the fundamental problems of former Yugoslavia and search for solutions; the wars and cruelties are the result of misguided conflict understanding and management. Second, they should devote their energies to rewarding those who want peace rather than punishing those who promote hate, ethnic cleansing, nationalism, criminality, and warfare.

Third, they should offer economic and other types of aid to those who lay down their weapons. The promise of economic reconstruction can serve as an important stimulus for conflict resolution. They should take care not to fall into the trap of seeking revenge or punishment; instead they should identify common interests, work against all violence, and respect the right of participation in conflict resolution for all actors, formal and informal.

They should work against the myth that "civilized" violence can stop "primitive" violence and thereby bring peace to Yugoslavia.

Next, third parties should use the Vance-Owen Plan for Bosnia-Hercegovina as a point of departure for new negotiations. It is far from ideal, but it is the best so far, short of turning Bosnia-Hercegovina into a UN protectorate. The alternatives, as we know, are either the dissolution of Bosnia into three ethnically homogeneous ministates, more fighting, or both. Fifth, they should push for either lifting the sanctions or for applying sanctions against all who violate one clear criteria, while tightening the arms embargo against all. Sixth, they should recognize the Federal Republic of Yugoslavia and reopen international forums, including the UN, and reinstall ambassadors to Belgrade. The federal government is not responsible for the wars and is clearly interested in dialogue. Seventh, they should boost the United Nations (UNPROFOR), the CSCE missions, and voluntary international and ex-Yugoslav NGO activities.

A functionally integrated force is needed and should consist of the following: First, there should be competent multinational battalions with only traditional self-defense and armored personnel carriers (APCs) roughly like those now in Croatia (sector West). And several thousand more are needed in Croatia, particularly in sectors East and South, and probably 50,000 more in Bosnia for a relatively short period. The purpose should be the simultaneous disarmament and demobilization of as many forces as possible. The size and quality of these battalions rather than their weapons will do the job.

Second, there should be many more civil police—four times as many more in Croatia and thousands more in Bosnia and areas such as Kosova and other trouble spots. They should fulfill a monitoring and preventive function and also carry out social and humanitarian tasks.

Third, there should be various civil affairs officers. They should include legal experts, economists, conflict resolution experts, social workers, negotiators, psychologists, agricultural consultants, technical experts, young volunteers from various parts of ex-Yugoslavia and abroad, and so forth. Together with the police they will have to remain for several years, working on peace building and reconstruction. Tens of thousands of people should be working with local communities everywhere on all aspects of reconstruction in society, among people, and in the psyche of the human beings involved.

It is revealing of the Western propensity for violence that the entire international debate on peacekeeping in Bosnia until now has focused exclusively upon military forces, not the need for police and civil affairs personnel.

The model for peacekeeping is the UNPROFOR in sector West of Croatia, which until May 1993 was able to integrate some of the aforementioned proposals, as well as the separate tasks of peacekeeping, peacemaking, and peace building. This must be rejuvenated and tried on a much larger scale in Bosnia-Hercegovina and, without any military component, in Kosova.

In addition, third parties should help dissidents and opposition all over former Yugoslavia to reach a wider audience. They should help install media and communications technology to permit human contact and more balanced images there and abroad. It is a human right to be able to express opinions. They should help victims, conscientious objectors, and others enter other European countries, for a period, until they can return. Safe havens should be created in former Yugoslavia and in Europe.

Third parties should try to build peace from below. They should establish parallel negotiations to those occurring in Geneva and New York—involving formal and informal actors, new themes, and new combinations of issues. They should oppose all talk about international military intervention and peace enforcement. That will not solve any problem, will kill more than it saves, and will force UNPROFOR to leave. Because there are no perfect solutions does not legitimize violence-promoting nonsolutions. They should also oppose all talk about final solutions for any region. Instead, they should help begin dialogue and trust at all levels and between all parties who want it. They should see beyond tomorrow and direct their energies to how they can help the 90 percent of all citizens of former Yugoslavia who want only normalization, reconstruction, and peace.

The creative arsenals of peace should also be employed, including: demilitarization, protectorates, trusteeship, informal and silent diplomacy, reconciliation, cooperative projects, humanitarian projects, local economic restoration, international assistance, voluntary labor, peace brigades, and so forth. There are no limits to what can still be done.

F inally, we should also learn from what has happened in Yugoslavia and let the death and suffering carry some kind of meaning. We should recognize certain facts. First, the creation of new states is a very complex process that usually leads to violence if not done with extreme care and solid planning. Second, the arms trade makes atrocities possible and prolongs wars. It is pathetic that the Security Council permanent members, which provide 80 percent of all major arms exports in the world, are also those that decide how to punish the importers who buy and use them.

Third, prevention is better than band-aid solutions. The UN must finally be equipped with personnel, organization, funds, and credibility to become what it was supposed to be—the world organization working systematically for nonviolent conflict resolution, security, and peace. Fourth, a complex integrated policy of fact finding, early warning, preventive diplomacy, peacekeeping, peacemaking, and peace building must be developed. Why is it that, for almost fifty years, we have had a UN peacekeeping budget that is only .3 of a percent of the world's war-making budget? Imagine what the UN, the CSCE, and NGOs could achieve with even a fraction of what a military intervention costs. Fifth, Europe badly needs new institutions and new capabilities to handle the new conflicts emerging after the Cold War.

To do some or all of this, rather than intervening militarily or using other realpolitik measures, is to "do something." Some of the proposals will help at some moment at some place; all of them, in various combinations, will help what was once Yugoslavia.

21

CONFIDENCE BUILDING IN ASIA-PACIFIC

ANDREW MACK

Does the end of the Cold War mean a more secure or less secure world? Some pessimists, nostalgic for the comfortable certainties of a bipolar past, believe that the security structures of the post–Cold War world will be more complex, less predictable—and very dangerous. They have a point.

In what was the Soviet Union and in parts of Eastern Europe, the collapse of repressive state control over different ethnic, religious, and nationality groups is allowing long-standing hostilities to emerge. The result has been upsurges of ethnic bigotry, anti-Semitism, and, sometimes, savage communal violence. Today's Yugoslavia, for instance, provides a chilling image of possible futures, not just for Eastern Europe and the USSR, but for countries like China, North Korea, Burma, and Vietnam when their repressive leaderships are also swept onto the scrap heap of history, as inevitably they must be. The Cold War, it might be said then, helped dampen other forms of conflict. The superpowers, for example, often restrained client states from embarking on military adventures out of fear they would be drawn into the resulting conflict. That constraint no longer exists. Thus, in 1991, South Korea can openly threaten military action against North Korea without causing undue concern in Washington. The United States knows that in today's political climate, a war between the two Koreas would not lead to a superpower confrontation as it might well have done even five years ago.

B ut those commentators who dwell on the possible risks of a multipolar future tend to ignore the very real costs and dangers of the bipolar past. We should not forget that it is less than a decade since the threat of global nuclear war was the waking nightmare of policymakers as well as citizens in both East and West. Today that fear has largely disappeared. The Cold War was also the source of an immense amount of human misery. In the United States, the militantly anticommunist official mind-set, which

This essay was first published in *Peace Review* 4:2 (1992).

was both cause and effect of the Cold War, led to McCarthyism at home
and bloody wars overseas. Today the era of anticommunist military interventions is clearly past; there will be no more Vietnams. Another was in
Afghanistan, Moscow's Vietnam, is equally inconceivable and for the same
basic reason. Freed from the perceived imperatives of global superpower
rivalry, the United States no longer has any incentive to support rightist
regimes simply because they have strong anticommunist credentials.
Similarly, a noncommunist Moscow no longer has any ideological or security interest in backing repressive and economically crippled Leninist states
like Vietnam, North Korea, and Cuba. The withdrawal of support for
repressive regimes of whatever ideological coloring should be applauded,
not least because it will speed their transformation. And finally, the lessen-
ing of ideological confrontation between states, while certainly not guaranteeing harmony, has at least removed a major barrier to communication. In
the 1990s, most nation-states are now speaking a similar economic and
political language.

President George Bush has talked a lot about a New World Order, but
to many people Bush's vision seems little more than the Old World Order
without the Russians. If the New World Order is exemplified by the orches-
trated exercise in international cooperation that defined the Gulf crisis we
have good reason to be pessimistic about the future. Students of realpolitik
who still believe that clubs are trumps—that military force remains the
final arbiter of relations between states—saw the stunning U.S. military
victory in the Gulf War as a dramatic vindication of their position. They
were, and still are, quite wrong. First, the proponents of military force
failed to demonstrate that war was necessary. The most obvious nonmilitary option—sanctions—was simply not given a chance to work. The economic blockade against Iraq had a better chance of succeeding than any
previous sanctions regime in history, because it was almost totally
leakproof and because the denial of critical exports and imports would relatively swiftly have brought the Iraqi economy to its knees. In other words,
the fact that the military option was successful does not demonstrate that
nonmilitary options would have failed.

Second, believers in the utility of military power tend to confuse winning a war with winning the peace. The United States had a brilliant plan
for winning the war against Iraq but gave little thought to winning the
peace. The Bush administration stated repeatedly that its war was with
Saddam, not the Iraqi people. Yet Saddam remains in power, while perhaps
200,000 Iraqis were killed in the war or its aftermath, and thousands more
still face death from starvation and disease. Third, in placing his ill-trained
forces in the open desert where they could not successfully be concealed,
and where civilian casualties from allied bombing would be minimal,
Saddam created a battlefield perfectly suited to the massive application of
U.S. military power.

The Vietnamese never made such an elementary mistake in their struggle against the United States, and there is little reason to assume that other states would follow Saddam's foolish military example. Fourth, it is doubtful whether in future crises the United States could count on its allies to hand over tens of billions of dollars to pay it to do the fighting. As Fred Bergsten has noted, the Gulf War was a unique example of collective action: "America acted—and America collected." The U.S. General Accounting Office recently reported that the United States actually made a profit from the war. The Gulf crisis was unique in other respects too. Saddam's brutish behavior and murderous past made him a perfect villain, while the end of the Cold War denied him his only influential friend.

Moreover, the act of aggression Iraq perpetrated against Kuwait was gross, and the breach of international law was unambiguous. More important, the seizure of Kuwaiti oil and the perceived threat to other Gulf producers meant that the issue was not simply one of morality and international law but directly affected the vital material interest of many of the world's richest and most powerful states. It is almost impossible to imagine any future conflict in which this combination of affairs would again be likely to prevail. In most armed conflicts—for example, Grenada, Nicaragua, Israel's Lebanon war, and Indonesia's takeover of East Timor—the legal rights and wrongs have been ambiguous, Western and other world opinion has been divided, and the material interests of rich and powerful states have not been at stake.

Gaining consensus at the UN for collective military action is normally extraordinarily difficult, and it is almost impossible to imagine any other circumstance in which a consensus like the one that was created for collective action against Saddam might again be built. But some commentators argue that since the United States has won the Cold War and the Soviets are no longer effective players on the world security scene, the United States is once again the unchallenged global hegemony. The New World Order is a unipolar one in which seeking international consensus is no longer necessary, because the United States can act successfully alone. Militarily this is probably true, at least in a technical sense, but it is also largely irrelevant. The United States certainly retains unique military capabilities, but its ability to use these capabilities in major crises is constrained by both economics and domestic political circumstances. Inside the United States, neoisolationism—the opposition to entangling and costly overseas commitments to countries that most U.S. citizens either do not care about or actively dislike—is growing. Last year, a poll indicated that the U.S. public rated Japan the biggest threat to their country. Confronted by massive deficits, a degenerating health service, a crisis-ridden education system, a crumbling physical infrastructure, and crime-ridden and violent cities, U.S. citizens are less and less willing to support expensive overseas military commitments. The United States used to be in Asia to contain communism, but communism is no longer a force that needs containing, and its demise removes the central rationale for continued U.S. presence. It also eliminates a major reason most Asian states wanted U.S. protection in the first place.

The end of the Cold War has had a highly positive impact on the regional security environment. There has been a radical improvement in relations between Moscow and Beijing and between both of the latter and South Korea. China and Vietnam are normalizing their relations after more than a decade of bitter hostility, and there is no doubt that the removal of the element of superpower competition from the Cambodian conflict helped achieve the recent settlement. Vietnam, once feared as the Asian Prussia, is out of Cambodia, is absorbed with salvaging its basket-case economy, and is making big cuts in its armed forces. And although it is true that Soviet-Japanese relations have not followed the trend of dramatically improving East-West relations, there has been some modest progress on the contentious sovereignty dispute over the Kurile Islands. And real rapprochement is possible if, as seems likely, Boris Yeltsin's government decides to make major concessions on the territorial issue in order to secure the massive infusion of Japanese aid the Russian economy so desperately needs.

Within ASEAN, the domestic insurgencies that were once a central focus of military concern have mostly disappeared or are declining. China, once seen as a subversive force in the region, facilitated the ending of the communist insurgency in Malaysia. And, notwithstanding the brutalities of Tiananmen Square, Beijing has reestablished diplomatic relations with Djakarta and Singapore. Indeed, only on the Korean peninsula are the armed forces of rival states deployed against known enemies.

Elsewhere in the region, defense planners face the novel and difficult task of planning future force structures without known enemies in mind, a problem with which Australian security planners are very familiar. Yet, given the inestimable improvement in the region's security environment, we confront the apparent paradox that as perceived threats decline, Asian defense budgets have been rising rapidly. In the United States, the USSR, and Europe, the end of the Cold War has reduced defense budgets. So why should Asia be different? Regional defense planners, of course, recognize and welcome the positive trends brought by the new East-West rapprochement. The source of their concern lies elsewhere and they almost never discuss it publicly: it is the specter of Japanese rearmament. There is an obvious parallel here between Asian concerns about Japan and European concerns about a militarily resurgent Germany. It used to be said of NATO that its key tasks were to "keep the Russians out of Western Europe, the Americans in, and the Germans down." Many Asian security planners see the U.S.-Japanese security treaty in similar terms. It is valued more as a means for restraining potential Japanese military resurgence than as an alliance for defending Japan from external threats. But while Germany is enmeshed in a multination security pact and a pan-European economic union that is achieving a high degree of political integration, there are no comparable multinational institutions enmeshing Japan.

A sian worries about a possible resurgence of Japanese militarism are heightened by Tokyo's apparent lack of contrition for its aggressive past; the contrast with Germany is again marked. And yet, in the 1990s, Japan's forces remain defensively oriented and lack an offensive arm with long-range strike aircraft or missiles or aircraft carriers or amphibious forces of any consequence. So although it ranks third in the world's military spending league, Japan lacks the capability to invade and occupy its neighbors. This fact, coupled with Japan's peace constitution, has helped to assuage regional concerns about a new upsurge of Japanese militarism.

Japan has not needed offensive forces to date because they are provided by its U.S. ally. But if the U.S. military presence either goes or becomes much diminished, Japanese defense planners may decide that they need a more balanced force structure—an offensive sword to complement their defensive shield. It is this prospect that so alarms South Korea, China, and many of the ASEAN states. Asian defense planners also worry that the power vacuum that a possible U.S. withdrawal would create might be exploited by other regional states, and in private conversations the names of China and India are frequently mentioned. So even though the current security environment in the region appears benign, the future seems uncertain and potentially dangerous.

Regional concerns about both the probability of U.S. withdrawal and its strategic consequence may, of course, be quite unwarranted. Indeed, those who worry about Japanese militarism rarely ask what interest today's Japan might have in military adventurism. Tokyo's global economic offensive has, after all, been far more successful than the military offensive that led to humiliating defeat in 1945. So why use guns when trade and investment seem so much more successful? But however valid such arguments may be, they are in a sense beside the point; what matters is not so much what the case is as what states perceive the case to be. And it is the perception of the dangers of a future without the United States that is the major factor driving the current military buildup in Asia.

From the conventional military perspective, which sees military strength as a necessary condition for security, such a buildup will seem not only prudent but necessary. If you want peace, so the saying goes, prepare for war. In today's mainstream security discourse, the idea that deterrence strategies enhance security continues to reign largely unchallenged. Indeed, making deterrence the central focus of security policy does make sense if the most probable cause of war is unprovoked aggression—if one confronts a Saddam Hussein or a Hitler. But in the late twentieth century, aggression of the type perpetrated by Saddam or Hitler is actually an infrequent cause of war.

This is so for a number of reasons. First, the global norm of national self-determination has made territorial aggression virtually impossible to justify—a sharp contrast to the values of the colonial era. The illegitimacy of conquest acts as an important constraint on states contemplating aggression. Second, economic power is an increasingly effective means of achieving national objectives in international relations. The economic disaster area that is the Soviet Union still has the largest armed forces in the world, but Moscow has simply ceased to be a serious actor on the global stage; Japan, by contrast, an island state incapable of invading its neighbors, is a major player.

Third, there is a growing body of evidence that suggests that military force is a decreasingly effective tool both of domestic governance and international policy. Some analysts argue that this is because modern warfare has become too destructive to achieve many useful ends. There is something to this argument. But there is an additional reason for believing that military force is of declining utility today. Complex and interdependent societies require a considerable degree of voluntary cooperation on behalf of their citizens if they are to function effectively. Brute coercion may be effective in simple social systems; it is much less so in complex modern industrial societies.

The fact that states need this voluntary cooperation gives citizens what might be called structural power within the system. It is thus no accident that unarmed citizens have played such a central role in bringing down military and other repressive regimes during the last two decades. The examples are obvious enough: Portugal and Greece in the 1970s; most Latin American states in the 1980s; Korea, Taiwan, and the Philippines in the past half decade; and, most dramatically and most recently, Eastern Europe and the Soviet Union. Military dictatorships appear to be a short-lived species in the modern world. The fact that governance by force is proving to be decreasingly effective within states creates a disincentive for aggression across borders as well. There is little point invading a country if you cannot subsequently control it—as the Soviets discovered in Afghanistan and the Israelis in Lebanon.

Unfortunately, the national security policies of Asia-Pacific states still focus overwhelmingly on combating aggression even though aggression is an improbable cause of future wars. In creating force postures to cope with aggression, regional defense planners pay insufficient regard to a more probable cause of war: that of a conflict escalating out of control and involving rival states in armed confrontations they did not originally seek. The fact that aggression is of decreasing utility in international affairs does not, however, mean that the incidence of war will necessarily decline; wars have many different causes and aggression is only one of them.

I n the 1990s, we need to pay more attention to the dangers of inadvertent war and relatively less to the threat of unprovoked aggression. The lesson of history of most relevance to defense planners today is not Hitler, Munich, and World War II, but Sarajevo and the outbreak of World War I. Second, where a conflict between a number of states already exists, the defensive preparations of one state may be taken as evidence of possibly aggressive intent by a rival state, which may in turn increase the rival state's defensive preparations, and so on.

The resulting conflict spiral will tend to increase mutual suspicion and hostility and could lead to an unrestrained arms race. The historical evidence suggests that there is a strong tendency for arms races to culminate in war. So we confront the irony that deterrence strategies involving military buildups may cause the very wars they are intended to prevent. Nations in conflict tend to see their opponent's military capabilities as the measure of the threat they confront. Threat perceptions increase when the force postures and strategies of rival states have a strongly offensive character. Such strategies create incentives for shooting first in crises and for escalation once the threshold to violence has been crossed. They are, in the language of contemporary strategy, destabilizing.

A sensible security policy needs to strike an appropriate balance between, on the one hand, deterring potential aggressors and, on the other hand, reassuring nonaggressive adversaries in order to reduce the risk of conflict spirals and inadvertent war. The balance is delicate because the two elements in such a security policy are often antithetical. Too much reassurance could be perceived as appeasement by a would-be aggressor and actually increase the risk of aggression. On the other hand, too great an emphasis on deterrence can generate conflict spirals and lead to inadvertent war. Although judging the right mix between reassurance and deterrence will always be difficult, in the Asia-Pacific region it is a task that is rarely attempted at all.

Here the balance is skewed much too far toward the deterrence end of the spectrum. The dramatically increased regional defense budgets—some double what they were a decade ago—are paying for imports of modern weapons systems capable of striking with ever increasing lethality over ever greater ranges. And this buildup is not being accompanied by any of the sorts of policies the European states have evolved to reassure each other of their nonaggressive intentions in the post–Cold War world. European reassurance strategies involve a variety of confidence-building measures between military forces, constraints on provocative military exercises, and a stress on restructuring military forces so that, although they retain strong defenses, they cannot effectively be used for invading and occupying neighboring states. The Conference on Security and Cooperation in Europe (CSCE), which includes Eastern European and so-called nonaligned states as well as the Western European states, has been the institutional mechanism for introducing this new security philosophy into Europe.

It is true that CSCE has both problems and detractors, but its importance has been to institutionalize the concept of common security into the European defense discourse. Common security, as Gareth Evans frequently notes, is about seeking security with other states, not against them. Unfortunately, the concept of common security does not yet resonate strongly in the Asia-Pacific region, and when Gareth Evans canvassed the idea of a CSCA—a Conference on Security and Cooperation in Asia—last year, his proposal was greeted with indifference, suspicion, and, from the United States, downright hostility.

Asia was different from Europe, said the critics, and European institutions were inappropriate for the Asian region's security problems. Both observations were true but also largely irrelevant. It is true that it would make no sense to seek to impose the CSCE institutional model, which evolved the strategic context of a massive land confrontation in Central Europe, on the essentially maritime strategic environment of the Asia-Pacific. But no one, least of all Gareth Evans, was proposing this. It is not CSCE institutions that need to be transplanted, but rather the security philosophy that underpins and informs those institutions. And the strategic principles of the CSCE's common security philosophy are at least as relevant to the Asia-Pacific situation as to the European one—possibly even more so.

The fact that Evans's CSCA proposal and other calls for the creation of multilateral confidence-building regimes have thus far had a fairly cool official welcome is no ground for pessimism. Many of the ideas that were rejected outright only a year ago are now being quietly discussed in official and semiofficial forums, and even the United States has dropped its hard-line opposition to such issues being raised publicly. And we should not forget that the CSCE process in Europe took two decades to go from initial talks to the Vienna Treaty of 1990. Debates about the New World Order have, above all, been about how global security can be managed now that the comfortable simplicities of the Cold War era have disappeared. For a number of reasons, the security policies we pursue in the future should place a greater emphasis on reassurance and less on deterrence. If, as I have argued, the use of force in international relations is of decreasing utility, should we not be allocating more resources to nonmilitary approaches to enhancing regional and global security? Should not more tax dollars flow into the coffers of foreign ministries and fewer to defense departments? In countries like Australia, the ratio of defense to foreign ministry spending (not counting foreign aid) is around twenty to one—an extraordinary ratio even when one concedes that soldiers will always require more expensive hardware than diplomats.

The great command that defense bureaucracies have over human and financial resources compared with their diplomatic counterparts tends inevitably to privilege military approaches to security over nonmilitary ones—even when the latter are more appropriate. Yet surprisingly, the rationality of the twenty to one division of resources between Defense and Foreign Affairs has never been subject to cabinet discussion or review in Australia, despite the fact that, as Gareth Evans has noted, "implementation of a multidimensional approach to security requires adequate financial support for the non-military policy instruments." It is not helpful to be in a situation where there is a disproportionate allocation of government resources between those program areas and the defense budget.

If the (Australian) defense budget were cut by a mere 5 percent and the resulting savings transferred to Foreign Affairs, the latter's budget would be roughly doubled. Among other things, we could then afford to train our diplomats to speak the languages of the Asian countries to which they are posted. Currently, Foreign Affairs simply doesn't have the resources for proper language training. Yet the cost of providing such training would be only a tiny fraction of the cost of one of our FA-18 fighters. Which would be the better investment in our long-term security? The fact that questions as basic as these are never addressed by our political representatives is both extraordinary and depressing. To create a genuine New World Security Order we need some new thinking—at home, regionally, and globally. Not a bad way to start would be to require our politicians and security experts to tell us how they justify a post–Cold War security policy that continues to allocate a mere five cents to diplomacy for every dollar it spends on the military.

22

A MIDDLE EASTERN PEACE STRATEGY

ABDUL AZIZ SAID

This period following the Gulf War underscores the urgent need to develop a new U.S.-Arab relationship, one that recognizes both parties' interests, affirms the aspirations of the Arab people, and resolves the Arab-Israeli-Palestinian conflict. Although the United States' view—that instability in the Middle East threatens Western economic stability—is valid, viewing the conflict exclusively this way denies the many historically based problems that plague the Arab world and misses the opportunity to create a better future for everyone.

Let us shift the context of the Gulf tragedy away from Iraq's brutal occupation of Kuwait, from the threat to the ruling families of the Arab states of the Gulf, and from the needs of Western energy consumers, and toward the existential condition of 200 million Arabs victimized by their leaders, their declining quality of life, and the plight of Palestine in the midst of affluence. This way we can understand the poignancy of the Arab predicament. Since the rise of nineteenth-century European colonialism, Arabs have been excluded from history. Saddam Hussein, himself a symptom of this peculiar disease, turned into a messenger who cynically exploited the deep fears and frustrations in the collective Arab soul. Arabs are attracted by the pull of his message; the West is caught in the messenger's push.

The tutelage of the superpowers in the Arab world has historically been one of exploitation, acquiescence, and victimization. The colonial order in the Middle East, first established by Great Britain, France, and Czarist Russia and later assumed by the United States and the Soviet Union, is now approaching its end.

The rise of the system of Arab states after World War II brought discontinuity both with the traditional social structures and with the basic precepts and practices of Islam. Traditional Islamic institutions lost much of their effectiveness as organizers and safeguarders of social justice and

This essay was first published in *Peace Review* 3:2 (1991).

political participation. The West expected the new Arab states to be imitations of Western nation-states; so did the Arab leaders of the time. But the new Arab states were independent mainly in name.

Given the lack of legitimacy of the newly installed governments, power could only be maintained by corruption and despotism. Granted, some Arab governments are cosmetically better than others, and some are more benevolent; but all remain firmly authoritarian.

The Arab world will never be the same as it was before Operation Desert Storm. Iraq's humiliating defeat represents to millions of Arabs yet another generation lost, another front door to history slammed shut. Arabs may, as in the past, resort to backdoor politics, fundamentalism, and terrorism. Still, global and regional forces will have a growing impact in the region. Although the wave of democratization sweeping through Europe and Asia has so far bypassed the Middle East, broader public support will now be demanded of all Middle East governments. There will be no more security in obscurity for Arab princes and military dictators. The Middle East will be in the limelight for many years to come.

T he United States could facilitate the Arabs' reentry into history. Indeed, a U.S.-USSR-European coalition could support the Arabs in developing democratic forms appropriate to their needs, in rediscovering the life-affirming precepts of Islam, and in developing structures that promise a cultural future for the people. Now that the United States and the USSR are willing to jointly participate in a New World Order, they need to transcend the "imperial policing" mentality. A creative, farsighted policy could combine their expertise and experience to address legitimate Arab grievances and identify viable alternatives.

A workable peace strategy for the Middle East needs superpower support of six issues: the transfer and control of arms; an Arab-Israeli-Palestinian peace plan; social and economic justice; appropriate political participation; an Arab role in the emerging world order; and regional security under U.S. leadership. I will discuss each of these items in detail.

The introduction and proliferation of ballistic missiles and nuclear and chemical weapons have altered the Arab-Israeli power balance. The United States will have little success in reducing proliferation unless it holds Israel to the same standards it applies to Arab states. So far, the United States has sought to frustrate the transfer of new, more lethal weapons technology to the Middle East, hoping that the military balance would still favor Israel and other U.S. friends; local disputes would be resolved through peaceful negotiations; and the high cost of advanced weapons technology would prohibit states from achieving a security advantage. These hopes have been dashed as Middle Eastern governments continue to purchase conventional weapons while exploring opportunities to gain a qualitative advantage by acquiring chemical weapons and new ballistic missile systems.

In the context of the proliferation of nuclear weapons, new policy approaches are needed in the U.S. government. The United States needs to recognize that exclusive possession of weapons-related science and technology is a thing of the past. The United States should recognize that the Arabs have access to both technological knowledge of weapons and suppliers of military technology.

The United States has a particularly significant role to play in seeking to moderate the pace of missile and chemical weapons proliferation. For starters, the United States should make clear to Israel that continued transfers of missile technology to China, South Africa, and other nations cannot be tolerated. Past U.S. acquiescence in such transfers makes a mockery of U.S. participation in any missile control agreement and weakens Washington's credibility in seeking to secure European control over technology transfers to the Arab states and to Iran.

The United States should invite the Soviet Union into a peace partnership in the Middle East—the Soviets certainly have a stake in peace and stability in the region. Washington and Moscow can jointly offer incentives to Israelis, Palestinians, Syrians, and Lebanese grounded in an international legal framework. UN Security Council Resolution 242 of November 22, 1967, could be amended to include a call for Palestinian self-determination, peace negotiations under the auspices of the two superpowers (with the blessing of the permanent members of the Security Council), a recognition of legitimacy of the claims of all parties to the conflict, a moratorium on violence, and, finally, a U.S.-Soviet-sanctioned arms-free zone in the Middle East for the duration of peace negotiations.

The peace process could be conducted under the auspices of either a special authority created by the United Nations or a private nongovernmental organization such as the Harvard Mediation Team or Search for Common Grounds. In any case, Israelis, Palestinians, and other concerned parties should consult in selecting a mechanism for conducting the talks.

N o party should demand any concession of any other party as a condition for participating in negotiations. A condition could preclude options that might later prove fruitful. Initially, several possible maps would have to be drawn, and several formulas for limiting Palestinian and Israeli sovereignty within a confederation would have to be devised. The right of Jews to settle in some parts of their holy land would have to be recognized, as would the right of the Palestinians to settle in some parts of their ancestral land. These are rights of peoples, not of states.

The tension between the population-poor but resource-rich Gulf states and the surrounding resource-poor but population-rich countries can be resolved only by the Arabs themselves. Otherwise, the relation between people without resources and resources without people will trigger more violent confrontations. A developmental approach is needed, sponsored by the oil-rich Arab states, using oil revenues to support economic and social development in the Arab world. The rich Arab states should become the keepers of their less fortunate brothers and sisters and participate fully in the creation of an Arab economic community.

Both a public development authority and private assistance are needed. The former would include organizations such as an intra-Arab development bank; the latter would include an Arab trust fund to work closely with international economic agencies such as the World Bank. This private structure could fund and support approaches for helping the poor that have proven successful in other Third World nations. Small loans, for example, have been very successful for starting small businesses and making agricultural improvements. This development strategy has the added advantage of minimizing opportunities for graft and corruption and keeping the bureaucracy of implementation small.

Development is the process through which human beings choose and create their future, within the context of their environment. The goals of development are to realize the potential of human beings and human societies. Development in the Arab world cannot easily fit any prevailing Western model. Arab development can be reconciled with Islam once the concept of development is freed from the linear, rational idea of progress that has been canonized by the Western mind.

Development includes both modernization and humanization. Modernization is the process of adapting technology for the uses of the society and attempting to make that society more rational, efficient, and predictable, especially through the use of comprehensive planning, rational administration, and scientific evaluation. Modernization also carries the connotation of a more productive society, at least in economic terms. Humanization is the process of enlarging and making more equal the dignity, freedom, opportunity for creativity and community, and welfare of individual persons in society, as well as the restructuring of the society's institutions and culture to support these goals.

T he reconciliation of Islam and democracy is a crucial first step toward a new regional Arab order. Democracy—Western or Islamic—is not practiced anywhere in today's Arab world. Does this mean that Islam and democracy are not compatible? No.

The substance of democracy is a human society that has a sense of common goals, a sense of community, wide participation in making decisions, and protective safeguards for dissenters. The form a democracy takes is cast in the mold of the culture of a people. There is nothing in Islam that precludes common goals, community participation, and protective safeguards. It is true that Western liberal forms of democracy—with their provisions for political parties, interest groups, and an electoral system—are alien to Islamic tradition. But democracy is not built upon institutions; it is built upon participation. The absence of democracy in the Arab world is more the result of lack of preparation for it and less the result of a lack of religious and cultural foundations. There are democratic precepts in Islam as there are in other religions. There are also Islamic traditions, as there have been in other religions, that in practice result in transgressions against those ideals. In Islam, democratic traditions have been more commonly abused than used.

Arabs are forced by today's conditions to make the connections between democracy, modernization, and Islam. There is no model available now for "modern," "democratic," and "Muslim." At the close of the nineteenth century, when Egyptian liberal thinkers began to explore these concepts, they accepted the Western norm as the only reality. In so doing, they began to hang an Islamic garb on these concepts. It did not work then, and it is doubtful that it will work now.

Neither the Muslim fundamentalists nor the Arab secularists represent a genuine revival of Arab civilization, but rather negativism and identification with the enemy. What is required is an Arab alternative that is neither a superficial compromise nor a schizophrenic reaction: a response based on Islamic values that reflects the historical development of Islam and responds to the challenges of contemporary life. Mainstream Islam should regain the moral high ground and emotional momentum from fundamentalism. This can be done when Arabs gain self-respect as full-fledged citizens of the modern world. In the long run, it is better for the Middle East to develop through its own Islamic tradition. Otherwise, the people of the region will continue to suffer from the contradictions between traditionalism and secularism, fundamentalism, and Westernism.

T he oil-rich Arab states can contribute to a New World Order. Saudi Arabia, for example, can take the lead in planning for and promoting a long-term global transition from fossil fuels to nongreenhouse energy sources. The new Saudi oil discoveries could ease the transition with less risk of conflict over increasingly scarce oil. Without strong and enlightened leadership in the West, however, Western politicians will probably use the additional oil as an excuse to put off dealing with the energy problem. If that occurs, oil-rich Arabs will be increasingly at risk of armed conflict over control of dwindling oil supplies. It is very much in everyone's interest to promote a smooth transition.

The oil-rich Arabs can undertake three initiatives. First, Saudi Arabia can promote the development and use of environmentally responsible energy sources and energy-using technologies. A special emphasis should be placed on meeting the needs of developing nations, particularly in the Arab world. The goal would be to enable these nations to achieve economic development without risking the unacceptable environmental damage that the industrialized world is experiencing. This calls for new, more advanced, and environmentally benign technologies.

The Arab world can stabilize the oil market, and hence the world energy market, by negotiating a long-term agreement between OPEC and the oil-consuming world. This would transform the relationship between OPEC and oil-consuming nations from one of conflict and competition to one of cooperation. This goal is compatible with a smooth eventual transition from fossil to nonfossil energy sources. Those realists who would scoff at the possibility of productive cooperation between the producers and consumers of oil should consider the dramatic changes in international relationships away from competition and toward cooperation that have occurred in only the last two years. A key initial agreement would be a willingness to supply oil to the United States and other industrial nations, for their Strategic Petroleum Reserve, at a low and fixed price. This would begin to build mutual confidence that might facilitate a producers-consumers agreement.

If oil-rich Arab states were to help fill the Strategic Petroleum Reserve at a discounted price, a great contribution would be made toward building a cooperative world order. Currently, the United States and other industrial societies are caught in a paradox, facing both high prices, with extremely high uncertainty, and budget crises. Cheap oil would help alleviate both problems. Filling the Strategic Petroleum Reserve would provide greater security by reducing some of the price uncertainty, while also helping to balance the budgets.

There is a tremendous amount of thinking to be done by the United States about the Middle East. The great and glaring fact of international relations today is that an era has ended; a handful of states can no longer control what goes on in the world. Great Power strategy has become a historical curiosity. Today the only workable instrument for the ratification of interstate decisions is a broad consensus of governments and peoples.

Consensus—the distinctive political tool in relations among equals—has already gone far to replace armed force as the preferred instrument of national policy. Those international relations specialists who call themselves realists may object to the naiveté, the instability, or the shortsightedness of some manifestations of consensus, but it would be a sheer folly to challenge either its existence or its power. As a method of reaching binding international decisions, consensus is so new that mistakes and contradictions in its application are inevitable. But we have little in the way of alternatives; the emerging global order will either learn to live with mass opinion or it will not survive.

Today, the United States is challenged by the task of learning the requirements and accommodating to the demands of a New World Order. The victory that has proved so difficult to define and so elusive to achieve after World War II is here for the taking, under the condition, so congenial to the U.S. temper, of consensus among equals in a pluralistic environment. The adoption of a cooperative strategy carries the promise of security that is durable—not the elusive security with which we all are familiar. Enhanced security for one state requires improved security for all.

What are some characteristics of cooperation that would enhance security in the Middle East? One is the identification and acceptance by Arab people and governments, Israelis and Palestinians, the United States and the great powers, of shared objectives that can only be reached through cooperative efforts. Each party has to have an expectation of personal benefit from the cooperative effort. Parties are not obligated to contribute to an enterprise from which they expect to get nothing back. And there must be a fair distribution of the benefits and costs of cooperation. Heretofore, the people of the Arab world have carried most of the cost.

There is a crucial role here for U.S. leadership. Leadership is needed to establish mechanisms for cooperation in the Middle East, to coordinate the efforts, to monitor success. The United States could also establish mechanisms to determine the fair allocation of benefits and burdens and identify the roles and responsibilities of various actors in the cooperative enterprise. Finally, U.S. leadership could promote solidarity, which is necessary for the underlying norm of reciprocity to be effective.

The prevailing order of uncertainty in the Middle East could degenerate rapidly into chaos unless Arabs, Israelis, and Americans take the road to peace in the very near future. The current situation offers little predictability, and even less stability, and carries with it the risk of devolution into wholesale violence. Yet the Arab world is more inclined today than ever before toward coexistence with the Israelis. Washington's crisis and security managers, and the country's neoisolationists, can benefit from active diplomacy toward the Middle East.

PART 3
NEW IDEAS:
CREATING NEW MODELS

NEW IDEAS:
CREATING NEW MODELS

If you think that this is utopian, then I would ask you to reflect on why you think this is utopian.—Bertold Brecht

Reasonable men and women adapt themselves to the world. Unreasonable men and women seek to change it. Therefore all depends upon those who are willing to strive for the unreasonable.—George Bernard Shaw

Arguably, a just and lasting peace cannot emerge from the existing world order. Thus, if we are serious about making the changes necessary for creating a peaceful world, we cannot be content with minor, or even major, reforms Instead, the changes must be structural and fundamental. As George Bernard Shaw suggests, this is no time to be "reasonable." Only profound change, which will likely be viewed in mainstream thinking as unreasonable, will do. Yet what progress toward peace we have made through the ages has always seemed impossible or utopian when first proposed. The trick is to ask why.

This section presents new ways of thinking about domestic and international relations. It emphasizes the importance of establishing alternative models of peaceful participation and nonviolent behavior. It will begin to show, among other things, why it is necessary to break free—fully, not merely partially—from mainstream security studies models.

Consistent with the book's theme, we begin by suggesting the means for developing a new consciousness about global affairs. For example, obviously we have great expectations for peace studies; what can education actually contribute, beginning with what we teach our young children? What other aspects of culture can help us think differently about the world? With half the world illiterate, and the other half slipping off into the video age, can the written word still hold any power for positive change?

What's the role of language in altering our reality and in building real security? How can artists—from various realms—contribute to peace?

What is the role for the media; can they, for the first time, really act as watchdogs for the people rather than as lapdogs for the prevailing world order? And what about the largely unheard voices of women and people of color; what can they tell us about a more peaceful world?

Beyond developing a new consciousness, we can benefit from new models for more peaceful societies. For example, in this section we examine the concept of "civil society": the promising role of nonstate actors in the international system. We look at the right to peace, as it has been emerging in international law. We ask whether principles of alternative development can replace the conventional development model. Likewise, we question capitalism as the only alternative to communism: what other economic models, such as social democracy and democratic socialism, can we pursue? Can we develop a more participatory economics for the masses, not merely the rich?

Having already shown that violence and aggression are learned, not natural, what models can we adopt to reverse that learning or block it in the first place? Likewise, since military deterrence has proved to be both ineffective and counterproductive, can we develop alternative models, such as civil deterrence, based on nonviolent, popular noncooperation? And, what about tinderboxes such as the Middle East? Since mainstream strategies have repeatedly failed to keep the peace, should we not consider alternative models?

NEW IDEAS:
NEW CONSCIOUSNESS

23

PEACE STUDIES AND THE AMERICAN ETHOS

JOSEPH J. FAHEY

In the late 1960s when a handful of professors from various disciplines were meeting at Manhattan College to plan the bachelor of arts program in peace studies, a former dean of our college said to us, "You don't want these kids to be peacemakers; you want them to be troublemakers!" Our response was to assure him that peacemaking was at heart a reconciliatory process and that, in fact, we were trying to teach our students not to be troublemakers. But the dean was more perceptive than we were; at heart a peacemaker is a troublemaker, especially in the twentieth century.

As one looks back, one can see how naive we all were. The United States was in the midst of the war in Indochina, Martin Luther King's non-violent life had been taken by violence, and increased nuclear arms production was the cornerstone of international peace and security. The U.S. public for the most part still hated the Russians, Cubans, Chinese, and anyone at home who expressed an interest merely in talking to these people. Our colleges were preparing students for careers in weapons design and construction and transnational corporate investment, and the Reserve Officer Training Corps programs were turning out thousands of graduates to satisfy the nation's military appetite. How could the peacemaker be anything but a troublemaker?

To a very large extent, I think, peace studies has not thus far fulfilled its promise of making trouble for our culture, our nation, and the academy. This is, of course, not a criticism because it would be foolish to expect a field that is still in the midst of defining itself (social justice? human rights? conflict resolution? security? international relations?) to challenge—in just twenty or thirty years—the various forms of exploitation that have dominated our planet for the last several hundred years. But at heart peace studies does pose some very significant challenges to the American ethos and we do well to pause and reflect on the salient features of this culture.

First, we are a messianic nation. From the arrival of Christopher

This essay was first published in *Peace Review* 2:2 (1990).

Columbus in 1492, through the landing at Plymouth Rock in 1620, to the establishment of Puritan individualism as the basis of American philosophy, the leitmotif of American culture has been that we are the light to the nations, the city on the hill, the new Jerusalem. The dominant white males believed that God had sent them to these shores to concuer the savages, to tame the land, and to set a moral example for the rest of the world to emulate. The old European order was in the midst of decay and the American experience was to be the world's savior. Violence and messianism came to be inseparable. The gun became the symbol of American masculinity and power and whether it be gunboats or the Strategic Defense Initiative, the nation continues to believe that it could not survive without the threat to go to war with somebody. Militarism was the logical expression of the nation's Manifest Destiny messianism. Militarism was the means through which the new nation would spread its gospel of freedom (for investment) and peace (Pax Americana).

The new American messiahs set about on a de facto policy of genocide to the native population, of exploitation of the land, and of the pursuit of wealth through the acquisition of African slaves. Both during the colonial period and extending through the 1989 invasion of Panama, American messianism has dominated United States foreign policy. From the shameless record of the exploitation of the aboriginal population; through the stealing of large tracts of land from Mexico and the acquisition of Cuba, Puerto Rico, the Philippines, and Hawaii in 1898; through the use of U.S. marines in Nicaragua and other areas of Central and South America, the American messianic spirit has dominated our brief history as a nation. Above all, Americans to this day firmly believe that it is our divinely ordained obligation to save the rest of the world from itself (witness the asserted 80 percent popular approval of the invasion of Panama).

C apitalism was both a means and an end in American messianism. God had not just given this land to the white males because of the moral superiority of their personal lives; God intended that the men should use this new land to get rich. The American capitalists shared the view of their Calvinist forebears that the possession of material wealth was a sign that God had predestined one for salvation (while poverty was to be equated with damnation). Thus, the medieval restrictions against usury (the taking of interest on loans) and the traditions of a fair price and a fair wage were inimical to a market economy that was to be based on the divinely established laws of supply and demand. In the new order people were now free to make money in any manner they pleased, from anyone they could, and through any means available.

Capitalism existed in its pure form in the nineteenth century during the industrial era. People worked ten- to twelve-hour days six to seven days a week; they labored in unsanitary and badly lit work areas; children and women were paid much less than men for equal work; and workers had no rights—even to a coffee break. Labor unions were outlawed, and the women and men who tried to work for even minimum justice were jailed, beaten, killed, tortured, and otherwise persecuted by the factory and mine owners with able assistance from the local police, the National Guard, and cooperative local and national politicians and judges. Women were denied the right to vote, to own property, and even to share joint custody of their children in divorce—to which they also had no right. And the fishes, birds, wolves, buffalo, air, and water were, of course, completely without rights.

Anti-intellectualism characterized the pioneers, the farmers, the industrialists, and even the labor movement. Intolerance has characterized much of American history, whether in the form of the execution of dissenting women in the colonial period; of antinomian Jacksonian primitivism; of the persecution of abolitionists, feminists, socialists, and pacifists; of the Red scares following World Wars I and II; of people who express counterculture sexual preferences; or of the Reagan know-nothings and scoundrels. Philosophers and social scientists are regarded with a good deal of suspicion either because they are irrelevant or subversive. Americans know the intellectual only as expert or as ideologue, and no serious intellectual social criticism (by pacifists, socialists, feminists, or environmentalists, for example) is permitted on the airwaves. The life of the intellect is simply not esteemed in the American ethos.

There are, of course, many positive dimensions of the American character, and peace studies must also take these into account in fashioning its academic philosophy and programs. Reform has dominated American life. If American history had lacked persons who believed in reform, reconstruction, and transformation, the nation would hardly have survived this long. From the beginning of the American experiment there were people who argued against American messianism, who condemned the greed of the capitalist, and who believed that the pursuit of truth was more valuable than the exercise of fanatical religion. Throughout American colonial and national history, Quakers and others treated the Native Americans with respect, abolitionists opposed slavery, feminists sought equity for women, pacifists pursued world community, socialists labored for a democratic economy, and environmentalists urged recognition of the rights of nature.

In a real sense, the vice of anti-intellectualism has also proven to be a virtue in American life, since adaptability is at the heart of pragmatism and this ability to adjust and to change made it possible for so many reforms (and some reconstruction) to occur without revolution. It should be stressed, however, that almost every major reform in American history has been effected through the influence of those abolitionists, populists, socialists, feminists, and pacifists. Reform has almost never come from within, but it has nevertheless consistently played a major role in American social history. What justice there is in the United States today is a result of the reformers and progressives. Their continued pursuit of a nation characterized by egalitarianism and social justice may, in the end, result in a significantly modified American ethos.

It is in the context of the American penchant for arrogance, selfishness, and pragmatism along with the nation's elasticity and tolerance of reform that the advocates of peace studies must understand their mission. First, peace studies should stress the positive in the American experience. While the beginning point must be a frank admission of the flaws in the American experience, some of which I have already mentioned, it should be recognized that there is much that is positive about the American ethos. To the acceptance of reform we must add the almost naive optimism of Americans who believe that even the impossible can be accomplished almost through the power of will alone. The Puritan belief in hard work, thrift, and individual accountability contributes to the American faith that the future has in it more promise than peril. Americans are a friendly, cheerful, and informal people, and their talent for inventiveness and creativity in the face of adversity are extremely positive traits in the American character.

Perhaps it is the practical, optimistic strain in the American ethos that is responsible for the heavy focus many peace studies programs place on the social sciences as core disciplines. Despite some Puritan views to the contrary, many Americans believe in the fundamental goodness and redeemability of human nature, and so a heavy focus on process (nonviolent strategies, conflict management and resolution) characterizes many research and education programs. Indeed, many believe that peace studies is uniquely American because of its heavy concentration on such practical matters as dispute settlement. The archetypal American—Benjamin Franklin—would be proud.

Second, peace studies must be authentically intellectual in nature. The life of the intellect is distinguished by the quest for truth rather than its application, the preference for the creative over the practical, and the ability to criticize the essence of an idea rather than its mere manifestation. The virtues of the intellectual life are playfulness, piety, humility, and passion. An intellectual loves to play with ideas for their own sake, approaches all learning with a deep sense of mystery along with a keen awareness of what she or he does not know, and possesses a commitment to the quest for truth for which she or he will sacrifice reputation, livelihood, or life itself. An intellectual approaches new ideas with a sense of awe and wonder and understands that the essence of humor is not exterior laughter but the interior ability to comprehend the absurdity of the historical moment. An intellectual lives for ideas rather than off them.

If peace studies falls into the trap of pursuing purely professional or applied studies, it will make little contribution to the American culture. As long as the academy, the corporation, and the political sphere are assured that peace studies represents no substantive challenge to business as usual, it can expect to flourish and even prosper in the American ethos. The study of the humanities—philosophy, history, art, religion, literature—should serve as the foundation of a peace studies program rather than exist at its periphery. It is the idea of peace that is the question before us, and if there is no serious debate as to the nature of peace, the academy will make no lasting contribution to a people's ethos. In the best tradition of the intellectual spirit, peace studies must turn answers into questions and challenge the very basis of culture along with its social institutions.

Third, peace studies must focus on social justice. While there is far more that we do not know about the science of peace than we do know, we are at least aware that societies that tend to undervalue civil, political, and economic rights tend also to be violent societies. Wars result from acts of injustice rather than from the pursuit of justice. The periods of reform in American history were always periods in which progressive people challenged the country to an expanded definition of human rights. It lies before us to assert that human beings have a right to the democratic control of their political and economic destiny, a right to work, a right to housing, a right to medical care, and a right to a university education.

The concept of peace in many religious traditions is always in part understood to be justice or fulfillment. Theologically, the biblical and other religious traditions hold that salvation cannot be achieved without the entirety of creation becoming integrally united in harmony and oneness. It is this deeper sense of justice that should characterize our work. From every discipline we must examine the integrity of creation and realize that we humans are merely guests here in the universe and that the ownership of the small planet on which we live is as wide as the cosmos itself. Justice demands that we recognize the inherent rights that are conferred upon us by nature rather than by the political or economic system of the moment.

Fourth, peace studies must assist in the formation of a world community. The fall of the Berlin Wall symbolized far more than merely the reunification of a sadly divided people. It symbolized the end of the nation-state. While this 400-year experiment in human social organization has produced some benefits to the human species, it has also been responsible for a great many wars, which continue to threaten to annihilate the species itself. The fall of the Wall means nothing to the war planners. It merely changes the location, tactics, and weapons systems of the next war. We need to be completely realistic about this: As long as sovereign nations exist, war will exist.

The United States has fought more than 200 wars in its history—

almost all undeclared by Congress. The vast majority were wars of expansion against the Native American nations and the Mexican people. Today the conquest extends to the oceans and to outer space. Peace studies should assist in helping people to include all people and animals as their sisters and brothers. Peace studies cannot be content merely to resolve the conflicts between national actors or to seek security in the midst of the anarchy that reigns internationally. The study of the United Nations—its functions, promise, and future reorganization—should be an essential part of every peace studies program. The United Nations presently represents the unity of the species and planet on a morally symbolic level; the future United Nations organization must serve as the juridical home to the globe's species.

Finally, the strongest contribution that peace studies can make to the American ethos is to help the culture cease being exclusively American in nature. Citizens of the United States should celebrate the global origins of their own culture and realize that a world culture is emerging that is based on the unity of all creatures, the democracy of nature. Peace studies has a unique contribution to make to this realization.

24

WRITING AS AN ACT OF HOPE

ISABEL ALLENDE

In every interview during the last few years I have encountered two questions that forced me to define myself as a writer and a human being: Why do I write? And who do I write for?

In 1981, in Caracas, I put a sheet of paper in my typewriter and wrote the first sentence of *The House of the Spirits:* "Barabbas came to us by sea." At that moment I didn't know why I was doing it, or for whom. In fact, I assumed that no one would ever read it except my mother, who reads everything I write. I was not even conscious that I was writing a novel. I thought I was writing a letter—a spiritual letter to my grandfather, a formidable old patriarch, whom I loved dearly. He had reached almost one hundred years of age and decided that he was too tired to go on living, so he sat in his armchair and refused to drink or eat, calling for Death, who was kind enough to take him very soon.

I wanted to bid him farewell, but I couldn't go back to Chile, and I knew that calling him on the telephone was useless, so I began this letter. I wanted to tell him that he could go in peace because all his memories were with me. I had forgotten nothing. I had all his anecdotes, all the characters of the family, and to prove it I began writing the story of Rose, the fiancée my grandfather had, who is called Rose the Beautiful in the book. She really existed; she's not a copy from García Marquez, as some people have said.

For a year I wrote every night with no hesitation or plan. Words came out like a violent torrent. I had thousands of untold words stuck in my chest, threatening to choke me. The long silence of exile was turning me to stone; I needed to open a valve and let the river of secret words find a way out. At the end of that year there were five hundred pages on my table; it didn't look like a letter anymore. On the other hand, my grandfather had died long before, so the spiritual message had already reached him. So I thought, "Well, maybe in this way I can tell some other people about him,

This essay was first published in William Zinsser, ed., *Paths of Resistance* (Boston: Houghton Mifflin, 1991). © Isabel Allende, 1989.

and about my country, and about my family and myself." So I just organized it a little bit, tied the manuscript with a pink ribbon for luck, and took
it to some publishers.

In the process of writing the anecdotes of the past, and recalling the
emotions and pains of my fate, and telling part of the history of my country, I found that life became more comprehensible and the world more tolerable. I felt that my roots had been recovered and that during that patient
exercise of daily writing I had also recovered my own soul. I felt at that
time that writing was unavoidable—that I couldn't keep away from it.
Writing is such a pleasure; it is always a private orgy, creating and recreat-
ing the world according to my own laws, fulfilling in those pages all my
dreams and exorcising some of my demons.

B ut that is a rather simple explanation. There are other reasons for
writing.

Six years and three books have passed since *The House of the Spirits*.
Many things have changed for me in that time. I can no longer pretend to
be naive, or elude questions, or find refuge in irony. Now I am constantly
confronted by my readers, and they can be very tough. It's not enough to
write in a state of trance, overwhelmed by the desire to tell a story. One has
to be responsible for each word, each idea. Be very careful: the written
word cannot be erased.

I began to receive academic papers from American universities about
the symbols in my books, or the metaphors, or the colors, or the names. I'm
always very scared by them. I just received three different papers on
Barabbas, the dog. One of them says that he symbolizes the innocence of
Clara because he accompanies her during her youth, and when she falls in
love, symbolically, the dog dies in a pool of blood. That means the sexual
act, it seems. The second paper says that the dog represents repression—the
militarists—and the third paper says that he is the male part of Clara, the
hidden, dark, big beast in her. Well, really, Barabbas was just the dog I had
at home. And he was killed as it was told in the book. But of course it
sounds much better to answer that Barabbas symbolizes the innocence of
Clara, so that's the explanation I give when somebody asks.

Maybe the most important reason for writing is to prevent the erosion
of time, so that memories will not be blown away by the wind. Write to
register history, and name each thing. Write what should not be forgotten.
But then, why write novels? Probably because I come from Latin America,
a land of crazy, illuminated people, of geological and political cata-
clysms—a land so large and profound, so beautiful and frightening, that
only novels can describe its fascinating complexity.

A novel is like a window, open to an infinite landscape. In a novel we
can put all the interrogations, we can register the most extravagant, evil,
obscene, incredible or magnificent facts—which, in Latin America, are not

hyperbole, because that is the dimension of our reality. In a novel we can give an illusory order to chaos. We can find the key to the labyrinth of history. We can make excursions into the past, to try to understand the present and dream the future. In a novel we can use everything: testimony, chronicle, essay, fantasy, legend, poetry and other devices that might help us to decode the mysteries of our world and discover our true identity.

For a writer who nourishes himself or herself on images and passions, to be born in a fabulous continent is a privilege. In Latin America we don't have to stretch our imaginations. Critics in Europe and the United States often stare in disbelief at Latin American books, asking how the authors dare to invent those incredible lies of young women who fly to heaven wrapped in linen sheets; of black emperors who build fortresses with cement and the blood of emasculated bulls; of outlaws who die of hunger in the Amazon with bags full of emeralds on their backs; of ancient tyrants who order their mothers to be flogged naked in front of the troops and modern tyrants who order children to be tortured in front of their parents; of hurricanes and earthquakes that turn the world upside down; of revolutions made with machetes, bullets, poems and kisses; of hallucinating landscapes where reason is lost.

It is very hard to explain to critics that these things are not a product of our pathological imaginations. They are written in our history; we can find them every day in our newspapers. We hear them in the streets; we suffer them frequently in our own lives. It is impossible to speak of Latin America without mentioning violence. We inhabit a land of terrible contrasts and we have to survive in times of great violence. Contrast and violence, two excellent ingredients for literature, although for us, citizens of that reality, life is always suspended from a very fragile thread.

The first, the most naked and divisible form of violence is the extreme poverty of the majority, in contrast with the extreme wealth of the very few. In my continent two opposite realities coexist. One is a legal face, more or less comprehensible and with a certain pretension to dignity and civilization. The other is a dark and tragic face, which we do not like to show but which is always threatening us. There is an apparent world and a real world—nice neighborhoods where blond children play on their bicycles and servants walk elegant dogs, and other neighborhoods, of slums and garbage, where dark children play naked with hungry mutts. There are offices of marble and steel where young executives discuss the stock market, and forgotten villages where people still live and die as they did in the Middle Ages. There is a world of fiction created by the official discourse, and another world of blood and pain and love, where we have struggled for centuries.

In Latin America we all survive on the borderline of those two realities. Our fragile democracies exist as long as they don't interfere with imperialist interests. Most of our republics are dependent on submissiveness. Our institutions and laws are inefficient. Our armed forces often act as mercenaries for a privileged social group that pays tribute to transnational enterprises. We are living in the worst economic, political and social crisis since the conquest of America by the Spaniards. There are hardly two or three leaders in the whole continent. Social inequality is greater every day, and to avoid an outburst of public rancor, repression also rises day by day. Crime, drugs, misery and ignorance are present in every Latin American country, and the military is an immediate threat to society and civil governments. We try to keep straight faces while our feet are stuck in a swamp of violence, exploitation, corruption, the terror of the state and the terrorism of those who take arms against the status quo.

But Latin America is also a land of hope and friendship and love. Writers navigate in these agitated waters. They don't live in ivory towers; they cannot remove themselves from this brutal reality. In such circumstances there is no time and no wish for narcissistic literature. Very few of our writers contemplate their navel in self-centered monologue. The majority want desperately to communicate.

I feel that writing is an act of hope, a sort of communion with our fellow man. The writer of good will carries a lamp to illuminate the dark corners. Only that, nothing more—a tiny beam of light to show some hidden aspect of reality, to help decipher and understand it and thus to initiate, if possible, a change in the conscience of some readers. This kind of writer is not seduced by the mermaid's voice of celebrity or tempted by exclusive literary circles. He has both feet planted firmly on the ground and walks hand in hand with the people in the streets. He knows that the lamp is very small and the shadows are immense. This makes him humble.

But just as we should not believe that literature gives us any sort of power, neither should we be paralyzed by false modesty. We should continue to write in spite of the bruises and the vast silence that frequently surrounds us. A book is not an end in itself; it is only a way to touch someone—a bridge extended across a space of loneliness and obscurity—and sometimes it is a way of winning other people to our causes.

I believe in certain principles and values: love, generosity, justice. I know that sounds old-fashioned. However, I believe in those values so firmly that I'm willing to provoke some scornful smiles. I'm sure we have the capacity to build a more gentle world—that doing so is our only alternative, because our present equilibrium is very fragile. In literature, we have been told, optimism is dangerous; it flirts with simplicity and is an insurrection against the sacred laws of reason and good taste. But I don't belong to that group of desperate intellectuals. Despair is a paralyzing feeling. It only benefits our enemies.

My second novel, *Of Love and Shadows,* tells about the *desaparecidos,* "the disappeared ones." It's based on a political massacre that took place in

Chile in 1973 during the military coup that put an end to 150 years of democracy. The novel denounces repression and the impunity of the murderers, and it had a warm reception from the most readers. But some said it was too political and sentimental and not very objective, as if one could be objective about the crimes of a dictatorship. Maybe these critics would have forgiven me, as other writers have been forgiven, if the book had only been a story of horror and bitterness. They didn't like the fact that in the novel solidarity and hope prevail over death and torture. If the main characters, Irene and Francisco, had died in a torture chamber, or at least if the violent experiences they endured had drowned them in despair and destroyed forever their capacity to love and to dream, these critics might have been more tolerant. Evidently it's hard to accept in literature that love can be stronger than hatred, although it frequently is in life.

If my books are going to be classified as political, I hope readers will find out that they are not political for ideological reasons only, but for other, more subtle considerations. They are political precisely because Alba Trueba, in *The House of the Spirits,* who has been raped, tortured and mutilated, is able to reconcile herself with life; because Irene and Francisco, in *Of Love and Shadows,* make love in spite of terror; because in my third novel, *Eva Luna,* Eva defeats the odds of her fate with generosity and candor; because these characters search for truth and have the courage to risk their lives.

I suppose I have the secret ambition to become a great writer, to be able to create stories that will resist the passage of time and the judgment of history. Yes, I know, it's terribly pretentious! But I'm more interested in touching my readers—as many of them as possible—on a spiritual and emotional level. To do this from a feminine point of view is a beautiful challenge in the society I live in. The political literature that some women writers have begun to create is so revolutionary that no wonder many critics are scared. Women are questioning the set of values that have sustained human society since the first apes stood on their feet and raised their eyes to the sky. After centuries of silence, women are taking by assault the exclusive male club of literature. Some women have done it before, of course, struggling against formidable obstacles. But now half of the novels published in Europe and the United States are written by women. Our sisters are using the cutting edge of words to change the rules we have always had to obey. Until now, humankind has organized itself according to certain principles that are considered part of nature: we are all born (it has been said) with some original sin; we are basically evil, and without the strict control of religion and laws we would devour each other like cannibals; authority, repression and punishment are necessary to keep us in line. According to these theories, the best proof of our perverse nature is that the world is what it is—a round rock lost in the cosmic nightmare, where abuse, war, inequality and hatred prevail.

But a small group of women and young men are now making the most astonishing statements. Fortunately, most of them work in the best universities, so even if they are only a few, their voices have great impact. These people are questioning everything, starting with our own image as human beings. Until now, men have decided the destiny of this suffering planet, imposing ambition, power and individualism as virtues. These values are also present in literature. Critics, most of them men, as you probably can guess, have determined what is good in literature—what is valuable or artistic, according to our aesthetic, intellectual and moral patterns—leaving aside the feminine half of the human race, whose opinions on this or any other matter don't interest them. I think it's time to revise this situation. But it is not the Old Guard who will do it. It will be done by women and by young men who have nothing to lose and therefore have no fear.

In the process of analyzing books, critics have exalted all kinds of literary experiments, some of them quite unbearable. How many books have you tried to read lately and haven't gotten past page fifteen because they were simply boring? Flamboyant literary techniques win awards even though the subject is deplorable. The worst vices are glorified if the writing is elegant. Lies, bitterness and arrogance are forgiven if the language is original and the author already has his laurels. Pessimism is in fashion.

But many novels that don't fit that pattern are now being written by women and by some brave men, not all of them young—for example, García Marquez, who wrote that incredible and sentimental book *Love in the Time of Cholera,* which is a sort of magnificent soap opera about two old people who fall in love, and they love each other for eighty years. It's wonderful.

Those writers are shaking the literary world nowadays because they propose a completely new set of values. They don't accept the old rules anymore. They are willing to examine everything—to invent all over again and to express other ethical and aesthetic values; not always to replace the prevailing ones, but to complement them. It's not a question of changing male chauvinism for militant feminism, but of giving both women and men a chance to become better people and to share the heavy burden of this planet. I believe that this is the true political literature of our time.

All political systems, even revolutions, have been created and directed by men, always within the patriarchal regime. Important philosophical movements have tried to change man and society, but without touching the basis of human relations—that is, inequality of the sexes. Men writers of all periods have written political literature, from utopia to parody, but feminine values have been scorned and women have been denied a voice to express them.

Now, finally, women are breaking the rule of silence and raising a strong voice to question the world. This is a cataclysm. It is a new literature that dares to be optimistic—to speak of love in opposition to pornography, of compassion against cruelty. It is a literature that's not afraid of colloquial language, of being sentimental if necessary; a literature that searches the spiritual dimension of reality, that accepts the unknown and the unexplainable, confusion and terror; a literature that has no answers, only questions; a literature that doesn't invent history or try to explain the world solely with reason, but also seeks knowledge through feelings and imagination. Maybe, this literature says, it's not true that we are perverse and evil. Maybe the idea of original sin is just a terrible mistake. Maybe we are not here to be punished, because the gods love us and are willing to give us a chance to decipher the clues and trace new paths.

The effect of these books is hard to measure, because the old instruments are no longer useful. Probably the strongest literature being written nowadays is by those who stand unsheltered by the system: blacks, Indians, homosexuals, exiles and, especially, women—the crazy people of the world, who dare to believe in their own force. We dare to think that humanity is not going to destroy itself, that we have the capacity to reach an agreement, not only for survival but also to achieve happiness. That is why we write—as an act of human solidarity and commitment to the future. We want to change the rules, even if we won't live long enough to see the results. We have to make real revolutions of the spirit, of values, of life. And to do so we have to begin dreaming them.

So I will continue to write: about two lovers embracing in the moonlight, near an abandoned mine where they have found the bodies of fifteen peasants, murdered by the military. Or about raped women and tortured men and families who sell themselves as slaves because they are starving. And also—why not?—about golden sunsets and loving mothers and poets who die of love. I want to tell stories and say, for example, that I care more for the free man than the free enterprise, more for solidarity than charity. I want to say that it's more important for me to share than to compete. And I want to write about the necessary changes in Latin America that will enable us to rise from our knees after five centuries of humiliations.

Much skill will be needed to write about these things eloquently. But with patience and hard work I hope to acquire that skill. I suppose I'm being very ambitious. Well, most writers are, even women writers.

Now, for whom do I write? When I face a clean sheet of paper, I don't think of a large audience or of the people who would raise their knives to cut me in pieces. If I did, terror would paralyze me. Instead, when I write, a benevolent image comes to my mind—that of Alexandra Jorquera, a young woman who lives in Chile whom I scarcely know. She has read my books so many times that she can repeat paragraphs by heart.

In fact, she knows them better than I do. She quotes me and I don't know she's quoting me. Once she told me that she had discovered in my books the history of Chile that is denied by the official textbooks of the dictatorship—the forbidden and secret history that nevertheless is still alive in the memories of most Chileans.

This is the best compliment my work has ever received. For the sake of this girl I am very demanding with my writing. Sometimes, tempted by the beauty of a sentence, I am about to betray the truth, and then Alexandra comes to my mind and I remember that she, and others like her, don't deserve that. At other times I'm too explicit, too near the pamphlet. But then I step back, thinking she doesn't deserve that either—to be underestimated. And when I feel helpless against brutality and suffering, her candid face brings back my strength. All writers should have a reader like her, waiting for their words. They would never feel lonely, and their work would have a new and shining dimension.

In Latin America today, 50 percent of the population is illiterate. Among those who can read and write, only very few can buy books, and among those who can buy books, very few have the habit of reading. What, then, is the importance of a book in Latin America? None, would be the reasonable answer. But it's not exactly that way. For some strange reason, the written word has a tremendous impact in that illiterate continent. The totalitarian regimes have persecuted, tortured, sent into exile and murdered many writers. This is not an accident; dictators don't make mistakes in these details. They know that a book can be dangerous for them. In our countries most of the press is controlled by private enterprise or by inefficient governments. Eduardo Galeano, the great writer from Uruguay, puts it bluntly: "Almost all mass media promote a colonialistic culture, which justifies the unjust organization of the world as a result of the legitimate victory of the best—that is, the strongest. They lie about the past and about reality. They propose a lifestyle which postulates consumerism as an alternative to communism, which exalts crime as achievement, lack of scruples as virtue, and selfishness as a natural requirement."

What can writers do against this persistent and powerful message? The first thing we should try to do is write clearly. Not simply—that only works with soap advertising; we don't have to sacrifice aesthetics for the sake of ethics. On the contrary, only if we are able to say it beautifully can we be convincing. Most readers are perfectly able to appreciate subtleties and poetic twists and symbols and metaphors. We should not write with a paternalistic attitude, as if readers were simple-minded, but we should also beware of elaborate and unnecessary ornamentation, which frequently hides a lack of ideas. It has been said that we Spanish-speaking people have the vice of empty words, that we need six hundred pages to say what would be better told in fifty.

The opportunity to reach a large number of readers is a great responsibility. Unfortunately, it is hard for a book to stand against the message of the mass media; it's an unfair battle. Writers should therefore look for other forms of expressing their thoughts, avoiding the prejudice that only in books can they make literature. All means are legitimate, not only the cultivated language of academia but also the direct language of journalism, the mass language of radio, television and the movies, the poetic language of popular songs and the passionate language of talking face to face with an audience. These are all forms of literature. Let us be clever and use every opportunity to introduce ourselves in the mass media and try to change them from within.

I n Venezuela, José Ignacio Cabrujas, a playwright and novelist, one of the most brilliant intellectuals of the country, writes soap operas. These shows are the most important cultural phenomenon in Latin America. Some people watch three or four a day, so you can imagine how important that kind of writing is. Cabrujas doesn't elude reality. His soap operas show a world of contrasts. He presents problems such as abortion, divorce, machismo, poverty and crime. The result is quite different from "Dynasty." But it's also very successful.

I tried to put some of that soap opera stuff in *Eva Luna,* because I'm fascinated by that version of reality. The ladies on TV wear false eyelashes at eleven in the morning. The difference between rich and poor is that the rich wear cocktail gowns all the time and the poor have their faces painted black. They all go blind or become invalids and then they recover. Just like real life!

Many of the most important Latin American writers have been journalists, and they go back to it frequently because they are aware that their words in a newspaper or on the radio reach an audience that their books can never touch. Others write for the theater or the movies, or write lyrics for popular songs. All means are valid if we want to communicate and don't presume to be writing only for an educated elite or for literary prizes.

In Latin America a book is almost a luxury. My hairdresser calls me Dr. Allende because I usually carry a book, and she probably thinks that a doctorate is the minimum prerequisite for such an extravagance. In Chile a novel of three hundred pages can cost the equivalent of a laborer's monthly wages. In some other countries—like Haiti, for example—85 percent of the population is illiterate. Elsewhere in Latin America, nothing is published in the Indian languages of the majority. Many publishers have been ruined by the economic crisis, and the price of books imported from Spain is very high.

However, we should not despair. There is some hope for the spirit. Literature has survived even in the worst conditions. Political prisoners have written stories on cigarette paper. In the wars of Central America, little soldiers, fourteen years old, write poetry in their school notebooks. The

Pieroa Indians, those who haven't yet been exterminated by the genocide being carried out against the aborigines of the Amazon, have published some legends in their language.

I n my continent, writers often have more prestige than they do in any other part of the world. Some writers are considered witch doctors, or prophets, as if they were illuminated by a sort of natural wisdom. Jorge Amado has to spend part of the year away from Brazil in order to write, because people crowd into his house seeking advice. Mario Vargas-Llosa directed the opposition to Alan Garcia's government in Peru. García Marquez is a frequent middleman for Central American presidents. In Venezuela, Arturo Uslar Pietri is consulted on issues like corruption and oil. These writers have interpreted their reality and told it to the world. Some of them even have the gift of foretelling the future and put in words the hidden thoughts of their people, which of course include social and political problems, because it is impossible to write in a crystal bubble, disregarding the conditions of their continent. No wonder Latin American novels are so often accused of being political.

For whom do I write, finally? Certainly for myself. But mainly for others, even if there are only a few. For those who have no voice and for those who are kept in silence. For my children and my future grandchildren. For Alexandra Jorquera and others like her. I write for you.

And why do I write? Garcia Marquez once said that he writes so that his friends will love him more. I think I write so that people will love each other more. Working with words is a beautiful craft, and in my continent, where we still have to name all things one by one, it has a rich and profound meaning.

25

NATIONAL SECURITY NEWS

DAVID RUBIN

A common description of the journalistic process—one often advanced by journalists themselves to explain what they do—is the mirror-to-society metaphor. Journalists simply hold up a mirror to reflect both the good and the bad without partiality. In this comparison, journalism is a politically and ideologically neutral activity; reporters simply convey information to the public. This portrays journalism as a passive profession—a comfortable explanation for journalists wishing to avoid the responsibilities of power. Yet this seriously misconstrues the reporting process.

Journalists demonstrate their partiality, and their power, every day in every decision they make in constructing a news story. This begins with choosing the subject and selecting the sources on whom to rely. It continues in the story's organization and the selection of specific words to convey precise meanings. It concludes with the amount of time or space allocated and with the story's placement.

Anyone familiar with the central events of the Cold War and the U.S.-Soviet relationship since 1945 understands that the media-created reality describing these events often has been either incomplete or entirely false; it has obscured a hidden reality that clashes seriously with public impressions. Any peace studies curriculum designed to acquaint students with these events must, therefore, consider the news media role in structuring reality. Media consumers, citizen activists looking to change the media, and those wanting to work in the media must be taught that journalism has been an active player in constructing and maintaining the Cold War and the nuclear regime.

The press-as-player concept is central to understanding superpower competition and the arms race. Without print and electronic media support, the U.S. public would not be likely to support $300 billion annual spending on defense or accept the need for a vast nuclear arsenal to deter the Soviets. Nearly every major event in the historic U.S.-Soviet competition can be more clearly understood by examining the media's role.

This essay was first published in *Peace Review* 2:2 (1990).

The very first news release handed to reporters about the secret weapon that destroyed Hiroshima came from William L. Laurence, a respected science journalist working for the government, on leave from the *New York Times*. Laurence was given access to Los Alamos and to A-bomb secrets in exchange for adopting the role of a public relations man, agreeing to shape this story from the government perspective. His account of the bomb's building, testing, and dropping was widely published in the nation's press and helped establish the sympathetic framework within which atomic weapons were debated. Laurence won a Pulitzer Prize for his work, and the government won public acceptance, even admiration, for the weapon.

Soon after Laurence's journalism came General Leslie Groves's effort in the late 1950s to convince the public that the A-bomb was an important secret that should be kept from other nations, and that Communist spies had infiltrated the government to steal it. Groves enlisted the news media to spread these views, to help the military gain control of nuclear weapons, and to dampen public discussion of the role of nuclear weapons in U.S. defense policy. Journalists, both witting and not, actively promoted this deception, printing leaks of secret (and often incorrect) information that fed the public's appetite for spy scares and for an arms race with the Soviet Union.

Similarly, when the United States was conducting atmospheric tests of nuclear weapons in Nevada in the early 1950s, the press accepted the Atomic Energy Commission's assurances about public health. The few journalists, such as Paul Jacobs, who recognized radioactive hazards and challenged the government, were labeled unpatriotic by government officials and their fellow reporters. Weapons testing was represented as both safe and essential to national security.

The public has no way of checking reality in this realm, as compared to media coverage of local issues, such as crime or mass transit. Americans cannot easily challenge the press picture of the Soviet Union, or other enemies. Few U.S. citizens travel to the Soviet Union, Libya, or Iraq, nor do they speak the languages. Nuclear strategy and weapons development cannot be intelligently debated by the public either, given each administration's monopoly over information and their spoon feeding of secret data to the press.

An academic course on the press and national security should begin with the concept of framing. Students could profitably examine the first year's coverage of Mikhail Gorbachev by the U.S. media to see how he was presented to the public. They would find him widely described as just another Stalinist leader. His initiatives for reducing nuclear weapons were dismissed by officials and reporters as utopian, naive, or duplicitous. His glasnost program was mocked. His offer of an underground testing moratorium was viewed suspiciously and rejected by journalists and the Reagan administration (which urgently wanted to test the nuclear pumped x-ray laser, an SDI weapon candidate). While Soviet motives for the moratorium were framed in the least favorable light, similar skepticism was not applied to U.S. motives.

More recently, media coverage of the U.S. invasion of Panama illustrates how national security events outside superpower competition can be framed in Washington's terms. The invasion was widely reported as successful. It was a military operation executed with surgical precision, accomplishing its goal of capturing Noriega and returning Panama to democracy. Little space was devoted to uncomfortable subjects such as Panamanian civilian casualties, destroyed property, and U.S. weapons failures. Nor was much said about the legality of the invasion, how Noriega's capture would really help the war on drugs, or how the invasion would look from other countries. Rather, the invasion was framed as a Bush administration triumph. It again exemplified an essentially patriotic press corps, covering another, purported national security, story; with limited access to information, the press was manipulated into reporting the official line.

The media role in creating, through framing, an image of the enemy deserves special attention. Without a dangerous military adversary for the United States, the permanent crisis of the last forty-five years could not have been sustained. Until the late 1980s, U.S. journalists, at the government's urging, could be counted on to produce a uniform picture of the Russian Bear: an expansionist and illegitimate Soviet state bent on dominating Western Europe; a Soviet and Warsaw Pact military machine with an enormous conventional arms advantage offset only by the West's nuclear weapons; a Soviet people at odds with their government and hungry for capitalism and democracy; an aging and tyrannical Soviet leadership; a country of food shortages, lines, dissidents, and frigid temperatures.

In the last couple of years, the press has reversed itself and created a quite positive image of the Soviets and of Mikhail Gorbachev, now the Bush administration's political partner. (This may be similarly misleading, but the complexities of Soviet politics and economics do not fit the media's simple frames.) In the meantime, images of new enemies are now surfacing in the news media, often anonymously. The likeliest candidates have become the united Germans, the Japanese, drug lords, and terrorist states with germ, nuclear, and chemical weapons. These new enemy stories result from a partnership between government and a credulous press corps unable to escape government framing of events.

One reason for such little critical distance between press and government on national security issues comes from how journalists have defined news and newsmakers. In the national security area, the press has taken the statist view. Newsmakers are almost exclusively top government officials with access to secrets; they define what is news by selectively manipulating information. We rarely hear the voice of civil society in national security stories.

This has been so from the very beginning of the nuclear era. In the few weeks after the bombing of Hiroshima and Nagasaki, the U.S. press was open to discussion of the implications of atomic weapons by clergy, academics, and others outside government. But this window closed quickly once talk of A-bomb secrets, spies, and a hostile Soviet Union took over the channels of communication. Since then, the civil voice has occasionally erupted when government has temporarily lost the ability to frame events, such as during the 1950s debate over atmospheric testing, or when the nuclear freeze campaign seemed, in the early 1980s, to be forming into a politically potent grassroots organization. Normally, however, the statist voice drowns out whatever civil voice competes for news media attention.

It should be emphasized that U.S. journalism does not in all cases define news exclusively in government terms. This is a problem that is, perhaps, particular to the national security beat. Stories about the environment illustrate another situation. By the late 1960s and early 1970s, it was clear that government and industry officials were not the sole, or even the best, sources on questions of air and water pollution, toxic waste disposal, and the like. Citizen activists were routinely queried about these issues and were provided a platform in the news stories. It is now impossible to imagine a balanced story about an environmental hazard that does not include the views of the Sierra Club, the Natural Resources Defense Council, Greenpeace, and similar groups. They have been accorded source credibility by journalists.

This has yet to happen, however, on national security stories. Citizen activists and members of the peace community are largely ignored by national security reporters. Rarely are they permitted to initiate stories, and when they do appear in the coverage, it is often deep in the story, as a weak rebuttal—for the sake of objectivity—to the official perspective. The occasional feature story that appears on peace activists invariably portrays them as naive, disorganized, weak, and bumblingly ineffective. Until methods of sourcing change on this beat, and sources outside government are regarded as credible and newsworthy, the officials of State, Defense, the White House, and the intelligence community will set the public agenda on national security stories.

One weapon these groups hold over journalists is secrecy. Some of the information journalists need to explain military and diplomatic events remains closed to them because of the system of classification established by the executive branch. The press is also constrained by such statutes as the Atomic Energy Act and the Espionage Act, and by key judicial decisions that limit press freedom. A course on the press and national security must therefore describe the legal environment in which official secrecy can thrive despite the First Amendment.

While few would deny that a press free enough to challenge government on fundamental policy questions is necessary for democracy, the secrecy imposed by the nuclear regime limits that freedom in a number of ways. Although opposition to governmental prior restraints is central to the concept of a free press, such restraints have been sanctioned by the courts to protect national security. The system of classification that has grown up since the Manhattan Project and the end of World War II has created an enormous body of information that is off limits to the public and press. The Freedom of Information Act does not remedy this problem, as it contains a major exemption that keeps classified materials away from the public. Potential sources of classified information inside government are intimidated into keeping silent by employment contracts that limit their First Amendment rights, and by fear of prosecution under the Espionage Act and the Atomic Energy Act.

Journalists cannot publish what they do not know, yet the First Amendment has not been viewed by the courts as providing the press with any special right of access to gather information that touches on national security. Without accurate information on national security to print or broadcast, press freedom is a hollow liberty. Oddly, rather than fight against the regime of secrecy, the journalistic establishment has generally accepted the right of government to prior restraint of the press in time of national security threat, and it has reached an accommodation with the system of classification by accepting as a poor substitute the occasional leaked secret document.

T o encompass these various issues, an academic course on the press and national security might cover the following subjects:

- A discussion of the myth of journalistic objectivity, with examples of how the mirror-to-the-world model is inadequate to explain why stories are covered differently in different media
- A description of the many functions performed by the U.S. press, including that of occasional adversary to government, supporter of the status quo in foreign and defense policy, creator of the discourse that describes the nuclear regime, floater of trial balloons, tool in bureaucratic battles, framer of events, and reinforcer of the image of the enemy
- A discussion of the processes and traditions of journalism that govern the work of U.S. reporters, including patriotism, competition, careerism, deadline competition, definition of news, and self-censorship in the face of government pressure
- A presentation of case studies in which the quality of press cover-

age played a role in the outcome of an event with national security implications, such as the decision to deploy medium-range missiles in Europe in 1979, the Cuban missile crisis, the U2 affair, and the cancellation of deployment of the neutron bomb
- A historical review of coverage of the Soviet Union, with emphasis on the problems that have historically confronted U.S. journalists trying to report from Moscow and the changes under Gorbachev that have opened up the flow of information to the Western press
- An assessment of coverage of the peace movement, with an explanation of why the press has paid so little attention to its activities

By the conclusion of such a course, students should recognize how and why the government and the press have, together, limited the marketplace of ideas on national security issues. This should lead to a greater understanding of how policy has been made in this area and how information is a weapon that rivals the atom in its potency. The students should never again assume that any single product of daily journalism can provide an objective or dispassionate view of U.S.-USSR relations and the arms race or of developments in Eastern Europe. In short, they should become more sophisticated consumers of national security news and better equipped to participate in the shaping of policy, whether as activists, politicians, specialists, or journalists.

26

PREPARING CHILDREN FOR PEACE

LANA L. HOSTETLER

In the early childhood years, from birth until age eight, peace education is primarily a matter of providing high-quality experiences that ensure healthy growth and development. During these years, young children acquire the basic skills necessary to become lifelong thinkers and learners. They also begin to build value systems that will allow them to become life-long peaceful citizens. As children develop autonomy, trust, and positive self-esteem, they can also begin to develop empathy, compassion, and internal tools for peacefully resolving conflict.

Young children do not acquire these strengths by themselves. They require adult assistance with their emotional, social, cognitive, and physical development and for their basic survival. Indeed, if they cannot trust that others will meet their basic needs in a consistent, positive fashion, they may not be able to develop socially and emotionally. Children who do not trust themselves or others are less likely to develop skills that allow them to exist peacefully as adults.

Adults who care for young children, whether they are parents or child care professionals, must promote the development of the whole child. Group care settings such as a crèche, a preprimary classroom, a Head Start program, or a family day-care home frequently provide the child's first encounter with children in groups. In these settings, child care professionals should focus on the individual child's learning, problem solving and socialization. Too often, however, these environments focus primarily on the group's collective acquisition of academic skills and exclude other significant developmental needs. Children who must function as part of a group do not necessarily learn how to function within a group. When all the children in a group must simultaneously but individually perform the task, social interaction is limited and problem solving largely negligible. Inappropriate rules and time constraints may prevent these children from learning any social skills other than how to passively follow rules or aggressively defy them.

This essay was first published in *Peace Review* 2:2 (1990).

The National Association for the Education of Young Children (NAEYC) has outlined basic principles for managing and evaluating developmentally appropriate child care programs. The association advocates developing programs around children's needs rather than expecting young children to adapt to and learn well from any approach.

Developmentally appropriate practices are very helpful in preparing young children for peaceful living. These are experiences that allow children choices, provide hands-on exploration of materials and ideas, and let them work both independently and in small groups. Such practices assist all domains of the child's development: physical, cognitive, social, and emotional. The experiences help children gain confidence in their ability to succeed at appropriate tasks, which encourages them to engage in worthwhile endeavors with and for others. Adults can help young children state their problems and resolve them through peaceful means such as negotiation. With very young children, adults need to provide the words for expressing emotions, including anger. Adults should model appropriate social skills and provide examples of negotiation, mediation, collaboration, and nonphysical self-expression. For example, when two young children are sharing building blocks and they begin to quarrel because they both want all the blocks, they will often physically express their desires. They may even use blocks as weapons to ensure their own success. A teacher can coach the children with words such as, "Tell her you want some of the blocks too," while suggesting other problem-solving techniques, such as collaborating to build together. High-quality early childhood guidance is a major step toward preparing young children for peace.

Not all young children, however, have access to such programs. Not all elementary and secondary schools value the development of the whole child. And not all of a child's learning takes place in school or group care. To prepare all young children for peaceful living, we must consider circumstances at home, in the community, and in society at large.

In the United States, two disturbing trends influence early childhood development. First, an increasing proportion of young children live in poverty and are thus at risk educationally, socially, and in all other aspects. For these young children, positive experiences in group care may be offset by the day-by-day survival issues that they and their parents face.

A second disturbing trend is the increase of violence in children's experiences. For many young children violence is part of daily life in the home or the neighborhood. Other children watch violence on television. Children's programming has become increasingly violent in the last decade following deregulation by the Federal Communication Commission. Media research confirms this with two critical findings: The amount of air time allotted to war cartoons has increased from 1.5 hours per week in 1982 to 34 hours per week in 1986. The incidence of violent acts has increased from 18.6 per hour in 1980 to 26.4 per hour today. Effects of TV violence are exacerbated by interactive war games such as the Nintendo electronic battlefield, or combat figures like GI Joe and Teenage Mutant Ninja Turtles. Many of these figures have names and complete life stories. They are very real to young children who have difficulty separating fantasy from reality.

The effect of media violence on young children is well documented. NAEYC, in its position statement Media Violence in Children's Lives, states:

> Children may become less sensitive to the pain and suffering of others; they may become more fearful of the world around them; and they may be more likely to behave in aggressive or harmful ways toward others.

The statement recommends that policymakers and broadcasters, early childhood professionals, and parents take action to reduce both the availability and the effects of media violence for children.

Because young children's play and learning are deeply rooted in their experiences, violence profoundly effects them. Adults should minimize children's exposure to violence and increase the availability of experiences and materials that stimulate positive, imaginative play rather than imitative violence. I once asked a young child wearing a man's blazer in the dress-up corner of a classroom what he thought he could put in the inside pocket of the jacket. He replied: "A knife or a gun—that's what . . . you put there." Child care workers encounter such examples on a daily basis. They must be prepared to suggest alternatives that help the child value himself and his family. Adults must also go beyond the walls of the child care center to try to eradicate violence in the community or social systems. Otherwise, children can get the impression that violent actions are necessary for survival.

E arly childhood education must help children form good relationships with family members, classmates, and people within and outside of their immediate communities. Young children of all cultures learn the language and value system of their dominant culture. In today's global society, they must also learn how to join people who may be very different from themselves as part of a peaceful world. Such learning begins with nonbiased, positive information about the child's own group, setting, and community. Young children need to feel comfortable, knowledgeable, and secure in their own environment before they can understand others.

It is often difficult for people who work with very young children to envision the children as they will be rather than as they are. While parents and teachers may fantasize about what they hope the children will become as adults, those fantasies frequently project what the parents or teachers themselves are, living in the world as they know it today. Yet the world has changed dramatically since our own early childhoods and, indeed, during our adult lives. Consequently, we need to remember that we are primarily preparing children for change and for existence in a world that is becoming increasingly homogeneous and increasingly diverse.

The recent events in Eastern Europe illustrate this point. One's ideas about the Berlin Wall depend on one's age. For young children, the Wall is a concrete structure like the ones they erect with their blocks and knock down with their hands. For adults, the Wall is an abstract symbol and a physical barrier. We all must reappraise our perceptions of the Wall and restructure our fundamental beliefs, considering the events surrounding its dismantling. Our hopes for peaceful coexistence can be fulfilled. People we may have once considered enemies were in fact struggling to achieve this crucial juncture in world history. Sadly, many adults are not able to do such a restructuring. Their inability to assimilate and accommodate change may have roots in their early childhood, which illustrates the importance of preparing young children to be lifelong thinkers and learners who can cope with change, growth, and different people.

G ood early childhood programs teach young children how to work with people who are different from themselves. Young children can learn to appreciate and value differences. They are not born making guns with their fists, nor are they born believing that race, gender, nationality, religion, age, sexual orientation, or political philosophy create ladders of superiority and inferiority. These ideas are the result of interactions with adults, the media, their environment, and culture. Early childhood programs should promote antibias by discussing rather than ignoring the differences among children, and by highlighting the value of diversity rather than focusing the children on sameness.

Neither parents nor early childhood professionals can leave the task of preparing young children for change and peace to chance. Children's basic needs must be met and their self-esteem developed. They must feel valued, and they must believe their feelings, including their fears, doubts, and questions, merit thought and answers. The monster under the bed, the fear of an earthquake, or the fear of being taken hostage are very real for young children. They should not be dismissed by adults as mere imaginative fantasies. Young children I observed after a highly publicized hostage situation dramatized protective and flight behavior in their play at school and showed fear and clinging to their parents. Thoughtfully addressing fears such as these allays children's immediate trauma and develops their skills for living in harmony with themselves and others. It is important for children to be able to imaginatively explore their feelings by dramatizing a disaster. It is also important for them to resolve problems and ambivalences through play.

Adults can prepare young children for peace by cooperating with each other. Children mirror the problem-solving and negotiating techniques they see adults practice. If adults discipline children violently, or interact violently in the presence of young children, the children will accept violence as a natural part of the world. If discipline is punitive and inconsistent rather than directed toward self-control, the children may not be able to refrain from practicing violence themselves. If their environment is unpredictable and their basic survival needs are unmet, they may see the world as chaotic and responsive only to power and violence. If they feel themselves powerless, they may seek to exert power by exercising violence.

Early education for peace is thus not so much a matter of teaching young children *about* peace as it is enabling them to *be* peaceful. Fortunately, there are many resources available for adults who want to promote peace education in the early childhood years. Resources have been developed by organizations such as Concerned Educators Allied for a Safe Environment (CEASE), the Stop War Toys Campaign, the National Association for the Education of Young Children, the Association for Childhood Education International, and Action for Children's Television. Books such as *Discover the World* by Hopkins and *Who's Calling the Shots?* and *Helping Young Children Understand Peace, War and the Nuclear Threat,* both by Carlsson-Paige and Levin, provide parent and teacher materials for helping children become peaceful. The Association of Booksellers for Children is currently compiling an exhibit of children's books about peaceful living. They will print a bookmark with a short bibliography of significant books in this area for distribution in bookstores throughout the United States. These efforts are mirrored across the world as early childhood educators and parents grapple with the increasing need for resources that promote peaceful habits in children.

The Stop War Toys Campaign printed a poster that reads: "Peace Begins on the Playground." Becoming peaceful does indeed begin with the earliest childhood experiences. In order for these years to be the most positive, the most likely to nurture peaceful individuals, we must recognize our responsibility for arranging appropriate programs and experiences for young children. In addition, we must be sensitive to our role in advocating and providing all young children with the opportunity to grow into adulthood free from violence, hunger, and fear. Only when we are able to do so can we genuinely believe that all young children will have the desire, skill, and opportunity to participate in a peaceful world.

27

LISTEN TO WOMEN, FOR A CHANGE

BIRGIT BROCK-UTNE

Women working for peace today share three general characteristics: they use nonviolent techniques, actions and strategies; they value all life in nature, especially the life of children; and their work is transpolitical, often aimed at reaching people in the opposite camp. I would like to examine each of these characteristics and point out their effectiveness in various peace campaigns.

The radical feminist paradigm rests on the idea that one's personal beliefs generate political statements. The feminist movement does not attempt to overthrow any particular government but rather to displace one way of thinking with another. The tools of feminism are necessarily nonviolent, and they harken back to a long tradition of women's nonviolent campaigns.

A hundred years ago, the great Austrian peace hero Bertha Von Suttner said that if you want peace you must prepare for peace, not for war. She persistently debated her friend Alfred Nobel, who earned great fortunes on dynamite and weapons and who propagated the masculine and illogical idea that one gets peace by preparing for war. "I am doing more for peace with my cannons than you are doing with your speeches on peace and disarmament," Nobel once wrote to Bertha.

Von Suttner's famous pacifist novel *Die Waffen Nieder* (*Lay Down Your Arms*) inspired an outpouring of support for pacifist ideals. Leo Tolstoy wrote to Von Suttner, "[As] the book *Uncle Tom's Cabin* by Harriet Beecher Stowe contributed to the abolition of slavery, God give that your book will serve the same purpose when it comes to the abolition of war." The czar of Russia responded to *Die Waffen Nieder* by calling a peace conference, in 1898 in The Hague, to form an alliance of nations to abolish war. Pope Leo XI, in response to the book, advocated the same. So Von Suttner and other peace activists traveled from country to country promoting the czar's conference. A peace movement began, but the more offi-

This essay was first published in *Peace Review* 2:4 (1990).

cial its conferences became the less concerned they were with "the abolition of the instruments of murder" that Von Suttner advocated. Politicians
discussed arms reduction while, adhering to Alfred Nobel's illogical thinking, they rearmed for war. Military leaders argued that women should keep
quiet about important questions of war and peace. They labeled men who
did not want to go to war "men in petticoats."

Two world wars ensued, killing millions of people. Over a hundred
wars have since been fought around the world. Sexist slandering of pacifists persists. In societies where women are devalued, associating nonviolence with women has degraded the principle of nonviolence. Now, more
and more, women hold cabinet-level positions in governments and influential jobs in corporations. As women gain status, the status of nonviolence
also strengthens. Nonviolent strategies are generally attributed to people
like Mohandas Gandhi and Martin Luther King. But the most extensive use
of nonviolent strategies has been by women. Gandhi admitted that he
learned most of his nonviolent actions from women, in particular, British
suffragettes.

Europe is currently undergoing democratic changes brought about by
nonviolent means: disarmament, reductions in military spending, and
weapons dismantling. The Russian leadership now echoes the ideals Von
Suttner once shared with Tolstoy and the Russian czar. This new political
climate was not achieved by one leader alone; it grew out of strong popular
and government movements in both the East and the West. Women have
done much of the groundwork, even though their efforts tend to be over-
looked. In one case, for instance, where signatures on peace petitions were
collected mostly by women, a man officially handed over the signatures in
a televised ceremony.

N onviolent strategies call for creative application of the feminist belief
that means and ends are the same. Women find power in the everyday
activities of the powerless. Women recently applied the tedious chore of
shopping to strategically promote a caring market behavior in businesses.
When New Zealand's Labor government banned ships carrying nuclear
weapons from its harbors, newspapers reported that the U.S. government
planned to boycott New Zealand goods. Women in the United States and
Canada countered the boycott with a girlcott, staging rallies outside big
supermarkets to get women to request and purchase New Zealand goods.
While boycotts are effective ways to block products from oppressive or
exploitive producers, girlcotts encourage the purchase of goods from
socially beneficial sources.

Partnership societies tend to be the most peaceful and the least hierar-
chic and authoritarian, according to author Riane Eisler. In her book *The
Chalice and the Blade,* Eisler traces the roots of present global crises to a
fundamental shift in prehistory from life-sustaining technologies to tech-

nologies designed to dominate and destroy. Her book tells how Western culture originated in a male-female partnership, then veered into a bloody 5,000-year detour of androcratic rule. Eisler considers today's mounting global problems to be logical consequences of dominator societies that are also technologically highly developed. Because of their orientation, these societies cannot solve their problems.

Consider the field of forestry. Throughout the Third World forestry is conducted scientifically and unidimensionally, dominated by industrial plantations and reserve management. Vandana Shiva, in a report on environmental and developmental issues for women, claimed that the scientific approach often reduces forestry to calculations of timber yields that feed commercial and industrial demands. Ecologically, as well as socially, this approach takes a serious toll. Monocultures replace multispecies forests, disturbing natural balances that sustain people's, especially women's, needs.

To Third World women trees provide fuel, food, and fodder. These women learn which trees make the best fuelwood, which dry fast and burn well, which retain moisture in the soil, and which give the best foliage for fodder or fertilizer. Their knowledge and skills of natural resource management could contribute significantly to environmental rehabilitation. Women also work well collectively, which has enabled many women to run successful sustainable development projects. Some notable ones are the Kenyan Green Belts reforestation project and the Baldia sanitation project in Pakistan.

If peace is understood to mean the absence of structural violence, and we look at the world as a whole, the global status of peace is worsening. Recent surveys of poor Third World countries often attribute deteriorating social conditions to structural adjustment programs of agencies like the International Monetary Fund (IMF). It is important to find out who bears the burden of structural adjustments and who profits from them. Women and children continue to suffer from mounting debt burdens that favor cash crops. IMF conditionalities starve out the softer sectors of poor countries, such as health and education.

Virginia Woolf wrote, in her beautiful novel *Three Guineas,* "As a woman I have no country. As a woman I want no country. As a woman my country is the whole world." Since women often think of each other as mothers or daughters, and since they lack military training in defining enemies, women have developed a tradition of reaching out to other women in so-called opposing camps.

At the beginning of World War I, women from thirteen countries assembled in The Hague to protest the war and discuss ways to have it stopped. These women came from both warring and neutral nations. They formed the Women's International League for Peace and Freedom

(WILPF), writing a manifesto that included a proposal for a permanent institution of arbitration. The institution's first task would be to arbitrate between the two factions of the war. (This took place in 1915, before the League of Nations had been formed.) The meeting appointed two delegations of women to travel to warring and neutral states, presenting the manifesto to governments. The prime minister of one large nation replied to a delegation, "Your proposal is the most sensible which has come to this office." Another prime minister said, "I agree with you that it would be better to follow your proposal which could lead to an early end to this war than just to go on and waste more lives and damage more property."

As we know, the warring states did not adopt the WILPF manifesto. But WILPF persevered. They sent a proposal to the 1919 peace conference suggesting measures for avoiding more war. Emily Greene Balch, the first secretary-general of WILPF, received the Nobel Peace Prize in 1946. Gunnar Jahn, director of the Nobel Institute, said on presenting the prize: "It would have been extremely wise if the proposal WILPF made to the conference in 1919 had been accepted by the conference. But few of the men listened to what the women had to say. The atmosphere was too bitter and revengeful. And on top of this there was the fact that the proposal was made by women. In our patriarchal world, suggestions which come from women are seldom taken seriously. Sometimes it would be wise for men to spare their condescending smiles."

The recent history of peace activism includes many instances of women reaching out to nominal enemies. The Irish Peace Women organized tea parties for Catholic and Protestant women to get acquainted and summer camps that mixed children from both sides. In 1981, the Nordic Women for Peace invited women from the Soviet Union to join their march to Paris for peace. Unfortunately, the Soviet women who wanted to march were blocked by European governments that refused to issue them visas. Western military establishments later criticized the Nordic Women for marching in the West instead of in the Soviet Union where, the critics insisted, visas to peace marchers would be denied. So, in the summer of 1982, the Nordic Women staged a second peace march, this time to the USSR. The problems foreseen by the Western military never materialized. Still, this very successful march received little support from peace organizations that were run by men. The board of No to Nuclear Arms, for example, chose to neither endorse nor join the march, although some men who were members privately participated. Unfortunately, we are fighting male dominance within the peace movement as well as in other institutions. Establishing partnerships has only just begun.

In the future we need to work out what Riane Eisler calls a pragmatopia, which in Greek means a real place or a realizable future, in contrast to a utopia, which literally means no place. Pragmatopic-oriented women and men from the East and West, the South and North, must start building new systems on the three feminist principles of nonviolence, life as the ultimate value, and transnationalism. A pragmatopia would be governed by caring and life-enhancing values, not profit-seeking and conquering ones. Mapping out a pragmatopia that enhances the life of humans and the rest of nature can become easier if we all listen to women, for a change.

28

SAFE AS HOUSES?

PAUL CHILTON

Albert Einstein and Bertrand Russell, in their famous 1955 manifesto, told us that we have to learn to think in a new way. There was in fact a major shift in the thinking about security and foreign policy just after World War II. It was a response to the realization that physics had given us weapons that had changed the military reality. A second conceptual shift is under way now, under the influence of many factors, one of which is Soviet "new thinking."

The term "national security" has not always been with us. It was born in the 1940s in the effort to come to terms with the fact that no state could be an invulnerable, impermeable sanctuary in the age of the strategic bomber and the looming intercontinental missile. Under the new conditions there could be no defense in the traditional sense. In the aftermath of Pearl Harbor, Secretary of War Stimson asked himself whether "our basic theory of defense and reliance upon that fortress is not too static." In this awkward phrase he revealed the basis of the traditional conception of defense: the United States had been a gigantic, geographically protected fortress.

But it was not until the end of the war, in Senate hearings on the unification of the armed services, that the new concept began to be invoked as part of a policy formation process. "The abstract noun security has acquired a very concrete significance for us," remarked the chief of International Security Affairs, Joseph E. Johnson, only a few days before Hiroshima. Whereas in the House of Representatives committees of 1944 on the armed services, the term "national security" was scarcely heard at all, in the fall of 1945, in the Senate hearings, it served as a conceptual focus.

It is not uncommon for policies and actions to crystallize around some focal word or phrase. It is useful to ask what it was about the English word "security" that led Navy Secretary James Forrestal to say: "I am using the word 'security' . . . consistently and continuously rather than 'defense,'"

This essay was first published in *Peace Review* 1:2 (1989).

and Senator Johnson to tell him "I like your words national security." What was it indeed that made this word so acceptable to the political culture of the 1940s?

There are linguistic answers to this question as well as historical ones. If we want to understand what is going on when people express thoughts, new or old, we had better not shy away from the evidence of the words they use.

T he word "defense" and the word "security" make sense to us speakers of English because they are each associated with complex systems of concepts that are different but overlapping. First, defense has a distinct opposite, "attack," while security does not, and it tends to imply a static and morally approved posture on your own legitimate home ground. Second, defense is used predominantly only in a military (and sporting) context, while security has long been used in the civil, especially financial and psychological, domain. Third, and most important, security seems to be understood by reference to the basic spatial concept of the container. Many expressions in many languages utilize this concept. We are generally unaware of it but it explains why we have expressions like "secure in one's beliefs," "a hole in security," and even "security leaks" and "security penetrations," and most telling, "in the security of one's own home."

So we might guess that policymakers liked the word "security," and that the public was receptive to the word and the concepts it went with, for the following reasons. "Defense" was no longer appropriate to the new strategic realities, because it implied passivity and geographic limitations. Security on the other hand not only meshed with the civil sphere of commerce, domesticity, and well-being, it also had in common with the concept of defense the basic concept of the enclosing, embracing, and protective shell.

Its conceptual advantage in the new military age was twofold. First, security, like a container, has an inside and an outside: internal security or domestic surveillance of the enemy within, and external security or the guarding against outside forces. Second, security, like a container, has a boundary or perimeter. But this boundary or perimeter does not (unlike a traditionally understood national defense boundary) have to be the geopolitical frontiers of your national territory; it can be located where your national interests need it. It is no accident that the term "containment," promoted by George Kennan in 1947, should come to play such an important part in the U.S. foreign policy lexicon. The conceptual package that came with the word helped to structure the perceived international realities along lines discernible up to the present time.

I t has been said that Soviet President Gorbachev will for the first time pose for the West a conceptual challenge to this metaphor of security, asking: What do we want beyond the Cold War? Let us turn, then, to the most challenging concept that Gorbachev has thrown down: the "common European house." This phrase has been greeted with suspicion in the United States. Henry Kissinger has called it the most pernicious of escapist slogans. True, Gorbachev has seized some kind of initiative; it does not follow that he or any other Soviet can determine the conceptual outcome or the policies it may guide. Like the words "national security" and "containment," we have here a potent concept around which new policies can be structured.

The "European house" is a metaphor. Now metaphors are not just fancy ornaments for poets and orators. We use them every day for the intricate business of understanding the world and communicating with one another. There are two features of metaphor: one cognitive, the other interpersonal. From the cognitive point of view, metaphors are used in communication to understand situations we do not understand in terms of situations we do understand. Metaphors new and old tend to be built out of basic human concepts arising from bodily interaction with the environment: standing upright, being in a containing space, moving from one point to another. The container-based metaphors are, as we have seen, crucial in conceptualizing international relations. Moreover, you can utilize special sorts of containers significant to humans at basic level. The house is one of the most potent of these.

From the interpersonal point of view, metaphors are used in face-to-face interaction to lubricate the friction of contact between individuals—to create common ground with an interlocutor and to evade direct reference to a taboo or threatening subject.

Extrapolate to the political context and one can see immediately how metaphor is not an empty device in political rhetoric but may be an important diplomatic device. One of the reasons, moreover, why metaphor works to ease interpersonal contact is that it leaves room for the negotiation of specific meanings and references. It is this property that can be exploited by anyone engaging with Gorbachev's metaphor—indeed, it is being exploited to explore new thoughts about European security.

Houses are conceptualized differently from culture to culture. There are variable stereotypes as to size, shape, layout, surrounding space, and surrounding barriers; and there are also rules about coming and going, visiting and receiving, cohabiting, and so forth. A North American stereotype, for example, is probably a unitary boxlike structure containing a nuclear family, with a front and a back, a yard, a fence, and, increasingly, a security system. Map that onto states or groups of states, and certain kinds of thoughts are likely to follow.

What kind of house are we thinking of? Which of the many component features of the rich schema that makes up what we think of as a house are mapped into political realities? In particular, what does one make of the idea of a home that is common? In his book *Perestroika,* Gorbachev writes in response to this last question as follows:

> Home is common, that is true, but each family has its own apartment, and there are different entrances, too . . . it is only together, collectively, and by following the sensible norms of coexistence that the Europeans can save their home, protect it against a conflagration and other calamities, make it better and safer, and maintain it in proper order.

So the model here is not so much the suburban villa as the apartment block.

Three thorny issues about a new security for Europe that the metaphor raises can be bluntly put. First, is the United States going to stay there— that is, continue to define its own security space as having a perimeter running through the center of the European continent? Second, is the Soviet Union going to be brought into the European space—that is, continue to define its security interests as necessitating a colonial grip on the Eastern European countries? Third, what of German reunification? These questions tend to be intertwined in reality, and the interesting thing about the metaphor is that it makes it possible to think about them together.

Taking the third question first, the starting point for Germans was, it is true, the question of the dissection of Europe. The metaphor makes it possible to explore this matter. Gorbachev recounts how he asked the West German federal president what he understood by a common European home:

Weizsacker: "It is a reference point which helps us visualize the way things should be arranged in this common European home [doubtless he said Haus]. Specifically, the extent to which the apartments in it will be accessible for reciprocal visits."

Gorbachev: "You are quite right. But not everyone may like receiving night-time visitors."

Weizsacker: "We also aren't especially pleased to have a deep trench passing through a common living-room."

Not only is it taken for granted that the house here is an apartment block; that image makes it possible to raise questions about the free movement of peoples and about the post–World War II division of Europe in general and Germany in particular. The reason Gorbachev published this dialogue in his *Perestroika* was clearly to rebut more direct expressions of hopes for German reunification. Soviets dislike that prospect as much as Americans do.

The second question has recently been posed by the Bonn-based German-Soviet Forum. The conservative Alfred Dregger points out, for example, that the people of the Soviet Union live not only in a European but also in an Asiatic house. True, the Soviet Union is firmly linked geographically to Europe, but it is more than a European power, it is also a great Asiatic power.

This would mean that a new Europe should extend from Portugal not to the Urals but to the Polish-Soviet border; it would stand between the houses of the two superpowers. However, Dregger demands that in this European house there should be "open doors and windows—and no walls to . . . divide us as is still the case at the Brandenburg gate." There remains the problem of imagining that the Soviet Union has two houses. Moreover, in the thirty-five-nation Helsinki conference on European security issues, the Soviet Union has a claim to recognition as a participant in a wider European process. Conceptually, the problem is made difficult, because, despite Dregger's open doors and windows, the house is naturally conceived as a rigid structure or block that could dissolve one internal wall only to erect external ones. Both the United States and the Soviet Union resent this.

There are ways, however, of exploring these matters further, and it is within the conceptual schema of the house that the Germans have done so. The economic and potential political integration of Western Europe in 1992 leads them to ask whether a joining of the two Germanies becomes thereby closer or more remote. Chancellor Kohl, in an interview with *Die Welt,* has declared: "I consider it quite out of the question that we will come any closer to the unity of Germany, unless it be under a European roof." In subsequent articles, the newspaper asked quite reasonably what on earth this ambiguous utterance could be construed as implying, and proceeded to outline a scenario.

The joining of East Germany to West Germany (with renunciation of statehood), or association with the integrated European Community (with renunciation of adherence to the Warsaw Pact), is in the near term inconceivable. One scenario, which draws on signs of change in Eastern Europe and which is widely regarded as realistic, goes as follows. In the East, it is suggested, a similar development is in train as in the West. The Eastern European countries are drawing closer together, not to an integrated community, to be sure, rather to a club like the European Free Trade Association. Some countries are further advanced than others in this, and some are much more ready to look west.

According to this scenario, neither the Western nor the loosely knit Eastern countries relinquish their alliances and economic ties. The DDR remains in the Warsaw Pact and COMECON, the FRG in NATO and the European Community.

But cultural and economic ties grow denser along the lines of historic bonds. The clearest possible case at the present time, however, is not the two Germanys but the two halves of Austro-Hungary. Hungary's reformist Imre Posgay goes even further in orientation to the West, saying that the political division of Europe has been an error, that Gorbachev's idea of the common European house has "opened the doors," and that Hungary would in a literal sense want to purchase an entrance ticket!

Hungary's economic, demographic, and cultural ties with Austria make that a possibility when Austria applies for European Community membership in summer 1989. All this may point, frighteningly for some, to a German-speaking central core. One thing that can be said, however, is that it is not isolated but part of a general process of simultaneous loosening and reforming of ties across the continent. The German advocates of this model point out precisely that it is designed to avoid the justified fear in the East and West of a reunified German empire.

As *Die Welt* put it, this is not a closed container *(Gehause)*. It is still a house, but arrived at by focusing on the roof; Dregger's open windows and absent walls are beside the point.

The prospect of a new political, cultural, and economic grouping in Europe is what now promises security. This is a concept of domestic security, not military security. West German Foreign Minister Genscher, at the opening session of the talks on conventional forces in Europe in Vienna in March 1989, expressed agreement with Soviet Foreign Minister Shevardnadze that at these negotiations it is not merely a matter of arms reductions, but of overcoming the division of Europe. In other words, security will not lie simply in the negative absence of arms but in the positive domestic image of the house.

The point is made forcibly and urgently by none other than Henry Kissinger. On the one hand, Kissinger certainly regards Gorbachev's soothing metaphor of a home stretching from the Atlantic to the Urals as dangerous propaganda designed to undermine Franco-German military cooperation and the modernization of NATO short-range nuclear weapons. Nonetheless he does take up the conceptual challenge and makes specific policy proposals within the metaphorical framework of the house and not within that suggested by the other dominant container metaphor: "fortress Europe."

Like Genscher, Kissinger sees a process in which we must make at least conceptual links between arms control and a view of Europe's political future. The model looks like this. First, a European "home" from the Urals to the Atlantic is unthinkable. It must either include both superpowers or exclude both. The former is not dissimilar to the scenario discussed in the German press. The latter is not dissimilar to the position of the European peace movement and is what Kissinger calls a "road toward a stabler future." The "house" would, as in Dregger's model, extend from Portugal to Poland, which implies the abandonment of Russian control over

Eastern European countries. Third, the two military alliances would continue to exist but would be reduced in armaments and denied the right of intervention. Fourth, the "core of a new European construction" would be Western European integration, with Eastern European states having economic but not (for a while) political association.

By April 1989, the Kissinger concept was having some impact on the emergent new foreign policy of the Bush administration. On March 27, Secretary of State Baker announced that the administration was considering discussions with Moscow about a new political arrangement for Eastern Europe. The gist was that Moscow would loosen its grip over the Eastern countries in exchange for some sort of U.S. pledge that NATO would not move into Eastern Europe or undermine the Soviet Union. One question is whether such a deal implies a formalization of some new status for the Soviet Union. Another is what kind of interventions and underminings is the United States so generously offering to refrain from?

A lthough the Kissinger concept is a shift in the transition from the postwar national security and containment concept, it does not finally resolve the question of Europe's relation to the United States and the USSR. What it does do is make a new form of European security space between the two superpowers thinkable in the context of U.S. foreign policy. The house metaphor may help the Europeans themselves think of new relationships. Once you conceive of your land as a house, you are for one thing no longer merely in someone else's backyard.

It is odd to think of U.S. citizens living in the same house or having an apartment in the same block. The Russians could be neighbors in the same block or in the block next door. What is clear is that Europeans will not want their land treated as a piece of real estate, and they will not want any subleasing or absentee landlords. A European house must be managed by its occupants, indeed by the owner-occupants. The time is past for a condominium run by a superpower management corporation.

There are other salutary new thoughts to be had from the strangely bourgeois metaphor of domestic security. Cleanliness, order, and control over the dumping of garbage point to the environmental concerns that have already characterized new thinking about common security. But let us not forget that the house is a container image and that containers can imprison and shut out. We need images of openness, even though openness is also the conceptual basis of vulnerability. The Soviet press has already referred to a wider "common house"—the global ecology of which we are part. Let us not forget finally that metaphors mask basic experience. One day it may be possible to say national security and think not of survivable missiles but of the survival of real people in need of food, health care, and shelter.

29

AFRICAN AMERICANS
AND WORLD PEACE

JAMES N. KARIOKI

The world has recently witnessed on its TV screens the killing of tens of thousands of Iraqis in the southern Iraqi desert by the awesome high-technology weapons of the United States. Because the U.S. troops were never required to engage the enemy at close range, they experienced a death rate lower than that normally experienced by young men and women of that age back home. It is said that in the bars in the United States, which normally show football games on TV, the Gulf War was treated as an especially exciting game, with the patrons applauding the nightly news of the score.

It is possible that African Americans, both in the United States and on the ground in Iraq or Saudi Arabia, had a somewhat different perspective; after all, the people being killed were poor, unfree, and nonwhite. And as the major world conflict of the last years of the twentieth century shapes up as a conflict between the poor, and largely nonwhite, of the Third World against the massive power of the United States, it is possible that African Americans will be able to see the issues and dangers more clearly than their European American counterparts and feel a more poignant sympathy with the unfortunate of the world. And the experience of the African American has another useful attribute: that which concerns the effective use of nonviolence.

S ome months ago a Lithuanian spokesman was asked how his countrymen would react if the Soviet Union were to use military force to thwart their quest for independence. He retorted that they would respond nonviolently, and that they had learned their lesson from Martin Luther King, Jr. In his commentary several weeks earlier, John Chancellor on "NBC Nightly News" had also pointed to King's legacy among the Eastern Europeans who sang "We Shall Overcome" in tongues we did not understand but whose political sentiments were clear to us all.

When Martin Luther King, Jr. first took a public position in opposition

This essay was first published in *Peace Review* 3:2 (1991).

to the Vietnam War in April 1967, there was an outcry of criticism. The most pointed criticism against King was the claim that, by involving himself in the Vietnam controversy, he was overstepping his bounds. In short, speaking out on Vietnam was viewed not only as betrayal to the civil rights progress but, even worse, as unpatriotic. King was irritated but he did not retract. To project King in such a narrow perspective was misleading; it did injustice to his global vision and to the multidimensional aspects of the movement that he pioneered. To King's mind, the war in Vietnam and the domestic war on poverty were inseparable.

But what about actual involvement in international affairs? We think of King as having gone international in 1964 when he won the prestigious Nobel Peace Prize. This perception is correct to the extent that the prize was a recognition of King's contribution to peaceful social change. But the award was more; it was a challenge to continue to advance the cause of human welfare as a spokesperson for the downtrodden of the world. He accepted the challenge when he argued that the war was a betrayal to humanity in general and to him personally. The war constituted an injustice, and an injustice anywhere was a threat to justice everywhere. King felt that he had no choice but to speak out in search of a solution, for to do otherwise was to be complicit with evil. As he put it, there comes a time when silence becomes betrayal.

It may be that King's point of view was influenced by an earlier experience in his African ancestral homeland. In 1957, King was one of the dignitaries who attended the celebration of Ghanaian independence from colonial rule, Ghana being the first country to achieve self-rule in black Africa. On that occasion, Kwame Nkrumah proclaimed that the hard-won freedom for his country was meaningless and incomplete until *all* of Africa was free. Nkrumah envisioned an independent and federated Africa that stretched from coast to coast and from Cape to Cairo. White supremacy in Southern Africa stood in the way of the ambitious aspiration.

A gainst this background, it is fitting that the two most internationally visible African American personalities of the last two decades have been King's lieutenants: Andrew Young and Jesse Jackson. On the other hand, it is not entirely an accident that the international preoccupation of the two disciples turned out to be the issue of white supremacy in Southern Africa. After all, apartheid has been the most humiliating form of insult to justice and the most blatant affront to the humanity of the black race. It is in this region of the world that African Americans have shown most dramatically their sensitivity to the suffering of others.

For decades, apartheid supporters insisted that white supremacy was a South African internal matter. To the extent that the Republic of South Africa was sovereign, the argument went, the outside world was meddling in a domestic issue by decrying policies that led to racial injustice within its borders. But the Black World in Africa and the diaspora had a different perception. In its view, such a narrow definition of apartheid was unacceptable on the grounds that, like Nazism and slavery before it, institutionalized racism anywhere transcended political and legal designations. After all, apartheid violated the Universal Declaration of Human Rights. By this definition, apartheid may have been internal to white South Africa but, to the Black World, racism was supranational. The stage was set for a classic battle between an irresistible force and an immovable barrier.

The proapartheid strategy of claiming apartheid as an internal matter in white-dominated Southern Africa clearly has not worked. In the eyes of the proapartheid forces, the worst happened when their policy became a matter of global concern. If internationalization of apartheid was its omen for dangers to come, the question that comes to mind is: How did it transform into such a volatile universal issue? To put the same question in another way, how did apartheid break out of national horizons?

The antiapartheid movement traversed the line of "national" demarcations in 1957 when Nkrumah took the occasion of Ghana's independence day to proclaim that the cherished freedom for his country was incomplete and meaningless until the entire continent was free. As other African states became independent, African statesmen affirmed their allegiance to the doctrine of freedom indivisible for Africa by pledging that, like Nkrumah, they too would devote themselves to the liberation of the African "South." On that eventful day in 1957, apartheid took a giant step in the process of becoming African; it was well on its way to becoming a *continental* issue.

After 1963, the newly formed Organization of African Unity (OAU) became the collective body through which postcolonial Africa consolidated strategies against apartheid. At the United Nations, diplomatic efforts focused on demands that the Security Council declare apartheid a threat to international peace. As a result of this collective pressure, Western powers reluctantly imposed an arms embargo on South Africa in 1963. In time, the OAU became the continental organ to confer or deny political legitimacy to South African developments. Apartheid had entered full force the hallways of global, diplomatic intrigues.

South Africa turned into a profoundly embarrassing predicament for the Western democracies. Western powers found themselves victims to contradictions of their own ideologies. On the one hand, democratic principles suggested support for the antiapartheid thrust. On the other hand, imperatives of capitalism dictated otherwise. In the face of this Western dialectic (some say hypocrisy), Africans managed to force exclusion of South Africa from many international forums but, to their bewilderment, they fell short of convincing Western governments to impose economic sanctions against the Republic. Democratic justice was sacrificed on the altar of economic greed. Nonetheless, African pressure kept the issue of apartheid alive until tangible and wholehearted support arrived from their

ancestral brothers, the African American contingency in the United
States.

I n the 1970s, white supremacy in Southern Africa became a target for
President Jimmy Carter in the context of his crusade for global human
rights. South Africa accused Carter of irresponsibility; but a more painful
betrayal, from the point of view of the minority regimes of Southern
Africa, was Carter's appointment of Andrew Young as the U.S. ambassador to the United Nations. Elevation of an eloquent black man to the
stature of a superpower representative was more than white supremacy
could stomach. Young's version of statesmanship and his candor were too
much of an unveiled affront to the essence of apartheid. Particularly intimidating was Young's background of civil rights activism of the 1960s when
he was King's confidant. In white-dominated South Africa, alarm became
hysteria when Young made it clear that, despite his diplomatic assignment
in the UN, he intended to continue to speak out on race issues.

As fate would have it, Young's initial target became Southern
Rhodesia. His public call for the principle of one-man-one-vote in that
country prompted white Rhodesians to predict collective doom and to
retreat to a siege mentality. In their racial bigotry, they proclaimed Young a
threat to white people throughout the world, for "black power surgery"
could only mean a "terminal prognosis for the white man." Shortly thereafter, Rhodesia fell to black rule and became Zimbabwe. No holocaust has
occurred for whites.

In the 1980s, the Reagan administration accommodated apartheid by
its constructive engagement policy. Yet the pressure against apartheid did
not subside; it merely shifted from the White House to the U.S. Congress,
where antiapartheid forces were spearheaded by the congressional Black
Caucus and, in particular, by Representative Ronald V. Dellums of
Oakland, California, a district with a large black constituency.

The Black Caucus rejected as twisted the Reagan (and Margaret
Thatcher) logic that economic sanctions against South Africa would hurt
the blacks the most and the suggestion that apartheid would fade with economic growth. The Caucus supported the African stand that only sanctions
could bring apartheid to its knees once and for all. Comparatively, the argument went, transient economic hardships were a small price for black South
Africans to pay if the objective was abolition of apartheid. After all,
apartheid maimed and killed them spiritually and physically.

In 1986, the U.S. Senate overrode Reagan's presidential veto and
passed the Anti-Apartheid Act, the most restrictive legislation against
South Africa by a Western country. The Black Caucus had prevailed
against daunting opposition of the Reagan administration and the conservative elements in Congress. Less than four years later, apartheid showed the
first signs of cracking.

When George Bush took office in 1989, the U.S. political mood toward apartheid was significantly different from what Reagan had faced eight years earlier. The Black Caucus had established its credentials as the congressional conscience. On more than one occasion, it had demonstrated the political will to act as the guardian of justice for the black people of South Africa.

The U.S. public, also, was more politically aware of South Africa's brand of white supremacy, and offended by it, than it had been in 1980. Among public figures, the most vocal opponent of apartheid came to be Jesse Jackson, another African American. More than anyone else, Jackson attacked the violence of apartheid and made it an issue in the United States.

In his quest for the presidency, Jackson applied the universal ethic enunciated by his mentor, Dr. Martin Luther King: that injustice anywhere is a threat to justice everywhere. With this doctrinal proclamation, Jackson made apartheid a presidential matter, an item on the U.S. national agenda. Each of the contending presidential candidates was obliged to take a stand on apartheid. Jackson fell short of winning the nomination of his party, but on the issue of apartheid he was a victor to the extent that he forced the national Democratic Party to categorize South Africa as a terrorist state.

In the late 1970s, it was Andrew Young who had set the stage for the eventual end of white racism in Rhodesia. Almost exactly a decade later, Jackson jolted white South Africa into rethinking the future of apartheid by elevating the issue to the highest level of U.S. political debate. These black courageous "warriors" of peace were no strangers: they both were protégés of Dr. King. No doubt the latter's soul wept tears of joy and relief as Mandela walked into sunshine and freedom on February 11, 1990.

In his last published work, *Where Do We Go from Here?* King had expressed deep sorrow over our national indifference to the plight of the Third World. His concern was more than sheer altruism; he was alarmed over U.S. self-interests. He appealed for massive assistance for the Third World on the premise that to help others is, in the final analysis, to help ourselves. He felt a sense of danger for the United States—and the entire Western civilization—because of what he termed moral bankruptcy in its dealings with the less fortunate of the world. To his way of thinking, such stoic unkindness was symptomatic of an internal decay, a prelude to the demise of all great civilizations of the past.

King attributed U.S. indifference toward the less fortunate cohabitants of the earth to what he called the giant triplets: the unholy alliance of racism, materialism, and militarism. South Africa turned out to be the classic showcase of the decadence of the triplets-in action. But the Black World challenged the unholy alliance and, as a result, apartheid is now on borrowed time.

Yet there is a modern and more menacing peril to world peace than apartheid: the gross disparity in wealth between the developed world and the Third World. Saddled with a debilitating burden of debt, the Third World still fails to get a fair price for its commodities in the global market and is unable to make ends meet. Today, the Third World borrows huge sums of money merely to pay interest on old loans. As international debt has engendered economic paralysis in the Third World, it finds itself running desperately up the down escalator.

The United States has not been a kind and gentle nation at home or abroad. It is true that individuals and private organizations have extended substantial efforts to relieve suffering among crisis-stricken peoples such as in Ethiopia and the Sahel. It is equally true, however, that our financial and government institutions have played their part in perpetuating poverty around the world. Indeed, the United States has the dubious distinction of being at the vanguard of the forces keeping the Third World in what economic historians have referred to as "debt peonage."

The 1980s were once dubbed the "decade of despair" in Africa, most of Asia, and Latin America. A sense of helplessness, defeat, and frustration pervaded the Third World—occasionally erupting into explosive, collective anger. The Third World sentiments of the decade were summed up by Julius Nyerere of Tanzania when he asked a rhetorical but morally indicting question: "Must we starve our children to pay our debts?" In 1989, UNICEF reported that in the previous year, half a million Third World children actually died as a result of Third World public cutbacks in social services in desperate efforts to service international debts. In this sense, the debt has become a killer with psychological distance. Such is the human toll of this debt, a toll reminiscent of the evil triangle. Debt peonage is an old story in the African American experience.

After two centuries of chattel slavery, most African Americans graduated to tenants or sharecroppers enslaved by debt. "The country merchant was often the large planter," Barrington Moore, Jr. explained in *Social Origins of Dictatorship and Democracy* (1966). "By making large advances of groceries to tenant or sharecropper, charging much higher prices for them than ordinary retail prices, he kept control of the work force." The result, Moore concluded, was "to make the South even more of a one-crop economy (cotton in most places) than before, as banker pressed planter and planter pressed cropper to grow crops that would quickly be turned to cash." The same trend is evident on a global scale. Third World countries are forced by the international economic order to concentrate on single cash crops, whether in the form of bananas, coffee, cocoa, peanuts, soybeans, jute, or, for that matter, coca.

The same process can now be observed worldwide as it pushes Mexican *campesinos* into Mexico City, Brazilian *caboclos* into São Paulo, Filipino peasants into Manila, the landless of Kenya into Nairobi, and Egyptian *fellahin* into Cairo. The social consequences are the same throughout the world: creation of a frustrated, volatile, urban underclass with little chance for upward mobility. This condition is no different from the U.S. ghettos in Watts, Southside Chicago, Harlem, and elsewhere.

Frustrated aspirations often prompt self-negating behavior and destructive behavior against others. Certain sets of social circumstances enhance the potential for predictable actions by some fractions of populations experiencing those conditions. An observer could have predicted that hopelessness and despair in the U.S. ghettos would lead to drug abuse and violent crimes. Similarly, any honest social critic could have foreseen that frustrated aspirations would prompt young people to mass demonstrations in Manila, Seoul, and Soweto. If violence and disruption are the language of the unheard, the disinherited of the earth pose a danger to the human community as a whole.

African Americans are uniquely positioned, as Martin Luther King once suggested, to lead America toward more humane and enlightened foreign involvements. They are qualified because their experience in a persistent struggle to overcome oppression has endowed them with an insight into the plight of the suffering. African Americans are in fact fundamentally more akin to the Third World than to the First. The Third World, of course, comprises the overwhelming majority of the human race. Yet tension between the First and Third Worlds is more basic than the East-West divide.

African Americans have the additional capacity for open-mindedness in foreign relations to the extent that they have fewer vested interests in the global economic and political status quo than their white counterparts. What is more, they are less burdened by the condescending baggage of Western cultural arrogance. Americans of African descent share the widespread respect for the Judeo-Christian heritage, but they are not entirely awe-stricken by Hebraic and European traditions. Indeed, in their view, this tradition has much to be forgiven for. The survival of the Nation of Islam in the United States under immensely adverse conditions perhaps has a message of international significance. African Americans appear to have an affinity for Islam and, presumably, can show greater tolerance for other non-Western faiths and cultures.

To claim their rightful place as the educators of America for peace, African Americans will face impediments. The first step is to cast off parochialism. Circumstances have forced African Americans to be even more inward-looking than their white compatriots. The African American experience has been one of constant struggle to claim a rightful place in America, with little time or energy for foreign involvements. Restrictions on ventures beyond U.S. borders also have been part of the black tradition. Few opportunities have existed for African Americans in diplomacy, overseas journalism and business, international education, or even tourism. As a consequence, African Americans have tended to view foreign issues as foreign: irrelevant, intimidating, and remote to their American dream betrayed.

We have come a long way since W. E. B. Dubois claimed that black Americans were ashamed of association with Africa. It is fair to say, however, that most African Americans still consider identification with Africa eccentric and esoteric. These too must be made aware that we now live in what King called a "world house," and the destiny of the sons and daughters of Africa remains inexorably intertwined.

C onversely, uncritical approval of African leaders can be as damaging to African Americans' contribution to world peace as can uncritical rejection of other ethnic leaders. While the current oppressive Kenya regime, for example, is frequently cited by Amnesty International for human rights violations, the United States has recently become the largest supplier of arms to that government. Indeed, human rights abuses in Kenya have risen almost proportionally to the U.S. presence in that country.

In any case, other African leaders have been as distasteful as Uganda's deposed Idi Amin. In viewing the world scene, African Americans should heed the advice of the American philosopher William James that humans must be tenderhearted but tough-minded. Precisely because we are tenderhearted toward human rights, we must be equally tough-minded against those who abuse them.

Now that the Cold War has ended, the global issue that will bedevil the human race in the twenty-first century is that of distribution of resources between the haves of the North and the have-nots of the Southern Hemisphere. In the post–Cold War realignments—George Bush's New World Order—the Third World does not fit in the scheme of things. It is in this context that African Americans, as a substantial Third World contingency lodged in the North, have an opportunity and a duty to save the world from disaster by sensitizing the people of the United States to the harsh predicaments that face the dispossessed of Third World.

NEW IDEAS:
NEW MODELS

30

CIVIL SOCIETY IN TRANSITION

BEVERLY WOODWARD

In the period between the Warsaw Pact invasion of Czechoslovakia in 1968 and the momentous events of 1989, *civil society* emerged as an inspirational Idea for those determined to undermine the systems of social control that reigned in Eastern Europe. This Idea provided a conceptual framework not only for activists in this region but also for analysts in the liberal democracies intrigued by the courage and inventiveness of the Eastern European opposition. At times there was a sense of envy. Civil society did not always flourish in the West. Was it possible that citizen action had a greater potential under conditions of totalitarianism (or neototalitarianism) than under conditions of democracy?

Two and a half years later, discussions of civil society seem more confused and confusing. Some former dissidents have made the claim that "civil society is in power," but others lament the impotence of civil society in today's Eastern Europe. "Civil society has been deserted, fragmented, and demobilized," writes Tomaz Mastnak of Slovenia. The eruption of violence in the region is a further complication. In some parts of former Yugoslavia, society itself is on the verge of collapse and civility has been utterly abandoned. Nearby, outbreaks of xenophobic violence in parts of Germany stir up memories of a dreadful past.

Neither the conceptual confusion nor the political chaos can easily be sorted out. I shall take on a bit of the former here, convinced, as I am, that it impedes favorable developments in the region.

L et us consider some of the functions of civil society: to create a sphere of autonomous social activity, to campaign and agitate in behalf of political and social objectives, to provide a counterweight to governmental power, and to oppose the illegitimate exercise of governmental power. Most commentators also are of the opinion that by definition a civil society behaves civilly, i.e., nonviolently.

This essay was first published in *Peace Review* 4:4 (1992).

This view of the functions of civil society implies a distinction between civil society and government. Where there is a settled constitutional order, this order delineates, in theory at least, the space occupied by each. Prior to the events of 1989, however, the constitutional framework had little relevance in the Eastern European countries. Under Communist Party rule, the provisions of a constitution could always be twisted or suppressed to serve the aims of the party. The goal of the party was that there be no sphere of activity that was not under its control. In short, civil society was prohibited. In these circumstances, the first achievement of civil society was its autogeneration.

This process and the social formations that resulted were various in the many countries and regions of Eastern Europe. In some countries the manifestations of civil society were quite limited, involving, for example, restricted numbers of intellectuals, practitioners of religion, and guardians of nationalist sentiment. But even where there were no visible independent social institutions, movements, or groups, some autonomous social activity existed. Over time such activity eroded party control and altered the environment in which that control was exercised. In many countries civil society was too weak to provide a significant counterweight to governmental power. Nevertheless, it laid the groundwork for the collapse of governmental power.

The Quaker precept "speak truth to power" describes the most celebrated aspect of the activities that undermined the perceived legitimacy of the Eastern European regimes. A great deal of activity, however, was neither so overt nor so confrontational. Sometimes it seemed quite enough to "speak truth" to an audience of one in a closed room that had been checked for surveillance equipment. In other cases it was not truth that was emphasized but "difference" and the right to be different.

The fruits of all these activities often appeared negligible. "Dissidents" were praised as amazingly courageous or dismissed as foolhardy and unrealistic, or both. In the event, it turned out that they *had* been unrealistic—not in expecting too much from their activities, but in expecting too little. Many of the independent activists and groups had limited goals (or even no goal other than self-expression and/or moral survival), and nearly all were astonished when communist power collapsed.

There were many reasons for the collapse, but the steady alteration of consciousness produced by autonomous social activity was an indispensable element. The revolutionary events of 1989 were a testimony to the power of words and symbols—not just those of writers and artists, but of people from diverse backgrounds. The totalitarian aspiration to control belief and perception was undone by the public and semipublic expression of alternative beliefs and perceptions. These were manifested not just in works of art and literature, but in humor, graffiti, religious observance, and other activities in which citizens from many sectors of society could express themselves.

The decisive and inspiriting victories of 1989–1990 seemed to provide convincing evidence of the power of citizen resistance even under very unfavorable conditions. In some cases, individuals who shortly before had been in prison or threatened with prison found themselves in official governmental positions. This movement of dissidents into government led to the claim "civil society is in power," a claim that has been criticized as an expression of triumphalism and of antidemocratic sentiment.

Mastnak can be cited again: "Only a civil society *distinct from the state* could be conceived as a body able to exercise control over it and, consequently, to define and limit state action. Civil society in power, on the contrary, represents *unlimited power*. . . . The recent developments could be described as a shift from the *parallel polis* to *polis*. Civil society . . . is the new *polis:* the good men in power have formed the republic of virtuous men."

There are several complaints here: that the claim "civil society is in power" obliterates the distinction between society and government; that the identification of government and civil society eliminates, in theory at least, the basis for opposition to governmental power; that the virtue of individuals is equated (wrongly) with governmental virtue; that this presumption of virtue makes governmental power holders intolerant of opposition and insensitive to the needs and claims of societal interest groups.

The complaints target conceptual confusion and an antidemocratic orientation. To the extent that there is confusion, it is useful to analyze how it may have arisen. In the "bad old days" civil society was decidedly excluded from state power, and the distinction between the state and civil society was clear. With the beginnings of democracy, civil society was no longer so clearly out of power. Moreover, many who had played leading roles in civil society now played leading roles in government. Since participation in civil society had been equated with civic virtue, whereas participation in government had not been, there was a need to bridge the gap between old roles and new roles. One way to do this was to characterize government as civil society in power. Further, given the previous dichotomous ways of thinking—us versus them, and so forth—it was easy to conclude that civil society no longer being clearly out of power it must be in power.

A n absolute distinction between civil society and the state is most plausible under conditions of totalitarianism—in which case there is likely to be a profound shrinking of civil society. This condition no longer holds. But a complete overlap of civil society and of government would occur, paradoxically, only where the state—and in particular its distinctive capacities for the exercise of coercion—had withered away. The state, of course, has not disappeared in Eastern Europe. The new regimes are active

(indeed highly interventionary) and coercive in the manner of all governments, but also democratic, at least in some respects. Under these conditions, civil society and the state are intermingled, though still clearly distin-
guishable.

The point of overlap of the state and civil society is the democratic
election, in which civil society expresses its wishes with respect to governance. Jaroslav Sabata makes this point with a rhetorical question pertain-
ing to the first elections in Czechoslovakia: "Do those who were elected to
parliament in the first parliamentary elections in this country for forty-two
years belong to civil society or don't they? . . . As far as I'm concerned, the
legislative bodies which have been elected are the legitimate representatives of civil society."

Sabata's claim here is that parliamentarians elected in a valid democratic manner can be considered the representatives of civil society (or political society—he does not consider the distinction important). This claim has
prima facie plausibility. To represent civil society, however, is not to *be*
civil society. There is no relation of identity between the representative and
the represented.

The claim that civil society is in power should be rejected. The representatives of civil society exercise governmental power. While exercising
power, they continue to belong as individuals to civil society, but the power
exercised is not the power of civil society. Nor is the work of government
the work of civil society. The work of civil society is, above all, to create a
sphere of autonomous activity. This activity may be carried out alongside,
in collaboration with, or in resistance to government. Which sort of activity
or activities needs emphasis will vary according to the characteristics of the
regime and the circumstances of the moment. But even though resistance
(or, more precisely, civil resistance) is only one aspect of the activities of
civil society and is more appropriate in some circumstances than in others,
a capacity for civil resistance is always essential if fundamental rights are
to be protected and fundamental needs met.

When civil society opposes a great evil, the most active dissenters are
easily led to believe not only that they act virtuously but also that they
embody virtue. Perhaps some former dissenters now in government in
Eastern Europe have succumbed to this kind of self-deception. But "the
republic of virtuous men" about which Mastnak complains is not made up
only of former dissenters. Many who were formerly in the gray zone (neither actively resisting nor actively supporting the previous regimes) are
among those who might now be faulted for a somewhat self-righteous and
intemperate manner. The basis for these traits appears, therefore, not to be
simply a matter of individual biography.

T he current regimes of Eastern Europe are transition regimes. We know
what they are a bridge from; we think we know what they are a bridge

to, though the future may prove us wrong. For the time being we speak of these regimes as regimes engaged in democratization and the transition from centralized command economies to free market economies. Their structural features are neither those of their totalitarian (or neototalitarian) predecessors, nor are they those of the established democracies. These regimes are characterized by their instability, their exceptional decision-making powers, and, in a number of instances, by their weak societal support.

Where there is no societal consensus or settled constitutional framework governing property rights, distribution of political power, and the rights of individual citizens and of groups—where, in short, everything is "up for grabs"—antidemocratic tendencies are present that cannot be cured simply by elections. Some forms of consensus are a prerequisite for democracy rather than a consequence of it. At the time of the collapse of the communist regimes, the lack of consensus on basic issues was masked by widespread societal agreement that these regimes must go. It was masked also by these regimes' successful efforts over several decades to suppress differences and to suppress struggles for power.

Citizens and groups perceive that there are high stakes in this transitional situation, but they have few ideas about how to organize to protect their interests. For historical reasons ethnicity is now the most prominent and successful unifying factor for "subnational" groups in the Eastern European countries. Groups unified around this factor tend not to exclude violence as a means of pursuing their objectives. Divisions around ethnicity, therefore, generally fail to strengthen civil society. Once violence actually erupts, as it already has in some parts of the region, civil society is at risk of being overwhelmed and paralyzed by uncivil society. (This comment is not meant, however, to prejudge the legitimacy of the claims of any particular ethnic group.)

It is not just the threat of violence that undermines civil society in Eastern Europe. Acquiescence to the claims of economic experts tends to remove governmental economic decisions from the realm of citizen debate and to delegitimate citizen opposition to these decisions. Citizens are told that the experts have privileged knowledge, discussion is superfluous, and resistance to the technocrats' advice is unpatriotic—or even potentially disastrous to the well-being of the nation.

To many citizens in Eastern Europe, the new regimes may not seem so different from the old. Austerity programs and sacrifices for "the common good" are once again imposed by governmental fiat. Once again large-scale transfers of property ownership and management are initiated and regulated by governmental ministries. Once again "outside powers" dictate or appear to dictate the terms of economic life. Recently Gorbachev—in a broadside at Yeltsin—labeled this kind of governmental involvement in the economy "neo-Bolshevism." That is a distortion. To those citizens, however, for whom "capitalism" has brought increased economic hardship and little or no sense of increased political power, there is more than a grain of truth in Gorbachev's charge. (That Gorbachev himself is not popular is another matter.)

In fact, the primary experience of many Eastern European citizens continues to be one of insecurity and of minimal control over their material circumstances. Improvement of one's economic lot may appear to be obtainable only by actions that are semilegal or illegal, or at least outside the official economy (barter, domestic production). With respect to the former, one commentator has noted that "an underdeveloped banking and fiscal system and confused real estate law offer unprecedented opportunities."

Most current governments in Eastern Europe are in the anomalous situation of promoting capitalist rules and capitalist behavior while remaining themselves the largest property owners. Should a strike occur, "the boss" can bring to bear the power of government, the power of ownership, and the power of a sincere claim to virtue. (To be sure, the power of government is used less repressively by these regimes than by their predecessors.) Workers who strike have some limited economic power, but it is generally insufficient to prevail in such an uneven struggle. To prevail they need to demonstrate that they occupy the moral high ground. Of course, they may not, since not all worker demands are "reasonable." But the counterclaims of the governmental owners may be no more so.

In general, the new governments of Eastern Europe have manifested a lack of self-consciousness about the exceptional powers they are exercising. The prevailing rhetoric about market economies proclaims that they involve minimal governmental intervention. The market is portrayed as an independent self-regulating mechanism rather than as a complex social construct. In fact, in each of these countries a political economy is in the process of being constructed and critical economic policy choices are being made—heavily influenced, of course, by the international economy.

In a situation where governments exercise exceptional powers and there is no stable political/constitutional order, the articulation and mobilization of the nongovernmental sector proceeds with difficulty. Under the present Eastern European regimes, civil society generally is accorded some measure of legal protection, but not a fully favorable legal environment. (The situation varies from country to country.) This absence of adequate legal guarantees, combined with governmental impatience with—or even intolerance of—opposition, has inhibited the reconstruction of civil society since the revolutionary events of 1989. Unfortunately, neither the technocrats in power nor even the ex-dissidents in power (who become fewer in number) appear cognizant that the societal impact of a failure to create an adequate structural basis for a strong civil society may be as adverse as a failure to restructure economically.

Governments, of course, do not generally seek opposition, and civil society is correctly viewed as a potential source of opposition. Moreover, the experience of opposition in a totalitarian or neototalitarian setting may have taught the present political leaders in Eastern Europe lessons that are inapplicable or misleading in the new circumstances. The situation is not remedied by the constitutional advisers from the established democracies, since they tend to neglect the roles both of extraparliamentary opposition and of nongovernmental social support networks and to concern themselves mainly with establishing a basis for orderly transfers of power among political parties. Many Western political theorists in fact regard rather weak levels of political activity by the general population as desirable.

When social movements attempt to meet needs that governments will not or cannot fulfill, they may generate little controversy. But social movements with political objectives, those that pressure or oppose governments, tread a rockier path. Such movements in Eastern Europe face a paradoxical situation. Their governments profess a commitment to democracy and pluralism. But they also stress the need for unity if economic reconstruction is to be accomplished. Furthermore, the personnel of government do not have the habit of living with criticism, let alone confronting accusations of abuse of power. For their part, citizens may hesitate to criticize governments they have freely elected or may believe they have no power to affect them in any case (the latter phenomenon is partly a residue of the long period of communist rule).

Civil societies in Eastern Europe are in some disarray because there are few precedents (if any) for their situations. The effective functioning of a civil society requires an analysis of the strengths and weaknesses of the governmental and economic orders that embrace it. These vary from country to country. The modes of action, goals, and possibilities of civil society will differ accordingly. In Eastern Europe this work of analysis has barely begun. Because many of the previous generation of activists, those who paved the way for the events of 1989, are now engaged in the tasks of governmental and economic reconstruction, time will be required for new social movements and new leaders to emerge.

A cautionary word is in order. Although it is a precondition of democracy that there be legal supports for the activities of civil society, it is a mistake to conceive of civil society as solely a locus of civic virtue. Just as democratic government should not be equated with "virtue in power," so civil society and its components do not necessarily behave virtuously or rationally.

If the description of civil society as a locus of virtue and rationality is rejected, it is unnecessary to decide which popular (or "populist") movements belong in—as expressions of rational viewpoints—and which do not—because they express "irrational prejudices." In the last few years, some individuals and groups have thought it enough simply to invoke the name *civil society* to cover a cause with merit. This is an error. When *civil society* is used as an honorific, it tends to foster inflated claims and unrealistic expectations.

U nder totalitarian conditions unity was a hallmark of civil society. But diversity and conflict are the inevitable result of the initiation of democracy. The new social movements can be expected to pursue not only transsocietal objectives—such as guarantees of basic rights for all citizens—but also more particularistic interests. The emergence of such interests is not undesirable per se, since they often reflect important social needs. Their suppression by a government in the name of transcendent ideals—or simply national unity—should be viewed with suspicion, and certainly will continue to be in Eastern Europe, whose citizens have been subjected to decades of exhortation of this sort.

The received wisdom concerning the role of governments in balancing interests and moderating (or suppressing) conflict is put in question by the unhappy political experiences of this century. The mutual respect and mutual support that are the prerequisites of polity cannot, it appears, be imposed but require arduous work by citizen groups and social movements "from below." Respect for democratic processes, guarantees of basic rights as well as enhancement of participatory opportunities for all citizens, and attentiveness to the needs of diverse social groups can come about only if civil society, against all odds, pursues these objectives. In the Eastern European context, fully as much political imagination and courage are required in the present circumstances as in the past, and the stakes are as high as before, because the outcomes of the present transition processes are not in any way preordained.

31

THE RIGHT TO PEACE AFTER THE COLD WAR

KATARINA TOMASEVSKI

During the era of ideological warfare between the (ideologically defined) East and West, the terms "peace" and "human rights" were used like bullets. Human rights initiatives were identified as "Western" and peace initiatives as "Eastern." Human rights have in the meantime become accepted in the (ideologically defined) East, but the right to peace has not been included.

Let us recall that the proposal to include the right to peace on the agenda of the United Nations General Assembly originated during the Cold War and from the East. It was tabled in 1984 by Mongolia. The year 1986 was solemnly proclaimed to be the International Year of Peace. In reviewing its accomplishments, the General Assembly recently welcomed "the positive change in the international political climate from confrontation to cooperation." During its latest session, it adopted yet another resolution on the implementation of the Declaration on the Right of Peoples to Peace, "stressing that the emerging new positive trends and events in international relations are becoming increasingly conducive to strengthening universal peace and security." However, the General Assembly also identified numerous contemporary threats to this "universal peace" that deviate from these "new positive trends." Moreover, in its comprehensive review of the whole question of peacekeeping operations in all their aspects, the General Assembly noted that "increasing activities in the field of United Nations peace-keeping require increasing human, financial and material resources." Thus, it affirmed that, contrary to the high expectations raised by the end of the Cold War, peacekeeping and peacemaking remain a major expenditure item.

The end of the ideological warfare indeed seemed to promise peace to humanity. Cynics attributed that surge toward peacemaking to the

---

This essay was first published in *Peace Review* 3:3 (1991).

economic recession rather than to a genuine tendency to stop fostering and waging wars. The conflict dominating the global intergovernmental agenda changed from East-West to North-South, and neither side seems to champion peace. Moreover, the disappearance of the (ideologically defined) East as an entity meant also the loss of the traditional originator of peace initiatives on the global agenda. The agenda items intended to define peace as a human right are likely to survive on the agenda of the General Assembly, owing to the bureaucratic routine in dealing with the existing agenda items. A new impetus is unlikely, however, because neither changes in the peace agenda nor those on the human rights agenda seem conducive to asserting that there is such a thing as a human right to peace.

The right to peace can best be defined by two objectives: to protect people from warfare and to protect people in warfare. This logical order has been reversed in practice and much more effort focused at protecting people in warfare. The decade of the 1980s was marked by attempts to induce the United Nations to recognize that human rights continue to apply in armed conflicts and to set basic norms for their protection.

Human rights apply fully in peacetime conditions, while a much narrower protection, codified in (international) humanitarian law, applies in warfare. In addition, humanitarian law applicable to transboundary use of armed force is much more developed than for the use of armed force within borders. Moreover, using armed force within borders often remains outside legal norms of both human rights and humanitarian law. Much attention focused in the 1980s on this gray area between peace and war; the government typically derogates its human rights obligations, while warfare remains below the threshold of the application of humanitarian law. Neither peace researchers nor human rights lawyers have managed to elaborate a term that would encompass all the different phenomena that belong in this gray area. Their variety has been denoted by many terms, such as states of emergency, popular unrest, disturbances, civil strife, internal conflict, political violence, guerrilla warfare, ethnic conflict, pacification, military civic action, and low-intensity warfare.

Additions to the human rights agenda have included topics such as mercenaries or "adverse effects on the enjoyment of human rights of acts of violence committed by armed groups that spread terror among the population and by drug traffickers." Many have doubted whether such issues really belong to human rights; and they have been proven right because the human rights bodies have really not added anything new, nor have they developed a specific human rights perspective. Cynics have explained these additions to the agenda by pointing out that mercenaries, armed groups, or drug traffickers have often been used by governments as a convenient diversion from inquiries into the government's respect of human rights in actions against such groups in this gray area between peace and war.

The importance of the gap between human rights and humanitarian law was evidenced in the 1980s by the large number of efforts to lay down human rights norms for these neither-peace-nor-war situations: the Siracusa Principles on the Limitation and Derogation Provisions in the International Covenant on Civil and Political Rights (1984), the Paris Minimum Standards of Human Rights Norms in a State of Emergency (1984), the Oslo Statement on Norms and Procedures in Times of Public Emergency or Internal Violence (1987), and the Declaration of Minimum Humanitarian Standards (1990). Typically, these have all been scholarly or nongovernmental initiatives; the United Nations remained unresponsive. The General Assembly shied away from affirming a set of principles that would affirm that human rights continue to apply once peace has been lost, but it did make pronouncements relating to specific country situations. Thus, in 1984, the General Assembly urged the combatants in El Salvador to apply international humanitarian law "as the minimum standards of protection of human rights and humane treatment of the civilian population."

Surprisingly, the same United Nations that refused to affirm that human rights should apply to protect people from the use of armed force by their own government has recently organized and legitimated an armed intervention, founded exactly on this unrecognized principle. The Security Council, not a body involved in human rights before, became concerned "by the repression of the Iraqi civilian population" and "disturbed by the human suffering involved," and authorized the deployment of a United Nations Guard Contingent to ensure that humanitarian assistance meets "the critical needs of the refugees and displaced Iraqi population."

This radical step may or may not be applied to other countries, but the situation is paradoxical enough as it concerns Iraq. The United Nations human rights bodies were for years presented with evidence of human rights violations in Iraq—first dozens, then hundreds of well-documented cases—but Iraq escaped any and every condemnation for violations until it invaded Kuwait. Iraq was indeed a notorious case of the unwillingness of governments to condemn another government for human rights violations, when this government was a major commercial partner. Cynics might say that the condemnation of Iraq for human rights violations occurred only after sanctions had been imposed, which impeded further commerce.

To speculate whether the United Nations will pursue humanitarian assistance, backed by armed force, in other countries, one has to review the recently emerged international right to intervene to see how far it is likely to be developed further. This radical change took place in the late 1980s. As opposition to interference in internal affairs started withering away with the Cold War, the right to intervene *(droite à l'ingérence)* in disaster relief emerged. It included requesting the government to guarantee access to victims of disasters on its territory as a prerequisite for the alleviation of their suffering through international disaster relief operations.

A lleviation of human suffering is a tangible expression of human solidarity. Those that rush to help victims of disasters are deemed to act out a sense of responsibility for their fellow human beings and need unimpeded access to be able to help. The proposal for an international recognition of such a right originated from Médecins sans Frontières. It was defined by the General Assembly on December 8, 1988, in its Resolution 43/131 entitled Humanitarian Assistance to Victims of Natural Disasters and Similar Emergency Situations. What is included in "similar emergency situations" was, for obvious reasons, left undefined. In practice, little difference is made between natural and man-made disasters. Indeed, the very incentives for elaborating this "right to intervene" were man-made disasters, or silence imposed by governments on their "internal" natural or man-made disasters, or prevention of the delivery of disaster relief. In the case of Sudan, the General Assembly has explicitly joined "persistent natural disasters and armed conflict" as the cause of the international disaster relief, which represents "the principle of safe access for personnel providing relief for all in need."

This right to intervene to assist victims of natural and man-made disasters and thus alleviate human suffering has been subsumed under humanitarian rather than human rights law. Entitlements of victims are not legally recognized; there is no right to aid in general nor to humanitarian aid, although there have been numerous attempts to induce the United Nations to move in this direction. A general recognition of a right to aid, even for victims of natural or man-made disasters, remains unlikely. Proposals to recognize a right to aid may be adopted by the majority of the General Assembly but are opposed by the aid-providing countries. The current international policy gives the international (donor) community the right to choose whether and where to intervene. Recognition of a right to aid would enable all those in need of aid to articulate their needs, and choice would have to be made openly, which would necessitate some criteria to be developed and observed.

Moreover, recognizing a right to aid for minorities or other collective entities subjected to repression or victimized by man-made disasters would challenge the individualism of international human rights law. The rule is that only individuals may submit complaints for violations of rights conferred on individuals. This precludes the recognition of victims as a collective entity. One of the stumbling blocks to developing remedies for widespread and institutionalized violations, particularly those committed in the gray area between peace and war, is this individualism. In the human rights complaints procedures victims have standing only as individuals, even in conditions of mass victimization.

The United Nations instruments dealing with victims of abuse of power went further in asserting that victims are entitled to redress for the harm they have suffered, individually and collectively. The Declaration of

Basic Principles of Justice for Victims of Crime and Abuse of Power laid down the basic norms. The protection of victims of crime had been its initial focus, which made the exercise feasible; however, it would not have been accepted by the United Nations had the main target been victims of abuse of power.

The term "arms race" has disappeared with the Cold War from the global peace agenda. Although such rhetorical changes do not necessarily lead to changes of policy, in this case, proposals to include military expenditure in the criteria for allocating development finance to developing countries promise some real change. The International Monetary Fund has affirmed that excessive military expenditure constitutes abuse of resources, while the World Bank suggested that reducing military expenditure be considered as a condition in assisting developing countries that are "overspending" on the military, at the expense of investing in people.

There is nothing new in such an argument; all of it has been argued by scholars, peace activists, and nongovernmental organizations. Almost ten years ago, in *Current Research on Peace and Violence,* I wrote:

> We have become aware of the fact that preparations for waging wars (whether offensive or defensive) represents an institutionalized violation of human rights: deprivations resulting from resource allocation policies favoring military expenditure over welfare or agriculture can be substantiated nowadays by numerous data confirming that armaments and development and competing demands on public expenditures entail not only economic, but social costs as well.

The "peace dividend," which was expected as an instant product of the end of the Cold War, might be forthcoming through the disarmament of at least one of the superpowers to which "arms race" originally referred, if not both. The recent Group of Seven Economic Summit included the conversion of military to civilian industry in the USSR as one of the main areas of international assistance. The thrust of the peace dividend is targeted, however, to the developing countries, through the conditioning of aid by their reduced military expenditure. Current debates have revealed that 25 percent of the debt burden originates in military expenditure. Its toll is unknown. It is known that more than half of all African countries have been involved in one or more armed conflicts since their independence, but the overall human toll will never be known. The development toll of military expenditure has, however, now become a legitimate issue, thus opening the way for documenting the need for change and promoting it, if only in one part of the globe.

During the 1980s, the United Nations human rights bodies occasionally reiterated "the need for all concerned parties to realize the adverse effects of the arms race on the enjoyment of human rights," but disarmament and development were only given lip service on the intergovernmental agenda. Today disarmament and development have been placed on the intergovernmental agenda in the area of development finance by those who define the priorities in resource allocation internationally and thus can effect a change.

A lthough the right to peace has not progressed conceptually, in many instances norms from the area of peace have been borrowed to further protect human rights. An important reason for this is the heritage of international human rights law. Following the thrust of international law to regulate interstate relations, prohibitions were adopted for what states should not do to each other and to each other's population. As a corollary, rules of warfare were strict for interstate wars, while intrastate warfare remained for a long time outside international law. Due to this lack of application of international norms internally, the state's "own" population was protected by legal norms the last and the least.

It should be recalled that states introduced the first rudimentary forms of human rights to protect their nationals abroad. Protection of the rights of the state's own population emerged much later, and against much opposition, exemplified by the obstacle of interference in internal affairs—one of the prominent features of the Cold War period. A great deal of effort and time was needed to reject the notion that people were the property of the state, and this has not totally disappeared. On the international development agenda, people are still often referred to as human capital or human resources.

Much of the development of human rights focused on strengthening prohibitions of the abuse of power against the state's own population. The prohibition to kill was reinforced by subsuming summary and/or arbitrary executions and disappearances under globally prohibited acts, and there has been a growing momentum against the death penalty. Much as the abolition of the death penalty in a number of countries is considered a Northern-Western initiative, it is of global relevance because it rejects the notion that the state has the right to kill anybody.

Another significant development is a change in the United Nations' human rights work. The first steps, in the 1940s to the 1960s, laid down the main substantive human rights standards in order to develop a globally applicable yardstick. In the 1970s, international complaint procedures started operating, and individuals were permitted to pursue demands to investigate and condemn human rights violations by their own state in international tribunals. Critics of the international human rights system seldom stress this profound change: The government has lost the position of being the judge in its own case and can be held accountable internationally for what it does to its own people.

Moreover, condemning governments for human rights violations—

however ineffectively it is done in an intergovernmental system—always comes too late. Hence, procedures aimed at preventing the occurrence of violations were developed for those types of human rights violations that are universally accepted as violations: torture, summary and arbitrary executions, disappearances. This "right to intervene" of the international community has been developed as a humanitarian rather than human rights activity, and it has subsequently been broadened to disaster relief and even armed conflicts.

D espite numerous additions to human rights, the crucial part of the right to peace—an individual right not to take part in warfare—has not emerged as a recognized human right. Conscientious objection to military service is occasionally on the human rights agenda, subsumed under the agenda item "youth and human rights"; but it has not been declared to constitute a human right. Indeed, the 1989 Convention on the Rights of the Child shows that widespread opposition of governments to freedom from compulsory military service continues to impede any progress in this area. This convention is a unique example of retrogression in international human rights standards; the previous international norms to protect children from being drawn into warfare have actually been lowered by this convention.

One of the thorniest issues, throughout the ten years of drafting the Convention on the Rights of the Child, was the attempt by the drafters to keep the age of compulsory military service at eighteen. This effort failed. While the convention recognizes that children should enjoy protection to the age of eighteen, the sole explicit exception in the text of the finally adopted convention remains military service, where the minimum age has been lowered to fifteen. This provision reads as follows: "States Parties shall take all feasible measures to ensure that persons who have not attained the age of fifteen years do not take a direct part in the hostilities." Drafting the young into the military much before they are given the right to vote thus remains part of the international human rights law, and child soldiers remain an agenda item of human rights bodies.

Despite this failure to protect children from being drawn into warfare as soldiers by a globally applicable legal norm, the declarations of governments as they ratify this convention show that many continue to treat this as failure and remain committed to change. Thus, the government of Argentina declared "that it would have liked the Convention categorically to prohibit the use of children in armed conflicts." The governments of Uruguay and Germany declared that they would not recruit any persons below eighteen.

P eace was defined by the General Assembly as the right of peoples, not individuals, that is, a collective human right. This challenged the broadly accepted, but excessively individualistic, notion of human rights, previously championed by the West, today by the North. The failure to define who—or what—the peoples are is an obstacle to defining the first part of the right to peace: who can claim peace as a matter of entitlement. The notion of peoples developed in the context of decolonization does not help much, nor does the globally applied concept of the nation-state. Despite the growing awareness after the Cold War that the main challenges to peace will come from within states, human rights have not progressed in defining the rights, duties, freedoms, and responsibilities of groups, minorities, and communities that claim specific collective rights as entities. For lack of a better word, these are referred to here as "collectivities."

A notable step was undertaken in 1976 by the Universal Declaration of the Rights of Peoples (commonly referred to as the Algiers Declaration), but this represented too much of a challenge to the conventional human rights thinking to be followed up, even by the nongovernmental community. The only area in which a conceptual breakthrough has been made is indigenous rights. This has indeed been the most creative area of the human rights discourse in the 1980s. One possible reason is its relative freedom from Cold War politics. Indigenous organizations have changed the global human rights agenda by including collective and developmental rights, by arguing the necessity to move away from the individual and the state as the sole entities recognized in human rights.

Collective rights remain, however, hampered by the jealous adherence to the nation-state and to the territorial integrity of the existing nation-states). We may know that nation-state is a fiction that does not bear factual analysis, but it remains unchallengeable. Any recognition of ethnic, religious, or linguistic minorities is seen by states as a step toward redrawing national borders and is opposed by those who fear a loss of territory. Little progress has been made to move away from this obsession with territory as the symbol of statehood and collective identity. Although scholarly writings have suggested numerous ways and means of recognizing collectivities within states through various types and levels of internal self-determination, claims for self-determination are regularly perceived as territorial claims. The lack of procedures for articulating claims of collective rights impedes progress in this area. Moreover, there are no procedures for peaceful conflict solving, and this is certainly a contributing factor to peace breaking, so often caused by unresolved minority problems. Peacemaking efforts remain confined to stopping warfare, but creativity in problem solving of—still unresolved—minority problems is still lacking.

The right to peace could be conceptually developed, and thus help further the development of human rights, by elaborating procedures for peacefully solving problems and conflicts between various collectivities within states. After the Cold War, democracy is advocated as the global panacea, but it does not include procedures for negotiation and recognition of collective human rights, because it is confined to the conventional individual-state relationship. The role of the individual is confined to the exercise of electoral rights and political pluralism to a multiparty system within the nation-state. Democracy is thus conceived as the "will of the people," where people are treated as a single entity, accounting for majorities, while leaving out minorities. The gap left by the nonrecognition of human rights claims of groups, minorities, and communities could be filled by laying down procedural rules for articulating, negotiating, and settling such claims. This would greatly contribute to promoting peace, besides giving specific goals and contents to the right to peace. It would also enrich human rights by developing a much neglected field. The bulk of human rights work has focused on elaborating substantive standards, defining who is entitled to what; procedures to articulate and negotiate different and often mutually opposed claims have yet to be elaborated.

During the past decade, much has changed in human rights. Whether this improves or jeopardizes possibilities for including the right to peace among universally recognized human rights is an issue that needs careful consideration. Ten years ago, I wrote optimistically:

> Widening the scope of internationally proclaimed human rights by the inclusion of the right to peace would theoretically pose no insurmountable problem. It has been accomplished recently, both by UN resolutions and in scholarly treatises. However, in terms of conceptualizing such a right to peace, and especially assessing what its meaning would be as part of living law, not much progress has been made.

Nothing has changed since, and the conclusion about the lack of progress in conceptualizing the right to peace remains. Whether post–Cold War changes make defining and recognizing the right to peace easier or more difficult remains to be seen.

Human rights in the context of development have become the new global battlefield, much resembling the previous East-West confrontations, except that the divisive line has changed to North-South. Development has been added to the global human rights agenda against much opposition and is accompanied by never-ending disagreements about whether it really belongs there. Foreign debt and structural adjustment now figure prominently among obstacles to the realization of human rights in developing countries in the United Nations instruments, voted through by the majority of countries from the South and opposed by the North. The right to peace has been chronologically, if not conceptually, linked with the right to development; both reflect broad and global claims, though neither has resulted in a recognition of entitlements.

The North-South conflict inevitably challenges the universality of human rights because of wide disparities in the opportunities for human beings to enjoy their rights. Some are born into a community where access to education, health care, and employment is guaranteed. They often become lost, in the words of Roger Scruton, in the fog of self-indulgence. People whose luck of birth failed them have no access to education or health care unless they can pay for it; and most have no prospects of employment to enable them to pay. The luck of birth can be redressed by migration by some, but for the bulk of the population in poor countries there is no redress. A human right for which there is no remedy is of no practical use to anybody. The General Assembly has made no pronouncements relating to solidarity in the context of development. Solidarity has remained confined to disaster relief, accompanied by the recognition of the right to intervene in situations of widespread suffering. An exception is a brief resolution on human rights based on solidarity that stated that "the severe suffering of innumerable human beings through the world . . . calls for the strengthening of a common sense of human solidarity." Common sense would argue that preventing disasters—particularly man-made ones, which are inherently preventable—would prevent human suffering as well, and this could orient a "common sense of human solidarity." However, the United Nations response has been oriented toward developing early-warning systems for impending disasters rather than disaster-prevention mechanisms.

A decade ago, I argued, following the mainstream of international law doctrine, that peace constituted the supreme internationally protected value:

> It can be argued that peace is a supreme value of mankind and if not the supreme value cherished by international law, then certainly one of its supreme values. Thus, elaborating the notion of a human right to peace could be accorded a high priority. One line of reasoning is the scope and intensity of human rights violations occurring as a result of war, another one is a value of human life and irreversibility of its loss.

This had been challenged already in 1948 in the Universal Declaration of Human Rights, which asserted that the lack of protection of human rights compels people "to have recourse as a last resort, to rebellion against tyranny and oppression." Advocating peace may amount to cherishing the status quo. Arguments against changes in the unjust status quo, founded on the violation of the right to self-determination of peoples or on an exploitative economic system, continue. For example, Louis Henkin wrote in 1989 as follows: "Peace was more important than progress and more important than justice." Not everybody would agree that "unjust peace" is preferable to "just war." Arguments are made livelier by the lack of a shared view of what "unjust peace" or "just war" is even in theory, let alone in practice.

Much attention has been paid to ethnicity in thinking about unjust peace and just war, but little to development. Development is indeed an area where conflicts have not been envisaged but are due to affect the thinking about unjust peace. In the existing international human rights instruments relating to development, no mention is made of the fact that development is inherently conflict-prone. Realization of human rights requires recognizing conflicts between mutually opposed rights, conflicts between population categories whose rights are mutually opposed, and designing mechanisms for conflict solving.

Rather than setting a procedure for coping with such inevitable conflicts, the existing human rights instruments embody guarantees of substantive rights for all, but fail to provide guidance on how to deal with conflicting rights and conflicts of rights holders. This is particularly important because both individual and collective rights have been recognized in the United Nations efforts to define the right to development. The United Nations human rights bodies have recognized many times that "throughout the world there are serious problems arising from inter-ethnic and inter-group conflicts" and, as of 1988, are working to develop ways and means of facilitating peaceful and constructive solution of problems involving minorities. Designing procedures for peaceful articulation and negotiation of such conflicts could be the best contribution that the right to peace could make.

Declaration on the Right of Peoples to Peace, 1984

Reaffirming that the principal aim of the United Nations is the maintenance of international peace and security,

Bearing in mind the fundamental principles of international law set forth in the Charter of the United Nations,

Expressing the will and the aspirations of all peoples to eradicate war from the life of mankind and, above all, to avoid a world-wide nuclear catastrophe,

Convinced that life without war serves as the primary international prerequisite for the material well-being, development and progress of countries, and for the full implementation of the rights and fundamental human freedoms proclaimed by the United Nations,

Aware that in the nuclear age the establishment of a lasting peace on Earth represents the primary condition for the preservation of human civilization and the survival of mankind,

Recognizing that the maintenance of a peaceful life for peoples is the sacred duty of each state,

1. Solemnly proclaims that the peoples of our planet have a sacred right to peace;

2. Solemnly declares that the preservation of the right of peoples to peace and the promotion of its implementation constitute a fundamental obligation of each state;

3. Emphasizes that ensuring the exercise of the right of peoples to peace demands that the policies of States be directed towards the elimination of the threat of war, particularly nuclear war, the renunciation of the use of force in international relations and the settlement of international disputes by peaceful means on the basis of the Charter of the United Nations;

4. Appeals to all States and international organizations to do their utmost to assist in implementing the right of peoples to peace through the adoption of appropriate measures at both the national and international level.

32

DEVELOPMENT
WITH A HUMAN FACE

JEANNE VICKERS

Alternative adjustment packages (attempts to balance the consequences of development policy deficiencies) are needed to protect the vulnerable in the developing world while promoting growth. In many countries the position of the poor has worsened during adjustment, with deterioration in nutrition levels and educational achievement. Investment rates have frequently slowed or fallen. With reduced expenditure on both human and physical resources, the prospects for economic growth in the medium term have worsened.

S ome countries have managed to avoid many of the negative effects typically associated with adjustment and succeeded in maintaining and even improving standards of health and nutrition, resuming growth after only a short time. Botswana, South Korea, and Zimbabwe have all followed conventional but relatively expansionary macro policies, protecting the needs of the poor by measures to sustain their incomes and to reallocate resources to basic health and education. Botswana has placed great emphasis on employment creation through public works, and South Korea has also made use of public works to maintain incomes during economic recession.

In Zimbabwe, credit, marketing, and supplies have favored small-scale farmers, whose market production in consequence surged from 10% of the total in 1980 to 38% in 1985. Total government expenditure increased by over 60% in real terms from 1980 to 1984; the share of education and health in the total rose from 22% to 27% while the share of defense in recurrent expenditure fell from 44% to 28%. Preventive medicine rose from 7.6% to 14% in total health expenditure, and the share of primary education in total educational expenditure nearly doubled from 32% to 58%.

The experience of these three countries provides some important

This essay was excerpted from Jeanne Vickers, *Women and the World Economic Crisis* (London: Zed Books, 1992).

insights into how to achieve a satisfactory alternative, and demonstrates that it is possible to adopt adjustment policies which succeed in protecting the vulnerable while restoring growth. In the short run it is possible to protect the vulnerable without economic growth by careful policy interventions targeted towards the poor and needy. But prolonged economic stagnation undermines the possibility of sustaining the position of the poor, as the experiences of Ghana and Jamaica indicate. Consequently, the restoration of economic growth in the medium term must be a critically important part of achieving "adjustment with a human face." Moreover, the health, nutrition, and education of a nation is one of the most important determinants of its economic potential.

It must, however, be stressed that adjustment must take place in the industrialized countries, and in the international system, as well as in the developing economies. Major national imbalances may emerge from changes in the world economy without any deterioration in domestic economic management. Large changes of this sort occurred in 1982, for example, a fall in commodity prices, a rise in interest rates, a fall in the market for manufactures, or a decline in capital inflow.

Viewed from the perspective of international economic management, however, the appropriate adjustment may be not so much in the national economies, where the major and unsustainable imbalances emerge, but in the international conditions which gave rise to them—i.e., in the factors determining the world level of demand, commodity prices, interest rates, capital flows, and so forth. UNICEF considers that the need for adjustment in international conditions is of paramount importance because, for many countries, the extent of adjustment required under present conditions is clearly excessive, and for some may not be possible without intolerable sacrifice, not only of human and social conditions but also of democracy.

U NICEF has suggested the following major elements in adjustment with a human face:

1. More expansionary macro policies to sustain levels of output, investment, and satisfaction of human needs over the adjustment period, gradually moving to acceleration of development. This typically implies a different timing of adjustment, with more gradual correction of imbalances, requiring more medium-term external finance.

2. Meso policies designed to help fulfill priorities in meeting the needs of vulnerable groups and promoting economic growth, in the context of limited resources. These would include policies towards taxation, government expenditure, aid, credit, foreign exchange, and asset distribution, which together help determine the distribution of incomes and resources.

3. Sectoral policies to achieve restructuring in the productive sector within any aggregate level of resource availability, promoting opportuni-

ties, resources, and productivity in the small-scale sector, both in agriculture and industry and services.

4. Policies designed to increase the equity and efficiency of the social sector by redirecting effort and resources from high-cost areas, which do not contribute to basic needs, towards low-cost basic services, and by improving the targeting of interventions. Active support for a new range of initiatives which mobilize people for health and education, and for greater community action in such areas as housing, water, and sanitation.

5. Compensatory programs to protect the basic living standards, health, and nutrition of the low-income group during adjustment, before restructuring of production and economic growth have raised output and incomes sufficiently to enable the most vulnerable to meet minimum acceptable standards.

6. Monitoring of the living standards, health, and nutrition of the vulnerable during adjustment on a regular basis (quarterly for some items, as with much economic data), processed speedily so that progress can be assessed and the design of programmes modified accordingly. Monitoring of the human dimensions should be given at least as much weight as monitoring monetary variables.

A mong the structural adjustment strategies recommended by United Nations agencies is the need to give greater support to rural women. Despite the acknowledged predominance of women in agriculture in many parts of the world, women continue to be left out of agricultural strategies. In Africa, 85% of rural women are involved in agriculture, where they produce and process as much as 80% of family food consumption. Reduction in male wage employment and increasing landlessness have led to increased dependence on women's earnings in poor rural households. Where successful structural adjustment requires improving the balance of payments with regard to agricultural exports and food imports, then women must be part of that strategy. There are clear linkages between structural adjustment objectives to increase food supply, the economic and technical roles of women, and the welfare of children.

Many households in both Asia and Africa are headed by women, representing some of the poorest units. In Africa there are a growing number of households where the male is absent through out-migration. Most project and settlement schemes have denied women title to land, and women generally lack power, assets, and participation in formal institutions to make their views known and take their share of available resources. When given the opportunity they are vigorous entrepreneurial agents but often require a strengthening of their own organizations, such as savings groups, trade associations, and credit networks.

Resources have been directed towards men even in situations where women are the technical experts in crop production, as shown by research on irrigated and swamp rice in The Gambia, and subsequent investigations have confirmed this in other rice-growing African countries. Swamp rice cultivation in The Gambia is traditionally carried out by women, but when new projects were designed, the project management discussed proposals with men, not women.

Men were invited to take part in the construction work under food-for-work programmes so that the immediate benefits accrued to them. Because of the nature of "separate purses," no benefits were received by the women. As a result they had no interest in cultivating the new swamps because they had lost their traditional control over the crop, and because the siting and construction of the swamps, lacking their expertise, made their labor input especially high. When the project management involved women by asking their advice, they were impressed by women's all-round technical knowledge of rice cultivation and water control. As a result, some modifications have been possible in swamp construction and the provision of credit to women to enable them to purchase inputs.

UNICEF sees women as active agents in programme delivery; as organized groups playing significant roles in managing community resources and making decisions governing resource allocation; and as individuals serving the community as health and nutrition agents, water and sanitation monitors, adult literacy trainers, and family motivators.

UNICEF should help to support and/or expand their active role as producers, managers, educators, health agents, income earners, and so forth, and maximize the benefits derived by ensuring that services reach them and by supporting their participation in the planning and management of service delivery. Education is seen as a prerequisite and key factor in raising women's awareness and empowering them to become active participants in the national development process.

A priority concern of the UN Development Programme (UNDP) is to ensure the integration of women as participants and beneficiaries in all its developmental programmes and projects, not only because women are significant contributors to economic and social development, but also from the conviction that sustainable development is possible only if women are more effectively involved. In this it encourages concrete action related to commitments accepted by governments when they unanimously adopted the "Forward-Looking Strategies for the Advancement of Women" at the culminating conference of the UN Decade for Women in Nairobi in 1985.

A number of international institutions have taken action to monitor situations of concern to them, including WHO, ILO, and the World Bank. FAO has a Global Information and Early Warning System related to problems of food supplies and famine, and actively assists a number of countries in developing national early warning systems. Extension of the FAO system to economic crises, with greater use of data on the human dimension, could provide the basis for national and international early warnings of social stress.

Structural adjustment programmes insist upon strong export and market-orientation, and yet everyone—including the World Bank and the IMF—agrees that prospects for commodity prices are extremely bleak for the next few, possibly ten, years. Thus, a strong insistence on commodity-based export drives to stimulate economic growth would seem to be totally misplaced. It has become vital to explore different approaches to structural adjustment, both for the policy design and for the process itself.

The World Bank plans to double its lending for population, health, and nutrition as part of a six-pronged programme to improve the lot of women in the developing world. President Barber Conable has promised that the Bank would: design action plans in selected countries so that agricultural, industrial, educational, and health programmes promote women's progress along with other development goals; emphasize issues affecting women in dialogues with member countries; encourage development policies that provide adequate incentives for women and ensure that they have the means to respond; develop programme initiatives in agricultural extension and agricultural credit targeted for women, and expand credit and training for women to improve their employment prospects in other sectors; promote formal and informal education for women and girls.

In April 1987 the World Bank issued "Protecting the Poor during Periods of Adjustment." Originally prepared for the IMF/WB Development Committee, to serve as the basis for their discussion of the impact of adjustment measures on the poor and of how adjustment policies might be supplemented or modified to protect the poor, it has much in common with adjustment with a human face. Both accept the need for adjustment, for targeting the poor and vulnerable, and for extreme economy if realistic programmes are to be prepared and implemented at a time of severe constraints.

The Bank paper essentially concentrates on how to add compensatory measures focused on the poor to existing adjustment programmes, which it is at pains to protect from any disruption; it neither recognizes nor explores the extent to which the unqualified promotion of free market policies may conflict with the targeting and deliberate interference with the market needed to support employment, the informal sector, and protection of vulnerable groups. In contrast, the UNICEF report calls for more expansionary macro policies and underlines the need for restructuring policies in the productive and social sectors, as well as the need for meso policies to help direct more attention and resources to poor and vulnerable groups in general.

T he reaction of non-governmental organizations to the World Bank paper was one of disappointment that poverty was treated as a supplementary consideration, and that the paper allowed little scope for changing the design of adjustment programmes. It was felt that programmes which concentrate on human capital development and on agrarian reform could be efficient instruments of growth and effective with respect to equity, and that measures geared to increasing efficiency need not have a high social cost. Nevertheless, it was accepted that equity might have some cost in terms of growth.

The World Bank has shown itself very receptive to these comments, and values its continued collaboration with the NGO community. Nevertheless, the verdict of a group of NGO activists, which organized a Permanent People's Tribunal at the time of the IMF/World Bank meeting in Berlin in September 1988, was extremely critical of the policies of the two institutions, whose structural adjustment policies "caused a growing net transfer of resources from indebted countries to creditor countries. Consequently . . . living standards in indebted countries have deteriorated. The environment has been irreversibly damaged and living areas of indigenous peoples have been destroyed. The payment of reparations should therefore be considered."

In a statement to the UN Economic and Social Council in July 1988, the World Bank insisted that: "The question is whether there are ways in which the adjustment process can be designed and complemented to minimize the difficulties experienced by low-income and deprived groups, such as women. Two areas offer the greatest scope for doing this: ensuring that social expenditures, such as those in health and education, are cost effective and focused on the poor; and compensating the poor directly."

The statement made it clear that the World Bank had become an increasingly sensitive advocate of the importance of women's concerns in the developing world and the development process, and had identified this as a priority area for increased attention. Pointing out that women represent 50% of the adult world population and one-third of the official labor force, perform nearly two-thirds of all working hours for which they receive only one-third of world income, and own less than 1% of world property, the statement surmised that "development cannot advance far if women are left significantly behind."

S ince UNICEF first drew attention in 1987 to the need for adjustment with a human face, international recognition of the social effects of economic adjustment policies has been gaining ground. Michel Camdessus, Managing Director of the International Monetary Fund, expressed two convictions when issuing a recent IMF review of the impact on the poorest groups of Fund-supported programmes: ". . . adjustment does not have to lower basic human standards . . . the efforts of fellow agencies of the UN family to protect social programmes in the face of unavoidable budget cuts

and to make some programmes more efficient . . . exemplify the types of
things that are essential. [Also] . . . the more adjustment efforts give proper
weight to social realities . . . the more successful they are likely to be."

He continued to state the case bluntly: "People know something about
how to ensure that the very poor are spared by the adjustment effort. In
financial terms, it might not cost very much. Why? Because if you look at
the share of the poorest groups in the distribution of these countries'
income, it is a trifling amount. Thus, to maintain their share of global
income during an adjustment period, or even increase it, need not cost
much, contrary to what people say . . . the poorest 40% of the population in
many cases receives only 10% or less of total income. This 10% level can
be maintained or even increased by 10%—making it 11% for the poor—
only if everyone else makes a slight sacrifice. Unfortunately, it is generally
'everyone else,' and not the poverty groups, that is represented in government."

The UN Division for the Advancement of Women, in its "Update of
the World Survey," suggests that there is a general international consensus
that adjustment policies should be determined with full consideration of
their effects on people. How this can be done with regard to the advancement of women will require studies of national experience in this area.
Among approaches to examine would be:

- differential policies for rural and urban areas, including analysis of
  the effects of changes in subsidy or price control structures for
  essential goods;
- policies tailored to sectors in which women have significant participation;
- encouragement of women to enter sectors promoted by adjustment,
  and monitoring their status in these sectors;
- monitoring of policies to ensure that they do not have dispropor-
  tionately negative effects upon the poor;
- trade-offs between spending-reduction policies and compensatory
  programmes such as nutritional programmes;
- protection of programmes, such as education and training, which
  develop human capital and help promote equality;
- encouragement of sectors, such as food production and small-scale
  manufacturing, which already have significant participation by
  women;
- at the international level, a better balance between adjustment and
  financing, including debt rescheduling and cancellation and inter-
  est-rate concessions.

At its 29 March–7 April 1989 Session in Vienna, the UN Commission
on the Status of Women was told by the Director-General of the

United Nations Office in Vienna that evidence was mounting that "progress towards the full economic and political participation of women was slowing or had actually stopped."

Among the resolutions adopted at the session was one in relation to the question of women's unpaid work and activities in the informal sector. It invited UN agencies to give priority to the collection of information on women's participation in the informal and unpaid sectors of the economy of member states, and recommended that the report on statistics and indicators scheduled for submission to the Commission on the Status of Women at its 35th session should include suggestions for the determination of methods of including into the gross national product the economic value of work carried out by women in the informal sectors by using, inter alia, the work done by UN specialized agencies.

33

WHAT DO WE DO NOW?

LANE KENWORTHY

The demise of command socialism in Eastern Europe presents both an obstacle and an opportunity for those interested in constructing a just and effective economic system. The manifest economic failure of "really existing" socialism has convinced many people that laissez-faire capitalism is the only feasible form of economic organization. This is certainly a setback. At the same time, the door is now more fully open than ever before to new ideas about postcapitalist economics. No longer does the command model dominate in theory or in practice.

The left ought to take advantage of this opening to the greatest extent possible. Unfortunately, progressives of all stripes, particularly here in the United States, tend to be far too cavalier in their thinking about what kind of economic system they favor. We are more likely to focus solely on criticizing existing institutions. We have numerous convincing accounts of the ills of free-market capitalism but too few cogent suggestions about what to put in its place. If the left is to play a significant role in determining the future economic system in the United States and elsewhere, we need a much more explicit and sustained dialogue about where we would like to go.

This discussion should be pitched primarily at the level of economic systems rather than merely at policy options within the present system. Whereas the latter is unquestionably pivotal in orienting the left's near-term political strategy, the former can be neglected only at great peril. Short-run policy demands should be guided by a longer-term vision. The central themes in this system-level discussion ought to be planning and markets, public ownership, worker self-management, and equality.

In debating the institutional features of a postcapitalist economic system, progressives should concern themselves more directly and seriously with efficiency issues than they traditionally have. Partly this is to increase the size of the audience; after 100 years it seems clear that moral condemnations of capitalism are insufficient to generate widespread support for

---

This essay was first published in *Peace Review* 4:1 (1992).

alternatives. It is also because the Eastern European experience has demonstrated graphically the importance of "putting bread on the table."

We should also be more attentive to the benefits, rather than just the faults, of existing capitalist economic institutions. Any postcapitalism or socialism—especially one brought about through reform—will undoubtedly inherit many features from the economy it replaces. Institutional configurations tend to be sticky; they have an inertial quality. Capacities and resources get arrayed in ways that resist alteration. One of the chief lessons of the anticapitalist revolutions of this century (Russia, China, Cuba, Nicaragua, and so forth) is that economic systems cannot quickly be remade to fit the specifications of radical blueprints, regardless of the will of leaders and citizens.

S ince the mid-1800s, centralized planning has been the quintessential postcapitalist goal of the left. Most socialists have viewed planning as a precondition for the achievement of a number of desirable social goods, including efficiency (because it allows, in theory, a rational allocation of resources), economic growth without large fluctuations or cycles, full employment, and realization of the general interest over that of the particular.

During the past decade, however, a growing number of progressives have become convinced that the left should abandon the goal of genuine planning—at least insofar as that consists of extensive, coordinated, *ex ante* allocation of the majority of the economy's resources. This sentiment stems from a realization that planning has two inherent defects, both of which were borne out in the experience with centralized planning in the state-socialist countries during the past fifty years.

The first has to do with information. Because of the immense scale and numerous interdependencies involved, full-scale planning cannot be carried out effectively. Modern economies are composed of millions of different goods and services, and decisions about how much to produce and at what price depend upon what Friedrich Hayek has called "knowledge of the particular circumstances of time and place," which is constantly changing. The amount, complexity, interconnectedness, and instability of the requisite information are simply too great for a planning commission to aggregate and transform into a set of clear and coordinated directives for each enterprise.

Consequently, planning is bound to allocate resources with less than desirable efficiency. In addition, many directives will be infeasible for the enterprise to which they are given. A breakdown in plan fulfillment of producer goods in one firm leads to shortage at another, which causes another breakdown in quota fulfillment, and so on. As a result of shortages and delays of inputs, firms constantly have parts or workers sitting idle, waiting for supplies. This microlevel shortage phenomenon produces a substantial amount of aggregate waste in the economy. Moreover, in an effort to patch up problems, plans tend to be changed often, which only creates further bottlenecks and inefficiencies.

The second fatal weakness of planning has to do with motivation. There is a strong tendency under central planning for firms to be given what Hungarian economist Janos Kornai calls a "soft budget constraint." That is, enterprises do not face the threat of bankruptcy, of being shut down if they do not perform efficiently; instead they are guaranteed state support. This is probably an inevitable correlate of central planning, because if the state is ultimately responsible for decisions regarding each firm's output, wages, prices, etc., as is the case under centralized planning, then the state must take a good measure of responsibility if a firm fails economically. It will face strong pressure to keep the enterprise afloat.

A soft budget constraint leads to inefficient management practices. Without the threat of bankruptcy, firms have limited incentive to reduce costs. Soft budget constraints also impair efficiency in an indirect fashion, by encouraging firms to exaggerate their input requirements during the plan formulation stage. Any extra supplies the firm is able to get from the center can be hoarded, to be used in the inevitable event of shortages or delays of inputs later on. Since extra costs generally are borne by the government, there is no reason not to exaggerate one's needs. But rather than remedying the shortage problem, hoarding, for obvious reasons, only exacerbates it.

Soft budget constraints also impede innovation. The absence of effective competition and threat of bankruptcy dissolves the incentive for firms to innovate. Thus, while a centrally planned economy may be just as effective as a market-based economy in achieving large-scale innovations (such as putting a spacecraft on the moon), it will be less successful at producing the incremental company-level innovations that are at the heart of industrial advance.

Traditionally, the left argues that the poor performance of Eastern European planning results from distortions caused by the undemocratic operation of the planning process. The inefficiency could therefore be remedied by a healthy dose of democracy, both at the level of the firm and throughout the planning chain.

Alternatively, the left argues that informational difficulties resulting from scale and complexity can be solved by today's powerful computers. Michael Albert and Robin Hahnel have proposed that computers make possible a coherent and effective decentralized planning arrangement, in which firms coordinate production decisions in an *ex ante* fashion on their own, through a process of repeat bargaining.

The concept of planning is growing less popular, however—and for good reason. It is clear, based on the experiences of the Eastern European countries, that computers are not sufficient to remedy planning's deficiencies; there is simply too much information that changes too frequently.

Similarly, it seems quite unlikely that democratization and/or decentralization of the process could remove or even significantly alleviate the informational and motivational barriers to effective, efficient planning. A growing portion of the left is coming to believe that an attractive, feasible postcapitalist economy should be coordinated primarily by markets. For all their faults, markets appear to be the most effective available mechanism for allocating economic resources and stimulating innovation.

It is important to realize that market coordination of an economy need not imply that production and consumption are organized exclusively in the form of impersonal, arms-length, competitive transactions. Indeed, most existing market economies—especially Japan and the continental European countries—feature an assortment of quasi-market relationships between firms, often referred to as networks. Characterized by long-term, informal, personal, reputation-based interactions, networks not only increase the stability of market operations but also enhance efficiency in a variety of ways.

Reliance on markets as a coordinating device by no means implies a laissez-faire orientation by the government. As economists have long known, markets fail in many areas critical to economic performance. Unfettered—or, more to the point, unassisted—markets tend to undersupply investment in plant and equipment, research and development, new technology, and worker training. In some cases markets simply do not provide adequate incentives for sufficient investment; in other instances market incentives actually discourage investment. Countries such as Japan, France, South Korea, and Taiwan have exhibited considerable success at utilizing direct government steering to prevent or compensate for such market failures.

Many progressives are understandably unwilling to depart from the traditional socialist goal of socializing property ownership. The unrestricted accumulation of private property is the chief source of the widespread inequalities in wealth and power that pervade capitalism. In recent years, a number of innovative proposals have been developed for ways to combine markets with public ownership. Three are particularly worth mentioning here; in each, firms make their own production decisions and interact freely with their suppliers and customers, and property is publicly owned. The key differences lie in the way public property ownership is structured and in the mechanism through which finance is allocated to firms.

One market socialist proposal, advanced by John Roemer, features completely centralized control of finance. Credit would be allocated entirely by the state in the form of loans. By using differential interest rates, the political party in power could give priority to certain sectors and firms in the economy. According to Roemer, it is possible for a government economic bureau to calculate a set of interest rates such that a market interaction between firms and the state credit institutions would yield the desired allocation of resources. This arrangement would enable society to democratically determine its allocation of economic resources while still achieving optimal efficiency.

A second proposal, developed by Leland Stauber, features a more decentralized mechanism for allocating finance. Firms would continue to sell equity shares as they do now under capitalism, and this would constitute their principal source of finance. But the share purchasers—and thus owners of firms—would be public investment banks controlled by local governments. Ownership would remain decentralized in that each investment bank could purchase no more than 10 percent of the shares in any particular firm. The objective of Stauber's model is to approximate as closely as possible the allocative efficiency of a decentralized capital market, while removing ownership from private hands.

Public ownership of property is a central component of most conceptions of socialism. Traditionally, much of the left has assumed that public meant the state and that the transfer of property from private to public hands would occur largely in one fell swoop of nationalization. During the past several decades, however, social democratic strategists have drawn up proposals for gradually transferring capital ownership not to the state but to the work force. The best-known of these plans, the Swedish wage earner funds proposal of Rudolf Meidner, would require firms to place a small percentage of profits into a union-controlled fund. Over the course of fifty or so years, the bulk of the nation's capital would come under labor force control via its union organizations. Other proposals in this genre rely on alternative mechanisms—such as pension funds and employee ownership schemes—for socializing capital ownership.

Worker management of firms, like planning and public ownership, has long held a privileged place in progressive visions of a postcapitalist economy. Ethical concerns such as reducing alienation through participation, eliminating power asymmetry in the workplace, and, most important, extending democracy to the realm of work motivate the attraction to self-management. Proponents of self-management rightly insist that if democracy is justified in the political realm, it must be justified in governing economic enterprises. This relies on the age-old principle that what touches all should be decided by all.

Most enthusiasts of self-management also contend that, by increasing worker satisfaction and morale and reducing monitoring costs, workplace democracy enhances productivity and efficiency. Recent empirical studies on employee participation in decisionmaking within traditional capitalist firms have found participation indeed associated with higher productivity.

S till, there is a profound difference between participation and control, one that has a direct bearing on economic performance. Economists have demonstrated that, theoretically, an employee-managed economy—in which workers have full, rather than just partial, decisionmaking rights—

will tend toward underinvestment, inflation, and underemployment. Workers in self-managed firms face an incentive to pay out a high portion of profits to themselves in the form of wages, which reduces the quantity of funds available for reinvestment and results in price increases and inflation. Worker-managers may also be reluctant to reinvest profits because, if firms are collectively owned by the work force, individual workers cannot recover their share of such investments upon leaving the firm; hence, it is preferable to have that share paid out in the form of wages. Cooperatives can also be expected to keep their level of employment as low as possible, so that profit per worker is maximized.

Centralized wage setting among representatives of worker-managed firms—along the lines of that in corporatist economies such as Sweden and Austria—would help minimize wage exaggeration. Coordination promotes wage restraint by encouraging labor leaders to take into account the long-term interests of wage earners as a group.

Economist Saul Estrin has suggested that the tendency toward underinvestment of profits can be remedied by placing self-managed firms under the control of competing public holding companies. These companies, a prominent feature of Austria's economy, would provide external finance in the form of loans to the cooperatives, thereby surmounting the problem of insufficient reinvestment of internally generated funds. The public investment banks in Leland Stauber's market socialist proposal or the state credit institutions in John Roemer's model could serve the same function. An alternative mechanism for overcoming the underinvestment problem would be to give workers equity stakes in their firm, which could be redeemed only upon leaving the firm or retirement.

Finally, the employment-creation deficiencies of self-managed firms could be alleviated by having holding companies or some other government bodies encourage start-up cooperatives in profitable areas and/or offer incentives for existing firms to hire additional workers.

I f self-management is attractive and feasible, why are there so few cooperatives in existing capitalist economies? Skeptics contend this indicates that worker management isn't really so desirable or workable after all. Yet there are a number of plausible alternative reasons for the scarcity of cooperatives, ranging from biases in capital markets to risk aversion among workers under capitalist constraints. Because of the uncertainty inherent in evaluating its efficiency properties, the case for worker self-management must rest fundamentally on considerations of justice. Still, since self-management—unlike central planning—seems both practicable and potentially efficient, its ethical force should compel us at least to experiment widely with the institution.

Equality has always been a central concern of progressives and must undoubtedly be a key component of any just economic system. Does equality reduce efficiency? Although attempting to achieve perfect distributive equality would likely detract substantially from economic performance, there is little reason to think that equality greater than that now existing in most developed nations would have this effect. Income equality enhances and stabilizes demand, helping to perpetuate a virtuous circle of high wages, high growth, and high employment. And because of its fairness properties, distributive equity may improve worker motivation and cooperation, thereby enhancing productivity. Empirically, too, the evidence weighs against the conventional wisdom. The record of the sixteen most developed capitalist economies over the past thirty years offers no support for the notion of a trade-off between income equality and economic performance.

Does equality impede freedom? Libertarians such as Milton Friedman have forcefully articulated the position that freedom and equality are antithetical. This contention, however, relies on a rather limited conception of liberty as merely the absence of coercion. True individual freedom must consist of positive capacities, not just the absence of barriers. Greater equality of income, education, and power would enhance the capability of large numbers of people to generate and fulfill informed preferences and thereby augment their freedom. In this sense, equality and liberty are not only compatible, they are interdependent.

During the past twenty years, philosophers have debated the relative merits of the principles of equality of opportunity and equality of outcome. On purely philosophical grounds it is difficult to favor equal opportunity, since innate talents are surely a morally arbitrary basis upon which to justify differential outcomes. Nevertheless, no one has yet elaborated an even remotely feasible design for implementing a policy of strict equality of outcome (whether outcome refers to resources or to welfare). Furthermore, a limited degree of distributive inequality is not necessarily unjust. For these reasons, the goal of egalitarians should be to reduce end-state inequality to a reasonable, acceptable level, while attempting to achieve to the greatest degree possible a situation of equal opportunity.

In existing capitalist economies, the principal government measures used to reduce outcome inequality are social policy and progressive taxation. Although these measures helped equalize incomes in the United States during most of the postwar period, there are limits to the effectiveness of such policies. As noted earlier, accumulation of property is the chief source of capitalism's extreme resource inequalities. Although plainly there will have to be space for some private property ownership—for a sector of small-scale petty capitalists—in a desirable and feasible postcapitalist economy, the portion of property held in private individual hands must be restricted. As a rough estimate, perhaps 75 percent of employment should be accounted for by the public or socialized sector. (It is worth noting again here that public need not refer to the state.) We must develop a mechanism to reduce the inequality-producing effects of inheritance. One possibility is British economist James Meade's proposal for transforming the traditional inheritance tax system, giving people incentives to bequeath substantial portions of their wealth to those less well off.

A chieving equal opportunity requires, first, that access to skills and jobs be equalized. This would, of course, entail a restructuring of our existing educational system so that funding is more equally distributed. Also crucial is a serious government commitment to vocational training, retraining, and job placement programs. Sweden's active labor market policy is a model upon which postcapitalist policymakers could usefully draw. Equalizing access to jobs would also require the removal of the various impediments—present in all existing economies—to labor market equality for women and minorities. These include hiring discrimination, job segregation, and unequal pay for similar work.

A second precondition for true equality of opportunity is a guarantee of a basic degree of material security for all individuals. The most straightforward means of achieving this would be to distribute to every citizen a basic income grant sufficient to ensure a minimum standard of living, not contingent upon performing any work. Such a grant would have the additional salutary effect of forcing up the wages for, and/or increasing the mechanization of, society's most undesirable jobs.

Not everyone on the left will agree with these proposals. Nevertheless, an attractive, feasible economic system would arguably combine state-guided markets, substantial public ownership, worker self-management, and equality. What we need is a little bit of Japan, a little Austria, a little Yugoslavia, and a little Sweden nicely meshed together. Others, no doubt, hold different views. Further disagreement surely exists regarding strategy for how to get there from here. What perhaps we can all agree on, however, is that progressives need desperately to think, and talk, about what exactly we want in an economic system. The opportunity, and the necessity, for such discussion have never been greater.

34

AGGRESSION
REDUCTION STRATEGIES

ARNOLD P. GOLDSTEIN

Contemporary aggression takes many guises: violence and vandalism by juveniles in schools and in their communities; child and spouse abuse and other forms of domestic or familial violence; assaults, muggings, and homicides; rape and other sex-related crimes; politically motivated terrorism; racially or economically motivated mob violence; and aggression in many forms directly or indirectly initiated by the state. We could add athletic mayhem, clan blood feuds, ritual torture, police brutality, organized warfare, and much, much more. The variety, intensity, frequency, and overall prevalence of overt aggressive behavior throughout the world is appallingly high. Three popular strategies have been offered for reducing this aggression: control, catharsis, and cohabitation. Yet arguably, all three are destined to failure.

The first, *control theory,* is most popular in eras of political conservatism and can be illustrated by the response taken by the U.S. criminal justice system to violent crime. For example, in his book *Correctional Treatment,* Clemens Bartollas observes that

> proponents of the hard-line approach . . . see punishment as more likely to deter crime and to provide protection to society. They also claim that the establishment of law and order demands firm methods of crime control, such as a greater reliance on incapacitation, the use of the death penalty, the implementation of determinate and mandatory sentences.

But does deterrence in fact deter; do punitive means intended to control aggression in fact control? Most research says no. In the home and school, control of aggression is often sought through verbal or physical punishment techniques. The effectiveness of reprimands, spankings, or similar forms of punishment depends on various factors. Punishment will

---

This essay was first published in *Peace Review* 4:3 (1992).

more likely control aggressive behavior when it is more certainly and rapidly applied, when it is introduced at full rather than gradual intensity, when it is unlikely it can be avoided, when alternative means to goal satisfaction are less available, when levels of instigation or reward for aggression are low, and when the prohibiting agent is more potent. Given all that is required, it is not surprising that the main effect of most punishment is merely a temporary suppression of aggressive behavior. Punishment research also shows undesirable side effects of punishment, such as withdrawal from social contact, counteraggression toward the punisher, modeling of punishing behavior, disruption of social relationships, failure of long-lasting effects, selective avoidance (refraining from aggressive behaviors only when under surveillance), and the stigma of labeling. Even when punishment temporarily succeeds in inhibiting the unwanted behavior, it fails to teach the appropriate, alternative actions. Punishment instructs what not to do, not what one should do instead.

Catharsis is a second theory of how to manage aggressive behavior. This involves the draining, venting, or purging of emotions, an experience that purportedly occurs vicariously—by empathically identifying with another person, or directly—via one's own expressive behavior. Catharsis first appeared in the vicarious sense, with the reported emotional purging of the audience in early Greek drama. Later, in the direct sense, Freud wrote that "there is a continuous welling up of destructive impulses within the individual representing the outgrowth of the death instinct." Lorenz held that in both animals and humans, "aggressive energy is continuously being generated within the species member and seeks periodic release." In these hydrolic views, aggression is inevitable. All one can do is channel or regulate its periodic release via a socially acceptable, minimally injurious, aggressive act, such as debates, the space race, and competitive sports. Procter and Eckerd present this view in the *American Journal of Sports Medicine:*

> People's emotions are similar to steam locomotives. If you build a fire in the boiler of a locomotive, keep raising the steam pressure and let it sit on the tracks, sooner or later something will blow. However, if you take it and spin the wheels and toot the whistle, the steam pressure can be kept at a safe level. Spectator sports give John Q. Citizen a socially acceptable way to lower his steam pressure by allowing him to spin his wheels and toot his whistle.

The view of aggression as stored, constantly growing energy, which if directly or vicariously vented leaves less in the person's reservoir, is widely held; but is it correct? Here's what research has shown. Static comparisons simply compare the aggressiveness levels of people who do or do not regularly engage in aggressive activities. The catharsis theory would predict that those who do—having vented—should show less aggression. Yet one study, which compared contact sport (football, wrestling) to noncontact sport (swimming, tennis) athletes found no differences between them in aggression. Another study compared football players and nonathletes, and then tennis players and nonathletes. All results agreed: no between-group differences on aggression, i.e., no evidence that expressing aggression reduces it.

Before-after studies identify or randomly constitute two groups, but only one is given the opportunity to aggress. If catharsis is correct, that group should be less aggressive. Two studies of this type found no support for such an effect. More surprisingly, three other studies—one requiring subjects to hammer nails, another asking subjects to say aggressive words, and a third comparing football players and physical education students before and after the football season—found an opposite effect: greater aggression! Another study measured aggression levels in randomly selected fans just before and after an Army-Navy football game. Contrary to catharsis, fans of both winners and losers had increased aggression levels after the game. The investigators comment, "Exposure to the aggression of others seemingly acts to weaken one's internal mechanisms controlling the expression of similar behavior." Other research has confirmed this and also showed that fan aggression increased after (aggressive) football and hockey matches but not after (nonaggressive) swim meets.

Archival studies examine short- or long-term records of aggression-expressing sports and other events, which, if catharsis occurs, should reveal a decrease in aggression over the course of the event. Yet five such studies showed the opposite of catharsis: aggression increased as the event progressed. A similar result emerged in a report tracking aggression between two teams as they met over a season: more not less aggression took place. The early proponents of competitive sports as an ideal venting ground for human aggression saw sports, in their grand vision, as a substitute for war. Yet another study showed a positive relationship between the level of a society's competitive sports and its involvement in wars, conflicts, revolutions, and similar events. Other research found a positive correlation between a country's participation in the Olympics and the number of athletes it sent and both the number and length of the wars in which it participated.

Finally, in a laboratory study, one group of research subjects were shown either brutal, but staged, sports violence (e.g., the fight scene from the movie *The Champion*) or equally brutal actual fights from hockey, football, and basketball. In all instances, these subjects, as compared to non-viewing control group subjects, increased significantly in their own levels of aggression.

Catharsis is a myth. As Goranson notes in examining the effects of media violence:

> I think that this is one of those rare occasions in behavioral research where an unqualified conclusion is warranted. The observation of violence does not reduce aggressiveness. . . . Observed violence serves to facilitate the expression of aggression, rather than reduce aggression by draining off aggressive energy!

Cohabitation theory, yet another common strategy against aggression, takes the defeatist position that aggression is human nature, it will always be with us, and we have no choice but to live with it. Many holding this view live with it poorly. Thousands of city-dwelling elderly, for example, sentence themselves to solitary confinement every evening in response to their fear of becoming a violent crime victim. Millions more (perhaps all of us) increasingly desensitize themselves or tolerate, adapt to, or expect high levels of daily aggression as simply the way it is.

But, in fact, it is not the way it is. Much has already been accomplished in the laboratory and the community to successfully reduce child and spouse abuse, juvenile delinquency, sexual assault, school and sports violence, and other expressions of human aggression. We are learning of more and more effective aggression reduction strategies, but they all require a change in our customary thinking about aggression.

The can-do ethos of the United States makes us assume we will find the big solution for major social problems. Thus, we seek the one breakthrough program to wipe out poverty (e.g., the 1960s War on Poverty), cancer (e.g., various miracle cures), illiteracy (e.g., early education interventions), hunger and malnutrition (e.g., food stamps), and drug abuse (e.g., "Just Say No" campaigns). Likewise, the magic bullets aimed at aggression over the past few decades have included psychotherapy, behavior modification, medication, early detection and diversion, determinate or indeterminate sentences, selective incapacitation, and many other programs. They all miss the effective target. Complex problems like aggression have multiple causes and will yield only to complex solutions. When Johnny throws a book at his teacher (or draws a knife), we will not adequately explain this behavior (or reduce it) by blaming his aggressive personality, economic disadvantage, or other single cause.

Rather, aggression grows from an array of social and individual causes. They include: (1) physiological predispositions such as male gender and high-arousal temperaments; (2) cultural contexts such as social traditions that either encourage or restrain aggression; (3) immediate interpersonal environments such as parental or peer criminality or video, movie, and live-aggression models; (4) immediate physical environment such as temperature, noise, crowding, pollution, and traffic; (5) personal qualities such as self-control and prosocial behaviors; (6) disinhibitors such as alcohol, drugs, and successful aggression models; (7) means such as guns, knives, and other weapons; and (8) potential victims such as a spouse, child, or senior.

To have a chance of enduring success, interventions against aggression in a context like the schools, for example, must respond to the complexity of causes and thus be directed not only at the aggressor but also at the parent, teacher, school administration, and larger community context. An optimally complex intervention designed to reduce school violence must use a variety of channels.

An appropriately complex array of intervention modes works best if applied in a differential, tailored, individualized, or prescriptive manner. This holds for all types of aggression, although we have applied it most in interventions against juvenile delinquents. Prescriptive programming recognizes that different aggressors, including delinquents, will respond to different change methods. Instead of the usual one-true-light theory, which assumes that specific treatments can override individual differences and help heterogeneous groups, the many-true-lights theory explores which types of youth, meeting with which types of change agents, for which types of interventions will yield optimal outcomes.

U nderstanding, predicting, and controlling human behavior has been psychology's central objective since its inception almost 100 years ago. To accomplish this difficult task, our first step has been trying to more deeply understand the actor's personality. We might test for trait information about dependency, extraversion, and hostility. We would do so because psychology assumed, at least until the 1950s, that the primary determinants of human behavior lie within people themselves, i.e., within their personality or dispositional tendencies. Understand the personality better and the accurate prediction and control of behavior will follow.

Since the 1960s, however, psychology has increasingly recognized human behavior as a joint function of personal traits as they interact with each person's situational context. We can predict some future aggressive behavior, for example, if we know something about the hostility traits of a given athlete, student, or prisoner. But how much deeper our understanding, better our predictions, and more effective our intervention efforts are when we also consider situational research findings that show, for example: (a) that aggression in athletics is greater for home rather than visiting team members, greater later than earlier in a game or season, and greater when the team is in the middle rather than top or bottom of its league's standings; (b) that aggression in schools is greater in some locations (cafeterias, stairwells, bathrooms) than others (classrooms), greater at some times of the year than others (worst in March in the United States; worst on the last school day in Japan), greater the larger the school, and greater either the more autocratic or more laissez-faire the school rather than firm but fair; and (c) that aggression in prisons is greater the larger the prison, the more external (in and out) traffic, the more internal (within) traffic, and the more racially mixed or gang-dominated.

Situational characteristics such as location, physical arrangement, entrances and exits, illumination, temperature, noise level, timing, personal actions, norms, rules, goals, roles, tasks, themes, expectations, and ambiguities are each potential antecedents of aggressive behavior. None are in the potential aggressor, but all may substantially help us effectively understand, predict, and reduce human aggression.

Finally, we will be able to deal with aggression seriously only if we view such behavior as learned. As suggested, aggression does not derive basically from instinctive energy. Instead, recent research shows conclusively that a major (perhaps the major) source of aggressive behavior is human learning.

B ut learned where, and how? In most Western societies, and most clearly in the United States, there are three major classrooms for aggression: the home, the school, and the mass media. In the U.S. home, for example, although only 4 to 14 percent of parents physically abuse their children (e.g., burning, fracturing bones, inflicting concussions), 85 percent make at least occasional, and sometimes frequent, use of corporal punishment (e.g., spank, hit, slap). What happens when an adult hits a child? Often the child stops the offending behavior, at least temporarily. Negative reinforcement ends the aversive event and makes the adult more likely to use corporal punishment against the child's next transgression as well as against the transgressions of others. But from this not only the adult learns the adage "might makes right." So too does the child.

Aggression is learned either directly or vicariously. Direct learning (the adult aggressor in our example) follows from reinforced practice, i.e., the behavior is tried and produces the desired result. Vicarious learning (the victimized child in our example) comes from observing others behaving aggressively and being rewarded for doing so. Little Johnny learns not only not to pull his sister's hair again (at least not when his father is around) but also—by observing his father's successful aggression against him—that might makes right. He may well not counteraggress toward his father, but it should not surprise us if he goes out to play, sees a younger (smaller) friend with an attractive toy, and then forcefully takes it from him. Nor should we wonder when Johnny—like many other brutalized children—ends up abusing his own children as an adult.

The U.S. school is a second major place where aggression is taught. Not only does this result from the aggression practiced by many adolescent peer groups, but also from U.S. teachers—who often act in ways analogous to abusive parents. Abusive physical punishment of children by parents is illegal and can be reported, investigated, and prosecuted in all U.S. states, but not so teacher abuse of students. In fact, in twenty-eight states containing 51 percent of U.S. school children, corporal punishment is legal. Although usually constrained by rules that require the offended teacher to turn the offender over to the school's designated hitters (often vice-principals), they often set their own constraints about things like paddle size, the number and intensity of strokes, the presence of witnesses, and so forth. These regulations do little to lessen the great likelihood that when Johnny leaves the vice-principal's office, rubbing his behind, he will again have learned the lesson that might makes right.

Finally, Americans learn not only in the formal setting of their schools and the less formal setting of their homes. If sheer numbers are the guide, most learning occurs through the mass media—newspapers, books, comic books, radio, movies, and, in particular, television. The impact of the mass media on popular behavior in the United States is immense. The combined evidence suggests that, among other things, it has increased the level of violence in contemporary America. In particular, television viewing, which transmits a heavy, almost unceasing, diet of violence contributes substantially to overt aggressive behavior. Primetime, evening television in the United States during 1992 contained an average of nine acts of violence per hour, up from seven in 1982. Cartoon violence on Saturday mornings now contains twenty-five violent acts per hour. By age sixteen, the average U.S. adolescent who views thirty-five hours of television programming per week will have seen 200,000 violent acts, 33,000 of which are murders or attempted murders. No wonder some viewers engage in actual, copycat violence!

The pernicious effects of television violence also substantially decrease the sensitivity, concern, and revulsion to violence experienced by the general viewing audience. Higher and higher levels of violence become more and more tolerable. These and other aggression-enhancing or aggression-tolerating effects of U.S. television promote the worst in U.S. behavior.

Yet anything learned can be unlearned, and the very means by which aggressive, antisocial behaviors are typically learned (e.g., direct or observed reward experiences) can and have been used to teach prosocial alternative behaviors, such as sharing, empathy, cooperation, helping, and altruism. Since 1970, our research group has been developing, implementing, and evaluating three increasingly comprehensive interventions designed for chronically antisocial individuals. Working with aggressive adolescents, impulsive children, battering spouses, and others, our interventions—Skillstreaming, Aggression Replacement Training, and the Prepare Curriculum—have reaffirmed the effectiveness of the foregoing strategies. Aggression is best understood and most effectively controlled when seen as complexly caused learned behavior, with personality and situational determinants, which can be altered in an individualized, prescriptively based manner.

35

CIVIL DETERRENCE

CHRISTIAN MELLON
JEAN-MARIE MULLER
JACQUES SEMELIN

The French position on nuclear deterrence is well known: "France has no intention of undertaking offensive action against anyone whatsoever. . . . So we have a purely defensive situation. . . . We've made our capability so terrible that no-one would dare attack our country. That's what we call dissuasion." In these, and similar words, President Mitterrand has reassured his country throughout the 1980s that the little fellow—de Gaulle used to liken himself to the cartoon character Tintin taking on the grown-ups— won't get pushed around by any superpower bully.

It is called *dissuasion du faible au fort*—deterrence of the strong by the weak—and is founded on calculations of unacceptable damage and whether upwards of a thousand multi-Hiroshima weapons counts as nuclear sufficiency for France. The problem being that while the *weak* is perfectly able to destroy large numbers of enemy cities, the *strong* threatens retaliation that would not only constitute unacceptable damage but would leave France irreparable.

I s the risk morally, politically, and strategically acceptable? Philosopher André Glucksmann poses "the most serious and most banal of our modern everyday questions" when he asks: "Are we allowed to threaten civilian populations, ourselves included, with apocalypse? Does a civilization stay a civilization when it knowingly risks its own extinction?" Glucksmann, as we know, answers his own tragic question with a resounding yes, but we refuse to give our consent. Glucksmann's certitudes are too glib, given the probabilities of failure of deterrence somewhere along the line. It's neither realistic, nor rational, nor reasonable to be prepared to destroy ourselves to defend ourselves. And most French people know it.

Deterrence is not an international insurance policy; it's a gamble.

This essay is based on Christian Mellon, Jean-Marie Muller, and Jacques Semelin, *La Dissuasion Civile* (Paris: Foundation pour les Etudes de Défense Nationale, 1985).

There are so many ways it could break down. Even our nuclear strategists know—and sometimes actually admit—that there are threats to our independence and national sovereignty against which nuclear strategy is powerless. So we owe it to ourselves to think about the options. Prudence dictates that we envisage a scenario in which the president of the republic is left with no margin of maneuver to make the argument of our nuclear forces carry weight. What should we do then? The fallibility of nuclear dissuasion implies, at the very least, that it should not be the sole basis of our security.

Yet security is a fundamental need of every human community. This is the problem as we see it with proposals for immediate unilateral disarmament as a decisive contribution to peace. To the extent that any society's members feel that their security depends on the possession of armaments that are able to keep aggressors off their territory, the idea of unilateral disarmament can only lead to the most profound anxiety and insecurity. That is why our work is framed in terms of "transarmament," as a program that both fits in better with existing reality and is capable of creating a dynamic process to change it. Transarmament puts forward, as a priority, not the destruction of those weapons people believe ensure their security, but the importance of imagining other means of defense that might do the same job, at less risk. Whereas disarmament implies a negative prospect, transarmament suggests an essentially constructive project.

The important thing is to think in terms of means of defense that neither use nor even threaten to use homicidal violence as a tool. In other words, we have to seriously research the full range of nonviolent possibilities, not just in an ethical perspective but as a practical political activity.

Nonviolence is often thought of as an import from the East that does not easily transfer to Western culture. This just isn't true. Of course, Gandhi's example in India is particularly spectacular, but Gandhi himself was convinced that his was as much a Western as an oriental approach, and his method was certainly far from orthodox in terms of his own culture. Jacques Maritain and Emmanuel Mounier, writing in France in the 1930s, were converging on similar themes: "Violence is always an impurity, and a practical ideal of nonviolence should be the framework within which we work." Equally consistent was the rejection of fear and feebleness as components of nonviolence, which is instead defined as the politics of strong virtue. Nonviolent action always involves a struggle. One of its major roles is the awakening of active resistance in those suffering injustice, and even there it would be illusory to pretend that dialogue alone guarantees justice.

Our working hypothesis, therefore, does not envisage nonviolent civil defense as an alternative to armed defense but as a complement or extra resource. One advantage of this is that it permits joint research between those who have made a personal choice in favor of prioritizing armed defense and those whose ultimate aim is full-scale nonviolent defense.

Another is that it calls attention to the practical problems of the necessary transition.

On yet another level, it means that the credibility of a deterrence based exclusively on nonviolent civil defense is not at issue. What is worth noting, however, is the crucial difference between nonviolent civil dissuasion and nuclear dissuasion. If the latter fails, the means of dissuasion cannot be used as a means of defense—unless suicide can be construed as a defense. So there is absolute discontinuity between dissuasion and defense. Whereas if nonviolent civil dissuasion fails to deter an enemy attack, then the means intended for dissuasion can very effectively be put into operation as a means of defense. They are the very same. And not only can they be continued as long as necessary, but the enemy need have no doubt that we would be prepared to use them, which is more than can be said for the nuclear deterrent.

The more we "civilize" defense, in the sense of putting it in the hands of the civilian population, as well as in the sense of rendering it compatible with the behavior of an advanced civilization, the greater our dissuasive credibility. Isn't it the great weakness of nuclear deterrence, in fact, that it lulls people into believing that the whole business of defense has nothing to do with them? Of course, our governments go on about defense being a common concern and how the nuclear deterrent has no credibility without popular support. But what does it all mean? Passive acceptance? Nuclear consensus? Blind confidence in whoever happens to be the head of state at the time? The biggest risk for the country is that in a time of real crisis, there would be widespread panic. Civil society would break down before the bomb dropped. Government instructions, as we know from regular defense exercises, would be: Keep calm. Government interest would lie in immobilizing, not mobilizing, citizens.

What emerges from recent research is that people are much more interested than their governments realize in the business of defense, and that nonviolent civil defense is an option that corresponds to real aspirations. General Dominique Chavanat, reviewing a number of opinion polls on defense issues in *Défense Nationale,* came to the conclusion that "defense has been essentially a distant system, complex and frightening, outside people's control, but there are clear indications of a profound desire on the part of the French people to exercise a more direct responsibility." The responses show a majority (61 percent) affirming that "peace can be assured by other than military means."

The specific means we have in mind are all ones that correspond with these aspirations. Our basic model is a standard one, nevertheless—the strategic exercise is to deter, and if this fails, to defeat, a rational enemy who might decide to seize French territory as a means to an end. The following are the most probable ends: either to gain political control of our country by establishing a friendly government in Paris; or to suppress our democratic forms of organization for ideological reasons; or to exploit our economic resources, including technological expertise and labor force. It is on these three areas, then, that nonviolent strategy should concentrate.

Practical measures to deter and defend in the first category—political control—would aim at making French society ungovernable by any foreign power. Ungovernable because the enemy would be unable either to establish a lackey government that had the least trace of legitimacy in the eyes of the French people and the international community, or to effectively control the administration and police forces.

Heads of state may be the first to crack, so citizens need to be better trained to test and challenge the legitimacy of their leaders' moves. Pétain's solution of ambiguity in partitioning off the Vichy government in 1940 and Dubcek's undermining of the Czech people's nonviolent resistance in 1968—such accommodations have to be made constitutionally impossible, at least so we may recognize them when they happen. But there are other, legislative, steps to be taken in the protection of human rights and democratic procedures, which need to be given prominence now if they are to serve a useful purpose in the future. Nuremberg has taught us that we do need to think the unthinkable, juridically, to combat inhumanity effectively at every stage.

Local and administrative structures are potentially much more resistant than central government structures, and the risks incurred by individuals fewer. Here too, however, advance planning and training are essential for the automatic delegation of power down to the most decentralized levels, in the event of certain failures of resistance at the top. The sort of education in personal responsibility implied here cannot be achieved without some kind of collective thinking through of the demands made on the individual by a resistance movement. Bearing in mind the general aim of a civil resistance, which is to deprive the illegitimate power of people to carry out its orders, criteria would have to be drawn up for which orders could safely be obeyed, which ignored, which sabotaged, and so on. Only then would the individual, when the time came, be in a position to make his or her own choices.

What happens to the police force in these circumstances is determining. Eloquent enough the record of 1940–1944: Without the collaboration of the French police, the Germans would never have been able to accomplish their objectives, including the efficient rounding-up of French Jews. One of the most urgent matters for attention in the perspective of civil defense is the protection of police files from abuse. How secure are police records, particularly those of the *renseignements généraux* on the political activities and contacts of private citizens, from foreign takeover?

In the second category—ideological control—we surely have a powerful enough deterrent in the strength of our democratic practices and convictions and in the danger of our liberalizing effect on the subordinate elements of any totalitarian system that tried to absorb us! Nevertheless, ideology is the area in which we should properly examine the stakes of the game. What, potentially, are we fighting for? What are the values we most want to protect and would be ready to take risks for? What responsibilities are we willing to assume?

The role of "moral authorities" such as the churches can be an important indicator to a potential aggressor and directly affects the chances of civil resistance, as historic examples show. Hitler's plans for extermination of the mentally sick were effectively blocked by the religious authorities in Norway; whereas in Vichy the collaboration of the majority of Catholic bishops certainly weakened the Resistance; and for a contemporary example one has only to look at Poland.

In fact, the most serious problems encountered in planning for wartime cohesion on this ideological level are also the most serious problems of society in peacetime: the social or economic exclusion of large segments of the population; the gap between richest and poorest; the conscious or unconscious discrimination against racial and other minorities. The survival of the fittest is not a good model for a society that wants to defend itself and so survive. Objectively, the reduction of inequality is the surest way of creating a social consensus and reducing a society's vulnerability to ideological intrusion. In other words, there is a remarkable convergence between social justice and civil deterrence.

The third category—economic control—ought to be the simplest. How to resist economic exploitation is an area in which economists must have a great deal to offer but have not been given the incentive to produce it. The threat of a general strike that has been well prepared is not excluded a priori, but there are diverse forms of noncooperation that could come into play in any sustained conflict.

One such is the partial strike, in which strategic slowing down of key areas of production can be effected by quite small groups of workers. Where this is deemed too dangerous for the personnel, a more generalized go-slow might be preferred. Sabotage is a heroic-sounding act, but it encompasses many subtle and nonviolent forms; and the scope for inventively noncollaborative work, in the tradition of the *Good Soldier Schveik,* is infinite.

Key areas need to be prepared in great detail, however, if they are not to be wholly vulnerable to enemy manipulation. Electricity supplies are an obvious case in point. But there already exist very complex emergency plans for the selective supply of electricity in case of disaster, and war planning along these lines would be challenging and fun!

O ur conclusion is that it is possible to build up a system of nonviolent
civil defense initially as an adjunct to France's current strategic doctrine. It would be ready to take over in the event the deterrent failed. It
would be specifically trained to resist military occupation. And it would
meanwhile add important elements of civil dissuasion to our present one-
dimensional nuclear dissuasion.

The ideological foundation of civil deterrence is the capacity of the
population to refuse to collaborate with the authority that an aggressor
would wish to impose. This noncollaboration is expressed in disobedience
to the illegitimate authority, but it expresses first and foremost obedience to
the legitimate authority, which it continues to recognize. That is why the
civil disobedience we are recommending has to go beyond the spontaneity
of its historical precedents. It is not enough for the resistance to affirm its
political legitimacy; it has to be organized to realize the strategic capacity
needed to achieve its ends. Planning has to ensure the optimization of two
partly contradictory projects: maintaining the functioning of society on
behalf of the population; and paralyzing those activities that would profit
the aggressor in terms of either ideological influence, political control, or
economic exploitation.

The specifically civil form of deterrence we are advocating is quite an
innovation. Most of the normal categories of traditional defense thinking
would have to be rethought. For example, the state sector actually has
rather a small role in our society and would not suffice to mobilize a mass
civil defense. Yet at the same time, even within the state sector, it would be
no use organizing this kind of civil defense through the usual bureaucratic
rigmarole of executive decisions and taking orders from headquarters. The
organizational aspects of civil defense are much less mechanical that those
of military defense, and human factors have to play a more important role.

One of the most important things to consider is the responsibilities that
might be assumed by certain civil organizations that at present have no role
in defense: for instance, trade unions and professional associations, the
churches, political and social organizations. Local government should be
involved, to a far greater extent than it is at present, in the preparation of
this new civil defense. The kind of preparation we envisage is best
described as "social concert": an organic mutual agreement worked out
between the various socioeconomic partners in order to select and coordinate those methods that would be "best adapted" to the terrain. To be effective in a crisis, these would have to be worked out in advance. But it would
be folly to impose them from the top down.

W hat our initial research work has established is the feasibility of a
nonviolent civil defense in France. Like any social innovation, especially one that impinges on such a sensitive area as defense, it is bound to

meet with difficulties and obstacles, not least that changes in mentality as well as in fact are called for. But the key thing is to set the ball rolling in the right direction. In its favor are: the democratic pressure for fuller citizen participation in matters of defense; the minimal structural requirements of nonviolent civil defense; and the relatively small financial investment needed to set it in place.

Even more important, in our view, is the process by which such a system would be set in place. Over and over again, we have stressed the part that would have to be played—to promote not only the spirit of resistance, but also awareness of the means of resistance that we have at our disposal—by those institutions within which people daily live and work, share convictions and livelihoods, and participate collectively in the cultural, moral, economic and political life of their country. Each social movement and organization has its own internal logic favoring the sensitization of its members to the principles and methods of civil dissuasion.

Once this social dynamic is set in motion, who knows where the debate will end? What is really at stake for us as citizens, in our concern to defend our country and its values, whether with military or nonviolent means? We can ask, and maybe answer, some of these questions by refining our notion of civil deterrence.

PART 4

NEW STRATEGIES:
NEW IDEAS INTO ACTION

New Strategies:
New Ideas into Action

We have it in our power to begin the world again.—Thomas Paine

I can understand pessimism, but I don't believe in it. It's not simply a matter of faith, but of historical evidence. Not overwhelming evidence; just enough to fire hope, because for hope we don't need certainty, only possibility.—Howard Zinn

Good ideas and alternative models may fall short if we ignore how to get from "here to there." It also helps to believe that we can get from here to there, that change is possible. But change rarely comes from the top; rather it is most often achieved by pressures from the bottom, from the grassroots. Although often ignored, the world has a rich history of political and social movements. And while they do not always achieve their grandest goals, they have produced some remarkable progress—achievements once thought impossible, such as the end of slavery or the end of communist dictatorship.

Thus, this section examines how we might develop a more peaceful politics and economy in practice. We review various practical strategies for transforming our new thinking into political action and social change.

We begin by examining various forms of peace action. How are grassroots nongovernmental organizations promoting peace by working outside conventional political channels? Can citizens' assemblies such as those in Europe provide viable alternatives for official legislatures and bureaucracies? Can an industrial cooperative system such as the one in Mondragón, Spain, provide a viable, and more just, economic alternative for other parts of the world?

Can local governments, closer to the public "heartbeat," practice a kind of transnational, municipal diplomacy that transcends the debilitating politics of centralized and nationalist intergovernmental relations? Also, rather than merely hoping the media will more aggressively hold those in power responsible, can we learn to use or "frame" the media for more peaceful purposes? And what specific steps can we take to significantly reduce the practice of war? Indeed, much could be accomplished given the political will to do so.

Finally, we should examine the state of contemporary peace movements. For example, can the threat of nuclear war still motivate citizen activism? What is the role of insurgent movements for greater democracy in regions such as Africa and Latin America? Given its unique history since World War II, what are the contemporary challenges for the Japanese peace movement? And where does the U.S. peace movement stand, and what are the most promising directions for its future?

NEW STRATEGIES:
PEACE ACTION

36

A GRASSROOTS
APPROACH TO LIFE IN PEACE

—————— CHADWICK F. ALGER ——————

A grassroots perspective for overcoming peacelessness may be viewed as
either utopian or so long-term as to be useless. After all, people at the
grassroots have not controlled the world's instruments of violence. If we
want to stop violence, should we not focus on the power centers controlling
the world's firepower?

Perhaps, but past hopes that these centers might guarantee world peace
have not been fulfilled. Efforts to control violence through balance of
power, deterrence, collective security, peacekeeping, arms control, and disarmament have not always failed; nor should they end. But power centers
alone do not have the competence nor the will to save us from destruction.
Peace cannot be pursued primarily by using or controlling violence.

B eyond the morning headlines, there has been a global learning process
centered on: the United Nations system and related nongovernmental
organizations; transnational scholarly research and debate; and grassroots
movements. Increasing grassroots involvement shows that more people
now understand peace more deeply and the contribution grassroots activities can make, whether they are trying to free a political prisoner, denying
entry to armed nuclear ships, withdrawing investments supporting
apartheid, giving sanctuary to refugees, or organizing to prevent corporate
takeovers.

The global dialectic in peace thinking, reaching from the UN to the
grassroots, has produced three fundamental transformations. The first
broadens peace, as in the UN Declaration on the Preparation of Societies
for Life in Peace:

> the removal of institutional obstacles and the promotion of structural con-
> ditions facilitating the growth of socio-cultural, economic and political

———————

This essay is based on an article that first appeared in *Bulletin of Peace Proposals,*
18: 3 (1987).

trends, aiming at and leading to Life in Peace understood as both subjective life styles and objective living conditions congruent with basic peace values such as security, non-violence, identity, equity and well-being as opposed to insecurity, violence, alienation, inequity and deprivation.

The expanding UN membership, from 50 to 159 in forty years, has promoted a global dialogue on peace and thus broader definitions. People experience peacelessness from conditions such as sickness, poverty, oppression, war or threat of war, cultural threats, and pollution. Global progress toward peace requires overcoming simultaneously these diverse sources.

The second transformation recognizes that peace cannot be attained by a few leaders acting alone. A broader peace (both positive and negative) will emerge from diverse sectors and relationships. Government leaders and nongovernmental institutions cannot produce lasting peace without the knowledge, participation, and support of the world's people.

The third transformation sees peace as unfolding from the pursuit of peace. The further we move toward our present notion of peace, the more highly developed will be our image of peace and our ability to achieve it. This differs dramatically from peace as merely a return to prewar conditions, or as merely a resolution of isolated conflicts. Now we understand the diversity of human activities for pursuing peace, to which all walks of life can contribute.

S ome resist these transformations, insisting that stopping the violence or banning the bomb must precede concerns about social justice, economic well-being, or ecological balance. Of course, we must try to prevent further nuclear weapons deployment. But for millions of people, malnutrition, disease, poverty, racial and sexual discrimination, and cultural destruction are more tangible forms of peacelessness.

The seventy years of the League of Nations and the UN show that negative-peace strategies (stopping the violence) have had very limited success. Workers in these peace laboratories have therefore broadened the peace agenda to economic well-being, self-determination, human rights, and ecological issues. This is not an abdication, nor a diversion to easier tasks, but rather a recognition that negative-peace strategies rely on simultaneous positive-peace strategies.

The greatest potential for preparing societies for peace comes from the grassroots. Peace cannot be imposed but rather must grow from the bottom up. All aspects of peace—economic well-being, social justice, ecological balance, and limitations on violence—have been pursued by movements in both the industrialized and Third worlds. Yet the First World has focused on limiting nuclear weapons. In building coalitions around this objective, however, the peace movement has broadened itself to economic issues such as jobs for peace and military conversion.

On the other hand, development has been central to Third World peace thinking, assuming it would lead to economic well-being. The emerging focus on limiting the instruments of violence comes indirectly, from the view that arms production consumes resources and prevents development.

F irst and Third World movements both challenge traditional state prerogatives. Security policy has been controlled by a small politico-military elite, assumed to have special competence to know the national interest. Legislators in the formal democracies have deferred to this elite, but grassroots movements have not; bolstered by their own information and knowledge, they have challenged government security policies.

Simultaneously, development experts have been challenged by grassroots movements. Third World nations have long demanded freedom from external dependence to secure greater autonomy and self-reliance. Now the grassroots demand that these same nations give them greater autonomy and self-reliance for an alternative development.

These grassroots stirrings arise from dramatic changes in transportation and communications and their effect on production, marketing, investment, and military strategy. Even remote areas are now reachable by satellites, by nuclear or conventional explosives, by industrial pollution, and by economic intervention. This new sense of place in the world, and new interconnectedness, have pushed grassroots movements toward issues that were previously beyond local competence.

Grassroots peace movements could complicate the quest for global peace; already officials from 159 states, thirty UN agencies, and several hundred other international governmental organizations find it difficult to coordinate. Yet too many official covenants and peace declarations have had little impact. Many have been ignored; others haven't even been fully ratified; most people at the grassroots don't even know they exist. There must be greater grassroots participation.

B ut how can we do this? We cannot eliminate all territories between the grassroots and the UN. But people must unite to solve mutual problems from diverse communities—from neighborhoods, to cities, to provinces, and to larger configurations. People in different cultures must be able to connect to the world and yet preserve their own traditions.

Relatively few First World movements explicitly focus on peace. Only national leaders, not ordinary people, are expected to be involved. Formal education reinforces this socialization by limiting international relations study to state actions and ignoring the role of local communities in the world.

Some have pursued local peace initiatives nevertheless. Educational projects such as world affairs councils have sponsored symposia, study groups, and outreach activities in schools. Assistance programs have emphasized relief after cataclysmic events and long-term development aid. Refugee programs focus on refugees abroad and those needing homes in the local community. Exchange programs have emphasized youth but now adults as well. Sister cities or town twinnings link aspects of local life in cities across nations.

Unfortunately, most people-to-people programs do not challenge state policy but rather reproduce it, and they often deal with symptoms rather than causes. Some newer movements go further, focusing on weapons production (Nuclear Freeze, nuclear-free zones, military conversion), human rights (Amnesty International, political sanctuary, antiapartheid), and poverty (Bread Not Bombs, First World/Third World twinning).

Ordinary people can understand complicated issues such as economic conversion and weapons systems as well as foreign policy elites. They have developed innovative, direct action methods such as the antiapartheid campaign's divestment strategy against banks, universities, corporations, and governments connected to South Africa. Conversion plans have become participatory education exercises on organizing local peace economies. The sanctuary movement offers political refugees shelter in local churches. The Pledge of Resistance has organized retaliatory action against U.S. military intervention in Central America.

These movements also involve local governments. Bucking convention, 3,223 cities, counties, and provinces in nineteen nations have declared themselves nuclear-free zones, and others have adopted antiapartheid, sanctuary, and conversion legislation. In Europe, town councils have created policies for cooperating in Third World development activities. Bruges, Belgium, has an alderman for development, and Tilburg, Netherlands, has an advisory board on First and Third World inequalities. The mayors of Hiroshima and Nagasaki have convened a conference of world mayors against nuclear weapons.

Based on their distrust of governments and the media, people have been traveling abroad to observe situations directly. This people's foreign service movement includes visits to the Soviet Union, exchanges between U.S. and Soviet cities, and visits to Central America—particularly Nicaragua.

Just as First World peoples have been diverted from participating, Third World peoples have been led to believe that peace requires deference to national development policies designed by others. There is an assumption that the underdeveloped cannot lead a decentralized life without outside guidance. Majid Rahnema has pointed out that when the newly emerging states joined the bandwagon of development, they

> moved away from their peoples toward "privileged partnership" with metropolitan states. Development programmes became a label for the chan-

nels of negotiations and transactions of funds and equipment, never wholly free of corruption, seldom free of diversion into the repressive apparatus. "Development" made it all credible and respectable.

In contrast, new grassroots movements open alternative political spaces. Issues such as people's health, forest rights, community resources, and women's rights are now the subject of political struggle. Examples include the people's movement against felling trees in the Himalayan foothills, the miners' struggle in Chattisgarh, land reform activism in Andhra Pradesh, peasant organizing in Karnataka against granite mining, and a regional autonomy movement in the Bihar and Orissa tribal belt.

Given widespread dissatisfaction with development programs, calls for popular participation in development have blossomed. Nevertheless, Gilbert and Ward's study of community action by the poor in Bogotá, Mexico City, and Valencia (Venezuela) found each city deflecting opposition by making concessions, providing services, and coopting leaders; and they concluded that "there is certainly little sign of participation in the sense of growing control by poor people over the resources and institutions that determine their quality of life."

Others worry about decentralization becoming more a matter of form than substance. The Mexican scholar Hugo Zemelman, for example, distinguishes between participation with and without the power to decide. Participation with power "must include people's capacity to create forms of participation through the functioning of development projects." Others have distinguished between people-centered and production-centered development, with the former having settings that allow people to meet their own needs, self-organizing structures and processes, and local control of resources.

Locally initiated development has also stimulated nonformal education. Rolland G. Paulston and G. LeRoy have observed:

> If one seeks to find education that does more than legitimize and reinforce gross inequalities in life chances, then one must look outside formal schools to the educational activities of reformist collective efforts seeking individual and social renewal.

But this must be more than an adjunct to conventional schooling. Thomas J. LaBelle's study of seventy nonformal Latin American education programs found them not conducive to social change because they were man oriented, not system oriented. They focused on changing individual behavior but neglected the changes needed in socioeconomic structures. Instead, people must be involved in their own learning and link it directly to their everyday lives.

Grassroots peace movements challenge traditional assumptions, permeating education and the media, about the relationship between localities and the larger world. Our fixation on the powerful ignores people's growing involvement in global activities, depriving them of knowledge that could make their efforts more effective. People everywhere are immersed daily in a sea of worldwide transactions as they consume foreign goods, work for transnational corporations, absorb media originating in distant centers, breathe air from foreign factories, and are threatened by far-off weapons. But to act on these connections requires a new vision of people playing a more dynamic role in the world.

G rassroots activism in the United States illustrates the obstacles to establishing such a vision. Of course, it is clear that solutions to poverty, unemployment, energy, ecology, and human rights cannot be found in a single nation. But policy researchers working on these global problems cooperate very little with grassroots movements.

Some activists became actively involved strictly from local conditions, to which they have limited themselves. Although working on issues transcending state boundaries, they do not work with transnational movements nor do they view themselves as addressing global issues.

Some other activists have shifted from international to local issues but see their work as fulfilling global objectives. They have moved to the grassroots to build broader coalitions, sensing that people don't listen until they can see the link to themselves. For these activists too, state boundaries still limit their territorial reach, despite the worldwide networks working on these same issues.

A much less prominent prototype self-consciously blends local activism with global concerns. The co-op movement, for example, serves the local community with better food at lower prices, provides nutritional information, and evaluates misleading advertising. But it participates in a worldwide co-op movement as well. Members can meet their work quota not merely at the co-op but also by working on issues like nuclear proliferation and U.S. intervention in Central America. Also, local politicians in transnational groups such as Elected Officials for Social Responsibility define nuclear weapons control as a local issue because the weapons threaten their cities with annihilation and are a drain on resources. Others work on local campaigns against things such as apartheid and the global marketing of infant formula.

D espite local creativity in pursuing global issues, there is little vision in the United States of a future world toward which these actions might lead. In contrast, two Swedish economists, Friberg and Hettne, see the worldwide Green movement as an alternative to the Blue (market, liberal, capitalist) and the Red (state socialism, planning). It rejects mainstream development thinking preoccupied with the state, focusing on human beings or small communities instead, and pursuing self-reliance, cultural identity, social justice, and ecological balance.

In the Third World, Rajni Kothari questions the micro-macro split that artificially locates vested interests in local situations but pursues liberation from them in distant, nonlocal processes—the state, technology, revolutionary vanguards. Based on the Indian Lokoyan movement, Sheth finds a new politics (unconcerned with capturing state power) arising across regional, linguistic, cultural, and national boundaries—encompassing movements for peace and antinuclearism, for women, for the environment, for cultural self-determination, and for non-Western culture, science, and language.

Rahnema points to informal networks

> that link together the grass-roots movements of the South but also establish new forms of coaction between them and those of the North. . . . To sum up, new ways and means are to be imagined, mainly to allow each different group to be informed, to learn about other human groups and cultures . . . to be open to differences, to learn from them. . . . Only a highly decentralized, non-bureaucratic, intercultural rather than international network of persons and groups could respond to such needs.

Basing his analysis on his experience in Asia, Brian McCall calls for the "fuller participation of the non-governmental sector in the formulating, testing, operation and evaluation of alternative development strategies based on people's participation." He offers as examples the Asia and South Pacific Bureau of Adult Education, the Food Policy Study Group of the International Peace Research Association, the South East Asian Research Clearing House, and the Women's International Information and Communication Service.

Will the UN system respond to the needs espoused by grassroots movements? Majid Rahnema argues that contacts between UN organizations and developing populations are taboo: "They are contrary to the UN Charter (even though it begins with: We the peoples of the United Nations), and constitute an intervention into the internal affairs of sovereign nations." Short of a world people's movement to replace present UN development agencies, Rahnema asserts that grassroots movements still might legitimately expect the UN to "protect them against all disabling institutions and ideologies which keep them from improving autonomously their own life support systems." And Hungarian researcher Catalin Mamali suggests that this might be arranged through "a world network of people's assemblies, where the genuine representatives of all grassroots movements would meet and interact freely with each other."

H ow can we strengthen grassroots peace movements? First, local coalitions have developed across peace issues such as arms races, economic well-being, and human rights, which should be extended to help enlight-
en activists about the interdependence of peace issues. Second, work on
local issues such as civil rights, unemployment, and pollution should be
encompassed into local peace movements.

Third, grassroots movements in the North and the South should be
linked. Allies build confidence, and movements can learn from each other.
Fourth, and most difficult, officials in states, the UN system, and other
international governmental agencies must overcome the assumption that
security, peace, development, and related issues can be controlled only
from the world's centers. Instead, they must help liberate grassroots potential rather than merely lobby for plans formulated at global capitals.

Finally, international scholars and teachers should not mimic world
leaders but rather help illuminate how people's everyday lives and local
political, economic, and social institutions are immersed in worldwide
interactions. They should cooperate with grassroots movements for education to empower local people to overcome peacelessness in conventional
international and local relations. And they should help local movements
understand their connections to parallel movements in other parts of the
world.

37

THE EUROPEAN CITIZENS' ASSEMBLY

PATRICIA CHILTON
JIRI DIENSTBIER

Six years ago, a Czechoslovak dissident sat down and wrote a letter to the second European Nuclear Disarmament (END) Convention, a loose alliance of European peace organizations, meeting in Berlin. It was a meeting he was unable to attend because, like many East European political activists, he had been denied a passport. Quoting from the END Appeal, which had been circulating since April 1980 and which called for "the two superpowers to withdraw all nuclear weapons from European territory," he agreed that "we must commence to act as if a united, neutral, and pacific Europe already exists. We must learn to be loyal, not to East or West, but to each other, and we must disregard the prohibitions and limitations imposed by any nation state."

U ntil then, there had been little in the antinuclear debate of Western Europe to interest the long-fermenting social movements of the Eastern bloc. This link between a nuclear-free Europe and a choice of society for Europe's citizens was made in something like despair. Yet it inspired a citizen dialogue without which it would be impossible to imagine either the INF disarmament agreements of 1987 or indeed the Gorbachev new thinking.

One of the proposals Mikhail Gorbachev made in December 1988 at the UN was for some sort of global people's assembly: "The idea of convening on a regular basis, under the auspices of the UN, an Assembly of public organizations, deserves attention." It passed almost unnoticed. Almost as unnoticed was the fact that several initiatives of the kind were already under way when he spoke. One such initiative, originating from the same Czechoslovak dissident group, was for a European Citizens' Assembly that would span both East and West.

There had been a fraught meeting in Prague in June 1988. Most of the Czechoslovak organizers had been arrested and detained. All of the thirty-four foreigners attending had been summarily expelled from

---

This essay was first published in *Peace Review* 1:3 (1989).

Czechoslovakia. Nevertheless, a preparatory committee had been set up. It was convened again in Budapest in July 1989 to produce a draft constitution. In the meantime, there have been many events in Czechoslovakia that might be interpreted as inauspicious for the nurturing of this daring new democratic experiment. The Czechoslovak authorities have brutally repressed independent peaceful demonstrations in Prague. Playwright Vaclav Havel and peace activists Jana Petrova, Ota Veverka, Hana Marvanova, Tomas Dvorak, and others were put on trial. Yet plans have moved swiftly ahead to hold the first session of this pan-European parliament in Prague by the early summer of 1990.

What that will be like is still unclear. The one thing that is certain is that it has come about without government, or even UN, involvement. It does not rely on either the structure or the instrumentality of the nation-states from which its participants derive to legitimate its presence. This does not make the going easy. But it makes it possible.

Perhaps the most interesting feature of the prehistory of this people's parliament is the different routes by which the social movements of the East and West approached this common goal. For most of the Western European groups, the story begins with NATO's December 1979 decision on the deployment of U.S. cruise and Pershing missiles in Europe. Responses to that news were rapid and varied. Regional, ideological, class, and gender differences showed up. They still do. But there was a common rallying cry in the phrase "European Nuclear Disarmament." What that meant, the Western Europeans quickly realized, was that Eastern Europe had to be included and consulted too.

Even for some of the drafters of the original END Appeal, however, the reaching out to Eastern European movements was a tactical necessity rather than a blueprint for the future. They were not sure what they would meet on the other side and whether they would be speaking the same political language. The dialogue was uneven; messages were contradictory; misunderstandings occurred. Western European peace activists were left in no doubt, on the other hand, as to the vitality of independent citizens' movements in the Eastern bloc countries.

Most of these movements did not arise in response to questions of nuclear armament or disarmament. For many of them the surge of Western European antinuclear protest in the early 1980s remains purely incidental. It has had the practical consequence of making groups with widely differing backgrounds and agendas interested in each other. They recognize each other's landmarks but have not made the same journey. The Western Europeans, searching for a more relevant forum to enter than that of the U.S.-Soviet arms control negotiations, frequently groped their way back to something called the Helsinki process. Most of the Eastern Europeans acknowledged the Helsinki process as one of the early steps along their way. Helsinki became the natural common link between the two.

T he Conference on Security and Cooperation in Europe (CSCE) was convened in Helsinki in 1973. Members of the conference are the sixteen NATO countries, including Canada and the United States; the seven Warsaw Pact countries, including the Soviet Union, and the twelve neutral or nonaligned states in Europe, such as Austria, Switzerland, and Yugoslavia. Working groups from all thirty-five nations developed the Final Act, which was adopted in 1975. Technically, the Helsinki Final Act was not a treaty but a statement of common policy. It provided explicitly for a continuing multilateral process, including periodic conferences to review the implementation of the stated policies. Since 1975, there have been follow-on conferences in Belgrade, Madrid, and Vienna, and the three main baskets of issues discussed have been confidence-building measures, conventional arms reduction, and human rights.

The Helsinki Final Act Accords of 1975 did not change much at first. The governments that had negotiated them saw them as a strengthening of the status quo rather than a way of fundamentally changing international politics. In East and West, the "Helsinki process" was largely disregarded. Some considered it to be a capitulation in the face of Brezhnev's power politics. Others saw in it a greater guarantee of safety for the West, obtained through complicity with the inertia in the East.

So not surprisingly it was with a certain amount of dismay and mistrust that the new independent movements in the Eastern half of Europe were observed, and deemed by official commentators in both East and West to be destabilizing. It was too uncomfortable to think that the real source of destabilization might be the inertia with which Stalinism, exhausted and on its last legs, strives to delay its departure from the historical scene.

It was, in fact, these independent movements that uncovered the hidden possibilities in the Helsinki process. In several of the Warsaw Pact countries, committees were formed to monitor their own governments' observance—or rather violation—of the accords. From the international agreements on human rights (in basket three of the accords), ratified by Czechoslovakia in 1976, arose the founders of the Czechoslovak opposition group, Charter 77. Charter 77 already had a history, with its share of martyrs and exiles, when it began the dialogue with END in the early 1980s. Independent movements West and East, centered on peace and human rights, respectively, learnt swiftly from each other's new experiences.

The Prague Appeal, sent in 1985 by several dozen Charter 77 signatories to the fourth END convention in Amsterdam, was an attempt to synthesize their discussions so far by outlining a strategy for all independent groups. This appeal proposed that the Helsinki process should be used as a point of departure in preparing the common strategy. That strategy would represent a kind of Helsinki process from below.

The debate that followed produced a memorandum, Giving Life to the Helsinki Accords, signed by individuals, groups, and organizations from almost all of the Helsinki countries. This document was sent to the Vienna follow-up conference—the next stage in the Helsinki process—just as that conference was getting under way. European independent activists had agreed, among other things, that issues of peace and security, détente and cooperation, human rights, and self-determination were interconnected and could not be treated in isolation. It had also been agreed that concentration on a single issue at the expense of all the others (for instance, the issue of disarmament) was misleading and unproductive. It was necessary to overcome the division of Europe and it was essential to start at once. The current bipolar superpower manipulation of international politics had to be done away with and replaced by political unity in diversity. It was at the same time recognized that the work of governments was not enough. Independent civil activity was needed if political unity in diversity was to be achieved.

R egardless of all the problems associated with overcoming the rigid power structures and Cold War thinking, the international situation has become much more hopeful since 1985. There is now increasing opportunity for positive change. The Vienna Final Act, approved in January 1989, is good enough evidence of this; it amounts to a considerable breakthrough in the field of human rights. At the same time, it offers new opportunities for disarmament talks.

Governments alone are unable to transcend the existing situation, however. They are too closely bound to the notion of managing the current political status quo. They are captives of the existing internal and international structures. In pursuit of popular support, politicians often have to act in accordance with what they see as the momentary demands of the voting public. Deep-seated demands frequently turn out to be ill served by these political processes.

Independent activists and movements are free to formulate the social tasks that lie ahead much more openly and realistically, because they do not need to take heed of power and party politics. It is therefore essential that the Helsinki process at government level be complemented by an independent citizens' assembly that can consistently strive for the peaceful and democratic reunification of Europe. In the long run, it is only this kind of assembly that will be able to work toward the creation of a free, economically strong, ecologically oriented, and socially just society in Europe. And in North America and the Soviet Union.

The Helsinki process would thus be taken seriously at government level and be pursued by individual citizens. Activities on both levels should be parallel. There would need to be cooperation between both levels of the Helsinki process. Constructive criticism should be voiced. The independent assembly would be a continuous source of initiative. It would generate new proposals. It would be free to examine critically the ongoing Helsinki process from an independent standpoint. It would represent the grass-roots.

Representing differing political groupings and movements that are independent of governments, the assembly would naturally express a plurality of views. The minimal program of these groups would be the implementation of the agreements reached through the Helsinki process. They would seek to realize and extend the individual articles of these agreements in concrete terms. The ultimate aim would be a European unification on a new footing. The new unified Europe would be founded on two basic principles: not to disregard the dignity of individual human beings; and to pay special attention to environmental issues.

I f Europe were reunified in line with these principles, the impact would be major and worldwide. If Cold War structures and thinking were done away with in Europe, North America, and the USSR—an area that has a decisive potential for the further development of our civilization as a whole—and if people and nations in this area came to coexist in pluralist, democratic, and multipolar societies, it would have a strongly beneficial effect on the situation in the Third World. Conditions would be created for a more equal and sustainable development of the Third World.

Eligibility for the new European Citizens' Assembly would depend on the acceptance that relations between individuals and states should be based on democratic principles. Respect for human rights would therefore become the commonly accepted point of departure and mode of behavior in our civilization.

Supporters or advocates of terrorism could not be tolerated. If open political dialogue is to be the assembly's first principle, its members must be duty-bound collectively and openly to condemn all acts of terrorism, wheresoever they originate and whatever their political objectives.

The provisional agenda for the European Assembly is as follows: abolition of military and political blocs; gradual nuclear and conventional disarmament; implementation of consistently defensive military strategies; withdrawal of troops from countries that are not their own; free movement of persons; protection of the environment; and a transition toward an ecologically sound economy.

By devoting attention to these problems, the assembly would contribute to demilitarizing the international community as well as individual societies. It would help people to overcome outmoded prejudices and misunderstandings. It would work toward the creation of a cooperative and peaceful climate in the area of the Helsinki process and beyond.

It has been proposed that the seat of the assembly should be in Prague. Numerous significant events in European history are associated with this city. Czechoslovakia came into being in 1918 as a result of the victory of the democratic powers in the Great War. Munich 1938 not only heralded the destruction of the democratic Czechoslovak republic but paved the way for Hitler's attempt to conquer the world. February 1948, when the communists took power in Czechoslovakia, confirmed the division of Europe and led to the creation of the two power blocs. The Prague Spring of 1968 constituted a hope for socialism with a human face.

Now, twenty years on, that hope seems to have returned. Prague is at the geographical center of Europe. Of all the capitals of the countries in Europe's eastern half, Prague is situated nearest the borderline between the two blocs. Even the January 1989 events in Wenceslas Square, when riot police attacked peaceful demonstrators at the very time the Vienna Final Act was being signed, underlines the psychological importance of choosing Prague as the symbolic seat of the new assembly. The struggle for Prague is a struggle for the disposal of the debris of the rusty Iron Curtain.

T he debate about setting up the Helsinki grassroots parliament has now reached the stage when concrete proposals regarding organizational structure are being discussed. If the movements are actively to contribute to a major breakthrough in international relations, they must adopt higher forms of coordination. If the parliament is to become a politically productive forum, it will have to have governing bodies, a secretariat, and permanent working committees, as well as ad hoc committees to deal with specific questions as they arise. It will be necessary to provide technological backup and to set up press and documentation centers. Financial sources will have to be found that are not tied to political conditions.

It is therefore clear that setting up a Helsinki citizens' assembly will be a long-term task. It will depend on the ability of the individual working committees to gain authority and recognition through the concrete results of their work. There is no reason these committees should not tackle some of the simpler and more burning issues even before the whole assembly is set up. Indeed, they are tackling them already. However, the thrust of the assembly's international preparatory committee is to strive from the outset for the recognition of the assembly as an independent institution working within the framework of the Helsinki process.

At the same time, this goal seems much more realistic than it did a decade ago. Until recently, few people dared to dream about overcoming the postwar division of Europe. The idea that military and political blocs might be disbanded and that the safety of nations and states from Poland to Portugal might be safeguarded not by confrontation between blocs but by peaceful cooperation seemed idealistic. Now much more hardened realists are known to flirt with the idea of such an arrangement stretching from San Francisco to Vladivostok.

Until recently, Western European integration seemed nothing but an entrepreneur's pipe dream, not very likely to happen, and not very interesting if it did. Now the full economic integration of 1992 is hurtling into

Europe and opening up unexpectedly progressive political space as it goes. This shows in the unprecedented victories for Green and environmentalist candidates in elections to the (Western) European Parliament this June. It shows in the many pressures for extending the European Community to admit neutral Austria and communist Hungary, with Poland and East Germany not far behind in seeking to improve the special arrangements they already have. It shows in the sudden superpower concern to be a part of the new Europe, instead of each holding on to its own, divided Europe.

T he European Citizens' Assembly is still far out in front of the established political institutions of Europe in its experimentation with transnationalism. But the peace movements, human rights groups, environmental organizations, women's groups, churches, professional associations, trade unions, community groups, single-issue campaigns, and minority organizations that make up its present, ad hoc, embryonic membership have a notable advantage. They have been here before. They know the problems and they know the stakes. If the experiment succeeds, its effect on the political traditions of the new Europe will be obvious. And whether it succeeds, or fails, the repercussions will be global.

38

REIMAGINING FUTURE SOCIETY

ROY MORRISON

The world surprises. The astounding transformation of communist Europe and its global implications have changed everything except the way we consider the possibilities for the future. Both right and left seem to have lost their historic compass, their sense of destiny, and their confidence. The right wields power as though it believes the political changes of 1989 and 1990 did not happen. The left, in the face of revolution, is cowed.

The time has come for us to reshape our imaginations. The collective hesitation in the face of the sudden collapse of the Cold War and the gathering global environmental catastrophe is not merely an ideological and public relations problem. It reflects the underlying weakness in the foundations of the industrial state itself. The fundamental global task we face is to re-form the conduct of industrial civilization as a whole and to establish democratic, just, and ecologically sustainable societies. The Mondragon industrial cooperatives in Spain can help provide a basis for dramatic social transformation where existing capitalism and socialism have failed.

I ndustrial modernism arose with the entrepreneurial zeal in the latter part of the eighteenth century and swept all before it. The next century saw the triumphant consolidation of capitalist industrial modernism as the dominant world system. And what a leviathan it has proved to be. Its practice has been so powerful that its ideology has largely consumed the energies of socialists as well as capitalists; both march under the banner of industrialism that has more to do with production and power than with liberation. We are facing a monstrous social megamachine of our own creation, a machine that is not merely steel, plastic, and silicon, but flesh; a machine we serve not just as master and servant, but as working parts.

As the twentieth century draws to a close, the destructive legacy of industrial modernism, in both its capitalist and socialist manifestations, is all too apparent. A recourse to more of the same, to the further ministra-

This essay was first published in Roy Morrison, *We Build the Road as We Travel* (Philadelphia: New Society, 1992).

tions of bureaucratic technocracies, is a commitment to follow a trajectory leading to catastrophe—climatic change and global poisoning, precursors to ecocide and mass starvation; to social collapse; to nuclear obliteration. Saving change, fundamental change, must come from below, from the social practice of people fully engaged and in struggle with the forces of industrial modernism. The Mondragon cooperatives are an example of change from below. While they are not the answer, they are a relevant example of the kind of path we can choose to follow.

After the revolutions have ended and the dust of reality begins to settle, it will be tragic for those newly freed from the yoke of communist tyranny merely to recapitulate the forms and errors of capitalism. The "market" need not mean capitalism as we have known it. The Mondragon experience suggests that building a dynamic and just market economy does not require the stock markets or absentee owners that have been fundamental features of industrial capitalism. The existence of a labor-managed, democratic market alternative is a matter of global relevance, and not merely to the new European democracies or the advanced industrialized states.

The tension animating the crisis of industrialism is not the opposition between "freedom" and "planning." Mondragon's practice reflects an understanding that freedom and community are indivisible and that new democratic social choices must be made to reconstruct the nature of industrial society if it is to survive. Mondragon suggests that we can act creatively within our own communities to build social systems that embrace freedom, justice, and ecological sanity.

F rom its beginnings in the 1940s as a training school for apprentices, Mondragon has become the world's most significant cooperative system in an industrialized market economy. Once hidden in the Cantabrian Mountains of Guipuzcoa province, today Mondragon is a prominent element of the economy and society of the semiautonomous Basque region of Spain. The scale of Mondragon is impressive. Its 170 co-ops, including 100 cooperative businesses, have grown steadily, often spectacularly; they have used and developed sophisticated technologies and responded effectively to the fluctuations of the business cycle.

Mondragon includes a bank, the Caja Laboral Popular (CLP), with $2.9 billion in total assets and 180 branches; Ulgor, Spain's largest appliance manufacturer; Lagun-Aro, a social security and insurance system; Eroski, a retail co-op with more than $360 million in annual sales; Hezibide Elkartea, a collection of schools ranging from the elementary grades to universities and adult education that serves more than 45,000 students; and Ikerlan, an advanced technology research center. Overall, Mondragon encompasses industrial (including casting, forging, capital equipment, intermediate and consumer goods, and construction), agricultural, service sector, retail, housing, educational, training, and research cooperatives—all based on a system of cooperative entrepreneurship.

Mondragon is a dramatic departure from past social and organizational practice. The cooperatives reflect a social innovation called cooperative entrepreneurship—a process that allows ordinary people to shape humane, democratic, and prosperous societies.

Mondragon transcends conventional cooperative efforts now familiar in the United States, such as those in which workers buy out failing companies to save jobs or that offer employee stock ownership plans (ESOPs), which allow owners to sell their businesses and receive substantial tax benefits but often grant the worker-owners little control of their companies. Mondragon is basically different from the small (and usually undercapitalized) service, retail, or light industrial co-ops. Yet Mondragon's circumstances are not unique; conditions in the Basque country are not remarkably different from those elsewhere in industrial society. Mondragon is inspiring precisely because it has grown out of familiar conditions and because its basic elements are accessible to all working people.

The co-op's founding coincided with the start of the great Spanish economic expansion of the late 1950s, and growth was spectacular during the boom of the 1960s and early 1970s; it continued despite contraction of the Spanish and global economies in the 1970s. Today the Mondragon cooperatives have completed major restructuring and continue to prosper in a newly dynamic Spanish economy.

For example, in 1987, the Mondragon cooperatives had annual sales of about $1.57 billion; exports amounted to 20 percent of sales, or $310 million. Furthermore, the system has achieved the virtual elimination of long-term job loss and the minimization of business failures. Mondragon's concern for human dignity, and for the intangibles that translate into real community, is revealed in its process of employment creation and maintenance. The contrast with the surrounding economy is startling: even as the Basque region and Spain recovered from deep recession, Basque unemployment in 1986 was still 23 percent. Yet in 1986 and 1987, Mondragon created about 1,800 new jobs, and there are now 21,000 durable jobs in the co-ops. The Mondragon system has the highest productivity of all firms in Spain and the highest rate of profit—higher than in the largest capitalist corporations. Its efficiency stems from the cooperative structure; the high costs of supervisors are eliminated because workers, as owners, are already highly motivated.

Mondragon has faced severe economic trials but only three business failures. They include a fishing co-op with twenty-four operator-owned boats, which failed in 1973, and a small chocolate factory (converted from a capitalist firm) and a furniture veneering machine co-op, both of which failed in 1983 because of an economic slump. The flexible adaptation of the Mondragon cooperatives to economic hard times suggests the power of the cooperative solution to industrial modernist dissolution.

Mondragon's economic success, wrought by ordinary people with no significant material assets and living under the tyranny of Francisco Franco, is impressive; but even more significant, Mondragon's social success is a response to industrialism itself. While erecting factories and producing goods, the Mondragon cooperators were also creating, from below, a cooperative social reality, based on democracy and self-management; personal and collective risk taking through cooperative entrepreneurship; an enduring dedication to community; earnings available only to worker members, not outside investors; social choices to limit the destructive conduct of industrialism; and the democratic pursuit of *equilibrio* (balance), as well as harmony, poise, calmness, and composure in cooperative relations.

M ondragon embraces an ecological consciousness. Ecology, conventionally defined as the relationship of living things to their environment, is understood here to encompass social as well as biological reality, a kind of social ecology. The pursuit of *equilibrio* is connected to the basic ecological principle of diversity and unity or, in social terms, freedom and community. Mondragon reflects an emerging ecological postmodernism, a path of social development heading away from the destructive processes of industrial modernism toward the revitalization of human society and the integration of a sustainable social and natural ecology.

This represents not merely a separation from the cultural logic of late capitalism but a departure from industrialism as a whole in its capitalist or socialist manifestations. It is the process of healing the estrangement between people and nature (expressed socially through domination and oppression, and within ourselves by the separation of mind and body). The ethics and social choices of an ecological postmodernism are conditioned by the complexities of the living world and its social systems. In the view of social ecologist Murray Bookchin, "An ecological nature—and the objective ethics following from it—can spring to life, as it were, only in a society whose sensibilities and interrelationships have become ecological to their very core."

Recognizing the fundamental importance and ecological nature of Mondragon's pursuit of freedom and community may assist and help catalyze the future development of the global Green movement, which has been too often unable to connect its critique of industrialism with a constructive program for change. The Mondragon model presents environmental movements with a logical way to connect means and ends—and, for Mondragon itself, greater attention to explicit environmental concerns will help broaden, deepen, and strengthen the cooperative community.

O n the surface, the Mondragon accomplishment is clear. The cooperators have created an economically strong, democratic, and revolutionary social system from the most slender resources. While they have built up
impressive material and capital assets, the essential wealth of the system is
its community. In 1987, the first Cooperative Congress debated the basic
cooperative principles that guide the Mondragon experiment, thus fulfilling
the social goals of democratized knowledge and power and the search for
consensus and empowerment for both individuals and groups. As Alfonso
Gorronogoitia, one of the founders of the first cooperative, puts it: "What
surprises other entrepreneurs is the poetic-philosophical vein that we have
as entrepreneurs. . . . We could not be pure technocrats who know perfectly
the process of chemistry or physics or semi-conductors but nothing more.
We have never been pure technocrats. We see the development of these
firms as a social struggle, a duty."

But what is that struggle, that duty? The cooperators' experiment
began as a social response to the poverty and disempowerment they faced
as Basques and as workers under Franco and the large mill owners. Basic to
Mondragon is the struggle to continue making free choices that advance the
cooperators' idealism in practical ways, a process that continues today as
they engage the remnants of Franco's legacy and the common conditions of
industrial modernism in crisis.

The principles codified in the 1987 congress are a guide. They are
essentially labor-based and communitarian, rooted in a variety of movements and experiences: aspects of Basque cultural institutions and industrial heritage; the Catholic church's social doctrine; and socialist, communist,
and anarchist ideas. The principles affirm the freedom and empowerment
of working people and at the same time provide limits, characteristic of the
pursuit of *equilibrio,* in the interest of the community. This tension
between centralization and autonomy is fundamental to Basque political
life. The Mondragon system represents, in part, a creative resolution of this
tension.

M ondragon principles begin with the cooperative rules set down by
the nineteenth-century (British) Rochdale Pioneers. They have been
modified by the International Cooperative Alliance and by Mondragon's
own thirty-five years of practical experience. The principles include:

1. *Open admission* to all who agree with the basic cooperative principles without regard to ethnic background, religion, political
   beliefs, or gender.
2. *Democratic organization,* based on the equality of worker-owners.
   Workers must be members. Each cooperative is democratically
   controlled by one member, one vote; its governing structures are

democratically controlled and responsible to the general assembly or other elected body.

3. *Sovereignty of labor,* which is the essential transformative factor of society. The cooperatives give full power to the owner-workers to control the co-op and to distribute surpluses.

4. *Instrumental character of capital,* such that the co-op pays a just but limited return on capital saved or invested, a return that is not directly tied to the losses or surpluses of the co-op. Their need for capital shall not impede the principle of open admission, but co-op members must make a substantial, affordable, and equal financial investment in the cooperative—equivalent to a year's salary of the lowest-paid member.

5. *Self-management,* beginning with cooperation, which involves both collective effort and individual responsibility. Democratic control requires clear information on the co-op's operations, systematic training of owner-workers, internal promotion for management positions, and consultations with all cooperators in organizational decisions that affect them.

6. *Pay solidarity,* both internally and externally. Internally, the total pay differential between the lowest- and highest-paid member shall not exceed a factor of one to six. Externally, compensation is comparable to that prevailing in neighboring conventional firms.

7. *Group cooperation* on three levels: among individuals coorganized into groups, among co-op groups, and between the Mondragon system and other movements.

8. *Social transformation* through cooperation. José María Arizmendiarrieta, Mondragon's founder, wrote: "Cooperation is the authentic integration of people in the economic and social process that shapes a new social order; the cooperators must make this objective extend to all those that hunger and thirst for justice in the working world." The co-ops reinvest the major portion of their surpluses in the Basque community, including new job development, community development, social security, Basque worker solidarity, and Basque language and culture.

9. *Universal nature,* or the cosolidarity with all who labor for economic democracy, peace, justice, human dignity, and development in Europe and elsewhere, particularly with the peoples of the Third World.

10. *Education,* including the commitment of sufficient human and economic resources to cooperative education, professional training, and general education of young people for the future.

The peoples of Eastern Europe are now building, through collective and democratic action, a new social order from the wreckage of crumbling totalitarianism. In the midst of vivid moments of change, the old boundaries of the possible fade, and people discover themselves doing things that don't even have a name yet. In this atmosphere, the very meaning of the independent organs of civil society is in flux—a product of experiment, risk, and surprise.

In this ferment, there are openings to take up the Mondragon model. Refusing to embrace the socialist state does not mean adopting corporate liberalism. Social change here is not simply the collapse of a sclerotic socialism; it is part of the broader crisis of industrial modernism. In the view of Czechoslovak President Vaclav Havel, totalitarianism includes much of what is the common essence, East and West, of industrial modernism:

> The domination of a large group of powerless people by a small powerful group has long ceased to be its [totalitarianism's] most typical feature. Nowadays, what is typical is the domination of one part of ourselves by another part of ourselves. It's as if the regime had an outpost inside every single citizen. In an odd kind of way, the system pervades the whole of society, such that everyone at the same time supports it and helps create it ... by observing its various rituals and ceremonies.

Soviet totalitarianism is an extreme manifestation of a deep-seated problem that finds equal expression in advanced Western societies. The world is losing its human dimension. Self-propelling megamachines, and juggernauts of impersonal power such as large-scale enterprises and faceless governments, represent the greatest threat to our present-day world.

The evolutionary forces in Europe are but part of a great global movement from below. The instability of the system and the passion of those working for constructive change represent a challenge. What appears as the great omnipotent global reach and monolithic power of industrial modernism may, in retrospect, be as much a symptom of its transformation as of its longevity.

This is not simply hypothesizing that Mondragon-style structures shall arise in Eastern Europe, but rather that the strains upon industrial modernism will promote the rise of appropriate social structures of ecological postmodernism of which Mondragon is only an example. The new thinking of this homegrown brand of perestroika may even spread to the United States.

I n considering the future we should not limit ourselves to perpetuating the dominant trajectory of endless growth and despoilation. It is on the fringes, or the periphery, that the alternatives for our future can be seen to take shape. As the pursuit of profits and power enters into what we can describe as the zone of impossibility—that point where the environment, human society, and available material resources can no longer sustain its conduct—dramatic change is both possible and likely in a system increasingly far from equilibrium.

In these circumstances, instability and social transformation alternately seem to promise either redemption through change or disaster. An apocalyptic vision inclines us—particularly at the core in the United States—to the role of spectators. Industrial modernism is essentially incapable of developing solutions to problems that are the fundamental products of its own conduct. This leads us to demand that they do "something" about the intractable crises we face and, nearly simultaneously, to despair of our ability to find solutions created by our technology and our society. We can no longer afford to be mute witnesses to the bankrupt exercises of the status quo of Republican and Democratic parties, or of business as usual by transnational corporations. These are times, for better or worse, that bid us to participate actively and humanely in the processes of life and history.

39

Municipal Diplomacy

WILL SWAIM
MICHAEL SHUMAN

Although the conventional wisdom is that foreign policy is the exclusive domain of the central government of the United States, throughout the 1980s U.S. cities have played a critical role in damping some of the militarist excesses of the central government. Consider just three examples. When 120 cities refused to participate in the Federal Emergency Management Agency's post–nuclear war planning, the entire civil defense program was scrapped, undermining Reagan's nuclear war–fighting policies. The terrifying nuclear arms race of the early Reagan years gave way to serious arms control negotiations and ultimately the INF treaty only after 900 city, county, and state governments passed ordinances demanding a freeze in nuclear weapons production. And municipal opposition to U.S. support for the Nicaraguan contras—bolstered by nearly 100 U.S.-Nicaraguan sister cities that send thousands of observers and tens of millions of dollars in humanitarian assistance to Nicaragua—helped convince Congress to cut off the CIA's covert war on Nicaragua on February 3, 1988.

Once deemed the province of progressive cities such as Ann Arbor, Berkeley, and Cambridge, municipal foreign policy initiatives are increasingly common features of the public policy landscape. Today, more than 1,000 U.S. cities are actively participating in foreign policy, and their numbers are growing daily.

Together, these cities are becoming some of the most important peacemakers of our time. On South Africa alone, says *Foreign Policy* editor Charles William Maynes, U.S. policy "has not been made by [Assistant Secretary of State for African Affairs Chester A.] Crocker, it's been made by city councilmen."

While critics consider municipal foreign policies unwarranted meddling by local governments in national business, a growing number

---

This essay was first published in *Peace Review* 1:3 (1989).

of cities have concluded that peace is too important to leave to the National Security Council. They have been guided by three different rationales.

First, and most obviously, war is costly for cities. It is no accident that cities like Verdun, Berlin (East and West), Guernica, Dresden, Coventry, Hiroshima, and Nagasaki—all of them bombed or otherwise destroyed in wartime—also have some of the most active foreign policies. City leaders have come to realize that, inasmuch as their people and their buildings are held hostage to national security, it is their civic responsibility to ensure that war, especially nuclear war, never happens.

Second, even if the nuclear weapons themselves are never used, preparations for war are already inflicting grave economic costs on U.S. cities. When President Reagan came to office in 1981, the Pentagon's annual budget was $143 billion; when he left office eight years later, it was nearly $300 billion. Between 1982 and 1986, the United States borrowed more than $400 billion abroad to fund this buildup, transforming itself from the world's largest creditor to the world's largest debtor. While the federal government struggles to pay off the debt, it will also continue cutting vital local programs. According to the American Federation of State, County and Municipal Employees (AFSCME), the Reagan administration effectively cut nearly $160 billion from domestic programs helping, among others, families, children, the elderly, and the sick. Some programs that once benefited cities—such as General Revenue Sharing and Urban Development Action Grants—have been terminated altogether. The Bush administration has indicated that it too will sacrifice social spending to military production.

Any local elected official who says reversing the arms race is none of his or her city's business is fiscally irresponsible. That is why the National League of Cities and the U.S. Conference of Mayors have passed resolutions calling for a nuclear test ban and a redirection of Pentagon monies back to U.S. cities.

A third reason cities have come to favor peace is that peace pays. Peace means more lucrative trade and tourism. The rationale for city participation in international trade and tourism was perhaps best expressed by a 1983 National League of Cities (NLC) booklet, *International Trade: A New City Economic Development Strategy,* which argued:

> The fact that 20 percent of all U.S. jobs today are related to export production, a figure that is growing daily, is a reflection of (increasing) international interdependence. Equally significant is the fact that in 1982, a bad year for tourism, nearly 22 million foreign visitors came to the U.S. and spent nearly $14 billion, and foreign investment in the U.S. during the same period approached $60 billion. . . . World trade offers great local economic potential and will become an increasingly important element in the economic health of cities. The lure of economic rewards explains why offices actively promoting trade and multinational business can now be

found in city halls in Boston, Houston, Los Angeles, New Orleans, and New York.

M unicipal peace policies are essential components of ensuring a decent quality of life in U.S. cities. But can municipalities really deliver peace? Prevention of war and promotion of peace have been traditionally viewed as tasks exclusively reserved for the national government. Citizens with foreign policy concerns, the thinking goes, ought to address the federal government.

National peace efforts, however, are inevitably hamstrung by two inherent problems. First is the issue of accessibility. Most U.S. citizens have little contact, let alone influence, over their elected national leaders. Even when citizens have displayed broad opposition to federal foreign policies—like nuclear weapons or Central America policy—they have generally been ignored.

Relegated to occasional votes and letter writing in the face of what amounts to imperial disregard for popular opinion, U.S. citizens have increasingly lost faith in their ability to participate meaningfully in national politics—a fact reflected in declining voter turnout in presidential elections.

A second and more serious problem poisoning meaningful national political participation is the national security apparatus, which insulates national politicians from effective scrutiny and accountability. Most questions of peace and war are addressed by both the executive and legislative branches in secrecy. Operations of dubious legality especially flourish in such an atmosphere. Throughout the 1950s and early sixties, the United States deployed military or paramilitary force an average of once every eighteen months to overthrow a government or to keep an indigenous political movement from coming to power.

B ut for whom, as Noam Chomsky asks, were these actions covert? Certainly not for the perpetrators. Nor for the victims. These actions were covert only to the U.S. public. In many instances, U.S. leaders have used secrecy not to finesse adversaries abroad but to silence critics at home. A telling example is the U.S. Navy's policy of refusing to confirm or deny the presence of nuclear weapons on its ships. Because Soviet intelligence knows a great deal about the status of the ships it tracks, this policy results in the U.S. public knowing less about U.S. security policy than the Soviet military does.

The secrecy surrounding federal foreign policy affairs raises more than constitutional issues. It goes straight to the heart of local health and safety. Beginning nearly one year ago, for example, congressional investigators threw just a little light into the darkness of the U.S. government's forty-year effort to produce nuclear weapons that were said to be intended to deter aggression but that had, in the meantime, poisoned U.S. communities around the nation. Conservative estimates suggest that cleaning up the nuclear weapons plants and nearby communities will cost $150 billion. The burden of cleaning up the arms factories will surely fall upon the stooped shoulders of nearby local governments. In cities and towns in South Carolina, Colorado, Ohio, Washington, Idaho, Missouri, California, New Mexico, Nevada, Tennessee, Kentucky, Texas, and Florida, the arms race has truly come home.

A foreign policy based upon secrecy and inaccessibility has produced political apathy and environmental and economic disaster in the United States and policy catastrophes in Vietnam, Central America, and Lebanon. Many reasonable Americans react with a sense of despair and detachment to such a grim record. Millions of others facing the problems of inaccessibility and secrecy have already begun taking diplomacy into their own hands.

But as U.S. citizens increasingly enter the rough-and-tumble of international affairs, they are beginning to recognize that their powers as individuals or as members of nongovernmental organizations are quite limited. Unlike nation-states, which have vast treasuries derived from taxes, most individuals and nongovernmental organizations operate on financial shoestrings. The entire U.S. peace movement runs on about $300 million per year, about one-tenth of 1 percent of the size of the U.S. defense budget. Individuals and nongovernmental organizations also lack the color of authority of national diplomats and therefore are much less likely than national officials to get meetings with, let alone influence, powerful officials abroad.

How then can citizens trying to affect international relations, but outside the traditional national conduits of power, add money and legitimacy to their efforts? One answer is local government. Unlike the remote organs of U.S. foreign policymaking, local governments are relatively accessible—city council members are rarely more than a telephone call or a weekly meeting away. Local governments also are not insulated from public scrutiny by secrecy. Indeed, many local governments operate under Sunshine Laws that prohibit secret meetings and gavel-to-gavel cable television coverage, which makes them among the most open and accountable institutions in the United States.

Citizens have discovered that, unlike citizen diplomacy and nongovernmental organizations, local governments can confer both money and legitimacy on their foreign affairs activism. As financially pinched as U.S. cities are, were they persuaded to allocate 1 percent of their budgets to promote world peace, they could expand the entire U.S. peace movement more than tenfold. As for legitimacy, mayors may lack the same clout as national ambassadors, but they often receive red-carpet treatment when venturing into foreign affairs, far better than most citizens or organizations. That the then mayor of San Francisco, Diane Feinstein, and seven other mayors convinced the Soviet Union in early 1986 to allow thirty-six people to emigrate after so many analogous private initiatives failed can be attributed, in part, to the legitimacy of their offices. In sum, local governments have the right combination of accessibility, openness, money, and legitimacy that could make them into important peacemaking institutions.

It was exactly these characteristics of local government that made it the right launching pad for the environmentalist movement. In the 1950s and early 1960s, environmentalism was dismissed as largely a fringe movement populated by crazy tree-huggers. But one by one, states and cities began to create their own environmental agencies dealing with land management, toxic waste disposal, water protection, and air quality. As strange as they might have seemed twenty-five years ago, the California city of Palo Alto's Department of Recycling and California's State Energy Commission are today regarded as perfectly normal instruments for local policymaking. These institutions made environmentalism a multibillion-dollar-per-year industry, employing hundreds of thousands of lawyers, scientists, economists, and policy analysts.

And these jobs, in turn, have opened up dozens of university programs dealing with environmental law, science, economics, and policy. All of this is just as possible with the peace movement. If we start taking responsibility for promoting progressive foreign policies at the local level, if we create institutions for launching ambitious peace-oriented programs at home and abroad, we can finally make peace a multibillion-dollar-per-year industry too. Young people interested in international affairs careers will no longer have to choose between working for the Foreign Service or the multinational banks. Instead, they will find thousands of new, exciting jobs in their hometowns across America.

These institutions are beginning to be built. Cambridge, Massachusetts, and Washington, D.C., each have city-funded peace commissions. In 1986, Seattle created an Office of International Affairs (OIA) with an annual budget of $220,000 and five full-time staff. This office oversees the city's trade and tourism involvements, as well as its thirteen sister cities (which include Managua, Nicaragua, and Tashkent in the Soviet Union).

I magine 1,000 cities in the United States each spending between 25 and 50 cents per person on peace, roughly what the forty largest cities in the Netherlands spend for their peace efforts. At a minimum, this would pump tens of millions of new dollars into the peace movement. But consider all of the specific ways these expenditures could benefit peace.

If a thousand cities each analyzed the local economic impacts of the arms race, as the city of Baltimore has, we could substantially increase the consciousness of the U.S. public about the need for cutting defense spending. This could be further bolstered by a thousand cities preparing and distributing booklets entitled "Five Ways to Cut $50 Billion from the Pentagon," which might document the desirability of cutting first-strike nuclear weapons, Europeanizing NATO, and improving Pentagon management. In 1982, San Francisco sent every household a booklet describing the importance of a nuclear freeze.

A thousand city-paid lobbyists mobilized in Washington, D.C., could make a critical difference in banning nuclear testing, outlawing covert actions, reducing government secrecy, and strengthening congressional war powers. Currently the peace movement has about fifty lobbyists on Capitol Hill, comparable to the staff of a single major corporation's lobbying office. Is it any wonder peace legislation fares so poorly?

In the early 1980s, before it was abolished by the Thatcher government, the Greater London Council awarded tens of millions of pounds of grants to local peace organizations, funding rallies, buses, computer equipment, book fairs, museums, and so forth. A thousand cities in the United States could similarly each help support peace education and research centers in their own cities.

Over 160 cities and countries in the United States are now nuclear-free zones; half refuse, like the city of Chicago, to allow private nuclear weapons contractors to do business within the city. Internationally there are more than 4,200 nuclear-free zones in twenty-three countries. If 1,000 U.S. jurisdictions refused to give land-use permits to nuclear weapons contractors—as well as refused to enter municipal contracts with or divested city funds from these businesses—the nuclear weapons business could be brought to a standstill. More than 830 U.S. cities have 1,420 sister city affiliations that are using visits, cultural exchanges, and joint projects to promote global cooperation, understanding, and nonviolence. The forty official Soviet-U.S. sister cities (with another fifty or so in the pipeline) have played an important role in diminishing the Cold War. A thousand U.S. cities actively linked with cities in the Soviet Union could eliminate the Cold War once and for all. Moreover, these cities could help promote perestroika through joint business ventures and glasnost by shipping computers, videocassette players, microfiches, and other communications technologies to the Soviets.

The U.S.-Nicaraguan sister city movement has shown how municipal links can help sustain opposition to U.S. military intervention. Visitors from the United States can bear witness to the violence of covert wars, share their accounts with their neighbors, and help build pressure on Congress to cut off funding. In addition, because "freedom fighter" terrorists like the contras hate bad press, they will be reluctant to attack towns where Americans are staying and might be killed. Americans participating in official visits can help deter military aggression and human rights violations—not only in Central America, but in China, the Mideast, and Northern Ireland.

A thousand small-scale development programs and progressive trade policies with Third World towns could help eliminate the wretched poverty lying at the root of the radicalism, drug growing, and migration that the First World fears so much. Today, more than 500 European cities have these kinds of relationships, primarily with Africa.

A thousand U.S. cities could play a critically important role in preventing the environmental catastrophes threatening our (and every nation's) national security. The Center for Innovative Diplomacy, for example, is now bringing together cities in the United States and abroad to negotiate among themselves a treaty banning CFCs and other ozone-eating chemicals. By setting a good example, and lobbying their neighboring towns and national governments to follow suit, this treaty could move national governments to act more quickly to protect the atmosphere. Similar local initiatives in energy conservation and tree planting could help stop global warming—as well as get the United States off its dangerous addiction to Persian Gulf oil.

If we start taking responsibility for promoting progressive foreign policies at the local level, U.S. cities can help to reorient international affairs. None of the municipal foreign policies recommended here, of course, can be built quickly, easily, or cheaply. But if we begin to take peace and justice as seriously as filling the potholes, these goals will be within our reach. As Kenneth Boulding once wrote, "Cities of the world unite! You have nothing to lose but your slums, your poverty, and your military expendability."

40

FRAME OR BE FRAMED

JACKIE SMITH

A major consequence of the demise of the former Soviet Union is the need to redefine U.S. national security interests. One might expect that the end of the Cold War would have generated new and creative proposals for transforming conventional thinking about national security. There is little evidence that this is so. As Roger Peace suggested recently in *Peace Review:* "The Bush Administration is being allowed to define the New World Order by default."

There is a unique opportunity to exert political leadership in defining national security. Although traditional approaches to foreign policy prove increasingly ineffective, political leaders have failed to adopt more innovative responses to global conflicts. This leadership vacuum, combined with the breakup of traditional global alignments, calls for decisive efforts by peace activists to reshape the national security debate.

The links between public debate and actual policy are dubious, and the absence of such a debate allows political leaders—most notably the president—to choose which policies they wish to pursue. If leaders are to be held accountable for their foreign policy actions, the U.S. public must become more engaged in thinking about global problems and their possible solutions. Politicians and activists are keenly aware of the role mass media institutions play in shaping national debates on these issues.

P eace activists do not approach the contemporary situation as novices: Many have developed close ties with reporters or have employed other strategies for getting media coverage of their organization's activities. The work of peace activists in the 1980s has contributed much to what we know about the media and its coverage of peace and security issues. One major lesson is that peace groups are typically framed by the media as unruly, misinformed, and politically naive. Lacking deliberate strategies for shaping public debate on national security, the movement has allowed the media to define it rather than doing so itself. How might peace movement groups

This essay was first published in *Peace Review* 5:1 (1993).

work to actively shape the national security debate and avoid falling prey to reporters who almost inevitably portray activists in unfavorable terms?

Framing refers to the process by which a problem is defined as important or salient, its cause identified, and a solution proposed or implied. Social movement organizations engage in framing constantly, although few think of their work in these terms. Organizational newsletters, leaflets, literature, events, and even flyers announcing events help to articulate, reinforce, and disseminate various movement frames. Given the peace movement's goal of demilitarizing U.S. national security, influencing the mainstream media must be a central focus of activity.

Analysts cite many reasons for movements being unable to gain regular and favorable access to the national mainstream media. One framework for understanding how the media work is the "gatekeeper model," which views the media as organizations and interprets media activity in light of their organizational needs and constraints. It suggests that the media are probably more indifferent than hostile to peace groups. Thus, if activists better understand how the media work, they can devise better strategies to influence the way peace issues are framed by these institutions.

Media institutions are designed to make a profit. Thus, a major criterion for selecting material for coverage is the costs of acquiring information. The costs of covering foreign news are prohibitive for many media institutions, most of which rely on relatively inexpensive, centralized newswire sources.

The White House also serves as a key source of material for reporters covering foreign affairs and U.S. foreign policy. Extensive government resources are devoted to providing reporters with foreign affairs information in a form that responds to their various organizational constraints (for example, time, expertise). Indeed, throughout the past century, presidents have consciously cultivated the administration's capacity to influence the media, devoting extensive resources to this end. Executive press releases, regular press conferences, and other efforts to accommodate the media's needs have made the White House an invaluable information resource on U.S. national security policy and international affairs generally.

Besides having resources that allow it to provide daily information on a vast range of countries, the executive branch also enjoys privileged access to information on issues considered sensitive to U.S. security interests. It would be extremely difficult for any other actor to control a comparable wealth of information. As a result of the White House's efforts to shape national security policy, the president enjoys a disproportionate access to the national media, particularly on foreign affairs. In its efforts to expand the public debate over national security issues, the peace movement confronts a formidable opponent indeed.

While the playing field is far from even, peace movement actors might adapt their strategies to better meet the organizational concerns of reporters. A 1985 study by Women's Action for Nuclear Disarmament (WAND) found that few peace movement organizations had media strategies and practically none devoted even minimal resources toward this end. A stronger voice in the national security framing contest might be raised if more peace groups were to develop a conscious media strategy, provide personnel to work specifically on media relations, and offer the kinds of information reporters need (e.g., timely press releases that suggest an interesting "news pegs" in sound bite format).

R eporters follow particular routines in carrying out their daily tasks. They often rely on a relatively small collection of informants as their main sources on given issues. Editors will, at times, select reporters who know little about the issues they are reporting so as to ensure a heavy reliance on these sources for information. Sources are selected largely based on their positions, and government sources are typically viewed as the most credible—particularly on national security and foreign affairs issues. Movement sources, on the other hand, are usually seen as biased sources with insufficient access to information on the issue at hand. They are brought in by reporters usually only to show "the other side" of an issue.

The balance norm is a second reporting routine that should be considered by those trying to influence the media. This norm is only selectively applied by reporters when an issue is seen as "controversial." A reporter might either choose to frame an issue as controversial, or may be forced to when the issue is obviously so. Once an issue is defined as controversial however, the balance norm requires that "both" sides receive coverage. The assumption that there are always two sides to any dispute severely limits the range of relevant views having a chance of being covered. Typically, the sources selected to represent the "other side" are those with more moderate (read credible) views.

The pros and cons of various weapons systems are often the focus of national security debates, thus keeping the debate within the dominant frame that assumes deterrence strategy is indisputably effective. Thus, although the staging of mass demonstrations might be sufficient to bring the "balance norm" to bear on media coverage of an issue, those staging the demonstration are not likely to be consulted by the media for details of why they favor or oppose a particular policy. If demonstrators are consulted at all, the "news peg" they provide is likely to be the demonstration itself rather than the issues about which they protest.

Hence, in developing a strategy for influencing the national security debate, peace movement activists must recognize the concerns that shape the routine behavior of media representatives. Strategies that try to provide information that is timely, clear, accurate, and "credible" by standard media criteria will be more effective than those that do not.

T he general U.S. population is the ultimate consumer of the mass media, and the group whose views and activities peace movement actors hope to influence. Thus, it is important to understand this audience and its limitations. Social movement researchers have outlined two key dimensions along which movement actors are constrained in their attempts to frame issues: ideological and experiential.

Ideological constraints are determined by the nature of dominant national paradigms or world views. I am reluctant to talk about any such thing as a "national" paradigm, given the huge range of views and belief systems within any population; however, it can be said that most people within a given nation-state may share certain assumptions, values, and beliefs. These kinds of constraints were particularly salient for the peace movement during the Cold War, when it faced accusations of being a dupe of the Soviet Union. Anticommunism was a strong cultural theme in the United States, and it caused serious dilemmas for peace groups.

With the demise of communism, what further ideological constraints must be considered? The main one is the degree to which national security issues are salient for the general public. Foreign policy commands little attention among the broad U.S. population, and it rarely claims much time or space in the news media. To the extent that they receive media attention, international issues are often simplified for an audience with little background knowledge. National election campaigns very infrequently address issues of foreign policy.

Thus, peace activists are confronted with the problem of making issues of national security more central to the concerns of a broad population. The Freeze movement of the 1980s succeeded in this by mobilizing people around the concern about a nuclear war and the destruction it would wreak on one's family, children, and so forth. Peace activists must devise a frame that resonates similarly with the values, concerns, and beliefs that are manifest in people's daily routines. Doing this means constructing frames that communicate effectively and clearly the links between global security problems and people's core values and concerns.

A second barrier for peace movement framing is the fact that few in the United States have any direct knowledge or experience on issues of international politics and national security. Inexperienced audiences are more likely to uncritically accept media viewpoints on the subject. Without prior knowledge of international conditions, media audiences have nothing to filter the information provided by media sources. This is more likely the case for international than for domestic issues; many people have very direct experience with issues such as inflation, unemployment, health care costs, and so forth. Consequently, the peace movement faces a challenge unlike those of movements that focus on domestic problems.

Experiential constraints raise more difficult challenges for peace movement activists: How does one cultivate better popular understandings of international affairs so that people can independently evaluate the messages conveyed through the news media? The fact that the U.S. public has so little opportunity to participate in foreign policy decisionmaking explains much of this experiential gap. Peace activists must recognize this gap and confront it in innovative ways. Expanding the public debate on foreign policy calls for even broader efforts to expand democratic input into that policy process. Thus, an effective peace movement strategy should be multifaceted, focusing on institutions of communication as well as on those of policymaking.

G iven these formidable constraints, what might peace activists do to influence the mass media? The answer requires a strategy and specific projects.

Strategy suggests broad concerns that should be reflected in the various actions or projects undertaken. Peace activists should be interested in expanding public participation in the debates and decisionmaking on national security issues. Leaders must be held more accountable for their actions in the foreign policy arena. A public that is actively involved in thinking about foreign policy options can better ensure this democratic accountability. The peace movement also needs to define itself, or provide a "master frame" around which various peace groups organize. An appropriate master frame, for example, may be one promoting a positive, less militaristic role for the United States in an increasingly uncertain world.

Frames should be viewed as key resources for peace groups. The same kind of effort that goes into mobilizing other organizational resources must be put into developing effective organizing frames. These frames must be decidedly proactive: they must raise plausible, nonviolent policy responses to contemporary conflicts. Typically, peace movement frames have been defensive, trying to mobilize people against various wars or weapons systems. Such consistent opposition has brought frequent accusations that the movement is anti-American. Since the president is the commander in chief of the armed forces (as well as of U.S. international policy), movement efforts are typically in direct opposition to this national figurehead—thus making the movement look even more unpatriotic. A more proactive framing strategy might preempt unfavorable media coverage of peace activism by offering feasible new alternatives to deterrence-based policies rather than merely criticizing executive policy.

A participatory, proactive framing strategy should also explicitly cultivate the image of peace activists as patriots. Every effort should be made to avoid situations that might be framed as new examples of the peace movement's anti-Americanism. Peacetime press releases or rallies supporting, for example, U.S. cooperation with the United Nations or other movements toward collective security are tactics that might help deflect wartime criticisms of the movement as anti-American.

Beyond general strategy, the peace movement should develop specific projects. A resource-intensive but perhaps vital way of expanding national security debate would be to cultivate a national, regular (weekly?) newspaper. Such a publication might be organized by peace activists, but it should engage a broader range of people in debates about contemporary global issues. This would provide a regular forum for discussing alternatives to existing national security policies outside the confines of the executive branch frames.

A nother proposal would be to create a national security news service that would be an alternative to the White House as a reliable international news source. Although it would be impossible to match the information-gathering capacities of the U.S. executive branch, such a news agency could expand the national security debate beyond conventional limits. This could be further enhanced if peace groups promoted subscriptions to the news service by local papers, church or community newsletters, and so forth. A relatively new organization, the National Security News Service, has begun providing this service but could expand with greater cooperation from other groups. On a smaller scale, peace groups might provide regular columns for local papers that analyze contemporary developments on peace issues.

Finally, peace movement groups might work together to provide media training for activists. Skills in working with the news media, desktop publishing, and public speaking should be cultivated to improve peace activists' impact on the national security debate. Better communications should be considered a key peace movement objective. Efforts to provide more effective communication will help the peace movement frame security issues rather than having itself framed out of the debate.

41

ENDING THE SCOURGE OF WAR

DAVID KRIEGER

If we wish to abolish war as a legitimate means of settling disputes, what must we do? One can imagine this question guiding the drafting of the United Nations Charter. At the end of World War II, the founders of the United Nations certainly must have felt that the world had had enough of war. Some 50 million people had died in that war, more than half of whom were civilians. The most devastating war in history, it had included massive bombing of cities throughout Europe and Japan, culminating in the use of nuclear weapons. On June 26, 1945, representatives of fifty nations signed the new United Nations Charter, expressing their determination "to save succeeding generations from the scourge of war."

Now, nearly fifty years later, the United Nations has not succeeded in its primary mission of ending "the scourge of war." Since World War II there have been some 150 wars throughout the world resulting in some 22 million deaths. Each decade in the latter half of the twentieth century has witnessed an increase in the percentage of civilian deaths in warfare, reaching some 75 percent in the 1980s.

In part, warfare has continued in the post–World War II period because of flaws in the initial structure of the United Nations. The Security Council was given "primary responsibility for the maintenance of international peace and security." But the Security Council was often blocked from taking action to fulfill its responsibility by the veto power given to its five permanent members. Even without the veto power, the Cold War between East and West took precedence over ending the scourge of war.

The Cold War also led to obscene expenditures for armaments, and an accumulation of firepower capable of destroying the human population of earth many times over. The good news, of course, has been that the genocidal weapons of mass destruction, accumulated primarily by the five permanent members of the Security Council, have not been used on human populations since Hiroshima and Nagasaki.

With the Cold War ended, perhaps we can again seriously address the

---

This essay was first published in *Peace Review* 5: 3 (1993).

question of ending the scourge of war. To succeed in this goal will require individual commitment and global action. It will require changes in attitudes and institutions.

E instein warned that in the Nuclear Age "everything has changed, save our modes of thinking." By "thinking" I believe he meant our attitudes toward war, peace, security, and our fellow human beings. If humans could learn to abhor the once accepted institution of slavery, they can also learn to abhor war.

War has been seen as a means of resolving conflicts. Until the present it has largely been considered a legitimate means of doing so. This belief must change. Warfare must be delegitimized as a means of settling disputes. Within nations, the courts are relied upon as dispute resolution mechanisms. There are also the mechanisms of negotiations, mediation, arbitration, conciliation, and others. When justice fails within a polity, internal war or revolution is sometimes viewed as the only alternative. Thus, peace and justice will rise or fall together.

War must be viewed as too cruel and costly a use of human resources to be allowed. Mothers instinctively know this with regard to the participation of their own children in warfare, and fathers can learn too.

While learning to abhor war, we must learn new attitudes toward peace, most importantly that peace is more than the absence of war. It is a process that can be maintained only through active participation. Peace also requires justice. Justice, in turn, requires equal rights and opportunities for all.

Security in the Nuclear Age must be common security. The security of each of us depends upon the security of all of us. In the Nuclear Age we threaten ourselves and all of humankind with omnicidal weapons. A moment's reflection will reveal that this is a very dangerous and limited form of security. New security risks arise from environmental threats to the climate, oceans, atmosphere, forests, and ozone layer. We all need clean air and water and healthy food to be secure. The deterioration of the air we breathe, water we drink, and food we eat is an important issue of common security.

We must recognize that we share a common humanity. We are one species, homo sapiens, sharing a common origin. In this time of planetary communications and travel, the earth has become too small for hatred, prejudice, and distrust. As human beings we share common roots and a common destiny. To realize our potential as a species we must put aside our differences and celebrate our diversity. The basic value on which a just world order can be constructed is human dignity. If human dignity is not upheld, justice will not be possible and the resulting insecurity will lead to warfare.

Attitudes fit within a framework of beliefs and understandings about the world. To change attitudes—or, as Einstein suggested, "modes of thinking"—requires changing the way an individual views the world. This is a task for education at all levels.

Individuals must be taught that we all share a single, fragile planet and that there is a higher loyalty to humankind than to any nation. As the Hawaii state motto puts it, "Above all nations is humanity." Now that humans have sent emissaries into outer space, we know that while national boundaries may exist on our maps and in our minds, they do not exist on earth. They are artificial constructs, permeable to missiles, pollution, and ideas.

Our approach to security in the Nuclear Age has threatened the earth and our posterity. Our extravagant expenditures on weapons and armies have been a death warrant to those who need the basic necessities of life. Children starve in a world awash in high-tech armaments. Something is terribly wrong with this situation. It cries out for change, for education to raise the level of awareness and compassion.

Can attitudes change? Of course. We have only to look at modern attitudes toward slavery, a well-accepted institution only 150 years ago. More recently, during the past two decades, we have witnessed major changes in attitudes toward smoking, restricting individual rights to smoke when it would affect those who do not smoke. Even more recently, we have witnessed the positive attitude changes toward former "enemies" in the post–Cold War period.

Just as slavery was abolished, war too will someday be universally outlawed and controlled. As smokers' rights have been restricted in behalf of the innocent bystander, so too, the sovereign rights of states to make war will be increasingly restricted. These restrictions have, in fact, already begun. They are institutionalized in the United Nations Charter, which requires that all members "refrain from the threat or use of force in their international relations." The postwar Japanese constitution states that "the right of belligerency of the state shall not be recognized." The Costa Rican constitution abolishes the army as a permanent institution. Thus, changed attitudes toward peace and war have begun to find expression in various institutional frameworks within the international system. These changes point the way toward the future.

With the end of the Cold War there is an important opportunity to bolster international institutions to promote and preserve peace. In a 1992 report to member states, UN Secretary-General Boutros Boutros-Ghali called for strengthening preventive diplomacy, peacemaking, and peacekeeping by the United Nations. His report, "An Agenda for Peace," states: "The time of absolute and exclusive sovereignty . . . has passed; its theory was never matched by reality. It is the task of leaders of States today to understand this and to find a balance between the needs of good internal governance and the requirements of an ever more interdependent world." It might be added that it is the task of citizens to help and, if necessary, require their leaders to understand the limits on national sovereignty.

In the area of preventive diplomacy, Boutros-Ghali calls for increased emphasis on confidence-building measures, fact finding, early-warning systems, preventive deployment of UN forces, and use of demilitarized zones. In the area of peacemaking, he calls for all members to accept the general jurisdiction of the International Court of Justice: for the mobilization of assistance to curb the circumstances leading to disputes or conflicts, for good judgment in imposing sanctions, for agreements with member states to make armed forces available to the Security Council, and for the use of peace enforcement units to respond to outright aggression.

With regard to peacekeeping, the Secretary-General points out that between 1945 and 1987 thirteen peacekeeping operations were established, and since 1987 thirteen others have been formed. He emphasizes the cost effectiveness of these operations when compared to war:

> The costs of these operations have aggregated some $8.3 billion till 1992. The unpaid arrears towards them stand at over $800 million, which represent a debt owed by the Organization to the troop-contributing countries. Peace-keeping operations approved at present are estimated to cost close to $3 billion in the current 12-month period, while patterns of payment are unacceptably slow. Against this, global defense expenditures at the end of the last decade had approached $1 trillion a year, or $2 million per minute. The contract between the costs of United Nations peace keeping and the costs of the alternative, war—between the demands of the Organization and the means provided to meet them—would be farcical were the consequences not so damaging to global stability and to the credibility of the Organization.

The Secretary-General expressed strong support for the financing of peacekeeping contributions from the defense budgets of member states and offered additional proposals for financing peace-related activities of the UN.

Other studies have also offered proposals for strengthening United Nations and regional capabilities in maintaining peace and security. Among these are "Common Responsibility in the 1990s" by The Stockholm Initiative on Global Security and Governance (now continuing its work as the Independent Commission on Global Cooperation and Governance); "A United Nations of the Future" by the Transnational Foundation for Peace and Future Research; and "Supranational Decision-Making: A More Effective United Nations" by Nobel Laureate Jan Tinbergen. The Stockholm Initiative, for example, made the following proposals in the area of peace and security (which included strengthening the United Nations, holding regional security conferences, limiting arms trade, and reallocating the peace dividend):

1. Improved United Nations capabilities for anticipating and preventing conflicts, in particular the establishment of a global emergency system
2. The elaboration of a global law enforcement arrangement, in line with the United Nations Charter, focusing on the role of sanctions and on military enforcement measures
3. Organizational and financial measures to strengthen the United Nations capabilities for peacekeeping and peacemaking operations
4. Regional conferences on security and cooperation to be held in Europe and elsewhere
5. A stronger monitoring, particularly by the United Nations, of world arms trade, with the purpose of eventually agreeing on global norms, regulating and limiting trade in arms, and focusing on both supplier and recipient countries
6. A pledge by governments in the industrialized countries to allocate a specific part of the peace dividend for international cooperation
7. A commitment by governments in the South to substantially reduce their armed forces, with the purpose of creating a peace dividend to be invested in human development

The Stockholm Initiative offers additional proposals in the areas of development, environment, population, democracy and human rights, and global governance. Success or failure in each of these areas will ultimately be reflected in the ability to maintain a world at peace.

Institutions often change slowly, but when the circumstances are right, change can occur with amazing speed. This was the case with the ending of the Cold War and the fall of the communist regimes in the former USSR and Eastern Europe. We cannot count on creating the institutional changes necessary to end the scourge of war immediately, but we can create a Peace Action Plan and make a commitment to achieving its goals.

A Peace Action Plan for the last decade of the twentieth century should emphasize the following points:

1. *Control and ultimately abolish weapons of mass destruction.* The World Court Project, sponsored by the International Peace Bureau, the International Physicians for the Prevention of Nuclear War, and the International Association of Lawyers Against Nuclear Arms, is seeking a World Court ruling on the illegality of nuclear weapons. There can be little doubt that the use of nuclear weapons violates international law: They fail to discriminate between legitimate military targets and civilian populations,

spread poisonous materials, violate neutral territory, cause indiscriminate suffering, and so forth. The same is true, of course, of chemical and biological weapons and all other weapons of mass destruction. Initial steps in the control of these weapons include the following:

- The establishment of a long overdue comprehensive nuclear test ban
- The establishment of a nuclear nonacquisition regime to prevent all horizontal and vertical proliferation of nuclear weapons with strict international controls of all weapons-grade fissionable nuclear materials
- The creation of a scientific nuclear weapons dismantlement corps to aid the countries of the former Soviet Union in the dismantling of nuclear weapons
- The enforcement of the Chemical Weapons Convention
- The strengthening of the Biological Weapons Convention

2. *Control and ultimately abolish arms transfers.* The unrestrained transfer of armaments must cease. This process has begun with the establishment of the Arms Register by the United Nations to promote "transparency" in arms production and trade. The next step is to recognize that commerce in arms makes warfare both more costly and more likely and should therefore be made illegal. The largest arms importers are located in the Middle East, the most volatile region in the world. The largest arms exporters, to their disgrace, are the five permanent members of the UN Security Council—the same Security Council charged in Article 26 of the Charter with formulating plans "for the establishment of a system for the regulation of armaments."

3. *Implement the best proposals by the Secretary-General and others for strengthening the international structures for peace, including the United Nations' preventive diplomacy, peacemaking, and peacekeeping capacities.* Particular emphasis should be placed on preventing conflict from erupting into violence, such as through diplomacy and other nonviolent forms of conflict resolution. The sanctions for resorting to war should be well organized, well publicized, and effective. The jurisdiction of the International Court of Justice should be made mandatory for all UN member nations. The UN Military Staff Committee, referred to in Article 47 of the Charter, should be activated and given responsibility for devising plans for ending existing and potential conflicts through interventions, if necessary.

4. *Implement proposals to strengthen the international machinery for protecting the environment.* Security today depends on preventing environmental disasters such as destruction of the ozone layer, the release of radioactive pollutants, and the despoiling of the oceans and atmosphere.

Environmental disasters such as Chernobyl, the destruction of the ozone layer, and global warming are global problems requiring global solutions. No one nation can solve these problems alone, and they dramatically underline the limits of sovereignty. A start on improving international efforts to protect the environment was made at the Earth Summit in Rio in June 1992. To preserve a healthy environment is a common responsibility to ourselves and to future generations.

5. *Implement proposals to strengthen the international machinery for enforcing human rights.* In the post–World War II period, considerable international attention has been given to articulating human rights and organizing treaties to support those rights. Thus, we have treaties today prohibiting genocide, apartheid, slavery, and torture. Where the international community recognizes that these and similar conventions are being violated, sovereignty must not be a ban to upholding these rights.

6. *Enforce the principle of individual accountability for crimes under international law and establish an international criminal court.* The Nuremberg Principles adopted by the UN General Assembly after the International Military Tribunal at Nuremberg stated that "any person who commits an act which constitutes a crime under international law is responsible therefore and liable to punishment." The Nuremberg Principles go on to state that even heads of state are not relieved of responsibility for such acts and that "acts of State" and superior orders do not relieve an individual of responsibility if a moral choice was possible to him. The enforcement of individual accountability is a key missing element in today's world and allows aggressors such as Saddam Hussein to go unpunished. We also need to establish an international criminal court to take jurisdiction over major international crimes. The establishment of such a court is currently being considered at the United Nations. It would put on notice would-be violators of international law everywhere, no matter how elevated their position, that their acts are subject to scrutiny and that they may be held personally accountable for criminal acts under international law.

We shall soon be observing the fiftieth anniversaries of the end of World War II, the signing of the UN Charter, the dropping of atomic bombs on Hiroshima and Nagasaki, and the creation of the International Military Tribunal at Nuremberg. All of these events occurred in 1945, and their fiftieth anniversaries will be observed in 1995. In addition, in 1995 the Review Conference of the Nuclear Non-Proliferation Treaty will decide whether, and for how long, that treaty should be extended. Between now and 1995, a major campaign should be undertaken to underscore the important possibilities inherent in the end of the Cold War; it may help us achieve the primary objective of the United Nations of ending "the scourge of war."

When the UN founders wrote the Charter, they said they wanted "to save succeeding generations from the scourge of war, which twice in our lifetime has brought untold sorrow to mankind." Today we would have to say that the untold sorrow of warfare has brought sorrow on numerous occasions during our lifetime and continues to do so. We have based our security on threats of death and destruction of a scale that is scarcely imaginable. We owe it to all victims of warfare, to future generations, and to ourselves to commit ourselves to creating new global means of maintaining security and to abolishing warfare, our most primitive and uncivilized manner of resolving conflicts.

NEW STRATEGIES:
PEACE MOVEMENTS

42

THE BOMB, THE MOVEMENT, AND THE FUTURE

CHARLES HAUSS

The day I started writing this essay, September 12, 1989, was a typical one in the post–Cold War world. The *New York Times* carried a couple of pieces about improved Soviet-U.S. relations. But it also had four pages of articles on the Gulf situation, plus others on violence in South Africa, the continuing bloodshed in Liberia, ethnic strife in Yugoslavia, economic turmoil in the Dominican Republic, riots in Myanmar, crime in Hong Kong, and ethnic tension in Kashmir—thereby driving home the point that even though the Cold War has ended, this is anything but a peaceful and harmonious world.

That day's *Times* was also typical because it failed to mention what the peace movement was doing about any of these issues. The movement has not completely disappeared, of course. The group I have been most involved with, Beyond War, had already run an excellent advertisement in the *Times,* offering an alternative approach to the Gulf crisis. As the autumn wore on, the traditional peace groups weighed in, and more serious opposition to the U.S.-allied policy emerged. Among the rallies and demonstrations held around the world was one in my small town in rural Maine, which drew 500 people who braved the cold and winds of early December.

But, in any real sense, the peace movement that played such a vital role in ending the Cold War just a few short months ago has not been a significant factor in the debates about the crisis in the Persian Gulf or, for that matter, any of the other instances of violence that haunt this post–Cold War world. The peace movement's decline started in earnest with the signing of the INF Treaty in late 1987 and the beginning of the end of the Cold War. Other issues sped up that decline, ranging from the changed political situations in countries from Nicaragua to Namibia as well as our rediscovery of the damage we are doing to the global ecosystem on which all life depends.

This essay was first published in *Peace Review* 3:1 (1991).

Still, central to the peace movement's disappearing act is its inability to adapt to the needs of a changed but no less dangerous world. It isn't that its various wings haven't tried. In the spring of 1989, for instance, the World Federalists, SANE/Freeze, and others organized a massive conference in Washington that dealt with far more than just nuclear weapons and other Cold War–related issues and, in turn, laid the groundwork for wide-ranging cooperation by a broad spectrum of groups thereafter. In practice, however, little of that has come to pass, at least with any noticeable political impact.

It thus is very tempting to condemn the antinuclear weapons wing of the peace movement for leaving us unprepared to deal with the mammoth problems that remain. That is a temptation we should avoid for two reasons.

First, although such criticisms are largely accurate, the problems are far greater, part of a much larger cycle of boom and bust that has afflicted virtually every movement that has effectively spoken out in the name of peace—whatever that means—over the past forty-five years. Second, and in the long run perhaps more important, those criticisms mask a much more profound opportunity "the bomb" offers that could enable us to take the peace movement as a whole to a new and more sweeping stage in its evolution.

T here really is nothing unique about the anti–nuclear weapons movements of the 1980s. Like other movements of that decade, they grew and came to have a significant political impact largely because they focused on one issue of immediate concern.

With but few exceptions, the various organizations that make up the anti–nuclear weapons movements rarely were able to get their members and supporters to see the connection between the threat of nuclear war that had gained new urgency as the Cold War heated up again in the late 1970s and 1980s and the whole panoply of other problems that are also powder kegs with global implications.

To oversimplify things a bit—but only a bit—when the Cold War ended, those of us who had been working on the bomb found ourselves ill prepared to go on to the next phase in the evolution of the peace movement and deal with all those other frightening issues. Even more worrisome was the view that now that the United States and Soviet Union had learned how to resolve their problems, we would be entering a wondrous new era of global peace and harmony. When the Iraqi invasion of Kuwait occurred, U.S. and allied troops were sent to Saudi Arabia; the threat of war again lurked ominously close on the horizon and the populations of Europe and North America slid readily back into the we versus they thinking of old, with the exception that Saddam Hussein had now replaced the Soviets as our enemy.

Were we to stop at this point, we would miss what to me is the central lesson to be learned here. As the cliché has it, the situation really is like déjà vu all over again. For instance, those of us who spent the 1960s desperately trying to end the war in Vietnam found ourselves in the 1980s confronting an eerily similar situation in Nicaragua. Yet because the antiwar movement of the 1960s had done little to sink the kind of roots that would allow people to explore the problems of U.S. intervention in the Third World in general, for all intents and practical purposes, we had to reinvent the wheel in building opposition to U.S. support for the contra war.

The history of the Nuclear Age is filled with other examples of what we might call the Viet Nam trap. The anti–nuclear weapons movement had fallen into it before. After having built widespread opposition to atmospheric testing during the late 1950s and early 1960s, the Ban the Bomb movement lost its momentum, and most of its active members, once the Limited Test Ban Treaty was signed. The more recent version of that movement may have raised consciousness about the danger of nuclear war between the superpowers, but it did little to help people see that all war is obsolete in the Nuclear Age. Other groups have helped people see the evils and dangers of apartheid in South Africa, but they have made little headway in helping us understand, let alone struggle against, racism elsewhere in the world.

There is no need to add more examples to support what is an all too familiar point. The peace movement has scored some significant successes over the past forty-five years. Ironically, each success has been followed by a sharp decline in peace movement activity and, even more important, an inability to broaden its base in any substantial way beyond the initial issue; so once that issue receded from center stage, it was hard if not impossible for the organizations that dealt with it to move on with any degree of success. Perhaps the best way to understand that is to focus on a question I have intentionally left vague so far: what the peace movement itself is.

I have been talking, so far, about single-issue protest movements that have normally reacted against what governments around the world were doing. Such movements are not enough. Today we also need a very different kind of peace movement that can do three things these traditional groups have not been able to accomplish to help people see that peace is much more than the absence of war; the problems we face are global and affect every aspect of our lives and thus require an equally total response on our part; and we have to mobilize ourselves not just to deal with an immediate crisis but for a process of change that will take years and probably even decades to complete.

That is not to take anything away from the organizations and the protests that I—and probably you—have participated in over the years.

They have played an invaluable role in preventing atrocities and producing some remarkable changes for the global better. And there is no better way to grasp their importance than to see the costs of their absence, as in the debates during the first weeks and months following the Iraqi occupation of Kuwait.

Nonetheless, we do need to understand that our continuing reliance on single-issue and reactive movements has us in a rut. Because they tend to focus our attention on only one or at most a small set of related issues, they are by their very nature limited and are thus unlikely vehicles to create that kind of all-purpose and mobilizing peace movement the world is so desperately crying out for in these times of both tremendous hope and equally tremendous danger. The various antiwar and nuclear disarmament movements of the last four decades had only limited success and fell into the Viet Nam trap because they themselves were limited. Though their leaders may not have seen them in that way, they were all essentially single-issue movements, aimed at stopping aid to the contras, apartheid, or the renewed hostility toward the Soviet Union. Once those immediate issues receded from the front pages, so did the movements they spawned. In that sense, none of them really were peace movements other than in their opposition to this or that real or looming war. Maintaining the peace movement at that level condemns us to be continually falling into that trap and never moving on and meeting the challenges we face.

A real full-blown peace movement that carries with it the real hope of achieving a lasting peace has to go beyond that kind of single-issue focus and galvanize public attention and activities around a far deeper concern, perhaps best captured in the cliché "Peace is more than the absence of war."

I n a curious way, opposition to the bomb could also point the peace movement in a new and far more successful direction. To be sure, the bomb has lost much of its urgency now that the Cold War has ended and no less an authority than Barbara Bush has declared that the Soviet Union has become a part of the free world. Nonetheless, if we dig a bit more deeply into the dangers the bomb continues to pose, we can see that next stage begins to emerge. To start with, that means understanding that the Cold War and post–Cold War worlds are radically different from anything that came before them.

The situation in the Persian Gulf, the environment, the horrible violence of Liberia or South Africa, drugs, lives lived without dignity by the poor of the world from the Republic of Colombia to the District of Columbia—and, of course, the bomb—are interrelated and part of a single, interconnected global crisis. Each transcends national boundaries and can have devastating outcomes, including in some cases the destruction of civilization as we know it. None seems amenable to traditional politics that stress national solutions or the victory of one side over another. Put as simply as possible, each situation seems to require a new kind of politics that seeks and finds cooperative, multinational solutions.

Finding lasting solutions to these and other problems may well require a redefinition of how people and nations deal with each other that is even more radical than the one that ended the Cold War during these last two remarkable years. The newness of our age extends to its very roots, to the underlying values and assumptions we use in shaping our personal and global politics. Prior to 1945, what Einstein called our "modes of thinking"—whether left or right, Marxist or capitalist—were based on the often unspoken assumption that individuals, groups, classes, and nations were autonomous actors that were separate from each other and naturally pursued their interests in a hostile environment that often required the use of physical or other forms of violence and coercion.

Recently we have begun questioning that vision of reality in the light of a whole host of scientific discoveries and social problems. Indeed, we are lurking toward a worldview that stresses the interdependence of all life, which is exploding the underlying logic behind all those prenuclear theories. Rather than stressing our autonomy or independence, these theories take our interdependence as their starting point as both the source of our problems and our hopes. They see the root cause of the many issues we face and struggle against in a way of thinking that sees conflict in we versus they terms that inevitably leads to violence and that no longer seems capable of solving our problems. They stress, in particular, that war at everything from the interpersonal to the international level no longer serves the purposes for which it was invented: resolving conflict that could not be handled otherwise. And they stress that as our technological capacities have grown and the world has shrunk, the costs of our going to war—whether to our children or to our environment—have risen to unacceptable levels.

Those theories also use interdependence to point us in the direction of hope as well as despair. Because everything one does affects everyone and everything else, we actually have two approaches to resolving conflict. We can continue with we versus they thinking and the rest of business as usual. Or we can see that, at least in the medium and long term, our only viable option is the pursuit of win-win outcomes that benefit everyone involved. Concretely, that means pursuing a peace that is much more than the absence of war. It means creating a world that eliminates the injustices and prejudices that are at the heart of so many of today's hotspots. It means understanding that we cannot eliminate nuclear weapons or end war in the Persian Gulf unless we also address the social and economic issues of underdevelopment, overpopulation, and the rest of the North-South debate. In short, because the issues of the global crisis share a common cause, they cannot be adequately addressed separately or without addressing that common cause in the way we think and act. There is nothing new to these ideas.

In a sense, they do little more than empirically validate the golden rule and its equivalents found at the heart of all of the world's major spiritual traditions. In the political world, they have been around at least since the 1930s when visionaries like R. Buckminster Fuller started talking about "spaceship earth." Our challenge is to use them to build a strong and growing peace movement, which, in turn, can be used to build a world of peace in which people meet the evolutionary challenges of the world we created in the years after 1945.

That, of course, will be no mean feat. It will have to be multi-issue even though the Viet Nam trap suggests people have not been able to easily draw the connections between two or three closely related questions. It will have to be multinational even though attempts to make it so in the past—as in the various Ban the Bomb movements of the early 1980s—have rarely gotten very far. Yet if we learn to use the bomb a bit more creatively, it can open the door to building just that kind of movement.

For all the problems with the anti–nuclear weapons movements, the bomb remains our best metaphor or springboard for understanding the overarching realities of the post-1945, let alone the post–Cold War, world. If we can learn to be just a bit more creative, the bomb can be the vehicle that helps both ourselves and others see the dangers that persist and the new opportunities that are now presenting themselves. The fact that an all-out nuclear war would quickly destroy human civilization drives home the fact that we now live in an interdependent world in a remarkably effective, if stark, way. Put as simply as possible, the bomb best helps us see the new, and more complex, dangers associated with the interdependence of the Nuclear Age.

During the 1980s, the bomb also proved to be a good tool to use to help people see the opportunities that exist. Groups like Beyond War in the United States used the threat of nuclear war to probe the many dimensions of interdependence and helped hundreds of thousands of middle-class people in the United States see personal and political responsibilities of life in the Nuclear Age. More recently, a coalition of groups coordinated by SANE-Freeze has effectively drawn the connection between our military spending, the deterioration of our economy, and the need for widespread industrial conversion. Perhaps most important of all, the Greens in Germany and others have made considerable progress in helping people see these connections, especially those between war, the environment, and social justice.

Normally I find that academics lag behind activists in their understanding of political dynamics. Here, however, the university peace studies community may be ahead of the peace activists. For years, most peace studies curricula (though, I must admit, not always mine) have drawn those connections among the various issues and between the issues and basic social and political values and the need for and possibility of fundamental political change. One of the best recent anthologies includes articles on a wide variety of specific issues plus others that try to help the reader draw the connections among them, envision plausible alternatives to the global political status quo, and explore ways individuals can themselves make a difference.

The most recent text I received goes even further, combining ecological and economic security issues with the more traditional war and violence-based issues covered in peace studies courses. What's more, I am seeing an interesting change among students, a change confirmed by colleagues around the United States. The students are young enough to have no clear memories of the Cold War. Instead, their worldviews have been shaped by improved Soviet-U.S. relations, the new environmental movement, and our growing concern with social and economic woes around the world. As a result, they have little trouble seeing the importance of interdependence, the way global issues hang together, and the need for a long-term movement to forge cooperative solutions for those problems. We academics certainly do not have all the answers, but the fact that we have made some progress in building an intellectual base for the next phase of the peace movement leaves me with some hope. We academics have not found the ways to present this material quickly and effectively to a wide mass audience and in a way that mobilizes as well as informs. But that is what the peace movement has done quite well over the years, and its challenge is to find a way to use the bomb, all these other complexities, and the new perspectives about the world spewing forth from intellectuals inside and outside the academy to launch people into broader considerations of our interdependence and its political, economic, social, and ethical implications. This time we had better meet that challenge.

43

DEMOCRACY IN
AFRICAN INSURGENT MOVEMENTS

STEPHEN ZUNES

African governments are beginning to join their Latin American and Eastern European counterparts in making impressive moves toward democratization. A parallel movement appears to be coalescing in armed liberation struggles from the Horn of Africa to the Maghreb to the southern tip of the continent.

Marxism-Leninism has historically supplied the ideological and organizational orientation for most radical Third World nationalists. Despite its European origins, many African nationalists considered Marxism-Leninism a good framework for educating, mobilizing, and leading long-subjugated peoples to liberation. Marxism-Leninism helped explain the economic roots of colonialism and the material base of oppression, enabling many countries to make authentic social transformation rather than simply evolving to nominal independence under a neocolonial regime. Furthermore, a "vanguard party" built on strong leadership and a rigorous hierarchy of ideological and logistical command was believed to be crucial for organizing people accustomed to oppression into effective political and military forces.

In recent years, however, African liberation movements have moved away from Marxism-Leninism and toward internal democracy. Most shifts do not appear to be based on any lessened commitment to eliminating the last vestiges of imperialism, nor to any lessened commitment to socialism. Rather, liberation leaders are tapping into more appropriate and effective organizational and ideological modes. Three strong and long-standing African liberation movements aptly illustrate this trend: the Polisario Front of Western Sahara, the EPLF of Eritrea, and the ANC of South Africa.

Perhaps the most dramatic and successful example of decentralization and participatory democracy is in Western Sahara. The 1975 invasion of this country by Moroccan forces, just prior to scheduled independence, forced the majority of the population into exile in neighboring Algeria.

This essay was first published in *Peace Review* 3:4 (1991).

Today nearly 170,000 Sahrawis live in refugee camps in the desert south-east of Tindouf, in autonomy granted to them by the Algerian government. They have declared themselves the Sahrawi Arab Democratic Republic (SADR); they are a full member of the Organization of African Unity; and they are recognized by more than seventy nations. Meanwhile, guerrillas of the Polisario Front, Western Sahara's liberation movement, continue to wage war against the Moroccan occupation forces.

The Polisario made a conscious choice to decentralize their administration of refugee areas. Refugee camps are divided into *wilayas* (provinces), which are each divided into four *dairas* (cities) further divided into neighborhoods. The Polisario claims that this decentralism was simply a more pragmatic and efficient means of governance. This stands in direct contrast to the widespread assumptions—both in the West and in Marxist-Leninist systems—that whatever social advantages may come from small-scale governing units, centralization is far more efficient. This difference in attitude may stem from contrasting opinions of what government is for: If the goal is control, centralism is clearly preferable; if the real interest is in popular self-governance, including consensus decisionmaking, decentralism holds a clear advantage.

The political and administrative structures of both the Polisario Front and the SADR are based on participatory democracy. In the SADR, every citizen belongs to a functional committee of twelve to twenty people. Provisions committees distribute all food and basic necessities free of charge, based on need. Health and sanitation committees keep tabs on sanitary conditions and nutrition intake, make referrals to health professionals, and practice preventative medicine and out-patient care. Judicial committees, given the lack of crime, work primarily as mediation and conflict resolution services for family and other interpersonal disputes, in conjunction with the local *cadi,* the traditional Islamic judge. Children committees administer universal day care and other children's programs. Production committees are worker-controlled manufacturing centers, which make primarily handicrafts for domestic consumption, and agricultural centers, which cultivate irrigated vegetable gardens. All these committees operate on consensus.

Functional committees are quite active. For example, a representative of the local Health and Sanitation Committee visits every household regularly. Besides serving their stated functions, committees keep people busy in a refugee environment (which could otherwise lead to sullenness) and train the population in practical skills that can serve their country well after liberation. Each local functional committee chooses a member to serve on the local Popular Committee, which in turn selects a member to serve on the Popular Council of the *daira,* along with the popularly elected *daira* president. The Popular Council of the *wilaya* consists of presidents of daira councils and the elected *wilaya* head of each committee, presided over by a *wali* named by the minister of interior.

A Polisario leader named Brahim described a key advantage of this system:

> Our governing system was organized to ensure maximum participation. Authority doesn't change things, people do. To try to impose regulations would lead to our destruction. We have studied other liberation movements and have seen how factionalism has hurt them. Major disagreements in our movement would only help the Moroccans. The only way to ensure that we remain united is to allow for maximal popular input.

Since initiative appears to genuinely flow from the base rather than from above, committees and legislative bodies have a kind of vitality missing in most Marxist-Leninist systems, where they serve more of a legitimating function than an actual policymaking role. According to the governor of Dahkla:

> Liberation comes from inside the person. Thus, it is the collectivity of the individuals that is important, not a party or ideological line. Our political structure, therefore, must come from the people, from the base, not from some mastermind from above.

Since virtually all the inhabitants of SADR are refugees, the economy is limited. The production committees manage only small factories that make basic commodities for local consumption, such as straw mats and carpets, clothes, children's toys, and tobacco pouches. Virtually none of these items are exported—not even the beautifully designed carpets—due to the Polisario commitment to maximal self-sufficiency. All enterprises are publicly owned and completely worker managed. No one is paid. Work on a Production Committee, as on other committees, is voluntary. The state supplies major household items such as stoves; these are considered private possessions that can be kept by the family should they choose to move to another *wilaya*. Families that were able to bring personal possessions when they fled Moroccan-controlled zones are allowed to keep them. Some families own goats, and there is a small private market economy for selling or bartering personal items.

All food is free. Special care is taken to ensure that young children and pregnant and nursing mothers receive adequate nutrition. Records are kept of state-supplied provisions to each family; provisions are replaced on the average expected time of depletion. Distribution is based totally on need, regardless of a family's contribution to the system. This may be the nearest any society has come to actually implementing the philosophy "from each according to his ability, to each according to his need." This does not mean that these former nomads have leapt from primitive to utopian communism, skipping all the Marxist stages in between. What it does mean is that during the past decade, the Polisario has taken many thousands of homeless people in one of the world's most desperate living conditions and created a democratic and participatory system that meets people's basic needs.

Despite these impressive structures, which during more than sixteen years of exile have ensured a high degree of economic and social democracy, political democracy for most of this period has been limited. Many Sahrawis feel there is too much domination by one element in Polisario, and serious discrepancies between the movement's egalitarian line and the political reality. Polisario's Executive Committee makes all real political decisions; and they hand-pick many local political leaders. At a series of work stoppages and protests in 1988, democrats pressed for liberalization. Hardliners resisted, arresting democratic opposition leaders. Facing stiff opposition from the population, SADR went through several governments that autumn, still failing to satisfy the population. Continued popular resistance won the democrats a series of victories in 1990–1991. They now essentially hold power.

The June 1991 Polisario Congress, the largest ever and the first to include substantial representation from outside the camps, was dominated by democrats. Among other radical reforms, the Executive Committee and Politburo were replaced by a National Secretariat, with key positions held by reformers. There is now a new and more democratic constitution and an independent Human Rights Commission. Visitors have noted a more open atmosphere in the camps. Undoubtedly the already existing social and economic democracy made transition to political democracy possible. Indeed, it was an impressive testament to the Sahrawis that they were able to change the system instead of rupturing the organization and starting a new rival liberation organization, thereby splitting the movement on the eve of a UN-sponsored referendum that should shortly determine the fate of the disputed territory.

Ever since the defeat of the Ethiopian Dergue in the spring of 1991, the Eritrean People's Liberation Front (EPLF) has been the effective government of Eritrea. During this region's resistance against Emperor Haile Selassie in the 1960s, the EPLF broke from the original nationalist movement, the Eritrean Liberation Front (ELF), due to the latter's conservative social policies and strong Arab and Muslim orientation. The EPLF has since developed a membership that is largely representative of the religious, geographic, and ethnic makeup of the Eritrean population. By 1981, the EPLF had essentially eliminated the ELF as a major political force.

According to James Firebrace, a researcher on Eritrea, there are six major foci in EPLF political strategy: "the creation of a political consciousness, the transference of local political power in favor of the poorer peasantry and of women, land reform, new roles and rights for women . . . the structure of EPLF decision-making . . . [and] the military defense of the revolution." In each of these aspects of its political strategy, the EPLF seeks involvement and participation from an organized population, at the same time leading toward the goals of national unity, self-determination, and socialist transformation. EPLF cadre are trained to recruit and educate strong local leaders. Priority for leadership positions is given to women, minorities, and people from new areas of EPLF control. Recruits get two or three months of training, then return to their home communities where they are expected to lead and encourage mass organizations and village committees, while resuming their normal lives.

EPLF attempts to provide strong leadership while maintaining a high level of accountability to the general population. In attempting to transform Eritrean society, the EPLF balances two goals: maintaining the ideological and political direction of the revolution, and fulfilling the aspirations of the majority of the population so they will stay committed. EPLF describes this process as a revolution "from above and from below."

At the top, the EPLF has developed structures of overall administration and coordination. Cadres who received EPLF training are the "vanguard" that mobilizes people and encourages them to development new revolutionary structures. At the bottom, people elect their own local administrations. A traditionally hierarchical society and centuries of deference to large landowners and feudal chiefs make introducing a democratic social organization in Eritrea a difficult task. Unlike the Sahrawi nomads, who have a centuries-old tradition of participatory governance, democratic traditions in Eritrea are limited to some village councils of elders. In addition, unlike the relatively homogeneous Sahrawis, Eritrea contains nine distinct ethnic groups. Much EPLF effort has gone toward teaching people about democracy. Ironically, the enormous disruption caused by a generation of war has made the inculcation of radical ideas possible.

T he EPLF initiated democratic organization from the top down. In most places, the systems have taken root, with most local and some provincial governmental authorities exerting autonomy from the EPLF leadership and staging democratic elections. When the EPLF enters a new area, they hold village elections after a period of political education. Villagers nominate candidates, and the whole village population openly elects a temporary People's Committee, which might include former officeholders of an ELF or Ethiopian administration. The EPLF then carries out detailed studies of the village population, which it classifies into "social forces": peasants (poor, middle, and rich), women, youth, workers (in towns), and "professionals" (shopkeepers and artisans). EPLF establishes "mass organizations" from these groupings. In areas firmly under EPLF control, the mass organizations nominate candidates for their village's People's Assembly. The number of elected representatives from each mass organization is proportionate to the size of that social force, thus ensuring that poor peasants and women are well represented.

People's assemblies establish committees responsible for the range of governance functions in a society, including health and welfare, agriculture and land, development, the judiciary, cultural affairs, education, and security. In addition, mass organizations representing women, peasants, workers, youth, students, and professionals, along with the armed forces, elect delegates to the EPLF National Congress. The National Congress elects the Central Committee, which in turn elects the Politburo, creating a leadership ultimately accountable from below. Villagers can critique their leaders in regularly scheduled sessions. Critiques are usually on practical rather than ideological issues. This kind of accountability forces leaders to immediately respond to requests from constituents, by either carrying them out or explaining why they cannot be honored. Indeed, the overriding definition of democracy in Eritrean society is efficient and honest government.

The practical side of this is that by making people responsible for change, the EPLF does not have to be in charge of everything. This belief in pluralism dates back to the 1970s. Given the enormity of the challenges facing Eritrean society, maximizing creative input is a practical necessity.

In May 1991, the EPLF seized the final piece of Eritrea, an area of over 1 million people. Unconfirmed reports describe some authoritarian measures taken by EPLF authorities in this territory, particularly against non-Eritreans. In most cases, however, democratic structures appear to be intact, even as the EPLF assumes state power. A referendum on the final status of Eritrea will take place within two years.

S outh Africa's African National Congress (ANC) has gone through several ideological and tactical changes during its long history. Tendencies to move toward an explicit Marxist-Leninist orientation were periodically aborted by internal challenges. During 1968, for example, substantial numbers of ANC cadre in camps in Tanzania fled to Kenya and publicly criticized the opulence of ANC commanders, their increasingly pro-Soviet ideological line, and widespread favoritism. A meeting of the ANC and its supporters in Morogoro, Tanzania, in April 1969 led to a critical shift in ideology and structure toward greater internal democracy.

Within South Africa itself, the major problem facing organized opposition to the South African regime has been the vulnerability of the ANC leadership to arrest, exile, and assassination. Whenever a new generation of leaders emerged, the government effectively silenced them and therefore severely limited the ability of the organization to mobilize the South African masses. Through an elaborate and highly efficient police surveillance network, the "cutting off of heads" technique stifled the development of an internal revolutionary vanguard. Government repression against the ANC and the Pan-Africanist Congress (PAC) in the early 1960s demonstrated how, in a totalitarian situation, any liberation movement with too centralized a leadership can be largely paralyzed by the arrest of important leaders or the discovery and dismantling of new headquarters.

The Black Consciousness Movement (BCM) played a major role in organizing and mobilizing South Africans between the demise of the internal resistance movement in the early 1960s and the rise of the United Democratic Front, the trade union movement and the township uprisings of the 1980s. Black Consciousness began with the formation of the South African Students' Organization (SASO) in 1968, led by Stephen Biko. Like earlier orthodox African nationalists, SASO architects believed that oppression was largely a psychological problem, an inferiority complex instilled through centuries of European cultural imperialism. In order to overcome the subservient attitudes that had robbed most Africans of their self-assertiveness, Africans had to create, according to Biko, a convincing new identity for themselves that could engender a new pride evolving into a potentially revolutionary force. Biko's premise was that South Africa's 80 percent black majority could remain subjugated only as long as they accepted their inferiority and powerlessness, which were reinforced daily through contempt and condescension demonstrated by whites. Through Black Consciousness organizations, alternative institutions such as black-run medical clinics, cottage industries, and aid programs were established to raise black awareness.

While they were never in opposition to ANC or PAC, Black Consciousness activists often criticized the older leadership for having hierarchical organization and for abandoning the African tradition of exerting popular control on leaders. Hierarchy, they claimed, made it difficult to empower the masses, develop new leadership, or maintain organizational viability in the face of government repression. Black Consciousness organizations and institutions that the government banned or closed would reappear within weeks. Utilizing rotating facilitators instead of traditional leaders, the movement survived years of government repression and created a new generation of resistance leaders. Though the BCM was decimated by repression, its democratic legacies remain.

By the 1980s, ANC leadership and supporters came to recognize the importance of participatory orientation. Through mutual support with the United Democratic Front and trade union federations—loosely structured organizations themselves—it maintained a degree of resilience and unity in the face of the worst repression in South Africa's history. Scores of officially sanctioned local governments in black townships have collapsed, due to massive noncooperation. Most of the mayors and town councils have either resigned or are simply being ignored. Pro-ANC/UDF alternative governments have been established in the face of virtual military occupation.

One of the most striking examples is in the Alexandra Township near Johannesburg, which has a population of well over 100,000. Its alternative government starts at the level of the "yard," where three to five houses, each containing four to five families, share a courtyard. About six yard committees, representing up to twenty-five families, make up a block committee, which sends representatives to street committees. All of the street committees form the Alexandra Action Committee, which has become the township's de facto government. With the assistance of a white lawyer, they have drawn up a local constitution based on participatory democracy and have formed "peoples' courts," which deal fairly and effectively with matters such as petty theft, family violence, and interfamily disputes. When the Action Committee successfully led a rent strike, the official government cut off water supplies and the cleaning of the communal pit toilets. The Action Committee then formed its own committees, which took over these and other community jobs.

The ANC's first national conference since relegalization took place in early July 1991. Lively open debate occurred on some rather contentious issues. The conference elected a national 100-person executive, including a twenty-two person working committee to run the organization on a day-to-day basis. Many of those elected were less visible but highly competent activists from remote areas. It was clear the organization had changed in recent years and was now a well-functioning democratic entity. Still, it had not compromised its determination to redistribute economic power along with establishing majority rule.

Much of this increased pluralism grew out of years of quiet and consistent work by democratic elements within the organization. The democratic trade unions, which played a crucial role in mobilizing the antiapartheid movement, made clear they would not tolerate anything less. This did not come easy. During the first year and a half after the exiles returned, many maintained their top-down mentality. This clashed with an indigenous movement accustomed to democratic organization. As with the Sahrawi and Eritrean peoples, the democrats appear to have won out.

African liberation movements are moving in more democratic directions for a variety of reasons: following global democratic trends, getting in touch with peoples' indigenous democratic traditions, and recognizing the pragmatic advantages of democratic governance. These movements have demonstrated that, despite extremely harsh conditions, African peoples can organize themselves effectively and democratically while building genuinely egalitarian new societies. This phenomenon deserves greater study if for no other reason than it seriously challenges the traditional "realist" notions of human nature and social organization and provides hope for those who believe that exploitative and authoritarian societies need not be the norm. In addition, it offers an approach to Third

World development that rejects the traditional dichotomy between pragmatism and principle. What is striking is that these democratic modes of organization are justified not on ideological grounds as much as simply because they work best.

These movements are not without their problems and internal contradictions. Yet it is significant that although Western-style representative democracy in dependent neocolonial Africa has at best a mixed record, democracy based on principles of equality, growing out of indigenous culture and renewed by popular movements, can be quite successful. The impact of democratization on the quality of life for the African masses still depends largely on the creation of a new international economic order and related external factors. Still, these internal developments may be a harbinger for needed and positive changes in African political development.

44

CHALLENGING THE
JAPANESE PEACE MOVEMENT

KATSUYA KODAMA

It is almost half a century since the atomic bombs were dropped on Hiroshima and Nagasaki. Both cities were reduced to ashes and 200,000 people were killed outright or had died as a consequence of the bombs by the end of October 1945. For the survivors (the *hibakusha*), the horrors of the bombing (lingering radiation effects, socioeconomic and psychological damage) still haunt and handicap them. While the bombs induced much helplessness and hopelessness, many citizens of Hiroshima and Nagasaki, including some survivors, have managed to rise above the grief and hate to affirm hope in the future. There has been an affirmation of the essential unity of humankind and a declaration that there should be "no more Hiroshimas, no more Nagasakis, no more hibakusha." The experiences of Hiroshima and Nagasaki provided a powerful impetus for the emergence of the Japanese peace movement, the abolition of nuclear weapons, and confidence in the survivability of humankind. This essay provides a brief historical examination of Japanese peace movements and analyzes some of their internal and external problems.

B ecause of a press embargo imposed by the Occupation General Headquarters in September 1945, reports, commentaries, and studies dealing with atomic bomb damage in Japan were prohibited until the signing of the San Francisco Peace Treaty in 1951. This meant that little was known about the precise details and horrors of the bombs. Although literary personalities and intellectuals such as Sankichi Toge and Sadako Kurihara appealed for disarmament and peace, there were no mass peace movements in Japan until the mid-1950s. In 1954, crewmen of the Japanese fishing vessel *Lucky Dragon* were radiated by the hydrogen bomb test at Bikini Atoll. This shocked the Japanese public and aroused widespread opposition to nuclear weapons. It was through this incident that most of the Japanese public discovered the plight of survivors from Hiroshima and Nagasaki.

This essay was first published in *Peace Review* 4:2 (1992).

One of the important results of this concern was the Suginami Appeal, initiated by the Suginami Council in Tokyo in May 1954. It urged all Japanese to sign an appeal to ban hydrogen bombs, to spread the appeal to peoples and governments throughout the world, and to work to preserve the life and happiness of all peoples. Eighteen million signatures, from throughout Japan, were collected by November that year. The Suginami Appeal aroused national consciousness of the problems posed by nuclear weapons and resulted in the First World Conference Against the Atomic and Hydrogen Bomb held in Hiroshima on August 6, 1955. The testimonies from the survivors, Akihiro Takahashi of Hiroshima and Misako Yamaguchi of Nagasaki, profoundly moved the 30,000 participants gathered in the Hiroshima Peace Memorial Park. Building on this momentum, the first national peace movement, Gensui-kyo (the Council Against Atomic and Hydrogen Bombs) emerged in September 1955. The Gensui-kyo spanned the political spectrum from conservatives to radicals and enjoyed widespread national support.

B y the 1960s, however, Japanese peace movements experienced serious internal conflicts precipitated largely by Cold War divisions. Some members left Gensui-kyo and formed a new peace organization, Gensui-kin (Congress Against the Atomic and Hydrogen Bomb) in 1964.

The immediate causes of the split were controversies over whether nuclear tests by all countries (capitalist or communist) should be opposed and whether the Limited Nuclear Test Ban Treaty should be supported. The Gensui-kin, supported by the Socialist Party, insisted that nuclear tests by all countries should be opposed and the Limited Nuclear Test Ban Treaty should be supported. The Gensui-kyo, supported by the Communist Party, on the other hand, argued that Soviet nuclear missiles were essentially defensive and should not be opposed. It also opposed signing the Limited Nuclear Test Ban Treaty, arguing in favor of a comprehensive test ban instead. Since this break, the two organizations have been in conflict over a variety of disarmament and related issues.

These conflicts undoubtedly damaged the popular image of the Japanese peace movement, and many citizens, including the hibakusha, lost their zeal for them. The joint World Conference Against Atomic and Hydrogen Bombs (held in Hiroshima in 1977) improved the situation somewhat, and this joint conference continued every year until 1985. External influences have had a strong influence on the emergence of new peace activism in Japan. The upsurge of the Western peace movement—the Greens in Germany, CND in the United Kingdom, and the Freeze movement in the United States—was widely reported in the Japanese mass media as well as in academic circles.

Stimulated and encouraged by these overseas developments, the Japanese peace movement was reenergized after nearly twenty years silence. One notable trend was the emergence of energetic, grassroots movements. The 10 Feet Campaign, for example, carried out between 1980 and 1983, was a particularly impressive example of this new peace movement. The 10 Feet Campaign was aimed at buying back 85,000 feet of film depicting the casualties of Hiroshima and Nagasaki, taken by the U.S. Strategic Bombing Survey Committee, in order to make new documentary films from a peace movement perspective.

Each participant in the campaign paid 3,000 Japanese yen for ten feet of the 85,000 feet of film. Over 100,000 Japanese citizens joined the campaign. These numbers included many housewives, students, retired persons, and workers affiliated with neither the Socialist nor the Communist parties. This campaign represents a new wave of Japanese peace movement. Peace movements such as this challenged Gensui-kin and Gensui-kyo to resolve some of their conflicts and channel their energies toward becoming more effective national movements. They were able to do this for a few years, but by 1980 rifts were beginning to reappear between the organizations. There were conflicts over nuclear energy and Soviet nuclear tests; and heated divisions between the Socialist and Communist parties were also reflected within the peace movement. While both movements were able to coorganize the conference marking the fortieth anniversary of the Hiroshima and Nagasaki bombings, by 1986 the relationship had deteriorated so much that they found it impossible to organize a joint conference. At the moment there is no communication between the two movements, and Cold War divisions continue within the Japanese peace movement.

The end of the Cold War has also had a strong negative impact on Japanese peace movements. There are few obvious signs of vigor or enthusiasm. There are fewer peace events being organized and fewer people participating in them. Grassroots movements, like the 10 Feet Campaign, have either vanished or become very inactive. The media, in turn, seem to have lost interest in peace movement activity and carry fewer articles or reports about them. And in a sense this is not surprising. It might be easily surmised, based upon a merely casual observation, that many previously vital Japanese peace movements are simply dead. Peace researchers, therefore, need to analyze the current situation and discover whether this judgment is correct or whether the movements may be reactivated.

Conflict between different branches of the Japanese peace movement is clearly a major factor in its current paralysis. This is not, however, unique to Japan. In a comparative study of peace movements in Japan, Denmark, and Finland, similar conflicts were discovered in the Scandinavian countries. There was a central tension, for example, between peace movements oriented toward opposition to imperialism as opposed to those espousing radical pacifism. These two orientations generate conflicts over issues such as the significance of ex-Soviet nuclear missiles, the place of unofficial and official peace movements in the former Soviet Union and its satellites, and attitudes toward nuclear power plants. What distinguishes the Japanese peace movements from their counterparts in Europe is the depth of the conflict and consequent division, as well as an absence of communication and an inability to mount joint activities.

Although some tension between organizations is inevitable, in the case of the Japanese peace movements, such disputes result in very serious and often emotional conflict. This probably owes more to complex affiliations with specific political parties than individual differences between Japanese and European movements. Despite official declarations of independence, the informal links between the two major peace organizations and specific political parties are strong and taken for granted. Gensui-kyo is affiliated with the Communist Party, while Gensui-kin is affiliated with the Socialist Party. These political links generate serious conflict because the political parties are ideologically antagonistic.

The Socialist Party, for example, is separating itself from any residual Marxist ideology and strengthening cooperation with moderate and middle of the road thinkers. This means distancing itself from the Communist Party. This has generated intense conflict within the Japanese left, with the Communist Party severely criticizing the Socialists for their conversion and the Socialist Party leveling caustic criticism at the Communists for their "unrealistic and self-righteous" ways of thinking.

These conflicts have dominated discussions within the Japanese peace movement. The ideological attachment of Japanese peace movements to the Socialist or Communist parties is reinforced by financial and membership dependence on different trade unions, which are also split in their support for the Communist and Socialist parties. The external dependence of the peace movement on trade unions and political parties has generated internal problems and stagnation and makes it difficult to establish new agendas for the 1990s. There seems little chance of a resurgence of peace movement activity until the movements free themselves from the political parties.

I n addition to these organizational impediments, another problem afflicting Japanese peace movements is their narrow and rather restrictive view of peace. This flows in part from their close connections with Japanese political parties and trade unions that see peace almost exclusively in terms of "negative peace" and have some difficulty relating peace to other issues such as ecology, feminism, and social justice.

By contrast, Swedish peace movements, to take an example, not only challenge their government on military issues but also raise more fundamental questions about social structure, ways of thinking, lifestyles, and values. Their interests incorporate ecology and feminism. This comprehensive approach to peace issues is present in most other peace movements in

Europe and North America as well. It is not a coincidence that the Green Party in Germany started as an ecological movement but has now become one of the leading peace organizations. Their "alternative policy" as expressed by Rudolf Bahro is a central doctrine relating to both ecological and peace issues. The party is made up of social movements concerned with ecology, opposition to nuclear power, nuclear pacifism, antimilitarism, and youth questions.

These environmental movements in the West share some compatible goals and membership with women's, peace, and community movements. This is why sociologists classify these movements as "new social movements." Combining environmentalism, feminism, and peace is one of the important defining characteristics of these new movements.

When international tensions between West and East/North and South increase, these new social movements are likely to direct their attention to peace issues and to mobilize large numbers of people for peace actions. When the tension diminishes (at least in the eyes of the general public) and environmental awareness is raised because of events like Chernobyl or reports on global warming, there is renewed attention to environmental issues with a revitalization of environmental movements.

This certainly seems to be the case with peace movements in other parts of the world. As peace movement activity diminishes, environmental movements have expanded in response to nuclear and other pollution, viral infections of North Sea seals, and so forth. The shift away from narrowly defined security issues in the West has been accompanied by new concerns for "ecosecurity."

This process has not taken place in Japan. Japanese peace movements differentiate narrowly defined peace issues from ecology and other issues. The core activists remain concerned with nuclear disarmament and preventing further Hiroshima and Nagasaki disasters. This narrow focus is not of itself negative, but it becomes so when the peace movements exclude other issues from the peace agenda, thereby depriving themselves of the energy that flows from these new social movements. Japanese peace movements are not willing to accommodate ecological and feminist issues. Ideologically, there is a desire not to depart from the Hiroshima/Nagasaki peace movement traditions, as organizationally there is a perception that the new social movements challenge the authoritarian and hierarchical frameworks of the Japanese peace movement, the trade unions, and the political parties. All of these organizations are structured in a top-down fashion and differ markedly from the typical Western European grassroots organizations, which tend to be decentralized and democratic.

The central ideas of ecology and feminism, therefore, and the attitudes and activities of those who espouse them, do not mesh easily with Japanese peace movements. There is no strong integration between these concerns in Japan. This very narrow and exclusive approach to peace tends to undermine the ability of Japanese peace movements to resolve their internal problems and develop new strategies for the 1990s.

We can see then the relatively inactive and divided state of Japanese peace movements. If they are to resume a more central role in Japanese and broader regional or world peace processes, some significant changes must occur. First, Japanese peace movements must become independent from their "boss" organizations, namely political parties and trade unions. Without this autonomy there will always be conflicts within the peace movement that owe more to external political pressures than to a concern for peace. Second, Japanese peace movements should adopt a broader definition and understanding of peace. Now that the nuclear genie has been released, guaranteed nuclear disarmament is only possible in a "peaceful society" based on a "peaceful culture."

The end of the Cold War has made discussions about a postmaterialist, civil society—an alternative society—more plausible. Japanese peace movements, therefore, should acquire a broader historical and global perspective on peace. Solidarity with the environmental, feminist, and Third World movements (especially in the Asia-Pacific region) are essential to the revival of Japanese peace movements. This revival will require the imagination and creativity of peace researchers and peace movements if it is to have any short- or long-term political significance.

45

DIRECTIONS FOR THE
U.S. PEACE MOVEMENT

ROGER PEACE

The goals of world peace and justice are as important today as ever, but how relevant is the U.S. peace movement? Peace activists should be given credit for their efforts to hold the line against reactionary militarism in the 1980s. Major peace and justice campaigns were initiated to halt the nuclear arms race, stop the contra war in Nicaragua, end military aid to El Salvador, promote sanctions and divestment in South Africa, and pare down the military budget in favor of domestic needs. Today, however, short-term, oppositional campaigns are no longer enough. The peace movement needs a broader vision and common, long-range goals if it is to be effective in the post–Cold War era.

In the late 1980s, peace researchers and activists began to develop a broader vision as well as longer-range goals centered on the concept of common security (see Spring 1989 *Peace Review,* "Common Security, Common Threats"). Many national conferences and grassroots workshops were held around the country, culminating in a conference entitled "Common Security Through Structures for Peace" initiated by the World Federalist Association. Out of this conference, which was held in February 1989 and brought together over 100 peace organizations, emerged a new national peace network called the Alliance for Our Common Future.

When the Gulf crisis broke out in late 1990, however, the Alliance for Our Common Future proved to be no alliance at all. The World Federalist Association did not take a stand against the Gulf War—in contrast to virtually all U.S. peace groups. This set the leadership of the alliance apart from other peace groups and broke open an old division within the peace movement between liberal internationalists, on the one hand, and anti-imperialists and pacifists on the other. The split harkens back to World War I when liberal internationalists supported U.S. entry into the war while anti-imperialists and pacifists were jailed on sedition charges for speaking out against it.

This essay was first published in *Peace Review* 4:2 (1992).

The end of the Cold War also influenced the demise of common security as an organizing principle. The original concept of common security focused primarily on the military rivalry between the United States and Soviet Union; and when the Cold War faded, so did the idea of common security. Had the concept of common security been further developed to include a deeper analysis of the roots of militarism, it might have had more staying power.

The U.S. invasion of Panama in December 1989 should have been a catalyst for a major reevaluation and redefinition of common security, encompassing a historical perspective on imperialism, neocolonialism, and North-South relations; but this did not happen. The lack of historical perspective is evident in the "peace dividend" campaign today, which rides on the popular perception that the United States has maintained its military might over the last fifty years because of the Soviet Union's military challenge. More accurately, the Soviet Union provided a convenient rationale, a justification for U.S. neocolonial "world policeman" policies. The United States has not been making the world safe for democracy all these years, but rather for capitalism and U.S. geopolitical interests.

Today the movement for common security is almost invisible. While there are many visions and long-range goals among peace organizations, there is no agreement as to how these should be integrated, prioritized, and promoted. The Bush administration is being allowed to define the New World Order by default. Efforts to reap the peace dividend resulting from the end of the Cold War not only lack a progressive historical perspective; they are also not grounded in a wider understanding of the capitalist economic system, for the most part. Without a coherent critique of the capitalist system, peace activists cannot succeed in their larger goal of meeting human needs.

The peace dividend campaign, led by coalitions such as the Citizen Budget Campaign, Common Agenda, and the May 16 Mayors March on Washington (Save Our Cities, Save Our Children), makes the implicit assumption that human needs will be met if the military budget is cut and funds are redirected by the government to meet human needs. Yet the cause of unmet needs lies not in military spending, but in the nature of the capitalist economic system, designed primarily for corporate profitability. Blaming military spending for capitalism's failure to meet human needs is no more accurate than right-wing claims that unfair Japanese trading practices are the cause of our economic woes.

More realistically, the meeting of fundamental human needs and the development of a truly viable economy in the United States will require a fundamental restructuring of the present U.S. economic system:

- economic planning—designing the economy to meet human needs and protect the environment

- democratic accountability—an end to monopoly capitalism
- redistribution of income and wealth—progressive taxation and higher minimum wages
- guaranteed economic rights for all citizens—employment, housing, health care, education, and income security

Facilitating the conversion of military industries to peaceful uses is unlikely to occur without structural changes in the economic system. Given a world market already saturated with industrial goods, very few military industries will be able to convert to civilian production, particularly in recessionary times. Military industry workers face the same problem as auto industry workers. The issue of economic conversion thus needs to be approached from the point of view of economic rights, particularly the right to guaranteed employment at a livable wage, and comprehensive economic planning. Without an alternative plan for full employment, local workers and communities will try to hold on to military industries and bases, even pushing for arms sales abroad. Without comprehensive planning, peace conversion efforts are likely to turn into taxpayer subsidies for corporations and a bailout for military industries.

A s for the international economy, there is a widespread belief that making the United States more competitive is the answer to the U.S. recession. This viewpoint ignores the systematic inequities of the international capitalist economic system, however, and also contradicts the principle of cooperation for which the peace movement presumably stands. The international capitalist system has left Third World countries in a state of permanent underdevelopment, locking them into an export economy/debt cycle under the control of industrialized countries (the neocolonial system).

Alternative policies and strategies aimed at "self-reliant and people-centered development" have been put forward by the South Commission, chaired by Tanzanian President Julius K. Nyerere, in its report *The Challenge to the South* (Oxford University Press, 1990). In the United States, organizations such as the Institute for Food and Development Policy, Global Exchange, Nicaragua Network, American Friends Service Committee, and Interfaith Impact have been promoting alternatives to neocolonialism, emphasizing the idea of sustainable and equitable development. The peace movement as a whole needs to join this effort and offer a coherent critique of the capitalist economic system.

Developing a common vision for the peace movement is difficult because peace activists disagree on underlying issues, including how deep to go in probing the roots of militarism. Probing the roots of militarism is like peeling an onion. Beneath the outer layer of military and foreign policies are economic and political systems that reinforce oppression. Beneath these are cultural patterns that shape individual and social behavior (e.g., power elitism, racism, sexism). Going deeper, one finds ideological viewpoints that explain the world (e.g., the "free world"). At the core are spiritual beliefs about human nature and ethical values.

As a result, discussing deeper issues can be risky for activists because there is great potential for disagreements that may cause fragile coalitions organized around short-term goals to break down. This risk should be taken, however, both because the time is right and because the peace movement will otherwise forfeit the ideological struggle to the right.

Reactionaries are working hard to revive new security threats to the United States—Cuba, Libya, Iraq, North Korea, and Third World instability—while conservatives are working to ensure that the New World Order embodies the interests of U.S. elites and multinational corporations. The peace movement needs to be vigilant against reactionary U.S. interventionism but also must address the question of how to construct a New World Order in the post–Cold War era. As a starting point for discussion, I would offer the following three medium-range goals for the peace movement: replacing the U.S. world policeman role with international law and global institutions; supporting a consistent standard of human rights in U.S. foreign policies; and supporting the principles of economic rights and fairness.

International law and global institutions provide a constructive alternative to the traditional balance of power and national self-interest policies that feed arms races, nuclear proliferation, and excessive military spending. The promotion of human and economic rights ensures that peace will result in the fulfillment of human needs. Intermeshed with all three goals should be education and consciousness raising on the United States' historical role in the world and the nature of the capitalist system.

Regarding the first goal, the question of whether or not the United States should play the role of world policeman became headline news last March when a draft Pentagon planning paper advocating a lone U.S. superpower role was leaked to the *New York Times*. Senator Joseph Biden described the Pentagon paper as a prescription for "pax Americana," saying, "the Pentagon vision reverts to an old notion of the US as the world's policeman—a notion that, not incidentally, will preserve a large defense budget." The Bush administration, embarrassed by the negative reaction from U.S. allies, denounced the article as a "dumb report."

This is good news for the peace movement. The idea of the United States playing the role of self-assigned world policeman is being challenged in official circles. It is worth noting that the end of European colonialism began with the discrediting of the idea of imperialism in the early twentieth century (to be an imperial power was considered a sign of status previously). The peace movement should aim for a similar discrediting of the world policeman role as we move into the twenty-first century. Efforts should go toward creating a viable international security system under the auspices of the United Nations and World Court and based upon common security principles.

A s to the second goal of human rights, the peace movement must look beyond solidarity with people in specific countries (Salvadorans, Palestinians) and address U.S. foreign policies as a whole. We need to push for the U.S. government to adopt a consistent standard of human rights applied to all countries, whether considered allies or not. The United States is currently providing over $5 billion in military aid to other countries, many of whom abuse human rights, and billions more in economic aid, with little of that being used for true humanitarian needs.

In the summer of 1991, prompted by the end of the Cold War, Congress began a review of foreign assistance programs. Both the Senate and House agreed to rewrite the Foreign Assistance Act to affirm four basic objectives for foreign aid: poverty alleviation, broad-based economic growth; sustainable resource management, and promotion of democracy and human rights. Unfortunately, these objectives were not implemented, as the House and Senate voted in October 1991 to continue the same appropriations for foreign aid as the previous year.

On the positive side, Germany has begun placing conditions on its foreign aid. "We are going to be looking closely at the level of spending for arms, and also at factors such as human rights and economic freedoms in the various countries," said Carl-Deiter Spranger, German minister of economic cooperation, in August 1991. "This is the beginning of an international consensus on the way aid should be conditioned."

A s to the third goal, the demand for economic rights is growing stronger in the United States—health care, affordable housing, quality education, and income security; however, the economic system is less and less able to meet these needs for everyone. The peace movement can play a part in a larger progressive movement seeking to redress the inadequacies and inequities of the present economic system.

On the global level, the GATT (General Agreement on Trade and Tariffs) and NAFTA (North American Free Trade Agreement) talks are commanding attention from workers and communities who fear that companies will move abroad in order to take advantage of cheaper labor. Environmentalists and consumers are also concerned that U.S. environmental protection laws will be invalidated by international "standards" set at the lowest common denominator. Organizing against GATT and NAFTA is a coalition of labor, religious, environmental, development, and human rights groups (including some peace groups) called MODTLE (Mobilization on Development, Trade, Labor, and the Environment). Peace organizations can participate in this effort to promote alternatives to the reign of multinational corporations.

T o revitalize the peace movement, peace activists need to think like a movement. Little will be accomplished by each organization working separately. By sharing common, long-range goals and visions, the efforts of each campaign can be strengthened and sustained. Recognizing that there are many differences among activists relative to visions and goals, there are nevertheless a number of projects that could be initiated immediately. The following cumulative steps, to cite a few examples, can be taken:

Assess the current state of the movement on a regular basis. No movement strategy can be developed without knowing how many peace groups exist, their issues, resources, and philosophies. The last comprehensive survey of the U.S. peace movement taken in 1987 showed 7,000 peace-oriented groups, including over 300 national groups.

Develop a nationwide communication and information-sharing network available to all local and national groups. This can serve as a forum for discussing strategy among peace groups. (PeaceNet is presently serving this function for many groups.)

Develop a national weekly newspaper, providing the general public with peace movement viewpoints on current events and information on activities and campaigns. This could be the most important outreach tool for the movement. (For all the laments of peace activists about mainstream media coverage of their activities, the peace movement has yet to produce a national newspaper that gives voice to the movement.) Some agreement on editorial policy would be necessary, but the newspaper would also serve as a forum for differing viewpoints within the movement.

Develop other cooperative projects such as a nationwide legislative alert network, a national speakers bureau, and resource materials for discussion groups probing the roots of militarism. Such joint projects would again require some cooperation among national peace groups and foundations but would not necessitate formal association or long-term strategy.

Develop leadership and stable local groups through training and funding assistance. This could be one of the major outgrowths of a national network, building the grassroots base of the movement.

S uccess in developing cooperative projects would do much for the energy and confidence of peace activists and set the stage for a critical fifth step: building an alliance of national and local organizations with the aim of developing long-range goals and strategies, mapping out educational themes, and coordinating immediate issue campaigns. The combination of having a peace movement infrastructure and long-range goals would enable the peace movement to maintain momentum through the ups and downs of specific campaigns and to sustain the inspiration and commitment of volunteer activists.

Aside from these practical measures, thinking like a movement requires that activists understand their role in history. We are the heirs of those who have worked for peace and progressive social change in the past, and our efforts will carry forth into the future. We need, therefore, to function as a movement, with common goals, strategies, structures, and activities.

CONTRIBUTORS

DAVID ADAMS is a professor of psychology at Wesleyan University in Connecticut and chair of the Seville Statement on Violence support organization.

CHADWICK F. ALGER is a professor of political science at Ohio State University in Columbus and past secretary general of the International Peace Research Association.

ISABEL ALLENDE, the niece of Chile's assassinated president Salvador Allende, is the author of *The House of the Spirits, Of Love and Shadows, Eva Luna,* and *The Infinite Plan,* all published in the United States by Alfred Knopf Publishers.

ABDUL KARIM BANGURA is a professor of political science at Howard University in Washington, D.C.

BIRGIT BROCK-UTNE is a Norwegian social scientist who taught at the University of Dar es Salaam, Tanzania, for five years and now works at the Institute for Educational Research at the University of Oslo, Norway. She is the author of *Educating for Peace: A Feminist Perspective* and *Feminist Perspectives on Peace and Peace Education,* both published by Pergamon, London.

PATRICIA CHILTON is senior research fellow at the European Public Policy Institute at Warwick University in England, and is coauthor of *Defence and Dissent in Contemporary France* (Croom Helm, 1984). She is past chair of the European Nuclear Disarmament (END) movement and a member of the Helsinki Citizens' Assembly.

PAUL CHILTON teaches linguistics and international relations at the University of Warwick, England, and was a visiting fellow at the Center for International Security and Arms Control at Stanford University. He is the editor of *Language and the Nuclear Arms Debate* (Pinter, 1985) and author of *Orwellian Language and the Media* (Pluto, 1988) and *Security Metaphors* (Lang, 1994).

CHARLES DERBER teaches sociology at Boston College and is coauthor of *The Nuclear Seduction* (University of California Press, 1989) and of *Power in the Highest Degree* (Oxford University, 1990), and author of *Money, Murder and the American Dream* (Faber and Faber, 1993).

JIRI DIENSTBIER was a signatory of the *Charter 77* human rights declaration and a founding member of VONS, the Czechoslovak Committee for the Defense of the Unjustly Persecuted in Prague, for which he was imprisoned in the 1980s. He is now foreign minister of the Czech Republic.

LAYI EGUNJOBI is a senior lecturer and acting director of the Centre for Urban and Regional Planning at the University of Ibadan in Nigeria, and was a research fellow at the Nigerian Institute of Social and Economic Research.

ROBERT ELIAS teaches politics and directs the Peace and Justice Studies Program at the University of San Francisco, is the author of *The Politics of Victimization* (Oxford University Press, 1986) and *Victims Still* (Sage, 1993), and is the editor of *Peace Review*.

JOSEPH J. FAHEY teaches religious studies and is the director of the Peace Studies Program at Manhattan College in New York City, and is editor of *The Peace Reader* (Paulist, 1993).

H. BRUCE FRANKLIN is a professor of English and American Studies at Rutgers University in New Jersey and the author of *War Stars: The Superweapon and the American Imagination* (Oxford University Press, 1988).

JOSEPH GERSON is the regional program coordinator of the American Friends Service Committee in New England and has taught international relations at Holy Cross College and Regis College. He is the coeditor of *The Deadly Connection* (Institute for Defense & Disarmament Studies, 1987), and *The Sun Never Sets* (South End Press, 1990).

ARNOLD P. GOLDSTEIN is the director of the Center for Research on Aggression at Syracuse University and of the New York State Task Force on Juvenile Gangs. He is a member of the American Psychological Association on Youth Violence.

DONNA U. GREGORY teaches in the Writing Program at the University of California in Los Angeles and is the editor of *Nuclear Predicament* (St. Martin's, 1986).

CHARLES HAUSS teaches political science at George Mason University and is the author of *Beyond Confrontation* (Praeger, 1994). He taught at Colby College in Maine and has served on the staff of the Beyond War Foundation.

ARTHUR C. HELTON directs the Refugee Project of the Lawyers Committee for Human Rights, which has offices in New York City and Washington, D.C., and teaches at the New York University School of Law.

JEN HLAVACEK is a doctoral student in sociology at the University of Colorado, a board member of the American Sociological Association Section on Peace and War, and past managing editor of *Peace and Change*.

LANA L. HOSTETLER teaches childcare services at Lincoln Land Community College in Springfield, Illinois, and is president of the National Association for the Education of Young Children.

MARY KALDOR is senior research fellow at the University of Sussex in England, cochair of the Helsinki Citizen's Assembly, and author of *The Imaginary War* (Norton, 1990).

JAMES N. KARIOKI teaches political science at California State University, Chico. He was born and educated in Kenya.

LANE KENWORTHY is a research associate with the Midwest Consortium for Economic Development Alternatives (MCEDA) in Chicago.

JUDIT KISS is a development economist at the Institute of Development Studies of the University of Sussex, England, and a research fellow of the World Institute of Development Economics at the United Nations University in Helsinki, Finland.

KATSUYA KODAMA teaches sociology at Mie University in Japan, is editor of the International Peace Research Association newsletter, and is deputy secretary general of the Asia-Pacific Peace Research Association. He is author of *The Future of the Peace Movements* (Choubunsha, 1987) and *Life Histories of Atomic Bomb Orphans* (Lund University Press, 1989).

DAVID KRIEGER is coeditor of *Waging Peace: Vision and Hope for the 21st Century* (Noble Press, 1992), and president of the Nuclear Age Foundation in Santa Barbara, California.

LOUIS KRIESBERG teaches sociology and is director of the Program on the Analysis and Resolution of Conflicts at Syracuse University, is author of

International Conflict Resolution (Yale University Press, 1992), and is coeditor of *The Transformation of European Communist Societies* (JAI Press, 1992).

ANDREW MACK teaches international relations at the Australian National University in Canberra and is former director of its Peace Research Centre. His most recent books are *Asian Flashpoint* (Allen & Unwin, 1993) and *A Peaceful Ocean* (Allen & Unwin, 1993).

SAM MARULLO teaches sociology and codirects the Justice and Peace Studies Program at Georgetown University in Washington, D.C., is past chair of the American Sociological Association Section on Peace and War, and is author of *Ending the Cold War At Home* (Lexington, 1994).

CHRISTIAN MELLON is a Jesuit priest who is active in the French peace movement. He is the author of *Chretiens devant la guerre et la paix* (Le Centurion, 1984). He teaches at the Paris Catholic University, is on the Justice and Peace Commission of the French Catholic Church, and is an advisor to Pax Christi International.

MYRIAM MIEDZIAN teaches philosophy at Columbia University and is author of *Boys Will Be Boys* (Doubleday, 1992).

ROY MORRISON is author of *We Build the Road as We Travel* (New Society Publishers, 1992).

JEAN-MARIE MULLER is a professor of philosophy and author of *Vous avez dit pacifisme?* (Le Cerf, 1984).

JAN ØBERG is director of the Transnational Foundation for Peace and Future Research in Lund, Sweden, and chief of its conflict-mitigation mission to former Yugoslavia. He is author and contributor to several books on alternative security, nonviolence, world order, and sustainable development.

ROGER C. PEACE III is a writer and peace activist and the author of *A Just and Lasting Peace* (Noble Press, 1991).

MICHAEL RENNER is a senior researcher at the Worldwatch Institute in Washington, D.C. His research focuses on the links between peace and security and environmental issues.

DAVID RUBIN is the dean of the S. I. Newhouse School of Public Communications at Syracuse University. In 1985 he founded the Center for War, Peace and the News Media at New York University.

ABDUL AZIZ SAID teaches international relations, peace studies, and conflict resolution at the School of International Service of the American University in Washington, D.C. He is a member of several peace and human rights organizations, has been a consultant to the United States government and the United Nations, and has published several books on international relations and foreign policy.

WILLIAM A. SCHWARTZ is a doctoral student in sociology at Boston College and coauthor of *The Nuclear Seduction* (University of California Press, 1989) and *Power in the Highest Degree* (Oxford University, 1990).

JACQUES SEMELIN has taught history at the University of Paris and been a postdoctoral fellow at Harvard University. He is a political science researcher at the Centre National de la Recherche Scientifique in Paris and the author of *Unarmed Against Hitler* (Praeger, 1993). He is the coauthor of *La non-violence* (University Press of France, 1994) and editor of the journal *Alternatives non-violentes.*

MICHAEL SHUMAN is director of the Institute for Policy Studies in Washington, D.C., executive director of EXPRO, and former president of the Center for Innovative Diplomacy in Irvine, California.

JACKIE SMITH is a doctoral candidate in government and international studies at the University of Notre Dame and a research assistant at its Kroc Institute for International Peace Studies. She is cochair of the Student Section of the Consortium on Peace Research, Education and Development and a member of the American Sociological Association's Peace and War Section.

WILL SWAIM is an editor of *The Bulletin of Municipal Diplomacy,* the journal of the Center for Innovative Diplomacy in Irvine, California.

KATARINA TOMASEVSKI is a senior research associate at the Danish Centre for Human Rights in Copenhagen. Her publications include *Development Aid and Human Rights* (St. Martin's, 1989), *Women and Human Rights* (Zed, 1993), and *Children and Adult Prisons* (St. Martin's, 1986).

JENNIFER TURPIN teaches sociology and directs the Women's Studies Program at the University of San Francisco. She is the author of *Reinventing the Soviet Self* (Ablex, forthcoming), coeditor of the *Web of Violence* (University of Illinois Press, 1994), and the senior editor of *Peace Review.*

CYRUS VEESER is a PhD candidate in history at Columbia University in New York City and is completing his dissertation on private capitalist-State Department cooperation in controlling the economy of the Dominican Republic.

JEANNE VICKERS has worked with the UN Relief and Rehabilitation Administration in postwar Germany, with UNICEF, and with the Joint UN/NGO Group on Women and Development. She is the author of *Women and the World Economic Crisis* (Zed, 1991) and *Women and War* (Zed, 1993).

BEVERLY WOODWARD is a research associate in the Politics Department at Brandeis University and is coordinator of International Nonviolent Initiatives in Massachusetts.

STEPHEN ZUNES teaches politics at the University of Puget Sound in Washington. He is director of the Institute for a New Middle East Policy and writes and lectures on U.S. foreign policy, Third World politics, and social movements.

INDEX

ABOUT THE BOOK

With the development of the atomic bomb, Albert Einstein remarked that everything had changed except our thinking about the world. Einstein and Bertrand Russell warned us that "we have to learn to think in a new way. . . . Shall we put an end to the human race; or shall we renounce war?"

Unfortunately, we are facing the end of this century still in the midst of wars born of various motivations. In response, the editors of *Rethinking Peace* have compiled a collection of essays designed to encourage readers to think differently about the world and the prospects for peace. Based on rigorous scholarly work, these essays nevertheless have been written to be read by students—to make important points in a short space, and in plain English.

With an emphasis on new thinking and positive strategies for developing a more peaceful world, the authors explore why conventional politics and generations of peace movements have not quelled our fascination with militarism; how we got to where we are now; the kind of thinking that keeps leading us to war; and how we can fundamentally change our thinking so that a peaceful future is more than simply a pipedream.

The forty-five articles—fresh, timely, diverse, and controversial—are sure to provoke meaningful discussion and debate.